Patent
Law
and
Practice

Seventh Edition

To Nan and Becky

Patent

Law

and

Practice

Seventh Edition

Herbert F. Schwartz
Adjunct Professor, University of Pennsylvania Law School
Adjunct Professor, New York University School of Law

Ropes & Gray LLP
New York, NY

Robert J. Goldman
Ropes & Gray LLP
East Palo Alto, CA

BNA Books, A Division of BNA, Arlington, VA

Library of Congress Cataloging-in-Publication Data

Schwartz, Herbert F.
   Patent law and practice / Herbert F. Schwartz, Robert J.
Goldman.—7th ed.
         p. cm.
   Includes bibliographical references and index.
   ISBN 978-1-57018-973-9
   1.   Patent laws and legislation—United States. 2. Patent
practice—United States.   I. Goldman, Robert J.   II. Title.

   KF3120.S38 2011
   346.7304'86—dc23
2011036962

Published by BNA Books
1801 South Bell St., Arlington, VA 22202
bna.com/bnabooks

ISBN 978-1-57018-973-9
Printed in the United States of America

PREFACE TO THE SEVENTH EDITION

In the three years since publication of the Sixth Edition of this book, the patent laws have continued to evolve, procedurally and substantively, in response to developments in technology and the economics of innovation.

Since 2008, the Supreme Court's substantial changes to the law governing injunctive relief (*eBay*, 2006), declaratory jurisdiction (*MedImmune*, 2007), and invalidity for obviousness (*KSR*, 2007) have continued to create new bodies of law in the Federal Circuit and the District Courts. Both the Supreme Court and the Federal Circuit issued important opinions on the patentability of software algorithms and biotechnology inventions. And the Federal Circuit announced important changes to the law of patent damages, the defense of inequitable conduct, and the standard for adequate written description of an invention.

While the revised manuscript was being completed in September 2011, Congress passed and the President signed into law the Leahy-Smith America Invents Act. Many of the significant provisions of the Act will phase in gradually over time. For example, the Act provides new options for testing the validity of an issued patent in the U.S. Patent & Trademark Office (PTO) instead of in district court litigation. These options become available in September 2012. The much-publicized changeover of the U.S. patent law from a "first-to-invent" system to one that awards the patent to the "first-inventor-to-file" does not begin to take effect until March 2013, and then will apply only to patents issued on applications filed after that date. In response to the passage of the Act, I have revised the manuscript to highlight the changes to come, as well as those that have already taken effect.

I have also made a number of structural changes to the book. As the Federal Circuit passes its twenty-ninth birthday, it is no longer possible for a one-volume monograph to try to capture every pertinent decision in footnotes. Accordingly, the footnotes have been thoroughly revised with a goal of making them shorter and reflecting in all instances (1) one or more leading cases on a particular point and (2) one or more recent examples of how the Federal Circuit has applied the law. Also, in response to a request from a European colleague, where there is clearly a single leading case on a point—for example, the Supreme Court's *KSR* decision on obviousness or the Federal Circuit's 2011 *Therasense* decision on inequitable conduct—I have tried to quote the controlling language in the decision to give the reader the governing standard unvarnished by commentary.

I would like to acknowledge the contribution of several colleagues at Ropes & Gray in the preparation of this edition, including my partner Jeffrey H. Ingerman, and my associates Karen A. Doherty, Christopher P Carroll, Barna De, Gail A. Williams, and Adrienne P. Hale. Carol Hoffman, a Senior Research Librarian at Ropes & Gray and a member of the Special Libraries Association, provided substantial help, including the revisions to the closing material on additional resources. Jim Fattibene, Acquisition Manager for BNA, Karen Ertel, Senior Editor, and the BNA staff were supportive and understanding as deadlines loomed, occasionally passed and then loomed again. I thank them for being both professional and gracious.

Herb Schwartz read the manuscript at various intermediate stages and provided thoughtful comments and perspective as I worked through the revisions. But as the changes to the book have become more substantial, the responsibility for the ultimate statements, opinions and conclusions in this Seventh Edition has become increasingly my own.

ROBERT J. GOLDMAN

October 2011

PREFACE TO THE SIXTH EDITION

Early in 2008, Herb and BNA asked if I would like to join him in preparing the Sixth Edition of this monograph. I was pleased to do so. Having practiced with Herb for thirty years, we have spent much time trying to parse the patent laws, on behalf of clients and in preparation for our various teaching and speaking engagements. This was a logical next step in our work together, and it turned out to be a pleasant pursuit for both of us.

The purpose of the revisions for the Sixth Edition is to update the law, particularly in light of several recent Supreme Court decisions, but also in view of the continuing evolution of the jurisprudence of the Federal Circuit in areas such as willful infringement, claim construction and inequitable conduct. Herb's advice to me at the outset was typically concise: "Keep it short and make it right." What could be simpler than that?

For their help in the pursuit of "rightness," Herb and I would like to acknowledge the contribution of several of our colleagues at Ropes & Gray in the preparation of this edition, including our partners Jeffrey H. Ingerman, James E. Hopenfeld and Dalila Argaez Wendlandt, and our associates David S. Chun, Linda E. Rost, Reeta K. Whitney, Michael J. Chasan, Christopher W. Rauen, Monica P. Folch, Karen A. Christiansen, Henry Y. Huang, and Aisha O. Mohammed. Carol Hoffman, a Senior Research Librarian at Ropes & Gray and a member of the Special Libraries Association, provided substantial help, not the least of which was her role as a source of continuity with previous editions. James Fattibene and the BNA staff were particularly gracious to a newcomer, for which I thank them.

In each of the previous editions, Herb was careful to state that the ultimate statements, opinions and conclusions in this monograph were his. For this Sixth Edition, they are ours. This is far from the first time that Herb and I have had to sink or swim together on a challenging and worthwhile project. I hope that it won't be the last.

ROBERT J. GOLDMAN

September 2008

PREFACE TO THE FIRST
THROUGH FIFTH EDITIONS

The Federal Judicial Center is a part of the judicial branch that was created in 1967 by act of Congress (28 U.S.C. §620). Among its many functions, the Judicial Center develops and conducts programs of continuing education and training for judicial branch personnel, including judges. In furtherance of that mission, the Judicial Center publishes brief monographs about various areas of the law. In 1986, the Center asked if I would be willing to write a monograph about patent law. The request was a great honor and I accepted the task.

I understood that the goal of the Judicial Center's monograph series was to create a series of works, each of which could be read in a relatively brief period of time and help to educate a judge on the basics of the area of the law covered by the monograph. The task was challenging because there was little to serve as a guide for drafting a patent law monograph.

The majority of the relevant primers that existed in 1986 were too cursory in their treatment of patent law because they covered all aspects of intellectual property law (patent, trademark, copyright, and trade secrets). Further, none of the primers dealt with the issues that federal judges confront, e.g., when to stay a case involving a patent or when and how to bifurcate a patent case. The larger works on patent law were useful, but too ponderous for this purpose. They also lacked, among other things, an introduction to patent prosecution, i.e., the process of applying for and obtaining patents from the Patent and Trademark Office.

While the monograph was never intended to be a definitive reference work, I believed that its usefulness would be increased if it could point the reader to places where he or she could obtain more complete information. Accordingly, many footnotes and an annotated bibliography were included. Whenever possible, the source cited in a footnote (case, article, or book) was selected because it more fully explained the issues and case law concerning the matter footnoted.

The monograph, which was published in 1988 under the title Patent Law and Practice, appeared to fulfill the original goal of producing a short work that could be used to educate judges about the basics of patent law. It has been cited in many published opinions, up to and including the Supreme Court (*see Markman v. Westview Instruments,* 517 U.S. 370 (1996)), used as the text for judicial educational sessions, and referred to from the bench during trials. It has also been used to educate my students at the University of Pennsylvania Law School, and New York University Law School.

In 1993, the Federal Judicial Center asked if I would be willing to prepare a second edition. As in 1986, the request was a great honor and I accepted the task. Because the use of juries in patent trials had risen dramatically in the late 1980s and early 1990s, I decided that adding a chapter on jury trials might help judges consider ways to manage patent jury trials.

After the second edition of Patent Law and Practice was published in 1995, the Bureau of National Affairs, Inc., asked if I would be willing to make the monograph available to a wider audience. The Federal Judicial Center was enthusiastic about such a project. The BNA 1996 revised second edition was the result of support from these two organizations.

After the revised second edition, the United States Court of Appeals for the Federal Circuit, along with many federal district courts, had a significant impact on patent law and practice. Moreover, the decision by the Supreme Court in *Markman v. Westview Instruments, supra,* which had just come down at the time of the revised second edition, caused significant changes in the management and trial of patent infringement cases. By 1999, BNA felt that the time was right to begin a third edition. The Federal Judicial Center agreed. Given the importance of the Markman decision, I devoted a new chapter, Chapter 5, to the influence of that decision on substance and procedure in patent litigation.

As usual, important changes to patent law and practice have occurred since the last edition. In early 2003, I was asked by practitioners and judges when the next edition would be available. I asked the Federal Judicial Center and BNA if they would be interested in a fourth edition. Both organizations encouraged a new edition.

This fifth edition was prepared to keep the work current. Thanks go to James Canfield, who contributed significantly to its preparation. In addition, I would like to thank my associates, Ching-Lee Fukuda, Moriah Agovino, Padmaja Chinta and Matthew Traupman for their assistance. Once again, Jeffrey Ingerman deserves thanks for having contributed to the Patent and Trademark Office section. Our library, and in particular, Carol Hoffman, a member of the Special Library Association, has once again done a superb job. I would also like to thank James Fattibene and BNA Books, for their editorial assistance. In this edition, as well as in all other editions, the ultimate statements, opinions, and conclusions are mine.

I would like to thank my colleague, James T. Canfield, a member of the California and New York Bars, whose efforts were fundamental in the preparation of the fourth edition. Jim, who also had a large role in other editions, has been invaluable in seeing this edition come to life. Once again, the assistance of Janet M. Stark, a member of the American Association of Law Libraries, and Carol Hoffman, a member of the Special Libraries Association, has been superb. The contribution of my partner Jeffrey H. Ingerman on the Patent and Trademark Office section is particularly appreciated.

In connection with the third edition, the contributions of Jim Canfield, Carol Hoffman, Janet Stark, Jeff Ingerman, Jim Fattibene, and Brian Malsberger are appreciated.

In connection with the second edition, in addition to the contributions of Jim Canfield, Carol Hoffman, Janet Stark and Jeff Ingerman, the contributions of my partner Robert C. Morgan and my colleague Dr. Julie Blackman on the jury trial section are appreciated. Judge Avern Cohn's suggestions were also of great help in preparing the jury trial section.

In connection with the first edition, I am particularly indebted to Judges Howard T. Markey, Walter K. Stapleton, Avern Cohn, and William T. Conner for their comments on the draft. Again, in addition to Jim Canfield, Jeff Ingerman, and Janet Stark, I would also like to acknowledge the assistance of my former colleague Mitchell P. Brook and my wife, Nan B. Chequer, who is a member of the Connecticut Bar.

HERBERT F. SCHWARTZ

November 2008

SUMMARY TABLE OF CONTENTS

DETAILED TABLE OF CONTENTS

CHAPTER 1

INTRODUCTION

The Constitution gives Congress the power to promote the progress of the useful arts by securing for inventors the exclusive right to their discoveries for limited times.[1] The idea of granting exclusive rights to inventors was old and well-established when the Constitution was drafted in 1787. As early as 500 B.C., the Greek colony of Sybaris granted such rights.[2] Inventors were also given exclusive rights to their inventions by the Senate of the Republic of Venice pursuant to a law passed in 1474,[3] by the English and German empires on a regular basis in the middle

---

[1] U.S. CONST. art. I, §8, cl. 8. Regarding the history of this clause, *see* Edward C. Walterscheid, *To Promote the Progress of Useful Arts: American Patent Law and Administration, 1787–1836 (pt. 1)*, 79 J. PAT. & TRADEMARK OFF. SOC'Y 61, 63–71 (1997); *see also* Edward C. Walterscheid, *To Promote the Progress of Science and Useful Arts: The Anatomy of a Congressional Power*, 43 IDEA 1 (2002); Edward C. Walterscheid, *Within the Limits of the Constitutional Grant: Constitutional Limitations on the Patent Power*, 9 J. INTELL. PROP. L. 291 (2002); Edward C. Walterscheid, *Patents and Manufacturing in the Early Republic*, 80 J. PAT. & TRADEMARK OFF. SOC'Y 855 (1998).

[2] Ramon A. Klitzke, *History of Patents Abroad, in* THE ENCYCLOPEDIA OF PATENT PRACTICE AND INVENTION MANAGEMENT 384 (Robert Calvert ed., 1964); *see also* Howard I. Forman, *Two Hundred Years of American Patent Law, in* 200 YEARS OF ENGLISH & AMERICAN PATENT, TRADEMARK & COPYRIGHT LAW 21, 33 n.1 (ABA 1977).

[3] *See* Ramon A. Klitzke, *History of Patents Abroad, in* THE ENCYCLOPEDIA OF PATENT PRACTICE AND INVENTION MANAGEMENT 384 (Robert Calvert ed., 1964); *see also* Edward C. Walterscheid, *The Early Evolution of the United States Patent Law: Antecedents (pt. 1)*, 76 J. PAT. & TRADEMARK OFF. SOC'Y 697 (1994); Giulio Mandich, *Venetian Origins of Inventors' Rights*, 42 J. PAT. & TRADEMARK OFF. SOC'Y 378 (1960); Thomas A. Meshbesher, *The Role of History in Comparative Patent Law*, 78 J. PAT. & TRADEMARK OFF. SOC'Y 594, 601–02 (1996).

of the sixteenth century,[4] and by the colony of Massachusetts in 1641.[5]

Congress first exercised its constitutional power to grant exclusive rights to inventors in 1790, when it authorized the issuance of U.S. Letters Patent[6] to inventors.[7] Patents were a natural choice for conveying exclusive rights to inventors because of the English patent custom and because many of the American colonies and states previously had used patent-like grants for that purpose.[8] A patent confers on its owner the right to exclude others from making, using, offering for sale, or selling the

---

[4] *See* Ramon A. Klitzke, *History of Patents Abroad, in* THE ENCYCLOPEDIA OF PATENT PRACTICE AND INVENTION MANAGEMENT 384 (Robert Calvert ed., 1964). See also, regarding the English empire, Edward C. Walterscheid, *The Early Evolution of the United States Patent Law: Antecedents (pt. 2)*, 76 J. PAT. & TRADEMARK OFF. SOC'Y 849 (1994); DELLER'S WALKER ON PATENTS §§1–6 (2d ed. 1964); 1 WILLIAM C. ROBINSON, THE LAW OF PATENTS FOR USEFUL INVENTIONS §§3–10 (1890). See also, regarding the German empire, Hansjoerg Pohlmann, *The Inventor's Right in Early German Law*, 43 J. PAT. & TRADEMARK OFF. SOC'Y 121 (1961). Regarding the possible impact of natural law philosophy on the early evolution of patent rights, see Adam Mossoff, *Rethinking the Development of Patents: An Intellectual History, 1550–1800*, 52 HASTINGS L.J. 1255 (2001).

[5] Ramon A. Klitzke, *History of Patents—U.S., in* THE ENCYCLOPEDIA OF PATENT PRACTICE AND INVENTION MANAGEMENT 394 (Robert Calvert ed., 1964). Most colonial grants were issued by Massachusetts, Connecticut, and South Carolina. Edward C. Walterscheid, *The Early Evolution of the United States Patent Law: Antecedents (pt. 5)*, 78 J. PAT. & TRADEMARK OFF. SOC'Y 615, 630 (1996). No grants were issued by New Hampshire, Delaware, New Jersey, North Carolina, or Georgia. *Id.* Pennsylvania may not have issued any grants and fewer than 10 were issued by New York, Rhode Island, Maryland, and Virginia, collectively. *Id.* at 630–31.

[6] "Letters patent," from the Latin *literae patentes*, means "open letters." Historically, open letters were used by the English monarchy to bestow exclusive rights on people. In an open letter from the English monarch, the Great Seal was affixed so that the document could be read without breaking the seal. Similarly, U.S. Letters Patent, which are generally called patents, have a seal on the first page of the document. *See* Ramon A. Klitzke, *History of Patents Abroad, in* THE ENCYCLOPEDIA OF PATENT PRACTICE AND INVENTION MANAGEMENT 384 (Robert Calvert ed., 1964); *see also* Adam Mossoff, *Rethinking the Development of Patents: An Intellectual History, 1550–1800*, 52 HASTINGS L.J. 1255, 1259 (2001).

[7] *See* Ramon A. Klitzke, *History of Patents—U.S., in* THE ENCYCLOPEDIA OF PATENT PRACTICE AND INVENTION MANAGEMENT 394 (Robert Calvert ed., 1964); *see also* 1 WILLIAM C. ROBINSON, THE LAW OF PATENTS FOR USEFUL INVENTIONS §48 (1890). The first patent was issued to Samuel Hopkins. *See generally* David W. Maxey, *Inventing History: The Holder of the First U.S. Patent*, 80 J. PAT. & TRADEMARK OFF. SOC'Y 155 (1998).

[8] *See* Edward C. Walterscheid, *The Early Evolution of the United States Patent Law: Antecedents (pt. 5)*, 78 J. PAT. & TRADEMARK OFF. SOC'Y 615, 623–31, 665–85 (1996); Ramon A. Klitzke, *History of Patents Abroad, in* THE ENCYCLOPEDIA OF PATENT PRACTICE AND INVENTION MANAGEMENT 384 (Robert Calvert ed., 1964). Regarding the Continental Congress generally not granting rights to inventors, see Edward C. Walterscheid, *The Early Evolution of the United States Patent Law: Antecedents (pt. 5)*, 78 J. PAT. & TRADEMARK OFF. SOC'Y 615, 631–39 (1996). Regarding the deficiencies of nonfederal patent protection in the United States before 1790, see generally *id.* at 673–85. *See also* Edward C. Walterscheid, *To Promote the Progress of Useful Arts: American Patent Law and Administration, 1787–1836 (pt. 1)*, 79 J. PAT. & TRADEMARK OFF. SOC'Y 61, 63–71 (1997).

patented invention within the United States, its territories, and its possessions, or importing the invention into the same areas, for the life of the patent,[9] a right that is potentially very valuable to the inventor. Because a patent can be obtained only in exchange for full disclosure of the invention to the public,[10] patents provide an important incentive for people to invent and then to disclose their inventions. The public potentially can benefit significantly from such disclosure. As stated by Abraham Lincoln, who was a patentee: "The patent system added the fuel of interest to the fire of genius."[11]

The procedure for processing patent applications introduced in 1790 required the examination of all applications; that is, an examining board investigated each patent application and issued a patent only when it deemed the invention sufficiently useful and important.[12] In 1793, Congress changed the patent application procedure to a registration system.[13] Although patents supposedly were issued only for novel inventions under the Act of 1793, the government did not examine each application to determine novelty. Instead, the government accepted an applicant's oath that the invention was novel, and the courts were left to decide whether an invention was novel if the patent

---

[9] Additionally, if the invention is a process, the patent confers the right to exclude others from using, offering for sale, or selling throughout the United States, its territories, and its possessions, or importing into those areas, products made by that process. 35 U.S.C. §154 .

[10] See generally Edward C. Walterscheid, *The Early Evolution of the United States Patent Law: Antecedents (pt. 3)*, 77 J. PAT. & TRADEMARK OFF. SOC'Y 771, 777–802 (1995) (regarding the development of the English requirement for a specification).

[11] Lincoln received U.S. Patent No. 6,469 for a design that allowed a riverboat to navigate over the shoals. The quote is from a speech in Springfield, Illinois, on February 5, 1859. See THE STORY OF THE UNITED STATES PATENT OFFICE 1, 10–11 (Patent Office, Department of Commerce, 1972); see also Edward C. Walterscheid, *The Early Evolution of the United States Patent Law: Antecedents (pt. 4)*, 78 J. PAT. & TRADEMARK OFF. SOC'Y 77, 102–07 (1996) (regarding rationales for the English patent custom in the late eighteenth century).

[12] See Ramon A. Klitzke, *History of Patents—U.S.*, in THE ENCYCLOPEDIA OF PATENT PRACTICE AND INVENTION MANAGEMENT 394 (Robert Calvert ed., 1964); 1 WILLIAM C. ROBINSON, THE LAW OF PATENTS FOR USEFUL INVENTIONS §48 (1890); Edward C. Walterscheid, *To Promote the Progress of Useful Arts: American Patent Law and Administration, 1787–1836 (pt. 1)*, 79 J. PAT. & TRADEMARK OFF. SOC'Y 61, 71–72 (1997). The first examining board consisted of the Secretary of State (Thomas Jefferson), the Secretary of War (Henry Knox), and the Attorney General (Edmund Randolph).

[13] Edward C. Walterscheid, *To Promote the Progress of Useful Arts: American Patent Law and Administration, 1787–1836 (pt. 1)*, 79 J. PAT. & TRADEMARK OFF. SOC'Y 61, 72 (1997).

ultimately appeared in litigation.[14] The considerable uncertainty of the validity of patents created by this system[15] caused inventors difficulty in raising money to develop their inventions.[16] In 1836, Congress returned the patent application procedure to an examination system.[17] Despite the return to an examination system, the federal courts continued to have, and still have, an important role in deciding validity issues. They have this role probably because it is not uncommon for more complete, or better, evidence bearing on validity issues to be presented in an adversarial court proceeding than is presented in the United States Patent and Trademark Office (PTO) where applications are prosecuted by inventors ex parte.[18]

A relative increase in technological innovation throughout the rest of the world as compared with that in the United States became manifest by the late 1970s.[19] This led to important legislative and judicial actions in the early 1980s that tended to enhance the value of U.S. patents. For example, until these actions, it was perceived that there was little national uniformity in the interpretation and use of the patent laws because the regional courts of appeals expressed different attitudes toward patents.[20] Some studies suggested that the likelihood that a court would hold a patent invalid was greatly influenced by the regional circuit in which the case was tried.[21] National uniformity

---

[14] See 1 WILLIAM C. ROBINSON, THE LAW OF PATENTS FOR USEFUL INVENTIONS §49 n.2 (1890).

[15] See Ramon A. Klitzke, History of Patents—U.S., in THE ENCYCLOPEDIA OF PATENT PRACTICE AND INVENTION MANAGEMENT 394 (Robert Calvert ed., 1964); 1 WILLIAM C. ROBINSON, THE LAW OF PATENTS FOR USEFUL INVENTIONS §49 (1890); see also Edward C. Walterscheid, The Winged Gudgeon—An Early Patent Controversy, 79 J. PAT. & TRADEMARK OFF. SOC'Y 533 (1997) (telling the story of how the Superintendent of Patents (1802–1828) was sued for libel for stating that a patent he had issued was invalid and was being used to defraud the American people).

[16] See 1 WILLIAM C. ROBINSON, THE LAW OF PATENTS FOR USEFUL INVENTIONS §49 (1890); THE STORY OF THE UNITED STATES PATENT OFFICE 1, 5 (Patent Office, Department of Commerce, 1972).

[17] See 1 WILLIAM C. ROBINSON, THE LAW OF PATENTS FOR USEFUL INVENTIONS §50 (1890). A few other countries in the world now use a registration system. 1 IRVING KAYTON, PATENT PRACTICE, ch. 4 (6th ed. 1995).

[18] In 1999, Congress first created an optional inter partes reexamination procedure for patents already issued. See Chapter 2, §IV.C.

[19] 1 IRVING KAYTON, PATENT PRACTICE, ch. 4 (5th ed. 1993); see also Tom Arnold, Innovation and the Patent System Role in It: A Patent Lawyer's Point of View, 8 AIPLA Q.J. 131 (1980).

[20] See FRANK P. CIHLAR, THE COURT AMERICAN BUSINESS WANTED AND GOT: THE UNITED STATES COURT OF APPEALS FOR THE FEDERAL CIRCUIT 3–5 (1982).

[21] Id. at 11.

in the application of the patent laws was perceived as a method for reducing uncertainty regarding the validity of patents, and therefore increasing the value of patents. Increasing the value of patents, in turn, would increase the incentive to invent and to disclose, and would ultimately enhance technological innovation in this country.[22] The establishment of a national court for all patent appeals, a concept that had previously been advanced for over 100 years,[23] was vigorously pursued as one way to achieve these goals.

The Court of Appeals for the Federal Circuit was created in 1982. One of its primary goals was to create nationwide uniformity in the interpretation of various laws, including patent law.[24] By moving the vast majority of patent law appeals from the regional circuits to a single court, the creation of the Federal Circuit brought a stability to the patent law that, it was widely believed, would help spur investment in research and development and, thereby, economic growth in the United States.[25]

With an eye toward uniformity and creating stable law on which industry can rely, the Federal Circuit has tried, where possible, to elucidate bright-line rules in the patent law. Some of these experiments have endured, others have changed over time, and still others were modified by Supreme Court review. An example of a change that has endured is the Federal Circuit's decision that patent claim construction would be the job of trial judges, not of juries.[26] An example of evolving jurisprudence is the Federal Circuit's approach to the defense that an issued

---

[22] *Id.* at 3–5.

[23] Subcommittee on Patents, Trademarks and Copyrights, Senate Comm. on the Judiciary, 85th Cong., 2d Sess., Study No. 20 (1959).

[24] H.R. Rep. No. 97-312, at 20–23 (1981); *see also* Ellen E. Sward et al., *The Federal Courts Improvement Act: A Practitioner's Perspective*, 33 AM. U. L. REV. 385, 387–88 (1984); Sept. 13, 2006 address at Santa Clara University Tech Law Forum, by Judge Pauline Newman of the U.S. Court of Appeals for the Federal Circuit about the formation and history of the Federal Circuit, can be found at http://fora.tv/2006/09/13/Judge_Pauline_Newman.

[25] Antonin Scalia, *The Legacy of Judge Howard T. Markey*, 8 J. MARSHALL REV. INTELL. PROP. L. (Special Issue) 1, 2 (2009); Rochelle Cooper Dreyfus, *What the Federal Circuit Can Learn From the Supreme Court—And Vice Versa*, 59 AM. U. L. REV. 787, 789 (2010). The exceptions to the Federal Circuit's appellate jurisdiction in patent cases are discussed in Chapter 3, §VII.

[26] Markman v. Westview Instruments, Inc., 52 F.3d 967, 979, 983–88, 34 USPQ2d 1321 (Fed. Cir. 1995) (en banc), *aff'd*, 517 U.S. 370, 38 USPQ2d 1461 (1996). See Chapter 5.

patent should be unenforceable because of alleged inequitable conduct by the patentee in obtaining that patent from the United States Patent and Trademark Office.[27]

The Supreme Court has granted certiorari in instances where it found the Federal Circuit's patent jurisprudence at odds with the treatment of similar issues in other fields of law. An example of this was the Supreme Court's 2007 decision in *MedImmune, Inc. v. Genentech, Inc.*, which addressed the standards for applying the Declaratory Judgment Act to patent infringement disputes.[28] In addition, the Supreme Court has asserted its supervisory authority where Federal Circuit jurisprudence had strayed from established Supreme Court law, as in the interpretation of the requirement that, to be valid, a patent must claim "non-obvious subject matter."[29] The Supreme Court has also acted to resolve internal conflicts among the judges of the Federal Circuit, e.g., with respect to the scope and application of the "doctrine of equivalents" as a basis for finding patent infringement.[30]

In the past thirty years, in addition to creating the Federal Circuit, Congress has remained active in the field of patent law. For example, in 1984 Congress created both a safe harbor from charges of infringement for certain medical research activities and created a cause of action that permitted early resolution of controversies relating to patents affecting proposed generic drugs.[31] In 1988, Congress restricted the patent misuse defense, part of the balancing of the patent and antitrust laws.[32] In 2000,

---

[27]Therasense, Inc. v. Becton Dickinson & Co., 649 F.3d 1276, 99 USPQ2d 1065 (Fed. Cir. 2011) (en banc). See Chapter 7, §I.

[28]MedImmune, Inc. v. Genentech, Inc., 549 U.S. 118, 81 USPQ2d 1225 (2007). See Chapter 3, §I.B.

[29]KSR Int'l v. Teleflex, Inc., 550 U.S. 398, 418–19, 82 USPQ2d 1385 (2007). See Chapter 4, §I.D.

[30]Warner-Jenkinson Co. v. Hilton Davis Chem. Co., 520 U.S. 17, 41 USPQ2d 1865 (1997); Festo Corp. v. Shoketsu Kinzoku Kogyo Kabushiki Co., 535 U.S. 722, 62 USPQ2d 1705 (2002). On the subject of the relationship between the Supreme Court and the Federal Circuit, see Rebecca S. Eisenberg, *The Supreme Court and the Federal Circuit: Visitation and Custody of Patent Law,* 106 MICH. L. REV. First Impressions 28 (2007), and Rochelle Cooper Dreyfus, *What the Federal Circuit Can Learn From the Supreme Court—And Vice Versa,* 59 AM. U. L. REV. 787, 789 (2010).

[31]35 U.S.C. §271(e); Merck KGaA v. Integra Lifesciences I, Ltd., 545 U.S. 193, 74 USPQ2d 1801 (2005).

[32]35 U.S.C. §271(d). See Chapter 7, §II.

Congress authorized an optional inter partes reexamination of patents issued by the PTO, to supplement the ex parte reexamination process that it had enacted in 1980.[33] In 2004, Congress passed the CREATE Act, to facilitate joint research and development between companies.[34]

Most recently, on September 16, 2011, President Obama signed into law the Leahy-Smith America Invents Act.[35] This act eventually will result in a major change to the law of patent validity, changing the United States patent system from one in which the "first to invent" is entitled to a patent, to a system in which the rights will be awarded to the "first inventor to file" a patent application. This requires substantial changes to the statutory sections defining when an invention is novel and what prior acts can be used to invalidate a patent.[36] These changes, which will apply only to new patents issued from applications filed after March 16, 2013, are discussed in Chapter 4.

The America Invents Act also substantially enlarges the role of the PTO in reviewing the validity of issued patents through various "post-grant review" procedures. These changes, some of which are now in effect and others of which will take effect in the future, are discussed in Chapter 2. The other changes provided by the act are discussed where appropriate in the remaining chapters of this book.

The subject of what the patent law should become in the future is a topic of continuing study by Congress and the Executive Branch. The America Invents Act includes provisions for the continuing study of many aspects of patent law and policy, including the implementation of the new PTO practices and procedures, the scientific and medical ramifications of patents on genetic testing, ways to help small businesses seek international patent protection, and a study of "the consequences of litigation by non-practicing entities, or by patent assertion en-

---

[33] 35 U.S.C. §§301–307, 311–318 (2001 & Supp. 2005).

[34] Cooperative Research and Technology Enhancement Act of 2004 (Pub.L. 108–453) (2004); implemented in 35 U.S.C. §103(c)(2).

[35] Pub.L. 112-29, H.R. 1249 (2011). The legislative history of the act, H.R. Rep. No. 112-98 (2011), can be found online at http://judiciary.house.gov/issues/Patent%20Reform%20PDFS/CRPT-112hrpt98-pt1.pdf.

[36] Pub.L. 112-29, H.R. 1249 (2011), sec. 3.

tities."[37] In early 2011, the Federal Trade Commission published its second major study of the patent system in the past 10 years.[38]

This monograph is an introduction to U.S. patent law and practice as it exists today, including the changes that the passage of the America Invents Act will implement in the foreseeable future. Chapter 2 details the patent application process. Chapter 3 examines various procedural aspects of patent-related controversies. Chapter 4 discusses the conditions and requirements for a valid patent. Chapter 5 discusses substantive and procedural issues regarding claim construction. Chapter 6 examines the types of acts that are violations of the patent right (known as infringement) and examines defenses to a charge of infringement. Chapter 7 discusses equitable defenses. Chapter 8 explores the remedies available to a patent owner. Chapter 9 examines procedural issues relating to case management and the impact of juries on patent litigation.

---

[37] *Id.*, secs. 26, 27, 29, 31 and 34.

[38] Federal Trade Commission, *To Promote Innovation: The Proper Balance of Competition and Patent Law and Policy* (October 2003), available at http://www.ftc.gov/os/2003/10/innovation rpt.pdf; Federal Trade Commission, *The Evolving IP Marketplace: Aligning Patent Notice and Remedies With Competition* (March 2011), available at http://www.ftc.gov/os/2011/03/110307patent report.pdf.

Chapter 2

PROCEEDINGS IN THE PATENT AND TRADEMARK OFFICE

I. THE PATENT

The U.S. patent system was established by Congress in laws that are codified primarily in Title 35 of the United States Code. 35 U.S.C. §2 establishes the United States Patent and Trademark Office (PTO), within the Department of Commerce, as the executive agency responsible for the granting and issuing of patents and the registration of trademarks. Regulations issued by the PTO to govern its functions are codified in Title 37 of the Code of Federal Regulations. In addition, the PTO publishes the *Manual of Patent Examining Procedure* (MPEP)[1] to provide guidance to examiners, including a summary of the PTO's interpretation of the controlling legal authorities.

Three types of patents can be obtained. Utility patents are issued for "any new and useful process, machine, manufacture,

---

[1] The MPEP is available online at http://www.uspto.gov/web/offices/pac/mpep/mpep.htm. Although the MPEP does not have the force of law or the force of the PTO regulations, courts may take judicial notice of the PTO's understanding of the law as appropriate. MPEP, Foreword (8th ed. 2001, rev. July 2010); *see, e.g.,* Enzo Biochem, Inc. v. Gen-Probe Inc., 323 F.3d 956, 964, 63 USPQ2d 1609 (Fed. Cir. 2002); McKesson Info. Solutions, Inc. v. Bridge Med., Inc., 487 F.3d 897, 922–23, 82 USPQ2d 1865 (Fed. Cir. 2007).

or composition of matter, or any new and useful improvement thereof"[2] for a statutory term,[3] subject to the payment of quadrennial maintenance fees.[4] Plant patents are issued for "any distinct and new variety of plant" for a varying term.[5] Design patents are issued for "any new, original and ornamental design for an article of manufacture"[6] for a term of 14 years.[7] Generally, when legal literature refers to patents, it is discussing utility patents unless the description is otherwise qualified, expressly or by context. This monograph focuses on the utility patent.

A utility patent consists of a cover page that lists pertinent information, a written description, and one or more claims.

The information on the cover page includes the patent number and its date of issue, inventor's name, application number and date, title of the invention, assignee (if any), and other administrative details. All prior art and other references identified by the PTO as having been considered during the patent application process (as discussed more fully later) are also listed on the cover page. The cover page concludes with an abstract of the invention and a reproduction of the drawing that is considered most illustrative of the invention, if there are any drawings.

The written description of the patent (sometimes referred to as the specification) and drawings describe the invention, the preferred embodiment of the invention, and how to make and use it, so that the public has available the information needed to practice the invention. Upon expiration of the patent, the public may practice the invention freely.

The claims of the patent define the metes and bounds of the patent owner's exclusive rights during the life of the patent.

---

[2] 35 U.S.C. §101. The interpretation by the courts of the scope of the categories of patent-eligible subject matter is discussed in Chapter 4, §I.A.

[3] Under 35 U.S.C. §154(a), the term of a utility patent begins on the date that the PTO issues the patent and ends 20 years from the date on which the patent application was filed. If the patent application depends for priority (the date upon which the patented invention was made) on an earlier-filed application, the 20-year term may run from the application date of the earlier-filed application. The term of a utility patent can be extended in limited circumstances set forth in the patent statute. 35 U.S.C. §§154(b), 155–56. See this chapter, §IV.D, and Chapter 6, §I.F.

[4] 35 U.S.C. §41(b).

[5] *Id.* §161.

[6] *Id.* §171.

[7] *Id.* §173.

II. THE PARTICIPANTS

The PTO is headed by the Director, who is also an Undersecretary of Commerce. The Secretary of Commerce appoints, on the recommendation of the Director, a Commissioner for Patents to head the patent operations of the PTO.[8] The PTO examines patent applications and issues patents on some of those applications while rejecting others.[9] Patents are issued weekly by the PTO. The PTO also publishes weekly its *Official Gazette*, which contains abstracts of the patents issuing that week, as well as various other official notices.

The PTO currently receives more than 509,000[10] applications per year; each application is reviewed by one of approximately 6,225[11] examiners, all of whom have experience in some area of technology.[12] The PTO conducts initial and continuing training of examiners with respect to patent law and how to examine patent applications. Training is both technical and legal.

Although an applicant may proceed pro se before the PTO, most applicants are represented by a registered patent attorney or registered patent agent.[13] A patent application must be made

---

[8] Under the American Inventors Protection Act of 1999, enacted on November 29, 1999, the PTO was reorganized as of March 29, 2000. Before that date, the head of the PTO was the Commissioner of Patents and Trademarks, and the patent operations of the PTO were headed by the Assistant Commissioner for Patents.

[9] The PTO also examines trademark registration applications and registers or refuses to register trademarks on those applications.

[10] USPTO Performance and Accountability Report FY 2010, Filings Table, p. 53.

[11] *Id.* Table 28, p. 153.

[12] Examiners are divided among nine technology centers, each of which is divided into between four and eight examining groups. Each examining group, which is headed by a group director, covers a broad area of technology and has a number of subgroups, known as art units, that have responsibility for applications whose subject matter falls into subsets of that broad area. As of July 2011, there were approximately 280 art units in the PTO. Each art unit has primary examiners and assistant examiners and is headed by a supervisory primary examiner. Primary examiners have the authority to act on their own. Assistant examiners work under primary examiners and generally have less authority to act on their own. When an examiner is hired, he or she is assigned to an art unit that matches his or her technical background.

[13] Drafting and prosecuting a patent application requires special skill. Before someone can practice this skill on behalf of others, he or she must be registered with the PTO. To become registered, a person must pass an examination or have adequate experience as a patent examiner. PTO registration and practice are open to lawyers and nonlawyers. Registered lawyers are called patent attorneys and registered nonlawyers are called patent agents. As of July 2011, there were approximately 31,086 active patent attorneys and 10,262 active patent agents. *See* https://oedci.uspto.gov/OEDCI/.

in the name of the inventor.[14] If there is more than one inventor, each is referred to as joint inventor.[15] If an applicant transfers all or part of his or her interest in the invention to another, typically an employer, the transferee (or assignee) has the right to direct the course of the proceedings before the PTO on behalf of the applicant.[16]

Certain actions of the examiner in rejecting an application may be appealed to the Board of Patent Appeals and Interferences, which will be known as the Patent Trial and Appeal Board (PTAB or the Board) beginning on September 16, 2012. The Board also decides contests of priority, to identify the first inventor as between two or more applicants claiming the same invention. Such contests are referred to as interferences.[17] Decisions of the Board are reviewable by the federal courts.[18]

III. THE PROCESS

A. Preapplication Activities

Although the patent application process may be thought of as beginning with the drafting of the application itself, this

---

[14] 35 U.S.C. §111(a)(1).

[15] Although good faith errors in failing to name an inventor (nonjoinder) or incorrectly naming a noninventor as an inventor (misjoinder) can be corrected as late as the time of an infringement trial (35 U.S.C. §256), intentional misjoinder or nonjoinder can render a patent invalid or unenforceable. *See generally* Stark v. Advanced Magnetics Inc., 119 F.3d 1551, 43 USPQ2d 1321 (Fed. Cir. 1997). Only in certain limited circumstances, such as when an inventor is dead or legally incapacitated or when he or she refuses to sign an application, will an inventor not participate in the patent application process.

[16] 37 C.F.R. §3.71.

[17] Interferences are discussed in this chapter, §III.D.10. Under the Leahy-Smith America Invents Act, which was enacted on September 16, 2011, the PTAB also will conduct derivation proceedings, inter partes reviews and post-grant review. Under the Act, beginning on March 16, 2013, interference proceedings may only be brought for applications having a claim with an effective filing date before March 16, 2013, or for applications with a specific reference to another application with an effective filing date before March 16, 2013, that contained, at any time, a reference to such a claim. *See* Leahy-Smith America Invents Act, Pub.L. 112-29, H.R. 1249 (2011), sec. 3 (amending 35 U.S.C. §§134, 135, 145, 146, 154, and 305), sec. 6 (amending 35 U.S.C. §§301 and 311–319, and adding 35 U.S.C. §321–329), and sec. 7 (amending 28 U.S.C. §1295(a)(4)(A), 35 U.S.C. §§6, 141 and 143, 42 U.S.C. §2182, and 51 U.S.C. §20135).

[18] See this chapter, §III.E.

usually is preceded by other events. For example, an inventor may document (e.g., in a notebook) his or her conception of the invention and his or her reduction of that conception to practice. In addition, much dialogue may occur between the inventor and the person drafting the application. Another event that might occur prior to the preparation of an application is a prior art search. This search for relevant prior patents and technical literature may be carried out by the applicant or by a professional searcher on behalf of the applicant using online tools that are accessible through the Internet. Searches may also be done in the public search room maintained by the PTO in its Alexandria, Virginia location. An applicant is under no obligation to conduct a search before filing an application,[19] and indeed, not all applications are preceded by a search.

B. The Application

The statutory provision governing the contents of a patent application are 35 U.S.C §§111–122. The PTO regulations governing the contents of an application are set forth in 37 C.F.R. §§1.51–1.99. The MPEP discusses the content of an application in Chapter 600.

Each application that can mature into a patent[20] contains a specification, one or more drawings (if necessary), an oath or declaration, and the required filing, search, and examination fees.[21] The filing date of such an application is the date on which the specification and drawings (if necessary) and at least one claim are received at the PTO,[22] unless the specification and

---

[19] American Hoist & Derrick Co. v. Sowa & Sons, 725 F.2d 1350, 1362, 220 USPQ 763 (Fed. Cir.), *cert. denied,* 469 U.S. 821 (1984).

[20] An applicant may file a provisional application, which is not examined and cannot mature into a patent. A provisional application requires fewer parts. For example, the claims do not have to be included. A later-filed application for a utility patent can claim priority (i.e., the date of invention) from the filing date of the provisional application. 35 U.S.C. §119(e). A provisional application may also be converted into a non-provisional application, from which a patent may issue. 37 C.F.R. §1.53(c)(3); MPEP §601.01(c) (8th ed. 2001, rev. 2010).

[21] 35 U.S.C. §111(a)(3) (2001). These four components need not reach the PTO at the same time, but additional fees are incurred if some parts arrive later than others.

[22] This includes receipt of a paper application or an application filed electronically via the Internet using the PTO Electronic Patent Filing System—EFS-Web.

drawings are sent to the PTO using the express mail service of the U.S. Postal Service, in which case the filing date is the date that the specification and drawings were deposited in a U.S. post office as express mail. The specification and drawings can be insufficient in certain respects without affecting the filing date.[23]

1. Specification

The patent specification can have any format that the drafter desires, although the PTO prefers the following format:

1. title;
2. cross-reference to related applications;
3. statement regarding government rights;[24]
4. background: (a) field of the invention; and (b) description of related art;
5. summary of the invention;
6. brief description of the drawings;
7. detailed description of the invention, including the best mode (or description of the preferred embodiment);
8. claims; and
9. abstract of the disclosure.[25]

This suggested format usually is followed. The title usually is as short and specific as possible. The summary of the invention briefly states the nature and substance of the invention. The brief description of the drawings usually consists of one sentence for each drawing, describing very generally what is shown in that drawing. The abstract of the disclosure, printed on the cover page of the issued patent, enables the PTO and the public to grasp quickly the nature and extent of the disclosure.

---

[23] For example, the specification might not be in English, or the drawings might not be on the right kind of paper. These and other deficiencies can be corrected later, although correction of some deficiencies requires payment of additional fees.

[24] A statement of government rights identifies whether any government agency has rights under the application either because it was based on federally funded work, or because the subject matter of the application, e.g., atomic energy, vests title by statute in the United States Government. See Chapter 3, §I.A; 37 C.F.R. §1.77; MPEP §310 (8th ed. 2001, rev. 2010).

[25] 37 C.F.R. §1.77; MPEP §601 (8th ed. 2001, rev. 2010).

In the background section of the application, the applicant explains what he or she believes is the relevant field (art) and the state of that art before the making of the invention for which a patent is being sought. When appropriate, the inventor explains the problems existing in the art that his or her invention solves.

Inventors, registered patent agents, registered patent attorneys, and any others involved in the seeking of a patent are held to a high ethical standard in their dealings with the PTO, particularly with respect to disclosure of the state of the art to the extent that they are aware of it. This "duty of candor and good faith" for patent applicants, their attorneys, and others substantively involved in the prosecution of patents is set forth in 37 C.F.R. §1.56.

The high ethical standard is necessary because the patent application process is secret[26] and ex parte. An applicant should not be able to manipulate the process to obtain his or her exclusive rights merely because there is no one to state to the examiner the case against the application. Generally, this duty of candor and good faith is fulfilled by filing one or more Information Disclosure Statements[27] that explain the relevance of known information believed to be material.[28]

The detailed description of the invention constitutes the bulk of the specification. In addition to describing the invention sought to be patented, it must be written in terms sufficiently full, clear, concise, and exact to enable any person skilled in the

---

[26] 35 U.S.C. §122. Under the American Inventors Protection Act of 1999, an application loses its secret status if and when it is published (see this chapter, §III.D.11 regarding public use proceedings).

[27] An Information Disclosure Statement is generally accompanied by Form PTO/SB/08 (formerly known as Form PTO-1449), listing, in a prescribed format, the documents cited by the applicant. 37 C.F.R. §§1.97–1.98.

[28] The PTO defines materiality in Section 1.56 of the Rules of Practice in Patent Cases, 37 C.F.R. ch. 1. Before March 1992, information was deemed material if a reasonable examiner would have considered the information important in deciding whether to allow the application to issue as a patent. After March 1992, information is deemed material "when it is not cumulative to information already of record or being made of record in the application, and (1) It establishes, by itself or in combination with other information, a *prima facie* case of unpatentability of a claim; or (2) It refutes, or is inconsistent with, a position the applicant takes in: (i) Opposing an argument of unpatentability relied on by the Office, or (ii) Asserting an argument of patentability." 37 C.F.R. §1.56(b).

art to which the invention pertains to be able to make and use the invention.[29] This section must contain a disclosure of the best mode of carrying out the invention known to the inventor at the time of filing.[30] In this section, the drawings are discussed in detail.

The nonprovisional specification concludes with one or more claims that define particularly and distinctly the subject matter that the inventor regards as his or her invention. The claims set the metes and bounds of the patent owner's exclusive rights. Books have been devoted to teaching the patent practitioner how best to draft claims.[31] Each claim is the object of a sentence that usually begins with "I [or We] claim:" or "What is claimed is . . . ." The claims can be punctuated and laid out in whatever manner the drafter desires, except that there can be only one period and that must come at the end of the sentence. Words in the patent application are not necessarily held to their ordinary meaning. Each inventor, and his or her registered agent or registered attorney, can be his or her own lexicographer.[32] However, the application must define words being used in an uncommon manner.[33]

A patent application generally has more than one claim. The claims may vary in scope. Broad claims include fewer elements, or limitations, than narrow claims do and therefore cover a wider range of subject matter. Claims often are arranged in

---

[29] 35 U.S.C. §112, ¶1.

[30] *Id.* The Leahy-Smith America Invents Act, enacted on September 16, 2011, eliminates the failure to disclose the best mode as a basis in which a claim can be held invalid or canceled. Because the Act did not remove the best mode requirement in 35 U.S.C. §112, there remains a requirement to disclose the best mode. However, there appears to be no consequence, including inequitable conduct, or PTO proceeding, to address a failure to disclose the best mode. *See* Leahy-Smith America Invents Act, Pub.L. 112-29, H.R. 1249 (2011), sec. 15 (amending 35 U.S.C. §119(e)(1), 120, and 282).

[31] *See, e.g.,* THOMAS J. GREER, JR., WRITING AND UNDERSTANDING U.S. PATENT CLAIMS (1979); THE ART OF DRAFTING PATENT CLAIMS (Joseph Gray Jackson & G. Michael Morris eds., 1966); ROBERT C. FABER, LANDIS ON MECHANICS OF PATENT CLAIM DRAFTING (5th ed. 2004); EMERSON STRINGHAM, PATENT CLAIM DRAFTING (2d ed. 1952).

[32] See Chapter 5, §II.A.3.a.

[33] See Chapter 5, §II.A.3. Certain words have customary meaning in patent law. For example, the word "comprising" indicates that the claim is open (that is, that it covers the invention, including the elements set out in the claim, as well as any additional elements), whereas the phrase "consisting of" indicates that the claim is closed (that is, it covers the invention, including no more and no fewer than the listed elements). See Chapter 5, §IV.B.

order of decreasing scope (that is, the broadest comes first and the narrowest comes last). Claims can be in independent, dependent, or multiple dependent form. An independent claim is completely self-contained. A dependent claim refers back to an earlier claim and is considered to include all of its own limitations as well as those of the referenced claim. A multiple dependent claim refers back to two or more claims and is considered to include all of its own limitations as well as those of any one of the referenced claims.[34]

2. Drawings

Drawings are not always a necessary part of the application. If the invention is for a process or method of doing something, drawings usually are not required. If drawings are required, formal rules govern their acceptability.[35]

3. Oath or Declaration

A written oath, or declaration, is part of a nonprovisional patent application. Except in certain limited situations, it must be signed by the actual inventor or joint inventors.[36] In addition to containing the applicant's name, citizenship, residence, and address, the oath or declaration must state that the person signing (1) has reviewed and understands the content of the specification, (2) believes that he or she is the original and first

---

[34]For an example of an independent claim, see ROBERT C. FABER, LANDIS ON MECHANICS OF PATENT CLAIM DRAFTING §2:10 (5th ed. 2004). For an example of a dependent claim, see *id.* at §2:9. For examples of multiple dependent claims, see MPEP §608.01(n) (8th ed. 2001, rev. 2010). Currently, a patent application can be filed with an unlimited number of claims so long as the applicant pays additional fees for claims beyond a basic number.

[35]An applicant, for example, must petition to use color drawings. Photographs are not accepted, except in very limited situations. However, for plant patent applications, color drawings sometimes may be required and photographs are acceptable.

[36]37 C.F.R. §1.41. If the inventor is dead, insane, or legally incapacitated, a legal representative can sign the oath or declaration. *Id.* §§1.42–1.43. If the inventor is missing and cannot be found after diligent effort, or the inventor simply refuses to sign the oath or declaration, someone with a sufficient proprietary interest can sign it upon making the appropriate showing. *Id.* §1.47.

inventor of the claimed subject matter, and (3) acknowledges the duty to disclose material information.[37]

4. Filing Fees

The fees charged for filing a patent application vary depending on the number and form of the claims included in the application and the number of pages of the application. Additional fees may be incurred during prosecution of the application if the number or form of the claims is changed by amendment.[38]

C. Initial Processing of the Application

All papers arriving at the mail room of the PTO are marked with the date of receipt. Any papers purporting to be a new application, whether complete or incomplete, are marked also with an eight-digit application number, including a two-digit series code and a six-digit serial number.[39] Papers filed electronically are treated analogously. As of November 15, 2011, applications that are not filed electronically will incur an additional filing surcharge.

---

[37] Id. §1.63. The Leahy-Smith America Invents Act, which was enacted on September 16, 2011, includes a provision, having an effective date of September 16, 2012, that allows an assignee to provide a substitute statement for an inventor who is unable to provide an oath or declaration. The substitute statement may be included in an assignment executed by the inventor in lieu of providing the substitute statement. See Leahy-Smith America Invents Act, Pub.L. 112-29, H.R. 1249 (2011), sec. 4 (amending 35 U.S.C. §§112, 115, 118, and 251).

[38] A 50% reduction in filing fees is given to applicants who qualify as "small entit[ies]," namely, individual inventors, nonprofit organizations, and "small business concern[s]" as defined by the Small Business Administration specifically for this purpose. Id. §§1.27–1.28; 13 C.F.R. pt. 121. The Leahy-Smith America Invents Act includes a provision, effective on September 26, 2011, that creates a micro entity class that qualifies for a 75% reduction in PTO fees. To claim micro entity status, applicants must satisfy the small entity requirements and further state that (i) they were not named as an inventor on more than four previously filed applications, (ii) their annual income is not more than three times the U.S. median income, and (iii) the application has not been assigned or is intended to be assigned to an entity having an income above three times the U.S. median income. See Leahy-Smith America Invents Act, Pub.L. 112-29, H.R. 1249 (2011), sec. 10 (adding 35 U.S.C. §123).

[39] Traditionally, applications were referred to by the six-digit serial number. Serial numbers repeat every few years, so the filing date was needed to unambiguously identify an application. The PTO added the series code prefix to the serial number, which forms a unique application number. 37 C.F.R. §1.54; MPEP §503 (8th ed. 2001, rev. 2010). Many practitioners continue to refer to the application number as a serial number.

New applications are initially processed by the Office of Initial Patent Examination (otherwise known as the Application Division), which decides if an application is complete and meets all formal requirements.[40] Any drawings accompanying the application are forwarded to the official draftsperson, who checks to see if the drawings comply with the formal requirements. Any assignment of the application is forwarded to the Assignment Division, which records the assignment in its computer and microfilm records and returns it to the applicant with a notification of the reel and frame numbers in the microfilm records.

The Application Division may correspond directly with the applicant regarding certain informalities in the application. The applicant must respond before the application will be processed further.

The PTO maintains a detailed classification system that breaks down technologies into specific categories. Within the classification system are hundreds of classes, each class having at least dozens of subclasses. The Application Division determines the appropriate class and subclass of the application. It then forwards the application to the examining group in charge of that class and subclass. The forwarded documents were traditionally kept in a file jacket known as a file wrapper. The PTO has replaced this paper file with an electronic file. As of this writing, only certain old application files remain in paper form. The electronic file, known as an image file wrapper, is made up of the applicant's electronic submissions, if any, and scanned versions of paper submissions. The PTO's goal is to replace paper file processing with electronic file processing.

D. Examination and Prosecution

The statutory provisions governing examination of applications are 35 U.S.C. §§131–134. The PTO regulations governing examination are set forth in 37 C.F.R., beginning at Section 1.102. The MPEP discusses the examination process in Chapter 700.

---

[40] If an application is incomplete, the applicant is notified of the incompleteness and is given time to correct the defect. Depending on the type of defect, the application may or may not be accorded a filing date as of its date of receipt (see this chapter, §III.B). If a filing date is accorded, it may be lost if the defect is not corrected within the allowed time.

1. Formalities and Search by the Examiner

When a nonprovisional application reaches an examining group, it is assigned to the appropriate art unit and then to a particular examiner. The examiner first ascertains that the application contains the required elements, then reads the application to determine whether it is clear enough to be examined[41] and whether it contains more than one invention.

After determining that an application is sufficiently clear to be examined and contains only one invention, the examiner conducts a search for prior art relevant to the claimed subject matter, noting in a place provided on the file wrapper the classes and subclasses searched. Documents found in the search are called references. The search can be conducted in the examiner's private materials, in a library maintained by the examining group (which generally is restricted to classes for which the group is responsible), or in the PTO Scientific Library, which contains nonpatent technical literature and all patents issued by most major countries. However, most searching by examiners is now conducted electronically using online searching tools developed by the PTO for that purpose. The quality and thoroughness of the examiner's search are a function of his or her searching skill, the time allocated for the search, and the completeness of the libraries or files searched.[42]

2. First Office Action

After this initial activity by the examiner, he or she communicates in writing with the applicant or his or her attorney or agent, if one has been appointed. This communication is called an "Office Action." The Office Action includes at least two parts: a form cover letter, on which the examiner summarizes the action by checking the appropriate boxes and filling in the

---

[41] For example, an application filed by a foreign applicant might not conform to idiomatic English or U.S. practice. *See* MPEP §702.01 (8th ed. 2001, rev. 2010).

[42] 3 PATENT PRACTICE 11-4, 11-29 (Irving Kayton & Karyl S. Kayton eds., 6th ed. 1995).

correct blanks, and a typewritten explanation of the action. The Office Action also may include various attachments, which are itemized in the cover letter.

Restriction and election requirements. If the examiner determines that there is more than one invention claimed in the application, whether or not the examiner has searched any of those inventions, the first Office Action may list the inventions found by the examiner and include either a restriction requirement, if the inventions are clearly different, or an election of species requirement, if the inventions are related and at least one claim is generic to all inventions. In reply to either requirement, the applicant must choose one invention for prosecution. If there is a restriction requirement, the applicant who wishes to patent the nonelected inventions must present them in one or more divisional applications (see this chapter, §III.D.7). If there is an election of species requirement, the nonelected claims may be rejoined to the application if a generic claim is allowed.

Request for clarification. If the application is unclear, the first Office Action may request that the applicant clarify the application by correcting defects in its language. This is rare.

Substantive actions. The first substantive Office Action (which may be the second Office Action in situations in which a first action as described earlier was issued) can allow claims, reject claims,[43] object to claims, or object to the specifica-

---

[43] Chapter 2100 of the MPEP sets forth guidelines for examiners regarding the statutory requirements for patentability and the current court interpretations of those requirements. For example, in response to the Supreme Court's 2007 decision in *KSR Int'l Co. v. Teleflex Inc.*, 550 U.S. 398, 82 USPQ2d 1385 (2007), the PTO published Examination Guidelines for Determining Obviousness in 2007, and amended them again in September 2010 in light of Federal Circuit case law applying *KSR. See* MPEP §2141 (8th ed. 2001, rev. 2010). As a general matter, claims may be rejected if they are found to be anticipated by a reference (35 U.S.C. §102) or made obvious by a reference or combination of references (35 U.S.C. §103) (see Chapter 4, §§I.C and D, respectively). Claims may also be rejected under 35 U.S.C. §112 if they are too vague or indefinite to "particularly point[ ] out and distinctly claim[ ]" the exclusive right to which the applicant is entitled, so that a third party cannot be certain he or she is not infringing (see Chapter 4, §II.D). Less common grounds for rejection also exist. For example, a claim will be rejected as being drawn to "nonstatutory subject matter" if it is drawn to something not enumerated in 35 U.S.C. §101, §161, or §171. There are also several judicially created doctrines under which claims may be rejected (e.g., obviousness-type double patenting, where (for example) the subject matter of two applications filed by the same applicant are obvious in view of each other). *See* MPEP §804 (8th ed. 2001, rev. 2010).

tion.[44] It also may withdraw claims if the claims are drawn to an invention not elected in reply to a restriction or election requirement. The first substantive action may include notices of informalities. These informalities must be corrected within the time set by the examiner for reply to the substantive issues raised.[45]

3. Applicant's Reply

Within the period of time allotted for reply, which usually can be extended up to a maximum statutory period of six months upon payment of a fee, the applicant must reply to all of the examiner's rejections and objections or the application is abandoned.

Applicants may reply to claim rejections and objections by amendment of the claims, by argument, or by a combination of both. A reply usually includes both claim amendments and arguments designed to distinguish the invention as claimed from any prior art applied by the examiner. A reply also may include affidavits as to the nonobviousness of the invention, or affidavits establishing invention before the date of some reference cited by the examiner.

If the examiner rejects or objects to a claim as not being supported by the specification, the applicant may reply by amending the specification to reflect the language of the claim. The applicant also may amend the specification in reply to an objection asserting that it does not describe the invention with sufficient clarity.

In amending the application, and particularly in amending the specification, the applicant may not introduce new

---

[44]The specification may be objected to under 35 U.S.C. §112, ¶1, if it does not (1) describe the invention sought to be patented, (2) enable one skilled in the pertinent art to make or carry out the invention, (3) enable one skilled in the art to use the invention, or (4) set forth the best mode of carrying out the invention contemplated by the inventor (see Chapter 4, §II.C). If a specification is objected to under Section 112, paragraph 1, all claims directed to subject matter with respect to which the specification is objected to are rejected on that basis.

[45]Any substantive action (first or otherwise) can also include a Notice of References Cited (Form PTO-892), listing references found in the examiner's search and any Form PTO/SB/08 (formerly known as Form PTO-1449) that may have been submitted by the applicant with an Information Disclosure Statement, initialed by the examiner as evidence of having considered it.

matter, i.e., subject matter that was not disclosed in the application as filed.[46] An applicant seeking to add new matter to a specification may do so, if at all, by filing a continuation-in-part application.[47]

4. Reconsideration and Allowance

After the applicant submits a reply to the first Office Action, the examiner reconsiders the application. If the examiner is satisfied with the reply, he or she issues a Notice of Allowance. A Notice of Allowance is a form letter, the primary purpose of which is to inform the applicant of allowance of the application and to set a nonextendable three-month period by the end of which a statutory fee, called the issue fee, as well as publication fee if the application was published by the PTO during examination, must be paid to cause the patent to issue. The Notice of Allowance frequently is accompanied by a Notice of Allowability, which is similar to the cover letter of an Office Action and may have attachments such as an Examiner's Amendment (an amendment entered by the examiner, sometimes after consultation with the applicant), a Notice of References Cited, or initialed PTO/SB/08 forms originally submitted by the applicant. The Notice of Allowability also reminds the applicant of any drawing corrections that are required but have been held in abeyance pending allowance.

---

[46] 35 U.S.C. §132. New matter is defined by the PTO in MPEP §608.04 and §706.03(o), and is discussed further in MPEP §2163.06. If the specification is amended to support an originally filed claim, there is no problem of new matter because the originally filed claim is part of the original disclosure. *In re* Myers, 410 F.2d 420, 427, 161 USPQ 668 (C.C.P.A. 1969). However, if a claim is amended to overcome prior art, and in a second or subsequent Office Action the examiner says that the amended part of the claim is not supported by the specification, the applicant cannot add any material to the specification because such material would not be supported by any part of the original disclosure. *In re* Rasmussen, 650 F.2d 1212, 1214–15, 211 USPQ 323 (C.C.P.A. 1981); *In re* Winkhaus, 527 F.2d 637, 640, 188 USPQ 129 (C.C.P.A. 1975). Similarly, if the objection is based on nonenablement, it may not be possible to amend the specification without introducing new matter. However, if the specification is objected to because, for example, it originated in a foreign country and is not in grammatical English, it usually can be amended to correct the language without introducing new matter. *Cf. In re* Oda, 443 F.2d 1200, 170 USPQ 268 (C.C.P.A. 1971).

[47] Continuation applications are discussed in this chapter in §III.D.7.c.

5. *Interviews*

At any time from the issuance of the first Office Action until the issuance of a final Office Action, the applicant or applicant's representative is entitled to a personal or telephonic interview with the examiner for the purposes of clarifying the issues separating them and of reaching agreement leading to allowance of the application. After a final Office Action is issued, it is in the examiner's discretion to allow interviews and to consider replies. The examiner must make the substance of the interview of record by completing an Interview Summary form. The applicant also must file a summary of the interview.[48]

In March 2008, the PTO initiated a First-Action Interview Pilot Program in which an applicant may receive the results of a prior art search conducted by the examiner and then be permitted to conduct an interview with the examiner to discuss the search results before the first Office Action on the merits.[49]

6. *Reconsideration and Subsequent Office Action; Final Actions*

If the examiner is not satisfied by a reply, he or she may issue another Office Action. This second or subsequent Office Action may be made "final," except where the Office Action is based on a new ground of rejection, such as newly discovered prior art. A "final" Office Action does not mean that allowance no longer is possible. Rather, it means that: (1) although the applicant may present new amendments and arguments, the examiner no longer is required to consider them as of right; and (2) by six months from the date of the final Office Action, the application must be allowed or an appeal must be filed with the Board of Patent Appeals and Interferences or, after September 16, 2012, the Patent Trial and Appeal Board (the Board), or the application will be considered abandoned.[50]

---

[48] 37 C.F.R. §1.133(b); MPEP §713.04 (8th ed. 2001, rev. 2010).

[49] See http://www.uspto.gov/patents/init_events/faipp_landing.jsp. As of this writing, the First-Action Interview Pilot Program has been expanded to all utility art areas. The Full First-Action Interview Pilot Program will continue until May 16, 2012.

[50] MPEP §706.07 (8th ed. 2001, rev. 2010).

7. Replies to a Final Action; Request for Continued Examination

Replies filed after a final Office Action are answered by a Notice of Allowance, a Notice of Allowability, or an Advisory Action, which is a form letter on which the examiner checks a box indicating why an amendment after final rejection was not entered. For example, an amendment after final rejection may be refused entry if it raises new issues (as distinguished from new matter, which is always prohibited) or if it would require additional searching by the examiner. The examiner also may enter an amendment after final rejection only for purposes of an appeal by the applicant to the board.

After a final rejection by the examiner, the applicant is faced with a choice: the applicant can abandon the application, file an appeal with the board, take allowed claims and cancel the others, or file a Request for Continued Examination (RCE).

An RCE allows for continued examination of the application.[51] Upon filing of the RCE along with the appropriate fee, the finality of the final rejection will be withdrawn and the amendment submission will be entered and considered. After considering the amendment submission and the arguments submitted in reply to the final Office Action, the examiner can issue a Notice of Allowance or another Office Action. Examination will then continue in the same manner as outlined above.

a. Appeals

If the applicant files an appeal, he or she is given two months, extendable to seven months, to file an appeal brief.[52] After the appeal brief has been filed, the examiner must file an

---

[51] 37 C.F.R. §1.114.

[52] In July 2005, the United States Patent and Trademark Office (USPTO) established a pre-appeal brief conference program that offers a patent applicant an avenue to request a review of the legal and factual basis of the rejections in his or her patent application prior to the filing of an appeal brief. See New Pre-Appeal Brief Conference Pilot Program, 1296 OFF. GAZ. PAT. OFFICE 67 (July 12, 2005). Under this program, an applicant can submit up to five pages of arguments showing clear errors in the basis of the rejections at the same time as filing for the appeal. After reviewing the pre-appeal arguments the PTO will either (i) determine that the application remains under appeal, (ii) reopen prosecution of the application on the merits, or (iii) allow the application.

examiner's answer. No statutory or regulatory time limit applies for filing the examiner's answer. Within two months of the examiner's answer, the applicant may file a reply brief.

The applicant may request an oral hearing.[53] The appeal is then placed on the Board's calendar and assigned to a panel of three Administrative Patent Judges. When an appeal is set for oral hearing, the applicant is given notice of the date of the hearing and, at that point, may waive the hearing.

After an oral hearing, or if no oral hearing is requested, the appeal is considered by the Board. The Board may affirm the decision of the examiner in whole or in part, or may reverse it. After the Board reaches its decision, the application is returned to the examining group for further prosecution. If the Board affirms the examiner's decision, the applicant is in the same position as before the appeal—he or she must abandon the application or file a continuing application. If the Board reverses the examiner's decision, the examiner must issue a notice of allowance. If the Board affirms the examiner's decision in part, the examiner must issue an action reflecting that decision.

b. Cancellation of Claims

If an applicant faces final rejection of some claims, but allowance of others, whether or not the result of an appeal, he or she may decide to take the allowed claims and cancel the others. A notice of allowance would then be issued.

c. Continuing Applications

A continuing application is a generic term for three types of patent applications that are entitled to the filing date of an earlier (parent) application.[54] The application is said to have as an effective filing date the filing date of the parent application. If an application has an effective filing date earlier than the actual filing date, then prior art having a date between the

---

[53] The request must be filed within two months of the examiner's answer, but it can be filed at any time starting with the filing of the appeal. 37 C.F.R. §41.47(b).

[54] 35 U.S.C. §120.

effective and actual filing dates cannot be used against the application. The three types of continuing applications are continuation applications, continuation-in-part applications, and divisional applications. The requirements for claiming continuing status are that the application must be filed while the parent application is still pending (copendency), at least one inventor must be common to the two applications, and the text of the second application must refer back to the first.[55]

If an applicant faces a final rejection of all claims in an application or a final rejection of claims that were canceled to allow other claims to issue, or if there are nonelected claims in the application at the time of allowance, the applicant may wish to file a continuing application directed to the canceled or nonelected claims. In addition, there may be other reasons for filing a continuing application, as discussed later.

A **continuation application** is an application whose specification is the same as that of the parent application, but whose claims may be the same as or different from those of the parent application. A continuation application is entitled to the parent's filing date as to all subject matter contained in it. Several reasons exist for filing a continuation. For example, a continuation might be filed if all claims are finally rejected in the parent and the applicant has new amendments or arguments to present. A continuation application is particularly appropriate if the new amendments or arguments were presented in the parent after final rejection and were not entered because they raised new issues or required further searching, but the examiner gave some indication that the amendments or arguments had some merit.[56] A continuation also might be filed if only some claims were finally rejected in the parent. Those claims might be cancelled from the parent, allowing the other claims to issue. The cancelled claims may then be pursued, with or without change, in the continuation. Another reason for filing a continuation is that the applicant may have thought of a new way to claim the

---

[55] MPEP §§201.06, 201.07, 201.08, 201.11 (8th ed. 2001, rev. 2010).

[56] The need to file a continuation for this purpose was largely eliminated by the American Inventors Protection Act of 1999, which created the RCE, allowing an applicant, upon payment of a fee, to remove the finality of a final rejection and continue prosecution in the same application. 35 U.S.C. §132(b); 37 C.F.R. §1.114.

invention after allowance or final rejection of the parent, when claims may no longer be added directly to the parent.

A **continuation-in-part application** is an application that has some subject matter in common with the parent but also has new subject matter. A continuation-in-part is entitled to the parent's filing date as to any subject matter in common, but only to its own filing date as to the new matter. A continuation-in-part might be filed if the applicant had to add limitations to the parent claims to distinguish a reference or references, but the added limitations were not supported by the specification of the parent and the examiner would not allow supporting material to be added to the specification because it introduced new matter. The applicant could file a continuation-in-part to include the new matter. A continuation-in-part, including newly conceived material, also might be filed if the applicant conceives of improvements to the invention described in the parent. A continuation-in-part filed for this reason may be filed at any time, regardless of the status of prosecution of the parent case, as long as the parent is still pending. In such a case, the parent application might be allowed to continue. If the applicant thinks the invention as described in the parent is not commercially significant, he or she might abandon the parent.

A **divisional application** is a continuing application that is based on a parent application and has the same specification, except that the claims differ, usually because of a restriction requirement or an election of species requirement. The application is entitled to the parent's filing date for all purposes. A patent issued on the parent application cannot be used as prior art against such an application if division was made because of an examiner's requirement.[57] So-called voluntary divisions, by which the applicant selects different groups of claims and cancels some from the parent to be presented in a new application, are actually continuation applications. Voluntary divisional applications, like other continuation applications, are not protected from the possible prior art effects of a patent issued on the earlier application.

---

[57] 35 U.S.C. §121.

8. Postallowance Activity

After a Notice of Allowance is issued, amendments can be made only on a showing of good cause as to why they were not made earlier, and submissions of additional prior art by the applicant will be considered only if the applicant certifies that the art was not known to the applicant more than three months before the date it is submitted.[58] If an amendment is made to correct something in an Examiner's Amendment accompanying the allowance, it usually is entered if it does not change the meaning of the allowed application. Similarly, if an amendment is of no substantive consequence, such as an amendment to correct recently discovered typographical errors in the application, it will be entered. Even new claims may be entered, provided they are of the same scope as allowed claims and are supported by the specification. However, after the issue fee is paid, at which point preparations begin for printing the application as a patent and it becomes more difficult to enter changes, amendments may be entered only if the application is withdrawn from issue.

An application may be withdrawn from issue at the initiative of the PTO or on petition by the applicant on a showing of good cause, such as the discovery of new prior art that is relevant to the application. However, once the issue fee is paid, a patent will be withdrawn from issue on the PTO's own initiative only for "(1) [a] mistake on the part of the Office; (2) [a] violation of [37 C.F.R.] §1.56 or illegality in the application; (3) [u]npatentability of one or more claims; or (4) [f]or interference [see this chapter, §III.D.10]."[59] Similarly, after the issue fee is paid, the patent will be withdrawn from issue on applicant's petition only for unpatentability of one or more claims, for the filing of a request for continued examination, or for express abandonment.[60] If the application is not withdrawn, a patent usually will issue about three or four months after the issue fee is paid.

---

[58] 37 C.F.R. §1.97(d).
[59] Id. §1.313(b).
[60] Id. §1.313(c).

9. Foreign Priority

An applicant can claim the benefit of the filing date of an application filed abroad. Under the terms of the Paris Convention for the Protection of Industrial Property, and independently under relevant portions of the World Trade Organization (WTO) agreements resulting from the Uruguay Round of multilateral trade negotiations under the auspices of the General Agreement on Tariffs and Trade (GATT),[61] implemented in this country under 35 U.S.C. §119(a)–(d), the benefit of the filing date (referred to as priority) from the first application for an invention filed in any member country can be claimed in a U.S. application as long as it is filed within one year of the first application.[62] Priority can be claimed at any time during the pendency of an application. A claim of priority is perfected by filing a certified copy of the foreign application. Whether benefit is claimed from a domestic or foreign application, materials published between the priority date and the application filing date are not prior art to the application.[63]

10. Interferences

Until March 16, 2013, the United States will operate under a first-to-invent patent system, unlike the first-to-file system

---

[61] There are other relevant agreements as well. For example, before Taiwan became a member of the WTO, priority from a Taiwanese patent application could be claimed under a bilateral agreement between the United States and Taiwan.

[62] In addition to the application filed in a member country, an applicant (in certain circumstances) may rely on an "international application" filed pursuant to the Patent Cooperation Treaty (PCT), which is administered by the World Intellectual Property Organization (WIPO). The PCT is a multilateral treaty among more than 130 nations that is designed to simplify the patenting process when an applicant seeks a patent on the same invention in more than one nation. See 35 U.S.C. chs. 35–37; PCT APPLICANT'S GUIDE (WIPO, 1992, rev. June 2011).

[63] The one-year period of 35 U.S.C. §102(b) (discussed in Chapter 4, §II.B.1) is counted from the earliest effective U.S. filing date under 35 U.S.C. §119(e) or §120, but not from a foreign priority date under 35 U.S.C. §119(a)–(d). The exception that removes Section 102(b) prior art events from the protection of a foreign priority claim is explicitly written into Section 119(a). On the other hand, Section 119(e), which defines a provisional application's domestic priority, includes no such exception.

followed by most other countries in the world.[64] Thus, the first inventor may be the inventor entitled to a patent, even if another files a patent application earlier. If two or more applications claim the same subject matter, the applications are said to be interfering and the examiner, after determining patentability of the invention to each applicant, can declare an interference between them.[65] An interference can also be declared between a pending application and an issued patent. If the examiner does not declare the interference, the applicant can provoke an interference. An interference can relate to some or all of the claims in the application or patent. Beginning March 16, 2013, the United States will operate under a first-to-file system followed by other countries in the world. Regardless, interference proceedings may continue to be brought for applications having a claim with an effective filing date before March 16, 2013, or for applications with a specific reference to another application with an effective filing date before March 16, 2013, that contained, at any time, a reference to such a claim.

A patent interference is an inter partes proceeding in the PTO that includes the taking of testimony, the introduction of evidence, and the filing of motions. The purpose of an interference is to determine which of the parties was the first to make the invention.

Invention, at least for the purpose of interference, includes conception and reduction to practice.[66] Reduction to practice can be actual or constructive. Constructive reduction to practice is the filing of a patent application. The activities relied on to establish invention must take place in the United States, in a North American Free Trade Agreement (NAFTA) country,

---

[64]The Leahy-Smith America Invents Act includes a provision, having an effective date of March 16, 2013, that changes U.S. patent law to a "first-to-file" system. The Act also includes a provision, having the same effective date, that eliminates interference proceedings. However, the Act provides for derivation proceedings, as of the same effective date, to resolve a claim by the second inventor to file that the first inventor to file derived the application from the second inventor to file and therefore is not entitled to a patent. The derivation proceedings resemble the current interference proceedings in some respects. *See* Leahy-Smith America Invents Act, Pub.L. 112-29, H.R. 1249 (2011), sec. 3 (amending 35 U.S.C. §§100, 102, 119(a), 134, 145, 146, 154, 172, 202(c), 287(c)(4), 291, 305, 363, 374, and 375(a)).

[65]MPEP §§2304.04 and 2305 (8th ed. 2001, rev. 2010).

[66]35 U.S.C. §102(g).

or in a member country in the GATT-established WTO.[67] Therefore, an applicant whose invention was made outside the United States, Canada, Mexico, or a WTO-member country can rarely prove reduction to practice before the effective U.S. filing date of his or her application. For an invention made in a NAFTA or WTO country, the party who is both first to conceive the invention and first to reduce it to practice prevails.[68] However, if the first to conceive the invention is not the first to reduce it to practice, the additional element of diligence comes into play. If the party first to conceive but second to reduce to practice can prove he or she was diligently pursuing the invention between a time prior to the date of its conception by the other party and the date of his or her own reduction to practice, he or she will prevail.[69] Otherwise, the other party will prevail.[70]

11. Other Inter Partes Proceedings; Peer Review of Applications

Patent application proceedings are conducted ex parte.[71] A third party may become aware of the existence of a particular

---

[67] *Id.* §104. Before the effective dates of legislation implementing NAFTA and GATT, only activity that occurred in the United States could be relied upon to prove the date of invention. The effect of the law was not made retroactive. The GATT-based changes to Section 104, for example, did not become effective until January 1, 1996.

[68] Tibbetts Indus. Inc. v. Knowles Elecs. Inc., 386 F.2d 209, 211, 156 USPQ 65 (7th Cir. 1967), *cert. denied,* 390 U.S. 953 (1968).

[69] Gould v. Schawlow, 363 F.2d 908, 911, 150 USPQ 634 (C.C.P.A. 1966).

[70] *Id.* at 920–21, 150 USPQ 634.

[71] Before 1999, all patent applications were kept secret by the PTO until issuance. Under the American Inventors Protection Act of 1999, applications are now published under certain conditions, which apply to most applications (although they remain secret until publication). 35 U.S.C. §122; 37 C.F.R. §1.211; MPEP §1120 (8th ed. 2001, rev. 2010). No changes were made in the 1999 legislation to the ex parte procedures for patent examination. However, whereas third parties previously could institute inter partes proceedings such as protests (discussed in this section) against any application of which they became aware, regulations promulgated as a result of the American Inventors Protection Act of 1999 limit the filing of protests against applications that have been published. The Leahy-Smith America Invents Act includes a provision, having an effective date of September 16, 2012, that amends 35 U.S.C §122 to permit the public to submit patents and other publications before the earlier of (i) the date a notice of allowance is mailed, or (ii) the later of either six months after the application's publication, or the date of the first action on the merits. *See* Leahy-Smith America Invents Act, Pub.L. 112-29, H.R. 1249 (2011), sec. 8 (amending 35 U.S.C. §122). In addition, regulations implementing the publication of applications limit when an applicant may claim domestic or foreign priority under 35 U.S.C. §119 (see this chapter, §III.D.9) or benefit of an earlier United States filing date under 35 U.S.C. §120 (see this chapter, §III.D.7).

application, and if that third party is aware of prior art or public use that would affect the patentability of the invention, he or she may bring that prior art to the attention of the PTO.

Protest.[72] A protest is a paper submitted by a third party citing prior art and explaining why, in the third party's opinion, the prior art should prevent the issuance of a patent. The protester is not given any additional opportunity to communicate with the PTO regarding the application and is not informed of further prosecution of the application.[73] However, if the examiner in charge of the application believes that it is warranted, the applicant may be required to reply to the protest.[74]

Public use proceeding.[75] Prior art consisting of public use or sale by the applicant or his or her assignee may be made the subject of either a protest or a public use proceeding. Prior art consisting of public use or sale not by the applicant or his or her assignee must be made the subject of a public use proceeding. A public use proceeding is inter partes if the third party petitioner is the other party in an interference with the application, or if the application is a reissue application (see this chapter, §IV.B).[76] A public use proceeding involves the taking of testimony and exchange of briefs and, in an inter partes case, an oral hearing. The examiner's decision in a public use proceeding is not appealable unless it is the basis of a rejection, which may be appealed like any other rejection.

Peer review of applications.[77] The PTO has implemented a pilot program under which pending applications may be published for peer review. Under this program, members of the public are encouraged to submit prior art documents and comments related to these applications.

---

[72] 37 C.F.R. §1.291.

[73] *Id.* §1.291(c); MPEP §1901.07(a) (8th ed. 2001, rev. 2010).

[74] 37 C.F.R. §1.291(c); MPEP §1901.06 (8th ed. 2001, rev. 2010).

[75] 37 C.F.R. §1.292.

[76] MPEP §720 (8th ed. 2001, rev. 2010).

[77] 1319 OFF. GAZ. PAT. OFFICE 159 (June 26, 2007). After completion of the original two-year peer review program that applied to a limited number of technology areas, the PTO established a new one-year peer review program, expanding the number of technology areas to which the program applies. The new pilot program started October 25, 2010 and will continue until September 30, 2011. *See* http://www.uspto.gov/patents/init_events/peerpriorart pilotindex.jsp.

12. Quality Review

The PTO maintains an Office of Quality Review, which randomly checks the prosecution of allowed applications. This procedure is intended to improve patent quality and to increase the likelihood that patents will be held valid in the courts.[78]

A predetermined number of allowed applications are selected from each art unit. The selected applications are chosen at random by the PTO's computerized file management system. Applications already reviewed by the Board of Patent Appeals and Interferences or by a court are excluded. Each application selected is reexamined by a patentability review examiner, who reviews the file and may make an independent prior art search. If the review examiner has any questions about an application, the application is returned for further consideration by the group director of the examining group from which it came. The group director may resolve any questions on his or her own authority or may refer the application to a panel including the original examiner, the review examiner, the supervisory primary examiner, the director of quality review, and himself or herself. The group director renders the final decision. If warranted, the application may be withdrawn from issue (i.e., allowance rescinded) and prosecution reopened. For example, in 2010, 96.3 percent of applications allowed or finally rejected by examiners and reviewed were found to be compliant with quality standards.[79]

In 2000, the PTO established a "second pair of eyes" (SPOE) review, under which all allowances within certain technology areas are reviewed by another examiner. The purpose of this review is for the reviewer to quickly flag issues that may need further consideration by the examiner and/or the examiner's supervisor, before the allowance is processed. By 2002, the PTO extended SPOE review to more technology areas, which may have contributed to a reduction in overall allowance rates by

---

[78] MPEP §1308.03 (8th ed. 2001, rev. 2010).
[79] USPTO Performance and Accountability Report FY 2010, Patent Final Rejection/Allowance Compliance Rate Table, p. 19.

2008.[80] As of this writing, based on anecdotal reports, SPOE review continues to operate at a reduced level.

In 2005, the PTO added an additional in-process quality review that randomly checks the prosecution during the examination process.[81] For example, in 2010, 94.9 percent of applications subject to in-process review were found to be compliant.[82]

E. Appeals to the Courts

If an applicant is dissatisfied with a decision of the Board of Patent Appeals and Interferences or, after September 16, 2012, the Patent Trial and Appeal Board, in an appeal from a final rejection by the examiner, he or she may initiate a civil action against the director of the Patent and Trademark Office in the U.S. District Court for the Eastern District of Virginia.[83] A party to an interference that is dissatisfied with the decision of the board may have remedy by civil action against the other party.[84] In the district court, the question of the applicant's or the interfering parties' right to a patent is tried de novo. An appeal from the decision of the district court is taken exclusively to the Federal Circuit.[85] Alternatively, an applicant may appeal directly from the PTO to the Federal Circuit.[86] In practice, most appeals are taken directly to the Federal Circuit. Decisions of the Federal Circuit are subject to the certiorari jurisdiction of the U.S. Supreme Court, as are decisions of the other federal courts of appeals.

---

[80] *See* http://www.uspto.gov/web/offices/com/strat21/action/q3p17a.htm.

[81] USPTO Performance and Accountability Report FY2010, Performance Goals and Results, pp. 10–20.

[82] *Id.* Patent Non-Final In-Process Examination Compliance Rate Table, p. 19.

[83] Before enactment of the Leahy-Smith America Invents Act, the venue for de novo review of PTO decisions was the U.S. District Court for the District of Columbia. The Act changes the venue to the U.S. District Court for the Eastern District of Virginia. *See* Leahy-Smith America Invents Act, Pub.L. 112-29, H.R. 1249 (2011), sec. 9 (amending 35 U.S.C. §§32, 145, 146, 154(b)(4)(A), 293, and 15 U.S.C. §1071(b)(4)).

[84] 35 U.S.C. §§145–146.

[85] 28 U.S.C. §1295.

[86] 35 U.S.C. §141.

IV. POSTISSUANCE RESPONSIBILITIES

For the most part, the responsibility of the PTO ends when a patent is issued. However, in several limited circumstances, the PTO can act with respect to issued patents.

A. Disclaimers, Dedications, and Certificates of Correction

A patent owner may disclaim or dedicate to the public the entire term of an entire patent (all claims of a patent), the entire term of any complete claim (but not only part of a claim), or the terminal part of the term (that portion of the term beyond a certain date) of the entire patent (but not the terminal part of the term of only some of the claims of a patent).[87] Upon payment of a fee set by regulation, the PTO publishes a notice of the disclaimer or dedication in the *Official Gazette* and prints copies of the disclaimer or dedication for attachment to printed copies of the patent.[88]

If printing errors arise in the printing of a patent, the PTO must issue a certificate under seal, without charge, stating the nature of the error, and attach a copy of the certificate to each printed copy of the patent.[89] The issuance of a Certificate of Correction is published in the *Official Gazette*. The patent and certificate together have the same effect as to any actions arising after issuance of the certificate as the patent would have had it been issued correctly.[90]

---

[87] *Id.* §253. An entire patent, or the entire term of a complete claim, might be disclaimed if the patentee discovers that there might be a substantial question as to the validity of the patent or claim. The terminal portion of the term of a patent might be disclaimed if the patentee realizes that he or she has duplicate coverage in another patent. The terminal disclaimer would cause both patents to expire on the same day, avoiding a double patenting situation. Such a disclaimer is effective only for obviousness-type double patenting. *See generally* 3A DONALD S. CHISUM, CHISUM ON PATENTS §9 (2005).

[88] 37 C.F.R. §1.321.

[89] 35 U.S.C. §254.

[90] 37 C.F.R. §1.322. The Certificate of Correction is given no effect, however, in causes of action arising before it was issued. Southwest Software v. Harlequin Inc., 226 F.3d 1280, 1293–96, 56 USPQ2d 1161 (Fed. Cir. 2000).

An applicant is entitled, upon payment of a fee, to a Certificate of Correction for any clerical or typographical error that was the applicant's responsibility, as long as it is obvious that the error was made in good faith.[91] Such a certificate has the same effect as a certificate issued to correct PTO errors.[92]

The PTO will issue a certificate correcting the inventorship of an issued patent, either as a result of a court order in a case where inventorship was raised as an issue in litigation, or as a result of a petition by the patent owner.[93] In each situation, the error in naming inventors must have been made in good faith.[94]

B. Reissue

Section 251, 35 U.S.C., provides that a patent may be reissued by the PTO, upon surrender of the original patent, if the patent is "through error without any deceptive intention, deemed wholly or partly inoperative or invalid."[95] The types of error commonly forming the bases of reissue applications are (1) claims that are too narrow or too broad; (2) inaccuracies in the disclosure; (3) incorrect naming of inventors; (4) failure to claim or correctly claim foreign priority; and (5) failure to refer properly to a copending application, the filing date of which is claimed. The oath or declaration of a reissue application must set forth the error or errors forming the basis of the reissue application.

Claims may be broadened in a reissue application if the application is filed within two years of issuance of the patent, and if it is signed by the inventor.[96] After two years, a reissue application may be made only to narrow claims or to leave their scope unchanged. If claims are not being broadened, a reissue application may be signed by the assignee.

---

[91] 35 U.S.C. §255.
[92] 37 C.F.R. §1.323.
[93] 35 U.S.C. §256.
[94] 37 C.F.R. §1.324.
[95] 35 U.S.C. §251.
[96] 37 C.F.R. §1.172(a).

A reissue application must claim the same general invention as the original patent and cannot be used to recapture subject matter initially given up in order to convince the examiner to grant the original patent. No new matter (see this chapter, §III.D.3) may be added under the guise of correction. Since March 1, 1977, reissue application files have been open to the public. Any member of the public can file a protest against a reissue application (see this chapter, §III.D.11). From 1977 to 1982, a protester was allowed to participate in the prosecution of a reissue application. However, since 1982, participation by a protester has been limited to the filing of a protest.

The examination of a reissue application is not limited to the prior art considered in the original examination. The examiner of a reissue application can consider de novo all issues affecting patentability.[97] Examination for lack of deceptive intent will be done, but there is no examination for fraud or inequitable conduct.[98] When a patent is reissued, matter cancelled from the original is printed in brackets, and matter added is italicized. If reissued claims differ in scope from the original claims, any person who was practicing subject matter that was not covered by the original claims but is covered by the reissued claims may have intervening rights to the practice of that subject matter.[99]

C. Reexamination

1. Citation of Prior Art

Any person may cite patents or printed publications for entry into the file of a patent during the period of its enforceability in order to inform the PTO and the patent owner of such

---

[97] 37 C.F.R. §1.176.

[98] MPEP §1448 (8th ed. 2001, rev. 2010). An applicant's statement of lack of deceptive intent is usually accepted as dispositive by the PTO, *id.*, although the propriety of the PTO's decision to grant reissue may be challenged in later litigation.

[99] 35 U.S.C. §252.

prior art as it may affect the patent.[100] The submitter may remain anonymous. A copy of each citation of prior art is to be served on the patent owner, but in the absence of evidence of such service, the PTO notifies the patent owner that each such citation has been filed.

2. Reexamination

A citation of prior art under 35 U.S.C. §301 can form the basis of a request for reexamination.[101] Any person may seek reexamination, provided he or she pays the required fee.[102] The requester may be the patent owner. A request by the patent owner may include proposed amendments to overcome the prior art. Also, the PTO may initiate reexamination on its own.

A request for reexamination can be filed at any time during the period in which a suit for damages may be brought (see Chapter 6, §I.F). If an action for infringement has been filed, a request may be filed even after that period has run. The standard for ordering reexamination is that a substantial new question of patentability is raised by the cited art.[103] A decision on the request, based on that criterion, must be made within three months of the filing of the request. The decision gives the examiner's reasons for granting or denying the request. If the request is denied, the person making the request has one month to petition from the denial to the director. If the request is granted, an order for reexamination is issued.

If an order to reexamine is issued, the patent owner may file within two months a Patent Owner's Statement showing why the

---

[100] 35 U.S.C. §301. The Leahy-Smith America Invents Act includes an amendment, with an effective date of September 16, 2012, of 35 U.S.C. §301 to: (a) permit submission of written statements of the patent owner filed in a federal court or the PTO expressing a position on the scope of any claim of a patent in any post-grant proceeding and (b) exclude and keep confidential the identity of any person citing prior art or written statements from a patent file upon request. *See* Leahy-Smith America Invents Act, Pub.L. 112-29, H.R. 1249 (2011), sec. 6 (amending 35 U.S.C. §301).

[101] 35 U.S.C. §302.

[102] The fee is currently $2,520. 37 C.F.R. §1.20(c) (2007). It is set high to discourage frivolous requests. If reexamination is not ordered, $1,690 of the fee is refunded. *Id.* §1.26(c).

[103] *In re* Swanson, 540 F.3d 1368, 1375–79 (Fed. Cir. 2008).

claims are patentable and presenting narrowing amendments, if desirable.[104] After such a statement is filed, the requester, if other than the patent owner, may file a reply within two months.[105] A patent owner may refrain from filing a statement and thereby deny the requester an opportunity to be heard.

After the period for statement has passed, the reexamination proceeds ex parte in a manner similar to the prosecution of an application. The routes of appeal from a final rejection are also available except that, after September 16, 2012, an action in district court is no longer available following an appeal to the Patent Trial and Appeal Board. In reexamination, existing claims may only be narrowed, although new claims, no broader than the original claims, may be added. Upon completion of reexamination, a Notice of Intent to Issue a Reexamination Certificate, and subsequently the Reexamination Certificate itself, are issued.[106] The issuance of the certificate is published in the *Official Gazette*.[107]

Under the American Inventors Protection Act of 1999, a new inter partes form of reexamination was created alongside the preexisting ex parte form of reexamination. The inter partes reexamination provisions cover only patents issuing on applications filed on or after November 29, 1999. Under inter partes reexamination, a requester who is not the patent owner

---

[104] 37 C.F.R. §1.530.

[105] *Id.* §1.535.

[106] The certificate, when issued, will:
  (A) cancel any patent claims determined to be unpatentable;
  (B) confirm any patent claims determined to be patentable;
  (C) incorporate into the patent any amended or new claims determined to be patentable;
  (D) make any changes in the description approved during reexamination;
  (E) include any statutory disclaimer or terminal disclaimer filed by the patent owner;
  (F) identify unamended claims which were held invalid on final holding by another forum on any grounds;
  (G) identify any patent claims not reexamined;
  (H) be mailed on the day it is dated to the patent owner at address provided for in 37 C.F.R. §1.33(c) and a copy will be mailed to the third party requester; and
  (I) identify patent claims, dependent on amended claims, determined to be patentable.
  MPEP §2288 (8th ed. 2001, rev. 2007).

[107] A certain number of reexaminations will be reviewed by quality review examiners. See this chapter, §III.D.12.

may participate in the reexamination, but must accept certain estoppels as a condition of participation.[108]

Reexamination files are open to the public. Any interested person may file a citation of prior art during the reexamination. If such a citation is received before reexamination is ordered, the art cited will be considered in the reexamination. If it is received after reexamination has been ordered, the citation will be entered in the file after reexamination is completed, and no action will be taken on it. If the submitter of the citation wants the art to be considered further, he or she must file a new request for reexamination. Intervening rights can arise from reexamination, as they can from reissue (see this chapter, §IV.B).[109]

D. Patent Term Extension; Patent Term Adjustment

The term of a patent for a product, method of using a product, or method of manufacturing a product will be extended if the product was the subject of a regulatory review period before commercial use and the extension is applied for during the unexpired term of the patent.[110] The length of such an extension is generally equal to the period of regulatory review, subject to certain exceptions. A patent term can be extended only once, and only one patent for a product subject to any one regulatory review period can have its term extended.

The primary purpose of allowing term extension is to lessen the impact on patent owners of the lengthy regulatory

---

[108] The Leahy-Smith America Invents Act includes a provision, with an effective date of September 16, 2012, that revises the inter partes reexamination proceeding and renames it inter partes review (IPR). The Act also creates a new post-grant review (PGR) or opposition proceeding, as of the same effective date, in which cancellation of a patent may be sought on any ground of invalidity (not limited to patents or printed publications) within nine months after a patent issues. The Act also establishes a specialized form of post-grant review for "business method" patents, for a "transitional" period between September 16, 2012, and September 16, 2020. The Act further includes a supplemental examination provision, having the same effective date, that enables a patent owner to request the PTO to consider, reconsider, or correct information believed to be relevant to a patent. *See* Leahy-Smith America Invents Act, Pub.L. 112-29, H.R. 1249 (2011), sec. 6 (amending 35 U.S.C. §§301, and 311–319, and adding 35 U.S.C. §§321–329), sec. 12 (adding 35 U.S.C. §257), and sec. 18.

[109] 35 U.S.C. §307(b).

[110] *Id.* §156.

review periods for approval of new drugs and medical devices. Such reviews frequently consume a large portion of the statutory patent term, which limits the patent owner's ability to exploit his or her patent for the full term because the drug or medical device cannot be sold until it is approved.

A patent term can also be extended for up to five years to compensate for time lost from the patent term due to interference proceedings, imposition of secrecy orders, or when a decision of nonpatentability is reversed on appeal either by the PTO or by a federal court.

There are additional patent term adjustments, enacted by the American Inventors Protection Act of 1999, for administrative delays during prosecution.[111] Patent term adjustments are calculated by the PTO based on whether the examination of an application was performed within specified time frames.[112] The patent term adjustment period will be reduced by any time in which an applicant failed to engage in reasonable efforts to conclude prosecution of the application.[113] The Notice of Allowance includes notification of any patent term adjustment. A request for reconsideration of the patent term adjustment indicated in the Notice of Allowance must be filed before the payment of the issue fee.[114]

---

[111] Id. §154; 37 C.F.R. §1.701 et seq.
[112] 37 C.F.R. §1.703.
[113] Id. §1.704.
[114] Id. §1.705.

PROCEEDINGS IN THE FEDERAL COURTS

I. PARTIES

A. Who Can Assert the Patent Right

A patent gives its owner the right to exclude others from making, using, offering for sale, selling, or importing the patented invention in the United States during the term of the patent.[1] As a general rule, ownership of a patent vests initially in the inventor(s), i.e., the person(s) in whose name the patent application is filed.[2] Subject to patent misuse[3] and antitrust considerations, the patent owner can share or transfer this right through an assignment or grant permission for others to practice the invention through a patent license.[4] The assignment or license can be in whole or in part, which can result in many different parties with an enforceable interest in the patent.

Assignment: A patent owner can assign his or her ownership interest in the patent by (1) conveying the entire ownership

---

[1] 35 U.S.C §154(1).

[2] 35 U.S.C. §§111 (application shall be made by the inventor), 116 (joint inventors), 117 (application by the legal representative or a deceased inventor), 118 (filing by other than the inventor). There are statutory exceptions to the rule of ownership by the inventor, e.g., for inventions relating to nuclear power, 42 U.S.C. §2182, for inventions made pursuant to contracts with the National Aeronautics and Space Administration, 51 U.S.C. §20135(b)(1), and for certain inventions made under contracts with the Department of Energy, 42 U.S.C. §5909. In *Board of Trs. of Leland Stanford Junior Univ. v. Roche Molecular Sys., Inc.,* No. 09-1159, 2011 U.S. LEXIS 4183 (U.S. June 6, 2011), the Supreme Court construed the Bayh-Dole Act, 35 U.S.C. §§200–212, which governs patent rights arising from federally funded research, and concluded that the Act does not automatically vest ownership in the institution at which an inventor was working when the invention was made. Such an institution, however, may obtain an inventor's contractual agreement to assign patent ownership.

[3] See Chapter 7, §II.

[4] 35 U.S.C.A. §261 (2001) ("Subject to the [U.S. patent laws], patents have the attributes of personal property").

of the patent, (2) conveying a shared interest in the patent, or (3) conveying patent ownership for a specific portion of the patent territory.[5] The entire ownership is commonly transferred when an inventor assigns all of his or her rights in a patent to an employer.[6] The creation of a shared interest occurs, for example, when a joint inventor assigns his or her partial, undivided interest in the patent.[7] The third situation, a grant of patent ownership rights for a particular region of the United States, is relatively rare.

Licenses: A patent owner can exempt others from the exclusionary power of the patent by (1) granting an exclusive license to a portion of the patent right or (2) granting a nonexclusive license to all or a portion of the patent right.[8] Under an exclusive license, the patent owner agrees that the licensee will hold a subset of the patent monopoly.[9] The exclusive licensee may have the right to exclude others, including the patent owner, from a particular geographical area, field of use, time period, or type of practice (e.g., exclusive right to *make* a patented product), or a combination thereof.[10] If the exclusive license transfers all substantial rights under the patent, however, the license will be

---

[5] Waterman v. MacKenzie, 138 U.S. 252 (1891); Enzo APA & Son Inc. v. Geapag A.G., 134 F.3d 1090, 1093, 45 USPQ2d 1368 (Fed. Cir. 1998). An assignment does not include the right to recover for past infringement unless the assignment agreement shows intent to transfer this right. Minco Inc. v. Combustion Eng'g Inc., 95 F.3d 1109, 1117, 40 USPQ2d 1001 (Fed. Cir. 1996); Abraxis Bioscience v. Navinta LLC, 625 F.3d 1359, 1367, 96 USPQ2d 1977 (Fed. Cir. 2010), *cert. denied*, 2011 WL 4530371 (2011).

[6] An agreement to assign future patent rights does not immediately vest those rights in the assignee. Board of Trs. of Leland Stanford Junior Univ. v. Roche Molecular Sys., Inc., 583 F.3d 832, 841–42, 92 USPQ2d 1442 (Fed. Cir. 2009), *aff'd*, No. 09-1159, 2011 U.S. LEXIS 4183 (U.S. June 6, 2011).

[7] *See* Ethicon Inc. v. United States Surgical Corp., 135 F.3d 1456, 1465–68, 45 USPQ2d 1545 (Fed. Cir.), *cert. denied*, 525 U.S. 923 (1998). The co-owner scenario can be troublesome, because, absent agreement to the contrary, each owner has equal rights despite possible unequal shares (e.g., 1% and 99%). *See* 35 U.S.C.A. §262 (2001); 3 JOHN GLADSTONE MILLS III ET AL., 5 PATENT LAW FUNDAMENTALS §17:29 (2d ed. 2003).

[8] Morrow v. Microsoft Corp., 499 F.3d 1332, 1340–41, 84 USPQ2d 1377 (Fed. Cir. 2007).

[9] *Id.*; WiAV Solutions LLC v. Motorola, Inc., 631 F.3d 1257, 1264–65, 97 USPQ2d 1484 (Fed. Cir. 2010).

[10] *See, e.g.,* Intellectual Prop. Dev., Inc. v. TCI Cablevision of Calif., Inc., 248 F.3d 1333, 1345, 58 USPQ2d 1681 (Fed. Cir. 2001); International Gamco, Inc. v. Multimedia Games, Inc., 504 F.3d 1273, 1279, 84 USPQ2d 2017 (Fed. Cir. 2007); Prima Tek II, LLC. v. A-Roo Co., 222 F.3d 1372, 1378–80, 55 USPQ2d 1742 (Fed. Cir. 2000). A licensee may be exclusive, even if others retain the right to practice or license the patent in the exclusive area, as long as the alleged infringer cannot obtain a license from others. *WiAV Solutions LLC*, 631 F.3d at 1266–67. An exclusive licensee's standing to enforce a patent generally will extend only to the limits of the license grant. *Id.*

considered an assignment.[11] A nonexclusive or "bare" license does not convey any right to exclude others. Such a license is essentially a covenant by the patent owner not to sue the licensee for activities covered by the nonexclusive license agreement.[12]

Standing; necessary and indispensable parties: A patentee or assignee has standing to enforce the patent against infringers.[13] Co-owners are usually indispensable parties to an infringement suit and the suit ordinarily cannot proceed without each of them. Absent an agreement to join, an unwilling co-owner cannot be compelled to join the suit.[14] A patent owner may also be required to join any exclusive licensees, although the exclusive licensee can usually be compelled to join.[15]

An exclusive licensee has standing to enforce the patent in their exclusive area, but generally must join the patent owner even if the infringement appears to be only in the licensee's exclusive area.[16] A patent owner can often be compelled to join

---

[11] Vaupel Textilmaschinen v. Meccanica Euro Italia, 944 F.2d 870, 873–76, 20 USPQ2d 1045 (Fed. Cir. 1991); Alfred E. Mann Found. for Scientific Research v. Cochlear Corp., 604 F.3d 1354, 1359–62, 95 USPQ2d 1321 (Fed. Cir. 2010) ("To determine whether an exclusive license is tantamount to an assignment, we 'must ascertain the intention of the parties [to the license agreement] and examine the substance of what was granted' " (quoting Mentor H/S, Inc. v. Medical Device Alliance, Inc., 240 F.3d 1016, 1017, 57 USPQ2d 1819 (Fed. Cir. 2001)). The exclusive right to sue infringers is particularly dispositive in deciding if a license is effectively an assignment. AsymmetRx, Inc. v. Biocare Med., LLC, 582 F.3d 1314, 1319, 92 USPQ2d 1113 (Fed. Cir. 2009). A license must be in writing to be considered an assignment. *Mentor H/S, Inc.*, 240 F.3d at 1017, 57 USPQ2d 1819.

[12] Propat Int'l Grp. v. RPost, Inc., 473 F.3d 1187, 1193–94, 81 USPQ2d 1350 (Fed. Cir 2007).

[13] Waterman v. MacKenzie, 138 U.S. 252, 255 (1891); *AsymmetRx*, 582 F.3d at 1321, 92 USPQ2d 1113. Nunc pro tunc assignments will not confer retroactive standing unless there is evidence that standing was originally intended. Enzo APA & Son Inc. v. Geapag A.G., 134 F.3d 1090, 1093, 45 USPQ2d 1368 (Fed. Cir. 1998).

[14] Ethicon Inc. v. United States Surgical Corp., 135 F.3d 1456, 1467–68, 45 USPQ2d 1545 (Fed. Cir.) *cert. denied*, 525 U.S. 923 (1998); Israel Bio-Eng'g Project v. Amgen Inc., 475 F.3d 1256, 1264–68, 81 USPQ2d 1558 (Fed. Cir.), *cert. denied*, 551 U.S. 1141 (2007). In general, dismissal for lack of standing should be without prejudice. University of Pittsburgh v. Varian Med. Sys., Inc., 569 F.3d 1328, 1332–33, 91 USPQ2d 1251 (Fed. Cir. 2009) (reversing dismissal with prejudice for failure to join patent co-owner).

[15] Aspex Eyewear, Inc v. Miracle Optics, Inc., 434 F.3d 1336, 1344, 77 USPQ2d 1456 (Fed. Cir. 2006). An accused infringer in a declaratory judgment action generally will be required to join both the patent owner and any exclusive licensees. A123 Sys., Inc. v. Hydro-Quebec, 626 F.3d 1213, 1217, 97 USPQ2d 1257 (Fed. Cir. 2010).

[16] Intellectual Prop. Dev., Inc. v. TCI Cablevision of Calif., Inc., 248 F.3d 1333, 1347–48, 58 USPQ2d 1681 (Fed. Cir. 2001) ("As a prudential principle, an exclusive licensee . . . possesses standing . . . as long as it sues in the name of, and jointly with, the patent owner. . . "). An exclusive licensee may appeal, however, without the patent owner. Schwartz Pharma, Inc. v. Paddock Labs., Inc., 504 F.3d 1371, 1373–74, 84 USPQ2d 1900 (Fed. Cir. 2007).

as a defendant or involuntary plaintiff in a suit brought by an exclusive licensee.[17] The nonexclusive licensee has no standing to sue for infringement, because there is no legal injury when others practice the patent.[18]

B. Who Can Attack the Patent

A party sued for patent infringement may defend by asserting that the patent is invalid, unenforceable, or not infringed.[19]

An action seeking a declaratory judgment that a patent is invalid, unenforceable, or not infringed can be brought by any party, including assignees and current licensees of the patent.[20] However, an assignor of a patent, having previously asserted to the PTO that an invention was patentable, is generally estopped from attacking the validity or enforceability of that patent in subsequent litigation.[21]

With respect to standing to bring a declaratory judgment action to attack a patent, in *MedImmune, Inc. v. Genentech, Inc.*, the Supreme Court adopted for patent cases the flexible standard that governs jurisdiction under the Declaratory Judgment Act. The test for standing is whether, under all the circumstances, there is a substantial controversy between parties having adverse legal interests and of sufficient immediacy and

---

[17] Abbott Labs. v. Diamedix Corp., 47 F.3d 1128, 1133, 33 USPQ2d 1771 (Fed. Cir. 1995).

[18] Propat Int'l Grp v. RPost Inc., 473 F.3d 1187, 1193–94, 81 USPQ2d 1350 (Fed. Cir. 2007) ("A bare licensee cannot cure its lack of standing by joining the patentee as a party").

[19] 35 U.S.C §282.

[20] For public policy reasons, a licensee's promise not to challenge a patent is generally unenforceable. Lear, Inc. v. Adkins, 395 U.S. 653, 162 USPQ 1 (1969); Baseload Energy, Inc. v. Roberts, 619 F.3d 1357, 1361, 96 USPQ2d 1521 (Fed. Cir. 2010). Such a promise will be enforced, however, if it was made in settlement of litigation. Foster v. Hallco Mfg. Co., 947 F.2d 469, 474–75, 20 USPQ2d 1241 (Fed. Cir. 1991); Flex-Foot, Inc. v. CRP, Inc., 238 F.3d 1362, 1367–70, 57 USPQ2d 1635 (Fed. Cir. 2001); *Baseload Energy, Inc.*, 619 F.3d at 1361–62, 96 USPQ2d 1521. A claim for infringement is compulsory in the face of a declaratory judgment of noninfringement. Polymer Indus. Prods. v. Bridgestone/Firestone, Inc., 347 F.3d 935, 937–39, 68 USPQ2d 1626 (Fed. Cir. 2003).

[21] Diamond Scientific Co. v. Ambico, Inc., 848 F.2d 1220, 1224, 6 USPQ2d 2028 (Fed. Cir. 1988); Pandrol USA, LP v. Airboss Ry. Prods., Inc., 424 F.3d 1161, 1166–67, 76 USPQ2d 1524 (Fed. Cir. 2005).

reality to warrant the issuance of a declaratory judgment.[22] As phrased by the Federal Circuit, in the patent context, declaratory judgment jurisdiction will be found if a patent owner asserts that its rights cover certain ongoing or planned activity of a party and that party contends that its activity does not require a patent license.[23]

Courts have found facts sufficient to support jurisdiction where the patent owner has explicitly threatened suit, initiated license negotiations, sent a notice letter to an alleged infringer or its customers, or asserted that certain activities may infringe, even if no specific threat of suit was made.[24] The mere existence of a patent or enforcement activities against unrelated third parties are generally not sufficient to confer standing.[25] For there to be a controversy of sufficient immediacy and reality, the declaratory judgment plaintiff must have taken significant and concrete steps to engage in the infringing activity, beyond a fluid or indeterminate stage of activity.[26]

The party seeking declaratory judgment, the declaratory judgment plaintiff, bears the burden of proving facts to support jurisdiction by a preponderance of the evidence, and that the

---

[22] MedImmune, Inc. v. Genentech, Inc., 549 U.S. 118, 127, 81 USPQ2d 1225 (2007), construing 28 U.S.C.A. §2201(a) (2006).

[23] SanDisk Corp. v. STMicroelecs., Inc., 480 F.3d 1372, 1381, 82 USPQ2d 1173 (Fed. Cir. 2007). In patent infringement suits involving a generic pharmaceutical, declaratory judgment jurisdiction is governed not by the Declaratory Judgment Act, but rather by the Hatch-Waxman Act, 28 U.S.C.A. §2201(b) (2006). 21 U.S.C.A. §355(j)(5)(C) (Supp. 2007); *see also* Teva Pharms. USA, Inc. v. Eisai Co., 620 F.3d 1341, 1346–47, 96 USPQ2d 1808 (Fed. Cir. 2010).

[24] *See, e.g., SanDisk Corp.*, 480 F.3d at 1380–82, 82 USPQ2d 1173; Arris Group, Inc. v. British Telecomm. PLC, 639 F.3d 1368, 1373–75, 98 USPQ2d 1812 (Fed. Cir. 2011); Hewlett-Packard Co. v. Acceleron LLC, 587 F.3d 1358, 1362–64, 92 USPQ2d 1948 (Fed. Cir. 2009); Micron Tech., Inc. v. MOSAID Techs., Inc., 518 F.3d 897, 901–02, 86 USPQ2d 1038 (Fed. Cir. 2008); Sony Elecs., Inc. v. Guardian Media Techs., Ltd., 497 F.3d 1271, 1285–87, 83 USPQ2d 1798 (Fed. Cir. 2007). *But see, e.g.,* Creative Compounds LLC v. Starmark Labs., 651 F.3d 1303, 1316, 99 USPQ2d 1168 (Fed. Cir. 2011) (no jurisdiction where letter went to party's customers alleging infringement, but party had no obligation to indemnify customers).

[25] Innovative Therapies, Inc. v. Kinetic Concepts, Inc., 599 F.3d 1377, 1380–85, 94 USPQ2d 1307 (Fed. Cir.), *cert. denied*, 131 S. Ct. 424 (2010); Prasco, LLC v. Medicis Pharm. Corp., 537 F.3d 1329, 1338–39, 87 USPQ2d 1675 (Fed. Cir. 2008).

[26] Cat Tech LLC v. TubeMaster, Inc., 528 F.3d 871, 880–83, 87 USPQ2d 1065 (Fed. Cir. 2008). A significant length of time before the alleged infringing activity will occur factors against finding the requisite immediacy. *Id.* at 881–82.

other constitutional conditions for jurisdiction are present.[27] Even if the conditions for declaratory judgment jurisdiction are met, the court has discretion to decline to hear a declaratory judgment action.[28]

A patent owner can divest the court of jurisdiction by promising not to sue, provided that the covenant not to sue eliminates the controversy between the parties.[29]

The defendants in a declaratory judgment action for patent noninfringement, invalidity, or unenforceability generally must include any party who would have been a required plaintiff if it were an infringement suit.[30]

II. Jurisdiction

The federal courts have had exclusive subject matter jurisdiction over all cases arising under the patent laws since 1836.[31] This jurisdiction includes cases where federal patent law creates

---

[27] Benitec Austl., Ltd. v. Nucleonics, Inc., 495 F.3d 1340, 1344–45, 83 USPQ2d 1449 (Fed. Cir. 2007), *cert. denied*, 128 S. Ct. 2055 (2008); Edmunds Holding Co. v. Autobytel Inc., 598 F. Supp. 2d 606, 609, 91 USPQ2d 1221 (D. Del. 2009).

[28] Wilton v. Seven Falls Co., 515 U.S. 277, 289–90 (1995); *SanDisk Corp.*, 480 F.3d at 1383, 82 USPQ2d 1173. That discretion, while broad, is not unfettered. *Id.* ("[T]he exercise of discretion must be supported by a sound basis for refusing to adjudicate an actual controversy"). For example, a declaratory judgment action filed during ongoing, serious negotiations to sell or license the patent may be seen as a bargaining tactic and dismissed. EMC Corp. v. Norand Corp., 89 F.3d 807, 39 USPQ2d 1451 (Fed. Cir. 1996), *cert. denied*, 519 U.S. 1101 (1997); *Sony Elecs., Inc.*, 497 F.3d at 1287–89, 83 USPQ2d 1798.

[29] *Benitec Austl., Ltd.*, 495 F.3d at 1347–48, 83 USPQ2d 1449; Dow Jones & Co. v. Ablaise Ltd., 606 F.3d 1338, 1345–49, 95 USPQ2d 1366 (Fed. Cir. 2010) (no declaratory judgment jurisdiction where patentee offered covenant not to sue, despite judicial efficiencies if jurisdiction found). For cases involving generic pharmaceuticals, the efficacy of a covenant not to sue may raise additional issues under the Hatch-Waxman Act. Caraco Pharm. Labs., Ltd. v. Forest Labs., Inc., 527 F.3d 1278, 1291–94, 86 USPQ2d 1289 (Fed. Cir. 2008); Janssen Pharmaceuitca, N.V. v. Apotex, Inc., 540 F.3d 1353, 1360–62, 88 USPQ2d 1079 (Fed. Cir. 2008), *cert. denied*, 129 S. Ct. 1631 (2009).

[30] *See* A123 Sys., Inc. v. Hydro-Quebec, 626 F.3d 1213, 1217, 97 USPQ2d 1257 (Fed. Cir. 2010) ("In general, . . . an accused infringer must . . . join both the exclusive licensee and the patentee in a declaratory judgment action . . . .").

[31] 28 U.S.C.A. §1338(a) (Supp. 2005); Donald S. Chisum, *The Allocation of Jurisdiction Between State and Federal Courts in Patent Litigation*, 46 Wash. L. Rev. 633 (1971).

the cause of action or the plaintiff's right to relief necessarily depends on resolution of a substantial question of federal patent law (i.e., patent law is a necessary element of one of the plaintiff's claims).[32] Subject matter jurisdiction must be found in the well-pleaded complaint.

Before the enactment of the America Invents Act in 2011, courts had held that federal court jurisdiction cannot be based on patent law counterclaims.[33] However, for actions commenced on or after September 16, 2011, 28 U.S.C. §1338(a) has been amended to read that "No State court shall have jurisdiction over any claim for relief arising under" the patent laws. In addition, a new removal provision, 28 U.S.C. §1454, allows a federal court to retain jurisdiction over patent law claims while remanding supplementary matters to state court.[34]

Whether a particular case arises under the patent laws has already been decided for many common situations. For example, a breach of a contract to pay royalties due on a patent license does not arise under the patent laws and, thus, is a matter for state court jurisdiction.[35] Likewise, an action to remove a cloud on the title to a patent does not arise under the patent laws.[36] However, a claim that requires determination of inventorship (as

---

[32]Christianson v. Colt Indus. Operating Corp., 486 U.S. 800, 808–09, 7 USPQ2d 1109 (1988); see, e.g., Board of Regents, Univ. of Tex. v. Nippon Tel. & Tel. Corp., 414 F.3d 1358, 1363–68, 75 USPQ2d 1518 (Fed. Cir. 2005) (no jurisdiction); United States Valves Inc. v. Dray, 212 F.3d 1368, 1372, 54 USPQ2d 1834 (Fed. Cir. 2000) (jurisdiction). A district court may retain jurisdiction to enforce a settlement agreement. See, e.g., Schaefer Fan Co. v. J&D Mfg., 265 F.3d 1282, 1286–87, 60 USPQ2d 1194 (Fed. Cir. 2001).

[33]Holmes Grp. Inc. v. Vornado Air Circulation Sys. Inc., 535 U.S. 826, 62 USPQ2d 1801 (2002); Laboratory Corp. of Am. Holdings v. Metabolite Labs., Inc., 599 F.3d 1277, 1282, 94 USPQ2d 1224 (Fed. Cir. 2010); Golan v. Pingel Enter., Inc., 310 F.3d 1360, 1366–67, 64 USPQ2d 1911 (Fed. Cir. 2002).

[34]Leahy-Smith America Invents Act, Pub.L. 112-29, H.R. 1249 (2011), secs. 19(a) (federal court jurisdiction), 19(c) (removal), 19(e) (effective date).

[35]Schwarzkopf Dev. Corp. v. Ti-Coating Inc., 800 F.2d 240, 231 USPQ 47 (Fed. Cir. 1986). A breach of contract claim for a licensee's failure to notify the patent owner of infringement by a third party also does not arise under the patent laws. Bonzel v. Pfizer, Inc., 439 F.3d 1358, 1363, 78 USPQ2d 1136 (Fed. Cir. 2006). A suit for patent infringement brought after plaintiff terminated defendant's license, however, arises under the patent laws. Pixton v. B&B Plastics, Inc., 291 F.3d 1324, 1326–27, 62 USPQ2d 1944 (Fed. Cir. 2002).

[36]Jim Arnold Corp. v. Hydrotech Sys. Inc., 109 F.3d 1567, 1571–77, 42 USPQ2d 1119 (Fed. Cir.) (action to rescind patent assignment does not arise under patent laws), cert. denied sub nom., Baker Hughes Inc. v. Jim Arnold Corp., 522 U.S. 933 (1997); see Enovsys LLC, v. Nextel Comm., Inc., 614 F.3d 1333, 1342, 95 USPQ2d 1947 (Fed. Cir. 2010) (whether ex-spouse has title to patent is question of state law).

distinct from ownership) arises under the patent laws.[37] A claim for injurious falsehood arises under the patent laws when the alleged falsehood involves an accusation of patent infringement.[38] An action for declaratory judgment of patent invalidity, unenforceability, or noninfringement also arises under the patent laws, since jurisdiction is tested by reference to the hypothetical complaint that could have been brought by the declaratory judgment defendant.[39]

The federal courts have personal jurisdiction in patent cases generally under the same conditions as any other case: the state's long-arm statute authorizes jurisdiction and jurisdiction comports with due process.[40] The due process prong of this test may be based on specific jurisdiction (purposeful availment on the forum, claim arises out of those activities, and jurisdiction is reasonable and fair) or general jurisdiction (continuous and systematic contacts with the forum).[41] Personal jurisdiction may also be obtained by contractual consent.[42] The court will defer to the regional courts in its analysis of the long-arm statute.[43] The court will apply Federal Circuit law to examine the defendant's contacts in the state.[44]

---

[37] HIF Bio, Inc. v. Yung Shin Pharm. Indus. Co., 600 F.3d 1347, 1352–57, 94 USPQ2d 1286 (Fed. Cir. 2010) (inventorship is question of federal patent law, but, for pending patent application, dispute should be before PTO, not district court).

[38] Hunter Douglas Inc. v. Harmonic Design Inc., 153 F.3d 1318, 1328–31, 47 USPQ2d 1769 (Fed. Cir. 1998), *cert. denied*, 525 U.S. 1143 (1999).

[39] ABB Inc. v. Cooper Indus., LLC, 635 F.3d 1345, 1349–52, 97 USPQ2d 1885 (Fed. Cir. 2011); *Golan*, 310 F.3d at 1367, 64 USPQ2d 1911; Jacobsen v. Katzer, 535 F.3d 1373, 1377, 87 USPQ2d 1836 (Fed. Cir. 2008).

[40] Inamed Corp. v. Kuzmak, 249 F.3d 1356, 1359, 58 USPQ2d 1774 (Fed. Cir. 2001); Avocent Huntsville Corp. v. Aten Int'l Co., 552 F.3d 1324, 1329, 89 USPQ2d 1481 (Fed. Cir. 2008), *cert. denied*, 129 S. Ct. 2796 (2009).

[41] *Avocent Huntsville Corp.*, 552 F.3d at 1330–32, 89 USPQ2d 1481. Plaintiffs face a higher burden to establish general personal jurisdiction. *Id.* at 1330, 89 USPQ2d 1481. In a declaratory judgment action, making, using or selling products in a state can be the basis for general, but not specific, jurisdiction over a patentee. *Id.* at 1336, 89 USPQ2d 1481. The Federal Circuit has applied the stream of commerce theory. Beverly Hills Fan Co. v. Royal Sovereign Corp., 21 F.3d 1558, 30 USPQ2d 1001 (Fed. Cir.), *cert. dismissed*, 512 U.S. 1273 (1994). For an example of an application of the government contacts exception, see Zeneca Ltd. v. Mylan Pharms. Inc., 173 F.3d 829, 50 USPQ2d 1294 (Fed. Cir. 1999).

[42] *See, e.g.*, Monsanto Co. v. McFarling, 302 F.3d 1291, 1294–96, 64 USPQ2d 1161 (Fed. Cir. 2002), *cert. denied*, 537 U.S. 1232 (2003). Also, the defense of lack of personal jurisdiction can be waived. Rates Tech. Inc. v. Nortel Networks Corp., 399 F.3d 1302, 1307, 73 USPQ2d 1904 (Fed. Cir.), *cert. denied*, 545 U.S. 1141 (2005).

[43] Hildebrand v. Steck Mfg. Co., 279 F.3d 1351, 1354, 61 USPQ2d 1696 (Fed. Cir. 2002).

[44] *See id.* at 1355; Nuance Commc'ns, Inc. v. Abbyy Software House, 626 F.3d 1222, 1230–31, 97 USPQ2d 1351 (Fed. Cir. 2010), *cert. denied*, No. 10-1019, 2011 U.S. LEXIS 5011 (June 28, 2011).

III. Venue

Venue in patent controversies depends on the cause of action. When the plaintiff alleges patent infringement by a nonalien defendant, 28 U.S.C. §1400(b) applies.[45] When the plaintiff alleges any other cause of action involving a patent, the general venue statute applies.[46] Venue must be appropriate for each patent asserted in the case.[47] However, if venue is appropriate for one claim of a patent, then it will be appropriate for the entire patent.[48]

A. The Patent Venue Statute—28 U.S.C. §1400(b)

Section 1400(b) provides two independent tests to establish venue in patent cases involving a nonalien defendant: where the defendant resides, or where the defendant has committed acts of infringement and has a regular and established place of business.[49]

1. Where the Defendant Resides

Under the residency test for Section 1400(b) venue, the analysis depends on whether the defendant is an individual or a corporation. An individual defendant resides where he or she is

---

[45] Fourco Glass Co. v. Transmirra Prods. Corp., 353 U.S. 222, 113 USPQ 234 (1957); 28 U.S.C.A. §1391(d) ("[A]n alien may be sued in any district").

[46] 28 U.S.C.A. §1391 (2006).

[47] Digital Equip. Corp. v. Electronic Memories & Magnetics Corp., 452 F. Supp. 1262, 1266, 200 USPQ 448 (D. Mass. 1978); Schroeder v. Owens-Corning Fiberglas Corp., 326 F. Supp. 594, 597, 170 USPQ 62 (C.D. Cal. 1971).

[48] General Foods Corp. v. Carnation Co., 411 F.2d 528, 532, 162 USPQ 129 (7th Cir. 1969).

[49] The effect of this special patent venue statute, which had been interpreted as giving alleged infringers extra protection by allowing suits against them only in those districts that satisfy a relatively narrow definition of venue, was altered in part by the 1988 amendments to the judicial code, which changed the definition of "resides" as it applies to corporate defendants. See Schnell v. Peter Eckrich & Sons, 365 U.S. 260, 128 USPQ 305 (1961); VE Holding Corp. v. Johnson Gas Appliance Co., 917 F.2d 1574, 16 USPQ2d 1614 (Fed. Cir. 1990), cert. denied, 499 U.S. 922 (1991). For the history of §1400(b) and the impact of the 1988 amendment for corporate defendants, see Charles S. Ryan, The Expansion of Patent Venue Under the Judicial Improvements and Access to Justice Act, 77 J. PAT. & TRADEMARK OFF. SOC'Y 85, 87 (1995).

domiciled.[50] Domicile in a patent case is determined by permanent residence just as in any other case.[51] A corporate defendant, on the other hand, resides in any judicial district in which it is subject to personal jurisdiction at the time the action is commenced.[52] If the defendant is a corporate employee charged with personal liability for acts of infringement taken as an individual, then the venue requirements for an individual must be met.[53] However, if the defendant is a corporate employee charged with personal liability for actions taken by the corporation, then venue lies if the venue requirements for the corporation are satisfied, regardless of whether the corporate veil is pierced.[54]

2. Where the Defendant Has Committed Acts of Infringement and Has a Regular and Established Place of Business

Under the second test for Section 1400(b) venue, two elements must be met: the defendant must have committed acts of infringement in the district, and have a regular and established place of business in the district.[55]

a. Committed Acts of Infringement in the District

To find acts of infringement in the district, the question is whether acts occurred in the district, not whether the acts indeed

---

[50] Fourco Glass Co. v. Transmirra Prods. Corp., 353 U.S. 222, 226, 113 USPQ 234 (1957).

[51] See, e.g., BOC Group, Inc. v. CVC Prods., Inc., 8 USPQ2d 1278 (D. Del. 1988); T.P. Labs. Inc. v. Huge, 197 F. Supp. 860, 131 USPQ 13 (D. Md. 1961).

[52] 28 U.S.C.A. §1391(c) (2006), which the Federal Circuit has held to apply to 28 U.S.C.A. §1400(b) (1993). VE Holding Corp., 917 F.2d at 1584, 16 USPQ2d 1614; see Trintec Indus., Inc. v. Pedre Promotional Prods., Inc., 395 F.3d 1275, 1280, 73 USPQ2d 1587 (Fed. Cir. 2005). For states with multiple districts, the corporation resides in any district where its contacts would be sufficient to subject it to personal jurisdiction if that district were a separate state or, if there is no such district, in the district where the corporation has the most significant contacts. 28 U.S.C.A. §1391(c) (2006).

[53] Hoover Grp. Inc. v. Custom Metalcraft Inc., 84 F.3d 1408, 1410–11, 38 USPQ2d 1860 (Fed. Cir. 1996).

[54] Id. It is unclear whether the 1988 amendments to §1391(c) that affected venue for corporate defendants also affect venue when the defendant is a partnership, an unincorporated association, or a sole proprietorship. Cf., e.g., Kabb Inc. v. Sutera, 25 USPQ2d 1554 (E.D. La. 1992), with Injection Research Specialists v. Polaris Indus., 18 USPQ2d 1800, amended, 759 F. Supp. 1511 (D. Colo. 1991).

[55] See 14D CHARLES ALAN WRIGHT ET AL., FEDERAL PRACTICE AND PROCEDURE: JURISDICTION §3823 (3d ed. 2007).

constitute infringement.[56] Acts of infringement that satisfy Section 1400(b) include, for example, making, using, or selling an accused product or process in the district. They also include acts of inducement or contribution that are taken within the district to cause another to make, use, or sell an accused product or process.[57] Venue for defendants accused of inducing or contributing to infringement is appropriate only in the district in which the alleged acts of inducement or contribution occurred.[58]

b. Regular and Established Place of Business in the District

To find a regular and established place of business in the district, the question is whether the defendant conducts its business through a permanent and continuous presence in the district and not whether there is a fixed physical presence, such as an office or store.[59] Furthermore, the place of business does not need to be related to the alleged infringing act.[60]

B. The General Venue Statute—28 U.S.C. §1391

The general venue statute applies for all patent infringement actions that are not against nonalien defendants and therefore not subject to the special patent venue statue of Section 1400(b). For example, a case in which the plaintiff seeks a declaratory judgment that a patent is invalid, unenforceable, or not infringed invokes the general venue statute. Thus, even though this type of declaratory judgment action is the mirror image of a patent infringement case, a different venue statute applies.[61]

---

[56] *In re* Cordis Corp., 769 F.2d 733, 737, 226 USPQ 784 (Fed. Cir.), *cert. denied*, 474 U.S. 851 (1985) (merits of patent infringement are not reached in venue inquiry).

[57] *See, e.g.*, Liqui-Box Corp. v. Reid Valve Co., Inc., 672 F. Supp. 198, 5 USPQ2d 1372 (W.D. Pa. 1987); Gunter & Cooke, Inc. v. Southern Elec. Service Co., 256 F. Supp. 639, 149 USPQ 438 (M.D.N.C. 1966), *aff'd*, 378 F.2d 60, 153 USPQ 655 (4th Cir. 1967). See Chapter 6, §I for discussion of what constitutes making, using, or selling an invention under the U.S. patent laws. Activities made infringing by the GATT implementing legislation also may satisfy §1400(b).

[58] *See, e.g.*, Dover Corp. v. Fisher Governor Co., 221 F. Supp. 716, 139 USPQ 268 (S.D. Tex. 1963).

[59] *In re Cordis Corp.*, 769 F.2d at 737, 226 USPQ 784.

[60] Laitram Corp. v. Rexnord Inc., 226 USPQ 971 (D. Md. 1985).

[61] *See, e.g.*, General Tire & Rubber Co. v. Watkins, 326 F.2d 926, 140 USPQ 101 (4th Cir.), *cert. denied*, 377 U.S. 909, 141 USPQ 950 (1964); *see also* VE Holding Corp. v. Johnson Gas Appliance Co., 917 F.2d 1574, 1583, 16 USPQ2d 1614 (Fed. Cir. 1990), *cert. denied*, 499 U.S. 922 (1991).

C. Transfer of Venue

A patent case may be transferred from one district to another if the alternate forum is more convenient for the parties and witnesses and venue is otherwise appropriate. In reviewing convenience of forum issues, the Federal Circuit applies the law of the regional circuit in which the district court is located. For example, Fifth Circuit law divides the inquiry into private interest and public interest factors:

> The 'private' interest [convenience] factors include: (1) the relative ease of access to sources of proof; (2) the availability of compulsory process to secure the attendance of witnesses; (3) the cost of attendance for willing witnesses; and (4) all other practical problems that make a trial easy, expeditious and inexpensive. The 'public' interest factors to be considered are: (1) the administrative difficulties flowing from court congestion; (2) the local interest in having localized interests decided at home; (3) the familiarity of the forum with the law that will govern the case; and (4) the avoidance of unnecessary problems of conflicts of laws [or in] the application of foreign law.[62]

If most of the witnesses and evidence are closer to the proposed alternate venue, with few convenience factors favoring the current venue, then a trial court should transfer venue.[63] However, if there is no clear, preferred venue under the convenience analysis, a court may properly conclude that public interest or judicial economy favors a venue that is marginally less convenient.[64] Venue will not be supported by attempts to manipulate the convenience factors, such as setting up a shell corporation before trial or moving documents to the preferred venue.[65]

---

[62] 28 U.S.C.A. §1404(a); *see In re* TS Tech USA Corp., 551 F.3d 1315, 1319, 89 USPQ2d 1567 (Fed. Cir. 2008) (internal citations omitted) (granting mandamus to order transfer of an action from the Eastern District of Texas, applying Fifth Circuit law).

[63] *In re* Nintendo Co., 589 F.3d 1194, 1198–1200, 93 USPQ2d 1152 (Fed. Cir. 2009).

[64] *In re* Vistaprint Ltd., 628 F.3d 1342, 1346–47, 97 USPQ2d 1250 (Fed. Cir. 2010).

[65] *See In re* Hoffmann-La Roche Inc., 587 F.3d 1333, 1337, 92 USPQ2d 1861 (Fed. Cir. 2009); *In re* Microsoft Corp., 630 F.3d 1361, 1365, 97 USPQ2d 1734 (Fed. Cir. 2011).

D. Joinder of Multiple Accused Infringers

Before September 2011, the propriety of joining multiple accused infringers in a single action was governed by Rule 20(a)(2) of the Federal Rules of Civil Procedure. This often resulted in actions with many defendants whose only relationship is that they had all been accused of infringing the same patent.

For actions commenced after September 16, 2011, the Leahy-Smith America Invents Act adds a new provision to the patent statute, 35 U.S.C. §299, which expressly prohibits joinder solely on that basis. Joinder of multiple accused infringers is permitted only if (1) the patent owner's right to relief is asserted jointly or severally or if the action arose out of the same facts relating to the accused infringement, and (2) common questions of fact relating to all defendants will arise in the action.[66]

IV. PRESUMPTION OF VALIDITY AND BURDEN OF PROOF REGARDING VALIDITY

By statute, an issued patent is presumed valid. Each claim of a patent is presumed valid independent of the validity of the patent's other claims.[67] This presumption of validity is never destroyed but, rather, rests on any party asserting invalidity as a defense to a charge of patent infringement.[68]

---

[66] Leahy-Smith America Invents Act, Pub.L. 112-29, H.R. 1249 (2011), sec. 19(d). 28 U.S.C. §299 expressly does not apply to actions where a patent owner sues multiple defendants each of whom separately seeks FDA approval to make a generic copy of a patented drug before the expiration of the patents covering that drug. *Id.* (§299 does not apply in "an action . . . in which an act of infringement under section 271(e)(2) has been pled . . . .").

[67] 35 U.S.C. §282.

[68] *Id.;* American Hoist & Derrick Co. v. Sowa & Sons Inc., 725 F.2d 1350, 1359–60, 220 USPQ 763 (Fed. Cir.), *cert. denied,* 469 U.S. 821 (1984). When a challenger presents a prima facie case of invalidity, the patent owner has the burden of going forward with rebuttal evidence, but the presumption and ultimate burden of proof are not destroyed. Mas-Hamilton Group v. LaGard Inc., 156 F.3d 1206, 1216, 48 USPQ2d 1010 (Fed. Cir. 1998).

The burden on the party challenging validity is to show by clear and convincing evidence that the patent is invalid.[69] For example, a patent may be invalid if there is clear and convincing evidence that it was anticipated by, or obvious in view of, the prior art.[70]

Although courts are not bound by the PTO's decision to issue a patent, the PTO is due the deference given a qualified government agency that is presumed to have done its job properly.[71] Therefore, if a challenger comes forward with no evidence different from that reviewed by the examiner who considered the patent application, the challenger's task is difficult.[72] With respect to art that was not considered by the examiner, the Supreme Court stated in *Microsoft Corp. v. i4i Ltd. Partnership*:

> Simply put, if the PTO did not have all material facts before it, its considered judgment may lose significant force. And, concomitantly, the challenger's burden to persuade the jury of its invalidity defense by clear and convincing evidence may be easier to sustain. In this respect, although we have no occasion to endorse any particular formulation, we note that jury instruction on the effect of new evidence can, and when requested, most often should be given.[73]

---

[69] Microsoft Corp. v. i4i Ltd. P'ship, No. 10-290, 2011 U.S. LEXIS 4376, at *14–29 (U.S. June 9, 2011). A preponderance of the evidence is sufficient to establish invalidity if the assertion is premised on alleged prior invention by a copending patent application. Environ Prods. v. Furon Co., 215 F.3d 1261, 1265–66, 55 USPQ2d 1038 (Fed. Cir. 2000).

[70] See Chapter 6, §II.B for further discussion of patent invalidity arguments.

[71] *Microsoft Corp.*, 2011 U.S. LEXIS 4376, at *9–10; *Am. Hoist & Derrick Co.*, 725 F.2d at 1359, 220 USPQ 763. An example of this deference to the PTO in a different context is the standards of review set by the Administrative Procedure Act (APA). In 1999, the Supreme Court held that the APA applies to the Federal Circuit's review of PTO findings of fact. Dickinson v. Zurko, 527 U.S. 150, 50 USPQ2d 1930 (1999) (involving the Federal Circuit's review, pursuant to 35 U.S.C. §141, of a fact-based decision by the PTO not to issue a patent). *See, e.g., In re* Gartside, 203 F.3d 1305, 53 USPQ2d 1769 (Fed. Cir. 2000). The APA standard of review has no application in an infringement action originated in district court. Purdue Pharma L.P. v. Faulding, Inc., 230 F.3d 1320, 1329, 56 USPQ2d 1481 (Fed. Cir. 2000).

[72] *American Hoist & Derrick Co.*, 725 F.2d at 1359, 220 USPQ 763.

[73] *Microsoft Corp.*, 2011 U.S. LEXIS 4376, at *35; Tokai Corp. v. Easton Enters., Inc., 632 F.3d 1358, 1367, 97 USPQ2d 1673 (Fed. Cir. 2011). Where there is a dispute as to whether the challenger's evidence was, in fact, considered by the examiner, that issue may also be considered by the jury. *Microsoft Corp.* 2011 U.S. LEXIS 4376, at *35–36.

The clear and convincing standard cannot be met by the uncorroborated testimony of a single witness.[74]

V. Stays

A court may stay a patent infringement action based on the court's inherent power to control its own docket. Whether a particular case should be stayed and whether the parties before the court should be enjoined from participating in another proceeding in a different court are issues not unique to patent matters. The general factors to be considered were set forth by the Supreme Court in its 1936 decision in *Landis v. North American Co.*[75] However, deciding priorities between patent cases at times involves unique issues.[76]

A. Allowing Other District Courts to Proceed First

It is not unusual to have multiple copending cases involving the same patent in different jurisdictions.[77] For example, due to jurisdiction and venue considerations, a patent owner

---

[74]Finnegan Corp. v. International Trade Comm'n, 180 F.3d 1354, 1366–70, 51 USPQ2d 1001 (Fed. Cir. 1999); Lazare Kaplan Int'l, Inc. v. Photoscribe Techs., Inc., 628 F.3d 1359, 1374, 97 USPQ2d 1437 (Fed. Cir. 2010). Determining the sufficiency of the corroborating evidence is a separate issue. *Id.;* see Chapter 4, §I.C.3. Uncorroborated testimony may be used to rebut a challenge to patent validity, for example, to show deficiencies in the prior art asserted by the challenger. i4i Ltd. P'ship v. Microsoft Corp., 598 F.3d 831, 847, 93 USPQ2d 1943 (Fed. Cir. 2010), *aff'd*, No. 10-290, 2011 U.S. LEXIS 4376 (U.S. June 9, 2011).

[75]Landis v. North Am. Co., 299 U.S. 248 (1936).

[76]*See generally* Herbert F. Schwartz, *Competing Claims for Jurisdiction Between Federal Courts in Patent Suits*, 46 J. PAT. OFF. SOC'Y 685 (1964). By statute, a stay is mandated under certain circumstances involving a parallel infringement proceeding before the U.S. International Trade Commission. 28 U.S.C.A. §1659; Universal Tool & Stamping Co. v. Ventra Group Inc., 46 USPQ2d 1799 (N.D. Ind. 1998). A dismissal without prejudice may operate as an alternative to a stay. L.E.A. Dynatech Inc. v. Allina, 49 F.3d 1527, 1530, 33 USPQ2d 1839 (Fed. Cir. 1995). *See generally In re* Laughlin Prods., Inc., Patent Litig., 265 F. Supp. 2d 525 (E.D. Pa. 2003).

[77]Occasionally, the ownership of a patent will be at issue in a state court action at the same time as a patent infringement suit in federal court. *See, e.g.,* Moss v. Moss Tubes Inc., 44 USPQ2d 1309 (N.D.N.Y. 1997) (infringement suit stayed); Gen-Probe Inc. v. Amoco Corp. Inc., 926 F. Supp. 948 (S.D. Cal. 1996) (same). It is also possible for more than one action involving the same patent to be filed in the same court. *See, e.g.,* Biosite, Inc. v. XOMA Ltd., 168 F. Supp. 2d 1161, 1163–66 (N.D. Cal. 2001).

may file suit against the manufacturer of an allegedly infringing product in one district and the seller of that product in
another district. Multiple cases involving the same patent can
also result if a party files a declaratory action seeking a judgment of invalidity or noninfringement in one district and the
patent owner files an infringement suit against that party in
another district.[78]

Courts will look to the identity of the parties in deciding
whether to stay one case while another proceeds. In general, if
the parties in the suits are identical, the priority rule applies so
that the first filed suit proceeds while the second filed suit is
stayed.[79] For example, if the first filed suit is brought by the patent
owner against an infringing manufacturer, and the second filed
suit is for a declaratory judgment brought by that manufacturer
against the patent owner, then the second filed action is usually
stayed.[80] There may be sound reasons, however, that make it
unjust or inefficient to follow the priority rule.[81]

If the parties in the copending suits are not the same, the
decision of which suit, if any,[82] should be stayed is typically not
determined by priority alone. For example, if the first filed suit
is brought by the patent owner against a customer who uses an

---

[78] *See generally* Herbert F. Schwartz, *Competing Claims for Jurisdiction Between Federal Courts in Patent Suits*, 46 J. PAT. OFF. SOC'Y 685 (1964). It may also be that the patent owner has sued the same defendant in more than one district, where potential jurisdiction or venue issues are unre-solved at the filing date of the complaints. *See, e.g.*, Pfizer Inc. v. Sandoz Inc., No. 09-742-JJF, 2010 WL 256548, at *3 (D. Del. Jan. 20, 2010). The filing of a second action does not render the first action moot. In such a situation, the district court judges may coordinate their proceedings to avoid duplication of effort. Pieczenik v. Dyax Corp., 265 F.3d 1329, 1332, 60 USPQ2d 1305 (Fed. Cir. 2001).

[79] *See, e.g.*, Laboratory Corp. of Am. Holdings v. Chiron Corp., 384 F.3d 1326, 72 USPQ2d 1745 (Fed. Cir. 2004).

[80] *See, e.g.*, Pacesetter Sys. Inc. v. Medtronic Inc., 678 F.2d 93, 217 USPQ 36 (9th Cir. 1982); *see also* Kimberly-Clark Corp. v. McNeil PPC, Inc., 260 F. Supp. 2d 738, 741 (E.D. Wis. 2003) ("[W]here . . . nearly identical, actions are pending before two courts, it is the court in which the action was first filed that makes the determination of which court is to hear the case").

[81] *See, e.g.*, Electronics for Imaging, Inc. v. Coyle, 394 F.3d 1341, 1347–48, 73 USPQ2d 1528 (Fed. Cir. 2005); Serco Serv. Co., L.P. v. Kelley Co., 51 F.3d 1037, 1039–40, 34 USPQ2d 1217 (Fed. Cir. 1995).

[82] Alternatives to a stay include transfer pursuant to 28 U.S.C.A. §1404 (change of venue) or 28 U.S.C. §1407 (multidistrict litigation). See, e.g., *In re* Laughlin Prods., Inc., Patent Litig., 265 F. Supp. 2d 525 (E.D. Pa. 2003) (consolidated pretrial proceedings in 17 actions); with respect to multidistrict litigations, *see generally In re* Alfuzosin Hydrochloride Patent Litig., 560 F. Supp. 2d 1372, 1374 (J.P.M.L. 2008); and *In re* Rosuvastatin Calcium Patent Litig., 560 F. Supp. 2d 1381, 1383 (J.P.M.L. 2008).

infringing product, and the second filed suit is for a declaratory judgment brought by the product manufacturer against the patent owner, then the priority rule is usually not followed.[83] A significant factor in deciding which suit should go forward is whether the second filed suit involves both real parties in interest as plaintiff and defendant.[84]

B. Allowing the Patent and Trademark Office to Proceed First

It is becoming more common to have a patent infringement suit in district court at the same time that the patent is being reviewed by the PTO.[85] Both reissue and reexamination proceedings before the PTO involve the review of issued patents.[86] The PTO also can review an issued patent as part of an interference proceeding between a patent owner and a party who claims to be entitled to the patent as the actual first inventor.[87]

If an issued patent that is the focus of a PTO proceeding is also being asserted in a district court litigation, a litigant may request a stay until the PTO reaches its decision. A court may decide to grant a stay if, for example, the court finds that an ex parte reexamination will simplify litigation by resolving issues of patentability, and thereby ease discovery and trial, as long as

---

[83] William Gluckin & Co. v. International Playtex Corp., 407 F.2d 177, 160 USPQ 513 (2d Cir. 1969); *see also* Kahn v. General Motors Corp., 889 F.2d 1078, 12 USPQ2d 1997 (Fed. Cir. 1989). *But see* Air Prods. & Chem. v. MG Nitrogen Serv., 133 F. Supp. 2d 354 (D. Del. 2001).

[84] *See, e.g., William Gluckin & Co.,* 407 F.2d at 179–80, 160 USPQ 513; Codex Corp. v. Milgo Elec. Corp., 553 F.2d 735, 194 USPQ 49 (1st Cir.), *cert. denied,* 434 U.S. 860, 195 USPQ 466 (1977).

[85] Robert Greene Sterne et al., *Reexamination Practice with Concurrent District Court Litigation or Section 337 USITC Investigation,* 11 SEDONA CONFERENCE J. 1C (2010). The PTO reexamination has become more popular with accused infringers due to the PTO's formation in 2005 of a Central Reexamination Unit dedicated to resolving reexamination requests and changes in invalidity law that create new questions about whether a patent was properly issued. *Id.* at 4–5.

[86] See Chapter 2, §§IV.B and C for further discussion of PTO reexamination and reissue proceedings.

[87] *See, e.g.,* Wireless Spectrum Tech. Inc. v. Motorola Corp., 57 USPQ2d 1662 (N.D. Ill. 2001). See Chapter 2, §III.D.10 for further discussion of interference proceedings.

the reexamination is completed quickly.[88] Also, under current law, the patentee has the right to obtain a stay of any litigation involving the issue of patentability for any claims subject to an inter partes reexamination, unless the court determines that the stay is not in the interests of justice.[89] A court cannot compel reexamination or disturb the patent owner's choice of what documents to file during reexamination.[90]

Under the Leahy-Smith America Invents Act, which became law on September 16, 2011, the considerations relating to stays of litigation pending a PTO proceeding will change for patent infringement actions filed after September 16, 2012, i.e., one year after the statute took effect. First, several new PTO proceedings to review issued patents will become available. Second, as further discussed below, there will be some statutory limits on a district court's discretion to grant or deny stays.

Effective September 16, 2012: New PTO proceedings are available for post-grant review, inter partes review (which replaces inter partes reexamination), supplemental examination (which can lead to an ex parte reexamination), and transitional post-grant review for business method patents.[91]

Under the Act, a district court must automatically stay a declaratory judgment action challenging the validity of a patent if the challenger has already filed a petition with the PTO for

---

[88] *See, e.g.,* ScriptPro LLC v. Wal-Mart Stores, Inc. 83 USPQ2d 1062 (D. Kan. 2006); *In re* Laughlin Prods., Inc., Patent Litig., 265 F. Supp. 2d 525 (E.D. Pa. 2003); Pegasus Dev. Corp. v. DirecTV, Inc., No. 00-1020-GMS, 2003 U.S. Dist. LEXIS 8052 (D. Del. May 14, 2003). *See generally* Slip Track Sys. Inc. v. Metal Lite Inc., 159 F.3d 1337, 1340–41, 48 USPQ2d 1055 (Fed. Cir. 1998). *Compare* Viskase Corp. v. American Nat'l Can Co., 261 F.3d 1316, 1327–28, 59 USPQ2d 1823 (Fed. Cir. 2001) ("[W]here the copending actions are 'neither duplicative nor dependent on one another, there is neither any need nor any justification' for a stay") (quoting *Slip Track Sys., Inc.* at 159 F.3d at 1341); Fresenius USA, Inc. v. Baxter Int'l, Inc., 582 F.3d 1288, 1304–06, 92 USPQ2d 1163 (Fed. Cir. 2009) (Newman, J., dissenting), *cert. denied,* 130 S. Ct. 2120 (2010); *In re* Freescale Semiconductor, Inc., 290 Fed. Appx. 326 (Fed. Cir. 2008); Amphenol T&M Antennas, Inc. v. Centurion Int'l, Inc., No. 00-C-4298, 2001 U.S. Dist. LEXIS 13795 (N.D. Ill. Sept. 5, 2001); Agar Corp. Inc. v. Multi-Fluid, Inc., 983 F. Supp. 1126, 44 USPQ2d 1158 (S.D. Tex. 1997), *aff'd without op.,* 215 F.3d 1340 (Fed. Cir. 1999).

[89] 35 U.S.C.A. §318 (2001 & Supp. 2008); 145 CONG. REC. S14696, S14720 (Nov. 17, 1999) (section-by-section analysis). The optional inter partes reexamination process was created in 1999. *Id.*

[90] Emerson Elec. Co. v. Davoil Inc., 88 F.3d 1051, 39 USPQ2d 1474 (Fed. Cir. 1996).

[91] Leahy-Smith America Invents Act, Pub.L. 112-29, H.R. 1249 (2011) at secs. 3, 6, 12 and 18. See Chapter 2, §§III.D.10, IV.B, and IV.C for further details on the new PTO procedures.

post-grant review or inter partes reviews. The stay will last until the patent owner moves to lift the stay, or the patent owner files an infringement complaint or counterclaim.[92] On the other hand, a district court cannot stay disposition of a patent owner's preliminary injunction motion based on a post-grant review if the patent infringement complaint was filed within three months after the patent issues.[93]

For a transitional post-grant review of a business method patent, the district court has discretion to grant a stay pending PTO review, but the court must base its decision on the following four factors:

    (A)   whether a stay . . . will simplify the issues . . . and streamline the trial;

    (B)   whether discovery is complete and whether a trial date has been set;

    (C)   whether a stay . . . would unduly prejudice the non-moving party or present a clear tactical advantage for the moving party; and

    (D)   whether a stay . . . will reduce the burden of litigation on the parties and on the court.[94]

The Leahy-Smith America Invents Act does not alter the district court's current discretion to stay litigation pending an ex parte reexamination or reissue proceeding.

Effective March 16, 2013: "Derivation" proceedings, either in the district court or the PTO, will replace interference proceedings as the process by which a party alleging to be the actual first inventor can challenge an earlier-filed patent. The Leahy-Smith America Invents Act does not limit a court's discretion to grant stays of pending litigation where a derivation proceeding has been filed.[95]

---

[92] Leahy-Smith America Invents Act, Pub.L. 112-29, H.R. 1249 (2011), sec. 6(a) (provision 35 U.S.C. §315) and sec. 6(c) (provision 35 U.S.C. §325). The stay may also be lifted for purposes of a motion by the challenger to dismiss the declaratory action.

[93] *Id.* at sec. 6(f). As further discussed in Chapter 2, §§IV.B and C, a petition for post-grant review must be filed with the PTO within the nine-month period after a patent issues and can be based on any grounds for invalidity that are available as a defense to infringement under 35 U.S.C. §282(b)(2) and (3). A petition for inter partes review must be filed after nine months from patent issuance and must involve a challenge to the patent's novelty or nonobviousness.

[94] Leahy-Smith America Invents Act, Pub.L. 112-29, H.R. 1249 (2011), sec. 18.

[95] *Id.* at sec. 3.

VI. Prior Adjudications Regarding Validity

When a patent is infringed by more than one party, the patent owner may choose to sue the infringers in sequence, rather than simultaneously. Suing the infringers in sequence may be preferable due to the considerable expense of patent litigation or as part of a particular litigation strategy. Depending on the outcome of an earlier suit, the patent owner or another alleged infringer may try to use that result to its advantage in a later suit. For example, if the patent was held invalid in an earlier suit, a new defendant may argue that the patent owner is estopped from asserting that patent again.[96] On the other hand, if the alleged infringer in a prior suit failed to prove invalidity, the patent owner may argue that this prior adjudication weighs against finding invalidity in a later suit.

A. When the Patent Is Held Invalid in the Prior Adjudication

Before 1971, the rule of mutuality of estoppel was entrenched in the patent area; a party could not use an advantageous judgment for its benefit in a later suit if the party could not have been bound by the prior judgment had it been adverse. For example, a defendant could not estop a patent owner from asserting a patent that was held invalid in a prior suit unless the defendant was in privity with the accused infringer in the prior suit or in control of the prior litigation.[97]

The Supreme Court severely narrowed the requirement for mutuality in its 1971 decision in *Blonder-Tongue v. University Foundation*.[98] As a result, a patent owner is now collaterally

---

[96] The new defendant might also argue that a prior holding of unenforceability provides an estoppel. *See generally* Pharmacia & Upjohn Co. v. Mylan Pharms., 170 F.3d 1373, 1379, 50 USPQ2d 1033 (Fed. Cir. 1999).

[97] 18A Charles Alan Wright et al., Federal Practice and Procedure: Jurisdiction §4464 (2d ed. 2002).

[98] 402 U.S. 313, 169 USPQ 513 (1971).

estopped from asserting a patent that was held invalid in a final and appealable prior judgment, regardless of mutuality, unless the patent owner can show there was not a full and fair opportunity procedurally, substantively, or evidentially to litigate the issue of validity in the prior suit.[99]

The Supreme Court presented five factors relevant to deciding whether the patent owner had a full and fair opportunity to litigate, summarized as follows: (i) Did the patent owner pick the time and place to litigate (i.e., was the patent owner the plaintiff)? (ii) Did the patent owner have ample incentive to litigate? (iii) Did the court that held the patent invalid apply the proper standards (in particular, the test regarding nonobviousness)? (iv) Did the court that held the patent invalid completely fail to grasp the technical subject matter or the issues? and (v) Was the patent owner deprived of crucial evidence?[100] These factors are nonexclusive; however, a court cannot consider factors that do not relate to the issue of the full and fair opportunity to litigate.

The rule that a single holding of invalidity can estop later suits involving the same patent regardless of mutuality applies even when there are inconsistent prior adjudications regarding validity. For example, if a patent was not held invalid in one suit and then held invalid in a second suit, the patent

---

[99] *Id.;* Mendenhall v. Barber-Greene Co., 26 F.3d 1573, 31 USPQ2d 1001 (Fed. Cir.), *cert. denied sub nom.,* Mendenhall v. Astec Indus., 513 U.S. 1018 (1994); *see, e.g., In re* Cygnus Telecomm. Tech., LLC, Patent Litig., 536 F.3d 1343, 1349, 87 USPQ2d 1801 (Fed. Cir. 2008) (no estoppel), *cert. denied,* 129 S. Ct. 1906 (2009); *Pharmacia & Upjohn Co.,* 170 F.3d at 1379–80, 50 USPQ2d 1033 (estoppel). A very narrow exception might exist if invalidity ceased when a certificate of correction was issued. *See generally* Southwest Software v. Harlequin Inc., 226 F.3d 1280, 1297, 56 USPQ2d 1161 (Fed. Cir. 2000).

[100] *Blonder-Tongue,* 402 U.S. at 333, 169 USPQ 513; *see also* Dana Corp. v. NOK Inc., 882 F.2d 505, 11 USPQ2d 1883 (Fed. Cir. 1989). The full and fair opportunity inquiry is quite narrow, involving only the opportunity to litigate and not the correctness of the prior holding. *Pharmacia & Upjohn Co.,* 170 F.3d at 1380, 50 USPQ2d 1033. Invalidity determinations during preliminary injunction proceedings are not final and do not afford a patent owner a full and fair opportunity to litigate. Abbott Labs. v. Andrx Pharms., Inc., 473 F.3d 1196, 1202–08, 81 USPQ2d 1289 (Fed. Cir. 2007) (applying Seventh Circuit law).

owner could be collaterally estopped from asserting that patent in a third suit.[101]

B. When the Patent Is Not Held Invalid in the Prior Adjudication

Although a single holding of invalidity can be fatal to a patent, a single victory on the issue of validity does not confer invincibility. When a patent is not held invalid, it means that a particular challenger was not able to present clear and convincing evidence of invalidity. A different challenger may be able to present better evidence on the issue of invalidity. Therefore, any challenger must be allowed to present his or her evidence. A prior judgment finding insufficient proof of invalidity carries some weight, although the weight decreases as the quality and quantity of new evidence presented by a new challenger increases.[102]

VII. APPEALS AND CHOICE OF FEDERAL CIRCUIT VERSUS REGIONAL CIRCUIT LAW

For a case arising under the patent laws, an appeal from a final decision in district court goes to the Federal Circuit. The Federal Circuit was created in 1982 to alleviate the problems

---

[101] Mississippi Chem. Corp. v. Swift Agric. Chems. Corp., 717 F.2d 1374, 219 USPQ 577 (Fed. Cir. 1983); Stevenson v. Sears, Roebuck & Co., 713 F.2d 705, 218 USPQ 969 (Fed. Cir. 1983). Appealing an invalidity decision against fewer than all defendants in a multidistrict litigation does not estop the patentee from pursuing the appeal, even though a final judgment of invalidity was entered with respect to the non-appellee defendants. *In re* Cygnus Telecomm. Tech., LLC, 536 F.3d at 1349–50, 87 USPQ2d 1801. A judgment involving less than all the claims in a patent may estop the patent owner from asserting the nonadjudicated claims in a later suit. *See* Jervis B. Webb Co. v. Southern Sys. Inc., 742 F.2d 1388, 1399, 222 USPQ 943 (Fed. Cir. 1984); Interconnect Planning Corp. v. Feil, 774 F.2d 1132, 1135–37, 227 USPQ 543 (Fed. Cir. 1985).

[102] *See generally* Gillette Co. v. S. C. Johnson & Son Inc., 919 F.2d 720, 723, 16 USPQ2d 1923 (Fed. Cir. 1990); *Stevenson,* 713 F.2d at 711, 218 USPQ 969. *But cf.* Allen Archery Inc. v. Browning Mfg. Co., 819 F.2d 1087, 2 USPQ2d 1490 (Fed. Cir. 1987) ("The statutory presumption of patent validity . . . 'is not augmented by an earlier adjudication of patent 'validity' ' " (quoting Shelcore, Inc. v. Durham Indus., Inc., 745 F.2d 621, 627, 223 USPQ 584, 588 (Fed. Cir.1984))).

caused by conflicting decisions in the regional circuit courts involving patent law and the unwillingness of the Supreme Court to resolve these conflicts in a timely fashion.[103] The regional circuit courts decided appeals from cases arising under the patent laws from 1891 to 1982.[104]

The Federal Circuit does not have jurisdiction over all cases that involve a patent law claim. The appeal must be from a district court's final decision in an action that arises under the patent laws.[105] The courts had held that a counterclaim for patent infringement alone was not sufficient to confer appellate jurisdiction on the Federal Circuit.[106] However, the Leahy-Smith America Invents Act amended 28 U.S.C. §1295(a)(1) such that, for actions commenced on or after September 16, 2011, the Federal Circuit will also have exclusive jurisdiction over appeals "in which a party has asserted a compulsory counterclaim arising under" the patent laws.[107]

The Federal Circuit does have jurisdiction over appeals of nonpatent claims that accompany patent claims. For example, an appeal of antitrust claims will go to the Federal Circuit if the district court case also involved claims arising under the patent laws.[108]

The Federal Circuit applies its own law to deal with substantive issues of patent law and procedural issues relating to

---

[103] See Chapter 1, text accompanying notes 19–23.

[104] Initially, before the regional circuit courts existed, the desire for a national appellate court for patent appeals was caused by the congested docket of the Supreme Court. *Subcommittee on Patents, Trademarks and Copyrights, Senate Comm. on the Judiciary*, 85th Cong., 2d Sess., Study No. 20 (1959).

[105] Holmes Grp. Inc. v. Vornado Air Circulation Sys., Inc., 535 U.S. 826, 829, 62 USPQ2d 1801 (2002); Christianson v. Colt Indus. Operating Corp., 486 U.S. 800, 7 USPQ2d 1109 (1988); *see, e.g.*, ClearPlay, Inc. v. Abecassis, 602 F.3d 1364, 1369, 94 USPQ2d 1763 (Fed. Cir. 2010) (no appellate jurisdiction). Regarding what is a "final decision," *see, e.g.*, Procter & Gamble Co. v. Kraft Foods Global, Inc., 549 F.3d 842, 846–47, 89 USPQ2d 1085 (Fed. Cir. 2008); Pause Tech. LLC v. TiVo Inc., 401 F.3d 1290, 1292–93, 74 USPQ2d 1058 (Fed. Cir. 2005); Nystrom v. Trex Co., 339 F.3d 1347, 1349–51, 67 USPQ2d 1858 (Fed. Cir. 2003).

[106] *Holmes Grp. Inc.*, 535 U.S. at 834, 62 USPQ2d 1801; Telecomm Tech. Servs., Inc. v. Siemens Rolm Commc'ns, 295 F.3d 1249, 63 USPQ2d 1606 (Fed. Cir. 2002).

[107] Leahy-Smith America Invents Act, Pub.L. 112-29, H.R. 1249 (2011), sec. 19(b) (amending 28 U.S.C. §1295) and 19(e) (effective date).

[108] Golan v. Pingel Enter., Inc., 310 F.3d 1360, 1368, 64 USPQ2d 1911 (Fed. Cir. 2002); In re Spalding Sports Worldwide Inc., 203 F.3d 800, 803, 53 USPQ2d 1747 (Fed. Cir. 2000); Nobelpharma AB v. Implant Innovations, 141 F.3d 1059, 46 USPQ2d 1097 (Fed. Cir. 1998).

substantive issues in patent law.[109] The court decides proce-dural issues that are unrelated to the patent issues by applying the law of the regional circuit.[110] For matters of state law that are outside Federal Circuit jurisdiction, the court defers to state law.[111] Thus, in the appeal of an antitrust claim, the Federal Cir-cuit applies its own law when reviewing the patent issues and applies the law of the regional circuit court when reviewing the nonpatent elements of antitrust claims.

---

[109] The Federal Circuit applies its own law to procedural questions that: (1) pertain to patent law; (2) bear an essential relationship to the Federal Circuit's exclusive jurisdiction; or (3) otherwise clearly implicate the responsibilities of the Federal Circuit in a field within its exclusive jurisdiction. Bose Corp. v. JBL, Inc., 274 F.3d 1354, 1360, 61 USPQ2d 1216 (Fed. Cir. 2001), *cert. denied*, 537 U.S. 880 (2002); *see, e.g.*, Duro-Last, Inc. v. Custom Seal, Inc., 321 F.3d 1098, 1105–06, 66 USPQ2d 1025 (Fed. Cir. 2003) (sufficiency of pre-verdict motion under Fed. R. Civ. P. 50(a)); Eolas Techs., Inc. v. Microsoft Corp., 399 F.3d 1325, 1332, 73 USPQ2d 1782 (Fed. Cir.) (sufficiency of jury instructions on patent law issues), *cert. denied*, 546 U.S. 998 (2005); Fiskars, Inc. v. Hunt Mfg. Co., 279 F.3d 1378, 1381, 61 USPQ2d 1851 (Fed. Cir. 2002) (review of denial of motion for relief from judgment under Fed. R. Civ. P. 60(b)).

[110] Panduit Corp. v. All States Plastic Mfg. Co., 744 F.2d 1564, 1575, 223 USPQ 465 (Fed. Cir. 1984); Midwest Indus. Inc. v. Karavan Trailers Inc., 175 F.3d 1356, 50 USPQ2d 1672 (Fed. Cir.), *cert. denied*, 528 U.S. 1019 (1999); *see, e.g.*, Verizon Servs. Corp. v. Cox Fibernet Va., Inc., 602 F.3d 1325, 1332–35, 94 USPQ2d 1833 (Fed. Cir. 2010) (applying regional circuit law to issue of proper jury instructions). If the regional circuit has not spoken on an issue, the Federal Cir-cuit predicts how that circuit would decide the issue based on decisions in that circuit. *Panduit Corp.*, 744 F.2d at 1575, 223 USPQ 465. When necessary to maintain a nationally uniform patent law, the Federal Circuit will not defer to the law of the relevant regional circuit. *See, e.g.*, High-way Equip. Co. v. FECO, Ltd., 469 F.3d 1027, 1032, 81 USPQ2d 1120 (Fed. Cir. 2006); Regents of Univ. of N.M. v. Knight, 321 F.3d 1111, 1123–24, 66 USPQ2d 1001 (Fed. Cir.), *cert. denied*, 540 U.S. 820 (2003). *See generally* Vardon Golf Co. v. Karsten Mfg., 294 F.3d 1330, 1335–36, 63 USPQ2d 1468 (Fed. Cir. 2002) (Dyk, J., concurring).

[111] *See, e.g., Regents of Univ. of N.M.*, 321 F.3d at 1117–20, 66 USPQ2d 1001; BBA Nonwovens Simpsonville v. Superior Nonwovens, 303 F.3d 1332, 1337, 64 USPQ2d 1257 (Fed. Cir. 2002); University of W. Va. v. VanVoorhies, 278 F.3d 1288, 1296, 61 USPQ2d 1449 (Fed. Cir. 2002). *See generally* Deprenyl Animal Health v. University of Toronto, 297 F.3d 1343, 1349, 63 USPQ2d 1705 (Fed. Cir. 2002). As with regional circuit law, the Federal Circuit does not defer to state law when necessary to maintain national uniformity in patent law. *See, e.g.*, Rhone Poulenc Agro, S.A. v. DeKalb Genetics Corp., 284 F.3d 1323, 1327–29, 62 USPQ2d 1188 (Fed. Cir. 2002) (bona fide purchaser defense to patent infringement is a matter of federal law), *cert. denied*, 539 U.S. 957 (2003); Group One, Ltd. v. Hallmark Cards, Inc., 254 F.3d 1041, 1047, 59 USPQ2d 1121 (Fed. Cir. 2001) (§102(b) on-sale bar's offer for sale requirement is governed by federal law), *cert. denied*, 534 U.S. 1127 (2002).

PATENTABILITY

For an invention to be patentable, it must be (1) patent-eligible subject matter, (2) useful, (3) new, and (4) non-obvious. In addition, to obtain a patent for a patentable invention, the patent applicant must (1) be an original inventor, (2) file the application before certain statutory "time bars" arise, (3) adequately disclose the invention, and (4) distinctly claim the invention.[1]

---

[1] As discussed in Chapter 2, §III.B, an inventor also must satisfy the formal requirements of the PTO before a patent will be issued.

   As a roadmap, the requirements of patent-eligible subject matter and utility are set forth in 35 U.S.C. §101. Section 102 lays out the requirements of novelty and the "time bars" that will deprive an otherwise deserving applicant of the right to a patent. Section 103 describes the requirement of "non-obvious subject matter." The disclosure and claiming requirements for a patent application are set forth in 35 U.S.C. §112. The requirement that the applicant be the "original inventor" is set forth in 35 U.S.C. §102(f) and (g), and in the formal requirement that a patent application be filed in the name of the inventor(s) as described in 35 U.S.C. §§115-118.[2]

   On September 16, 2011, the Leahy-Smith America Invents Act became law.[3] The Act includes substantial revisions to 35 U.S.C § 102, along with corresponding related amendments to sections 101, and 103, inter alia. The purpose of these revisions is eventually to shift the U.S. patent system from one where the "first to invent" is entitled to patent protection as against subsequent inventors to a system where priority of the right to a patent will go to the "first inventor to file" a patent application.[4] **These changes, however, will not take effect until March 16, 2013, and then will apply only to patent applications *filed* after that date**.[5] Such applications may not issue for many months after March 2013. Patent applications filed and issued before that date will be governed by the law as it existed before the Act, for the life of those patents. Thus, the current validity rules will be with us for decades to come.

   Accordingly, the text of this chapter is organized around the "old" validity rules, which are still in effect.[6] Section III discusses

---

   [2] MANUAL OF PATENT EXAMINING PROCEDURE (MPEP) *available at* http://www.uspto.gov/web/ offices/pac/mpep/mpep.htm, published by the PTO as a guide for patent examiners, includes Chapter 2100, a summary of the PTO's interpretations of the requirements of patentability. Although the MPEP does not have the force of law or the force of the PTO regulations, courts may take judicial notice of the PTO's understanding of the law as appropriate. MPEP, Foreword (8th ed. 2001, rev. July 2010); Enzo Biochem, Inc. v. Gen-Probe Inc., 323 F.3d 956, 964, 63 USPQ2d 1609 (Fed. Cir. 2002).
   [3] Pub. L. 112-29, H.R. 1249 (2011).
   [4] *Id.*, sec. 3; *see also* H.Rep. No. 112-98, 112th Cong., 1st Sess, (2011) at pp. 40–43, 73–74.
   [5] Smith-Leahy America Invents Act, Pub.L. 112-29, H.R. 1249 (2011), sec. 3(n).
   [6] Changes to the "best mode" requirement of 35 U.S.C. §112 ¶ 2 take effect immediately. *See* Smith-Leahy America Invents Act, Pub. L. 112-29, H.R. 1249 (2011), sec. 15(c). These changes are discussed in this chapter, §II.C.4.

the differences between the old rules and the coming "first inventor to file" standard.

I. THE CONDITIONS OF PATENTABILITY

A. Patent-eligible Subject Matter

The U.S. Constitution grants Congress power to grant exclusive rights to inventors for a limited time "to promote the progress of science and useful arts."[7] Subject to the limitations of this grant, the 1952 Patent Act established as categories of patent-eligible subject matter any new and useful "process, machine, manufacture, or composition of matter, or any new and useful improvement thereof."[8] This "broad" and "permissive" definition was designed "to ensure that ingenuity should receive a liberal encouragement."[9]

There are three judicial limitations on the literal words of the statute. Inventions are not patent-eligible if they are directed toward "laws of nature, physical phenomena, and abstract ideas. . . . The concepts covered by these exceptions are 'part of the storehouse of knowledge of all men . . . free to all men and reserved exclusively to none.' "[10]

When determining whether a claim is directed to patent-eligible subject matter, the dispositive inquiry is whether the claim *as a whole* satisfies Section 101.[11] It is irrelevant that the claim may contain, as part of the whole, nonpatentable subject matter.[12] It is also irrelevant that a claim may be drafted to

---

[7] U.S. CONST. art. I, § 8; *see* Graham v. John Deere Co. 383 U.S. 1, 5–10, 148 USPQ 459 (1966).

[8] 35 U.S.C. §101.

[9] Bilski v. Kappos, 130 S. Ct. 3218, 3225, 95 USPQ2d 1001 (2010) (internal quotes and citations omitted).

[10] *Id.*, quoting Diamond v. Chakrabarty, 447 U.S. 303, 308, 206 USPQ 193 (1980) and Funk Bros. Seed Co. v. Kalo Co., 333 U.S. 127, 130, 76 USPQ 280 (1948). These exceptions, which find support in decisions dating to 1853, are also supported by principles of stare decisis. *Id.*

[11] Diamond v. Diehr, 450 U.S. 175, 188–89, 192, 209 USPQ 1 (1981).

[12] *In re* Bilski, 545 F.3d 943, 958, 88 USPQ2d 1385 (Fed. Cir. 2008) (en banc), *aff'd sub nom* Bilski v. Kappos, 130 S. Ct. 3218, 95 USPQ2d 1001 (2010); *see, e.g.*, Prometheus Labs., Inc. v. Mayo Collaborative Servs., 628 F.3d 1347, 1358–59, 97 USPQ2d 1097 (Fed. Cir. 2010) (unpatentable mental step did not make entire claim unpatentable), *cert. granted*, No. 10-1150, 2011 WL 973139 (U.S. June 20, 2011).

invoke a particular statutory category (e.g., a machine or a manufacture) when "the underlying invention" is actually in another category (e.g., a process).[13]

1. Processes

A process is a way to produce a result. For example, mixing A with B under conditions C to get D is a process. The inventor need not know why the process works. A patent is granted for discovering and disclosing the process, not for the scientific theory behind it.[14] Claims directed to a "method" are a type of process claim.

The patent-eligibility of method claims has been a recurring issue for the courts since the 1970s, in the context of the patentability of software algorithms.[15] More recently, this line of cases has been applied to patents on "business methods," and inventions relating to data collection and processing in the context of biotechnology, medical diagnostics, and similar fields.

In 2008, the Federal Circuit's en banc decision in *In re Bilski* established a test to distinguish patent-eligible methods from those that improperly sought to preempt all uses of an abstract idea or a fundamental principle of science or nature: "A claimed process is surely patent-eligible under §101 if: (1) it is tied to a particular machine or apparatus, or (2) it transforms a particular article into a different state or thing."[16] The court found two additional limitations in Supreme Court precedent: (1) "mere field-of-use limitations are generally insufficient to render an otherwise ineligible process claim patent-eligible"; and (2) "insignificant postsolution activity will not transform an unpatentable principle into a patentable process."[17]

---

[13] CyberSource Corp. v. Retail Decisions, Inc., 99 USPQ2d 1690, 1697 (Fed. Cir. 2011)

[14] *In re* Cortright, 165 F.3d 1353, 1359, 49 USPQ2d 1464 (Fed. Cir. 1999).

[15] *See* Diamond v. Diehr, 450 U.S. 175, 209 USPQ 1(1981); Parker v. Flook, 477 U.S. 584, 198 USPQ 193 (1978); Gottschalk v. Benson, 490 U.S. 63, 175 USPQ 673 (1972). The Federal Circuit's evolving understanding of these cases is discussed in *In re* Bilski, 545 F.3d 943, 961–64, 88 USPQ2d 1385 (Fed. Cir. 2008) (en banc).

[16] *In re* Bilski, 545 F.3d 943, 954, 88 USPQ2d 1385 (Fed. Cir. 2008) (en banc).

[17] *Id.* at 957, 88 USPQ2d 1385 (citations and internal quotations omitted).

Applying these principles, the Federal Circuit in *Bilski* affirmed the PTO's rejection of claims directed to methods of hedging risk in commodities trading.[18]

The Supreme Court's 2010 opinion in *Bilski v. Kappos* affirmed the rejection of the claims, but for a different reason. Justice Kennedy's majority opinion states that, while the "machine-or-transformation test is a useful and important clue, an investigative tool, for determining whether some claimed inventions are processes under §101," it is not "the sole test" for patent-eligibility. The majority also rejected the argument that "business methods" are *per se* unpatentable:

> Rather than adopting categorical rules that might have wide-ranging and unforeseen impacts, the Court resolves this case narrowly on the basis of this Court's decisions in *Benson, Flook,* and *Diehr,* which show that petitioners' claims are not patentable processes because they are attempts to patent abstract ideas.[19]

In a lengthy concurrence, Justice Stevens, writing for himself and Justices Ginsburg, Breyer and Sotomayor, found no guidance in the majority opinion as to how to define an "abstract" idea, and would have ruled more broadly that "methods of doing business" are not patent-eligible.[20]

Computer software: Following the *Bilski* decisions, the Federal Circuit reversed a judgment that a program directed to manipulating data to improve the display of computer graphics was not patent-eligible. The fact that the method claims included mathematical algorithms and formulas was not dispositive. Viewing the claim as a whole,

> [t]he invention presents functional and palpable applications in the field of computer technology. . . . Borrowing from the reasoning of the Supreme Court in *Diehr,* this court observes that the patentees here "do not seek to patent a mathematical formula. Instead, they seek patent protection for a process of" halftoning in computer applications.[21]

---

[18] *Id.* at 963–66, 88 USPQ2d 1385.

[19] Bilski v. Kappos, 130 S. Ct. 3218, 3225–31, 95 USPQ2d 1001 (2010).

[20] *Id.* at 3231–57, 95 USPQ2d 1001 (2010).

[21] Research Corp. Techs, Inc. v. Microsoft Corp., 627 F.3d 859, 868–69, 97 USPQ2d 1274 (Fed. Cir. 2010).

The court added this observation:

> Indeed, this court notes that inventions with specific applications
> or improvements to technologies in the marketplace are not likely
> to be so abstract that they override the statutory language and
> framework of the Patent Act.[22]

Where a claim is drafted to require that the method is
implemented on a particular machine, the machine must
" 'impose meaningful limits on the claim's scope' " and " 'must
play a significant part in permitting the claimed method to be
performed.' "[23]

Business methods: The Supreme Court in *Bilski v. Kappos*
identified the hedging of financial risk as " 'a fundamental economic practice long prevalent in our system of commerce and
taught in any introductory finance class' " and thus not patent-
eligible because it was abstract.[24] In its 2008 *Bilski* opinion, the
Federal Circuit identified "abstract constructs such as legal
obligations, organizational relationships, and business risks" as
potentially problematic.[25]

In *CyberSource Corp. v. Retail Decisions, Inc.,* the Federal Circuit affirmed a judgment that a method "for verifying the
validity of a credit card transaction" was unpatentable, even
when claimed as computer hardware programmed to perform
that method:

> [C]laim 3's steps can all be performed in the human mind. Such a
> method that can be performed by human thought alone is merely
> an abstract idea and is not patent-eligible under §101. Methods which
> can be performed entirely in the human mind are unpatentable not
> because there is anything wrong with claiming mental method
> steps as part of a process containing non-mental steps, but rather
> because computational methods which can be performed *entirely* in

---

[22] *Id.* at 869, 97 USPQ2d 1274.

[23] CyberSource Corp. v. Retail Decisions, Inc., 99 USPQ2d 1690, 1697–98 (Fed. Cir. 2011)
(citations omitted) (computer-implemented business method not patent-eligible). *But cf.* SiRF
Tech., Inc. v. International Trade Comm'n, 601 F.3d 1319, 1331, 94 USPQ2d 1607 (Fed. Cir.
2010) ("method of calculating an absolute position of a GPS receiver" patent-eligible).

[24] *Bilski v. Kappos,* 130 S. Ct. at 3231, 95 USPQ2d 1001 (citation omitted).

[25] *In re Bilski,* 545 F.3d at 962, 88 USPQ2d 1385 (Fed. Cir. 2008).

the human mind are the types of methods that embody the "basic tools of scientific and technological work" that are free to all men and reserved exclusively to none.[26]

Biotechnology/medical diagnostics: In *Association for Molecular Pathology v. U.S. Patent and Trademark Office,* the Federal Circuit affirmed that methods of "comparing" or "analyzing" genetic sequence information are not patent-eligible "because they claim only abstract mental processes."[27] A claim directed to a method of screening potential cancer therapeutics by measuring changes in cell growth rates were patent-eligible because they involved transformation of the cells being studied, and because the claim "is not so 'manifestly abstract' as to claim only a scientific principle."[28]

The court has also found that a "method of optimizing therapeutic efficiency" for treatment of an illness includes the requisite transformation of both the body that is being treated and the drug that is administered and metabolized. The Supreme Court will review this decision in its 2012 term.[29]

2. Machines

A "machine" is " 'a concrete thing, consisting of parts, or of certain devices and combination of devices. This includes every mechanical device or combination of mechanical powers and devices to perform some function and produce a certain effect or result.' "[30] To be patent-eligible, a machine must play a significant role in permitting the claimed method to be performed.[31]

---

[26] *CyberSource Corp.,* 99 USPQ2d at 1696 (method claim) and at 1696–99 (claim to "computer readable medium containing program instructions").

[27] Ass'n for Molecular Pathology v. U.S. PTO, 653 F.3d 1329, 1355–56 99 USPQ2d 1398 (Fed. Cir. 2011).

[28] *Id.* at 1358.

[29] Prometheus Labs., Inc. v. Mayo Collaborative Servs., 628 F.3d 1347, 1355–57, 97 USPQ2d 1097 (Fed. Cir. 2010), *cert. granted,* No. 10-1150, 2011 WL 973139 (June 20, 2011); *see also* Classen Immunotherapies, Inc. v. Biogen IDEC, Nos. 2006–1634, –1649, 2011 WL 3835409 (Fed. Cir. August 31, 2011).

[30] *SiRF Tech., Inc.,* 601 F.3d at 1332, 94 USPQ2d 1607 (citations omitted).

[31] *Compare SiRF Tech., Inc.,* 601 F.3d at 1332–33, 94 USPQ2d 1607 (Fed. Cir. 2010) (patent-eligible subject matter) *with CyberSource Corp.,* 99 USPQ2d at 1696–99 (programmed computer found did not place significant limitations on method to be performed by program).

3. Compositions of Matter

Compositions of matter "include 'all compositions of two or more substances and . . . all composite articles, whether they be the results of chemical union, or of mechanical mixture, or whether they be gases, fluids, powders or solids.' "[32] As with manufactures, discussed below, a product of nature can be the basis for a patentable composition of matter. The test is whether the composition resulting from the inventor's efforts has "markedly different" characteristics from that found in nature (and not whether the inventor combined matter in a way not found in nature).[33] For example, isolated DNA can be patentable subject matter where the isolated molecules have a distinctive chemical identity and nature from molecules found in nature.[34]

4. Manufactures

A manufacture, or an article of manufacture, is "the production of articles for use from raw or prepared materials by giving to these materials new forms, qualities, properties, or combinations, whether by hand-labor or by machinery."[35] A product of nature can be a patentable manufacture if it has

---

[32] Diamond v. Chakrabarty, 447 U.S. 303, 308, 206 USPQ 193 (1980).

[33] Ass'n for Molecular Pathology, 653 F.3d at 1351. (citing Diamond v. Chakrabarty, 447 U.S. 303, 206 USPQ 193 (1980)).

[34] Ass'n for Molecular Pathology, 653 F.3d at 1351. In a concurring opinion, Judge Moore distinguished cDNA molecules, produced in the laboratory, from isolated and purified DNA, which retains a structure more similar to native DNA. Id. at 1364–69. However, Judge Moore noted that the PTO has been granting claims to isolated DNA since the 1980s, and that principles of stare decisis suggested that a change in the law should come from Congress, not the courts. Id. at 1367–71. Judge Bryson dissented from the holding that isolated and purified DNA was patent-eligible subject matter. Id. at 1373–81. Cf. Intervet Inc. v. Merial Ltd., 617 F.3d 1282, 1293–95, 95 USPQ2d 1956 (Fed. Cir. 2010) (Dyk, J., dissenting-in-part) (questioning the patentability of gene patents). The Leahy-Smith America Invents Act includes a provision that prohibits the issuance of a patent "on a claim directed to or encompassing a human organism." See Pub.L 112-29, H.R. 1249 (2011), sec. 33. The amendment applies to all patent applications pending before the PTO on or after September 16, 2011, the effective date of the legislation.

[35] Chakrabarty, 447 U.S. at 308, 206 USPQ 193.

been altered by man.[36] As with compositions of matter, the pertinent question is whether the inventor's alteration causes the product of nature to be markedly different from what exists in nature.[37] Not all "manufactured" products are patentable. For example, printed matter is not a manufacture unless the structure of the printed matter, or the relationship between the printing and the structure of the printing medium, is patentable.[38]

B. Useful

To be patentable, a claimed invention must be "useful."[39] The invention must, at the very least, work,[40] although it does not have to work perfectly or even better than any competing products or processes that might exist.[41] "To violate §101 the claimed device must be totally incapable of achieving a useful result."[42] A product may be found to be useful on a lesser showing than would be required to obtain governmental approval to market that product.[43]

---

[36] *Chakrabarty*, 447 U.S. at 309–10, 206 USPQ 193 (genetically altered microorganism is patentable subject matter). Newly developed seeds and seed-grown plants are patentable subject matter. Pioneer Hi-Bred Int'l v. J.E.M. Ag Supply, 200 F.3d 1374, 53 USPQ2d 1440 (Fed. Cir. 2000).

[37] *Chakrabarty*, 447 U.S. at 310, 206 USPQ 193.

[38] 1 DONALD S. CHISUM, CHISUM ON PATENTS §1.02[4] (2011). Thus, a business form with headings for data to be recorded on the form is nonpatentable, whereas a railway transfer ticket with a detachable coupon is patentable. *Compare* U.S. Credit Sys. Co. v. American Credit Indem. Co., 59 F. 139 (2d Cir. 1893) *with* Cincinnati Traction Co. v. Pope, 210 F. 443 (6th Cir. 1913).

[39] 35 U.S.C. §101.

[40] Process Control Corp. v. HydReclaim Corp., 190 F.3d 1350, 1358–59, 52 USPQ2d 1029 (Fed. Cir. 1999), *cert. denied*, 529 U.S. 1037 (2000). Utility is closely related to enablement under 35 U.S.C. §112, although utility is a question of fact while enablement is ultimately a question of law. *Id.; see, e.g., In re* '318 Patent Infringement Litig., 583 F.3d 1317, 1327, 92 USPQ2d 1385 (Fed. Cir. 2009) (finding no utility, thus no enablement).

[41] Stiftung v. Renishaw PLC, 945 F.2d 1173, 1180–81, 20 USPQ2d 1094 (Fed. Cir. 1991); Juicy Whip Inc. v. Orange Bang, Inc., 185 F.3d 1364, 1366, 51 USPQ2d 1700 (Fed. Cir. 1999) ("The threshold of utility is not high. . . .").

[42] Brooktree Corp. v. Advanced Micro Devices, 977 F.2d 1555, 1571, 24 USPQ2d 1401 (Fed. Cir. 1992); Juicy Whip Inc. v. Orange Bang, Inc., 185 F.3d 1364, 1366, 51 USPQ2d 1700 (Fed. Cir. 1999) ("The threshold of utility is not high. . . .").

[43] *In re* Brana, 51 F.3d 1560, 1567–68, 34 USPQ2d 1436 (Fed. Cir. 1995).

Nevertheless, not all products or processes that work are considered useful. For example, products or processes that can be used only for immoral or illegal purposes may not be considered useful.[44]

An additional set of "utility" issues arises in the context of inventions where something has been discovered or developed, but the inventors do not yet know what it will do. For example, the technology to identify polymeric structures or genetic sequences led to the discovery of many such structures and sequences whose actual function is as yet unknown. In *Brenner v. Manson,* decided in 1966, the Supreme Court established the requirement that, to be patentable, such inventions must exhibit "specific" and "substantial" utility at the time of the filing of the patent application:

> The basic *quid pro quo* contemplated by the Constitution and the Congress for granting a patent monopoly is the benefit derived by the public from an invention with substantial utility. Unless and until a process is refined and developed to this point—where specific benefit exists in currently available form—there is insufficient justification for permitting an applicant to engross what may prove to be a broad field.[45]

The Federal Circuit elaborated on these requirements in the context of genetic sequences in its 2005 decision in *In re Fisher*:

> Courts have used the labels "practical utility" and "real world" utility interchangeably in determining whether an invention offers a "substantial" utility. Indeed, the Court of Customs and Patent Appeals stated that "'[p]ractical utility' is a shorthand way of attributing 'real-world' value to claimed subject matter. In other words, one skilled in the art can use a claimed discovery in a manner which provides some *immediate benefit to the public.*" It thus is clear that an application must show that an invention is useful to the public as disclosed in its current form, not that it may prove useful at some future date after further research. Simply put, to satisfy the "substantial" utility requirement, an asserted use must show that that claimed invention has a significant and presently available benefit to the public.[46]

---

[44] *See Juicy Whip Inc.,* 185 F.3d at 1366–68, 51 USPQ2d 1700.

[45] Brenner v. Manson, 383 U.S. 519, 534–35, 148 USPQ 689 (1966).

[46] *In re* Fisher, 421 F.3d 1365, 1371, 76 USPQ2d 1225 (Fed. Cir. 2005) (internal citations omitted).

"Specific" utility requires more than usefulness as a tool for further research. In this regard, the Federal Circuit endorsed the PTO's 2001 Utility Examination Guidelines as "comport[ing] with this court's interpretation of the utility requirement of §101."[47]

C. New

Because patents are granted to promote progress, an invention is not patentable unless it is new. An invention is not new if all the claimed elements are present in a single piece of relevant prior art, as prior art is defined in 35 U.S.C. §102. Such an invention is said to have been "anticipated" by that prior art "reference." As the Federal Circuit has explained:

> Although §102 refers to "the invention" generally, the anticipation inquiry proceeds on a claim-by-claim basis. To anticipate a claim, a single prior art reference must expressly or inherently disclose each claim limitation. But disclosure of each element is not quite enough—this court has long held that "[a]nticipation requires the presence in a single prior art disclosure of all elements of a claimed invention *arranged as in the claim*."[48]

With respect to anticipation by inherency, "[i]t is well settled that a prior art reference may anticipate when the claim limitations not expressly found in that reference are nonetheless inherent in it. . . . Under the principles of inherency, if the prior art necessarily functions in accordance with, or includes,

---

[47] *Id.* at 1372, 76 USPQ2d 1225. The PTO Utility Guidelines are found in the MANUAL OF PATENT EXAMINING PROCEDURE (MPEP) at §2107, *available at* http://www.uspto.gov/web/offices/pac/mpep/mpep.htm.

[48] Finisar Corp v. DirecTV Group, Inc., 523 F.3d 1323, 1334–35, 86 USPQ2d 1609 (Fed. Cir.) (citations omitted), *cert. denied*, 555 U.S. 1070 (2008); Billups-Rothenberg, Inc. v. Associated Reg'l & Univ. Pathologists, Inc., 642 F.3d 1031, 1038–39, 98 USPQ2d 1578 (Fed. Cir. 2011) (reference can be anticipatory even if it disparages the later-claimed invention); Net MoneyIN, Inc. v. Verisign, Inc., 545 F.3d 1359, 1369–71, 88 USPQ2d 1751 (Fed. Cir. 2008) (elaborating on "arranged as in the claim"); *see also* Structural Rubber Prods. v. Park Rubber Co., 749 F.2d 707, 714–16, 223 USPQ 1264 (Fed. Cir. 1984).

the claimed limitations, it anticipates."[49] If, however, the claimed features will sometimes occur and sometimes not, there is no inherency.[50] A prior art reference can inherently anticipate even if a person of ordinary skill in the art would not have appreciated the inherent property at the time.[51]

In order to be anticipating, a prior art reference must be enabling so that the claimed subject matter may be made (in the case of a composition of matter, a machine or manufacture) or used (in the case of a process) by one skilled in the art.[52] Enablement in this context means that the reference would have allowed one of ordinary skill to make the invention without undue experimentation. There is a rebuttable presumption that a prior issued patent contains an enabling disclosure.[53]

A single piece of prior art may also incorporate other material by reference. The mere reference to another application, patent or publication is not sufficient to incorporate everything found therein. Rather, the host document must identify "with detailed particularity," from the point of view of a person with ordinary skill in the art, what material is incorporated and clearly indicate where that material is found.[54] The court must determine what material in addition to the host document constitutes the "single reference" needed to serve as the basis for an

---

[49] *In re* Cruciferous Sprout Litig., 301 F.3d 1343, 1349–50, 64 USPQ2d 1202 (Fed. Cir. 2002), *cert. denied sub nom.* Brassica Prot. Prods. LLC v. Sunrise Farms, 538 U.S. 907 (2003) (internal quotations and citations omitted); King Pharms., Inc. v. Eon Labs, 616 F.3d 1267, 1274–76, 95 USPQ2d 1833 (Fed. Cir. 2010).

[50] MEHL/Biophile Int'l Corp. v. Milgraum, 192 F.3d 1362, 1365, 52 USPQ2d 1303 (Fed. Cir. 1999); *In re* Oelrich, 666 F.2d 578, 581–82, 212 USPQ 323 (C.C.P.A. 1981).

[51] *See, e.g., In re* Omeprazole Patent Litig., 483 F.3d 1364, 1374 (Fed. Cir. 2007); Abbott Labs. v. Baxter Pharm. Prods., Inc., 471 F.3d 1363, 1367–68, 80 USPQ2d 1860 (Fed. Cir. 2006).

[52] *In re* Gleave, 560 F.3d 1331, 1335–36, 90 USPQ2d 1235 (Fed. Cir. 2009). Enablement for purposes of showing anticipation has a different meaning from enablement for satisfying the disclosure requirements of 35 U.S.C. §112 ¶1, which are discussed in Section II.C.2. of this chapter. *See id.;* Rasmusson v. SmithKline Beecham Corp., 413 F.3d 1318, 1325–26, 75 USPQ2d 1297 (Fed. Cir. 2005).

[53] Impax Labs., Inc. v. Aventis Pharms., Inc., 545 F.3d 1312, 1314–16, 88 USPQ2d 1381 (Fed. Cir. 2009).

[54] Advanced Display Sys. v. Kent State Univ., 212 F.3d 1272, 1282–84, 54 USPQ2d 1673 (Fed. Cir. 2000), *cert. denied,* 532 U.S. 904 (2001); Calloway Golf Co. v. Acushnet Co., 576 F. 3d 1331, 1345–46, 91 USPQ2d 1705 (Fed. Cir. 2009), *cert. denied,* 130 S. Ct. 1525 (2010).

alleged anticipation.[55] Anticipation is a question of fact, including whether material is inherently disclosed in the prior art.[56] The extent to which material is incorporated by reference in a prior art reference is a question of law.[57]

Not everything that is "prior" to a patent at issue is prior art. Under the laws of most other countries, priority is measured for all purposes by reference to the filing date of the application for the patent in suit. U.S. patent law uses two dates. With respect to the "novelty" requirements of 35 U.S.C. §102(a), (e) and (g), the statutory touchstone is the date of "invention" by the patent applicant. The time bars of §102(b) and (d) are measured by reference to the date on which the patent application was filed, as discussed in Sections II.B.1 and 3 of this chapter.

The Leahy-Smith America Invents Act redefines the categories of prior art for patents granted on applications that will be filed after March 16, 2013. The prior art/novelty issue will turn on the "effective filing date" of the application for patent, not the date on which the claimed subject matter was invented. This is discussed, *infra*, in §III of this chapter.

In an addendum at the end of this chapter, the current version of 35 U.S.C. §102 is set out in full text. The text as amended by the America Invents Act is also set forth, for comparison.

In the discussion that follows, all references are to the pre-Act version of the patent statute, unless otherwise indicated, i.e., the version of the statute that is in effect as this book goes to press.

1. Section 102(a)

According to 35 U.S.C. §102(a), "[a] person shall be entitled to a patent unless the invention was known or used by others in this country, or patented or described in a printed publication in this or a foreign country, before the invention thereof

---

[55] Commonwealth Scientific & Indus. Research Org. v. Buffalo Tech., Inc., 542 F.3d 1363, 1371–72, 88 USPQ2d 1564 (Fed. Cir. 2008).

[56] Atlas Powder Co. v. Ireco, Inc., 190 F.3d 1342, 1346–48, 51 USPQ2d 1943 (Fed. Cir. 1999); Minnesota Mining & Mfg. Co. v. Johnson & Johnson Orthopaedics, 976 F.2d 1559, 1565, 24 USPQ2d 1321 (Fed. Cir. 1992).

[57] *Advanced Display Sys.*, 212 F.3d at 1282–84, 54 USPQ2d 1673.

by the applicant for patent." Based on this, prior knowledge, use, patents, and publications can be relevant prior art.

"**[T]he invention was known . . . by others in this country . . . before the invention thereof by the applicant for patent.**" "Known" has been interpreted to mean knowledge that was accessible to the public.[58] Such knowledge must have been sufficient to enable one with ordinary skill in the art to reduce the invention to practice.[59] Private or secret knowledge is not within the scope of Section 102(a) prior art and therefore cannot anticipate a patent claim.[60]

"**[T]he invention was . . . used by others in this country . . . before the invention thereof by the applicant for patent.**" "Used" has been interpreted to be publicly accessible use,[61] which means use in the absence of affirmative steps to conceal.[62] The non-secret use of a claimed process in the usual course of producing articles for commercial purposes is a public use.[63]

The publicly accessible use must have been of the invention reduced to practice.[64] The invention need not have been commercially perfected, but it must have been beyond the experimental stage.[65] It is irrelevant that the publicly accessible use may not have enabled one to make and practice the claimed

---

[58] Minnesota Mining & Mfg. Co. v. Chemque, Inc., 303 F.3d 1294, 1301, 1306, 64 USPQ2d 1270 (Fed. Cir. 2002), *cert. dismissed*, 538 U.S. 972 (2003); Woodland Trust v. Flowertree Nursery Inc., 148 F.3d 1368, 1370, 47 USPQ2d 1363 (Fed. Cir. 1998). An oral presentation may be the basis for knowledge. Ecolochem Inc. v. Southern Cal. Edison Co., 227 F.3d 1361, 1369–70, 56 USPQ2d 1065 (Fed. Cir. 2000), *cert. denied*, 532 U.S. 974 (2001).

[59] *Minnesota Mining & Mfg. Co.*, 303 F.3d at 1301, 1306, 64 USPQ2d 1270.

[60] Connecticut Valley Enters. v. United States, 348 F.2d 949, 146 USPQ 404 (Ct. Cl. 1965). For example, knowledge presented under government security classification is not typically within Section 102(a). Del Mar Eng'g Labs. v. United States, 524 F.2d 1178, 186 USPQ 42, 187 USPQ 656 (Ct. Cl. 1975).

[61] *Minnesota Mining & Mfg. Co.*, 303 F.3d at 1301, 1306–07, 64 USPQ2d 1270; *Woodland Trust*, 148 F.3d at 1370, 47 USPQ2d 1363.

[62] MPEP at §2132.01, *available at* http://www.uspto.gov/web/offices/pac/mpep/mpep. htm. For example, a machine operated in an open field is a publicly accessible use even if no one sees the machine. Rosaire v. Baroid Sales Div., Nat'l Lead Co., 218 F.2d 72, 74–75, 104 USPQ 100 (5th Cir.), *cert. denied*, 349 U.S. 916, 105 USPQ 518 (1955). In contrast, if the machine is operated in a windowless building and all who enter the building are sworn to secrecy, then the use probably is not public. *See, e.g.,* Kimball Int'l Inc. v. Allen Organ Co., 212 USPQ 584 (S.D. Ind. 1981).

[63] W. L. Gore & Assocs., Inc. v. Garlock, Inc., 721 F.2d 1540, 1548–49, 220 USPQ 303 (Fed. Cir. 1983), *cert. denied*, 469 U.S. 851 (1984).

[64] *See, e.g., Kimball Int'l Inc.*, 212 USPQ at 589.

[65] *Rosaire*, 218 F.2d at 73–74, 104 USPQ 100.

invention, or that the presence of the later-claimed invention was not appreciated at the time by those who used it.[66]

"[B]y others in this country." To anticipate, both prior knowledge and prior use must have been by others and in this country. "By others" is a requirement that more than just one person other than the inventor knew about or used the invention.[67] The requirement that prior knowledge and prior use must be "in this country"[68] means that a re-invention by a U.S. applicant will not be anticipated by prior public knowledge or prior public use of that invention in a foreign country.[69] However, use or knowledge in countries that are members of the World Trade Organization (WTO) or have ratified the North America Free Trade Agreement (NAFTA) may be used to prove prior invention in certain circumstances.[70]

"[T]he invention was . . . patented . . . in this or a foreign country, before the invention thereof by the applicant for patent." If a patent is published, it is like other printed publications discussed in the following section. All U.S. patents are published, but not all foreign patents are published. A published patent places all that it claims and discloses into the prior art that is relevant to deciding novelty, whereas an unpublished patent places only the material actually claimed into the prior art.[71]

For the purpose of deciding novelty, an invention is generally considered patented as of the date when the patent both is

---

[66] Lockwood v. American Airlines Inc., 107 F.3d 1565, 1570, 41 USPQ2d 1961 (Fed. Cir. 1997); *W. L. Gore & Assocs., Inc.,* 721 F.2d at 1548–49, 220 USPQ 303.

[67] MPEP §2132.01, *available at* http://www.uspto.gov/web/offices/pac/mpep/mpep.htm.

[68] Roemer v. Simon, 95 U.S. 214 (1877).

[69] An opposite result would have obtained under the Acts of 1790 and 1793. *See* Edward C. Walterscheid, *Novelty in Historical Perspective* (pts. 1–2), 75 J. Pat. & Trademark Off. Soc'y 689, 777 (1993). The reasons given for ignoring foreign knowledge or use are (1) the difficulty of proving foreign knowledge or use and (2) the belief that foreign knowledge or use are not readily accessible to those working in this country. Gayler v. Wilder, 51 U.S. (10 How.) 477, 496 (1850); Chambers & Mendham v. Duncan, Wilson, & Lauder, 9 Off. Gaz. Pat. Office 741 (Comm'r Pat. 1876).

[70] *See* 35 U.S.C. §104(1), (3); 37 CFR §1.131; *see, e.g.,* Scott v. Koyama, 281 F.3d 1243, 1246 n.2, 61 USPQ2d 1856 (Fed. Cir. 2002). Ratification of the North American Free Trade Agreement (NAFTA) and the General Agreement on Tariffs and Trade (GATT) in the mid-1990's meant that the United States could not discriminate against member-country patent applicants, which led to revisions to the patent statute and PTO regulations.

[71] 1 Irving Kayton, Patent Practice, ch. 4 (8th ed. 2006).

publicly available (not necessarily through publication) and confers legal rights. These events can occur on separate dates.[72]

"[T]he invention was . . . described in a printed publication in this or a foreign country, before the invention thereof by the applicant for patent."

"Described" means disclosed sufficiently to satisfy the tests for anticipation, as discussed in Section I.C. of this chapter.

> Because there are many ways in which a reference may be disseminated to the interested public, "public accessibility" has been called the touchstone in determining whether a reference constitutes a "printed publication". . . . "A reference is publicly accessible upon a satisfactory showing that such document has been disseminated or otherwise made available to the extent that persons interested and ordinarily skilled in the subject matter or art exercising reasonable diligence, can locate it.[73]

"Printed" has been interpreted broadly to mean all material accessible to the public in tangible form.[74] However, the internal documents of a company or a government agency, intended to be confidential, are not printed publications.[75]

The number of copies is not determinative. For example, a single book in a library is a publication if it is indexed and available to the public.[76] A single document in an electronic database that allows title searches by keyword is publicly accessible if a reasonably diligent searcher could locate it using keywords related to the invention.[77]

---

[72] *In re* Ekenstam, 256 F.2d 321, 118 USPQ 349 (C.C.P.A. 1958); *see* MPEP §901.05 and §2126, *available at* http://www.uspto.gov/web/offices/pac/mpep/mpep.htm.

[73] Kyocera Wireless Corp. v. U.S. Int'l Trade Comm'n, 545 F.3d 1340, 1350–51, 89 USPQ2d 1057 (Fed. Cir. 2008) (internal quotation and citations omitted); *In re* Lister, 583 F.3d 1307, 1311, 92 USPQ2d 1225 (Fed. Cir. 2009); SRI Int'l v. Internet Sec. Sys., Inc., 511 F.3d 1186, 1194–98, 85 USPQ2d 1489 (Fed. Cir. 2008).

[74] *See generally*, MPEP §2128, *available at* http://www.uspto.gov/web/offices/pac/mpep/mpep.htm. If a limited group of recipients of printed matter are asked to keep it secret, the material is not a publication. *But see* Cooper Cameron Corp. v. Kvaerner Oilfield Prods., 291 F.3d 1317, 1324, 62 USPQ2d 1846 (Fed. Cir. 2002) (focusing on whether only certain parts of a document were confidential).

[75] Northern Telecom, Inc. v. Datapoint Corp., 908 F.2d 931, 936–37, 15 USPQ2d 1321 (Fed. Cir.), *cert. denied*, 498 U.S. 920 (1990); MPEP §2128.01 (III).

[76] *In re* Hall, 781 F.2d 897, 900, 228 USPQ 453 (Fed. Cir. 1986).

[77] *In re* Lister, 583 F.3d at 1315, 92 USPQ2d 1225.

The date of a publication is the date when the reference was first available to the public.[78] Accordingly, although many scientific papers published in journals give the date the manuscript was received by the journal editor, the date the journal was published is the date the content was available to the public.

"[I]n this or a foreign country." Prior patents and prior publications from foreign countries can anticipate a later invention because these pieces of prior art are believed to be readily accessible to those working in this country and, as such, are part of the pool of knowledge available to a would-be inventor.[79]

"[B]efore the invention thereof by the applicant for patent." For knowledge, use, a patent, or a publication to be part of the prior art relevant to determining novelty, they must have predated the applicant's invention.[80] The applicant's date of invention is initially considered to be the filing date of the application, but can be carried back to the date of actual invention.

During patent prosecution, for example, if an applicant conceived an invention on February 1, 2005, after diligent effort reduced the invention to practice on March 1, 2005, and filed the application on March 1, 2006, the PTO will deem the date of invention to be March 1, 2006. The PTO examiner will search for Section 102(a) material prior to that date. If the examiner finds a publication by someone else on March 2, 2005, the inventor can submit an affidavit or declaration to prove the earlier, actual date of invention and remove the March 2, 2005, publication from the relevant prior art.[81] To do this during infringement litigation, the inventor must present evidence of an earlier date of invention,[82] which is weighed against the challenger's burden of persuasion.[83]

---

[78] *In re Bayer,* 568 F.2d 1357, 568 F.2d 1357 1361, 196 USPQ 670; *see, e.g.,* Mazzari v. Rogan, 323 F.3d 1000, 1003, 1005, 66 USPQ2d 1049 (Fed. Cir. 2003).

[79] *See, e.g., Mazzari,* 323 F.3d at 1005–06, 66 USPQ2d 1049.

[80] *See, e.g.,* Mahurkar v. C. R. Bard, Inc., 79 F.3d 1572, 1576, 38 USPQ2d 1288 (Fed. Cir. 1996).

[81] 37 C.F.R. § 131.

[82] *See* Loral Fairchild Corp. v. Matsushita Elec. Indus. Co., 266 F.3d 1358, 1363–66, 60 USPQ2d 1361 (Fed. Cir. 2001) (addressing whether the evidentiary standard for antedating a reference is the same as that for resolving priority disputes).

[83] *Mahurkar,* 79 F.3d at 1576–79, 38 USPQ2d 1288 (challenger must prove by clear and convincing evidence that the alleged prior art is actually prior to the invention date).

2. Section 102(e)

As discussed in the preceding section, the fundamental rule of novelty under the U.S. patent laws has long been that, to obtain a patent, the applicant must have been the first inventor of the subject matter claimed as an invention.[84] 35 U.S.C. §102(e) applies this principle to a prior inventor who applied for a patent before the invention date of the patent whose validity is at issue. Because patent applications are kept confidential until granted by the PTO or published by the PTO pursuant to 35 U.S.C. §122, the existence of the invalidating prior patent may not be known, conceivably until after the patent being challenged has issued. Under 35 U.S.C. §102(e), a patent claim is invalid if:

> the invention was described in (1) an application for patent, published under section 122(b), by another filed in the United States before the invention by the applicant for patent or (2) a patent granted on an application for patent by another filed in the United States before the invention by the applicant for patent . . . .

Both subsections require that, to be invalidating, the application must have been by "another." Where either the alleged prior art or the patent at issue names joint inventors, "another" means any difference in the named inventors, even if the groups are overlapping.[85] "What is significant is not merely the differences in the listed inventors, but whether the portions of the reference relied on as prior art, and the subject matter of the claims in question, represent the work of a common inventive entity."[86]

The date on which the alleged prior art was "filed" is its earliest "effective date," i.e., the date of the earliest application that sufficiently describes the subject matter at issue. Both provisional

---

[84] Alexander Milburn Co. v. Davis-Bournonville Co., 270 U.S. 390 (1926).

[85] *In re* Land, 368 F.2d 866, 875–81 (C.C.P.A. 1966).

[86] Riverwood Int'l Corp. v. R. A. Jones & Co., 324 F.3d 1346, 1355–57, 66 USPQ2d 1331 (Fed. Cir. 2003); Applied Materials, Inc. v. Gemini Research Corp., 835 F.2d 279, 281, 15 USPQ2d 1816 (Fed. Cir. 1987), *modified on reh'g* (1988) (disqualifying an alleged prior art reference by showing that the earlier work was done by the same "inventive entity"). The invention date at issue needs to be prior only to as much of the claimed invention is disclosed in the alleged prior art. *In re* Stempel, 241 F.2d 755, 759, 113 USPQ 77 (C.C.P.A. 1957).

and non provisional patent applications can be prior art under Section 102(e).[87]

3. Section 102(g)

As seen in the context of foreign knowledge or use under Section 102(a), the "novelty" condition of patentability is not absolute. A further example of this is found in 35 U.S.C. §102(g)(2), which provides, in part, that an applicant is not entitled to a patent if "the invention was made in this country by another inventor who had not abandoned, suppressed, or concealed it."[88] Thus, for purposes of §102(g), alleged prior invention in another country without more will not defeat novelty. If, however, the foreign prior invention was patented or disclosed in a printed publication, then novelty may be lost under §102(a).

Under §102(g)(2), a second person's invention may be deemed new if the first inventor abandoned, suppressed, or concealed his or her work.[89]

Abandonment, suppression, or concealment may be shown by affirmative acts of the first inventor,[90] or inferred from the first inventor's unreasonable delay in making the invention known to

[87] *In re* Giacomini, 612 F.3d 1380, 1383–84, 95 USPQ2d 1698 (Fed. Cir. 2010); *see also* MPEP §2136, *available at* http://www.uspto.gov/web/offices/pac/mpep/mpep.htm.

[88] Almost all countries resolve first inventor disputes in favor of the first to file an application, while the United States resolves in favor of the first to invent. 3 JOHN GLADSTONE MILLS III ET AL., PATENT LAW FUNDAMENTALS §16:1 (2d ed. 1986, rev. 2011); *see, e.g.,* Rosco, Inc. v. Mirror Lite Co., 304 F.3d 1373, 1381, 64 USPQ2d 1676 (Fed. Cir. 2002). However, as discussed above in the context of Section 102(a) prior art, passage of the America Invents Act currently before Congress would change the United States to a first-to-file system, eliminating the "first-to-invent" defense. However, an amended 35 U.S.C. §291 will authorize a civil action to determine whether the owner of a patent with an earlier filing date was "derived from the inventor" of a later-filed patent. In the alternative, the issue of derivation may be addressed in "derivation proceedings" in the PTO. *See* H.R. 1249, sec. 3(h), as passed by the House on June 23, 2011.

[89] *See generally* Paulik v. Rizkalla, 760 F.2d 1270, 226 USPQ 224 (Fed. Cir. 1985). Section 102(g) codified pre-1952 case law concerning the priority in favor of the first inventor. *Id.* The rationale for 102(g) is that, by abandoning, suppressing, or concealing an invention, a first inventor acts inconsistently with the goal of promoting progress of useful arts by prompt disclosure of inventions. *Id.*

[90] Aventis Pharma Deutschland GmbH v. Lupin, Ltd., 499 F.3d 1293, 1300 (Fed. Cir. 2007); Dow Chem. Co. v. Astro-Valcour, Inc., 267 F.3d 1334, 1342, 60 USPQ2d 1519 (Fed. Cir. 2001), *cert. denied,* 535 U.S. 989 (2002).

the public.[91] The first inventor needs to have recognized that the invention existed, but does not need to have been the first to appreciate the invention's patentability.[92] The question of abandonment, suppression, or concealment is fact specific.[93]

With one exception, the first person to "reduce the invention to practice" is deemed the first inventor.[94] The second person to reduce the invention to practice will be the first inventor if he or she was (1) the first to conceive the invention and (2) reasonably diligent in reducing the invention to practice from a time prior to the other inventor's conception of the invention.[95]

"Conception is the formation in the mind of the inventor of a definite and permanent idea of the complete and operative invention, as it is therefore to be applied in practice."[96] Conception requires that the inventor must have appreciated what was invented.[97] However, an inventor need not know that his invention will work for conception to be complete.[98]

"To show actual reduction to practice, an inventor must demonstrate that the invention is suitable for its intended purpose. . . . Depending on the character of the invention and the problem it solves, this showing may require test results . . . . Less complicated inventions and problems do not demand stringent testing."[99]

Priority of invention often is determined in an interference proceeding in the PTO.[100] In litigation, a party may seek to

---

[91] Eolas Techs. Inc. v. Microsoft Corp., 399 F.3d 1325, 1333, 73 USPQ2d 1782. The Federal Circuit has declined to create a presumption of abandonment, suppression, or concealment based on delay of a fixed length of time. *Dow Chem. Co.*, 267 F.3d at 1342–43, 60 USPQ2d 1519.

[92] Invitrogen Corp. v. Clontech Labs., Inc., 429 F.3d 1052, 1064, 77 USPQ2d 1161 (Fed. Cir. 2005); *Dow Chem. Co.*, 267 F.3d at 1341, 60 USPQ2d 1519.

[93] *Dow Chem. Co.*, 267 F.3d at 1342, 60 USPQ2d 1519.

[94] Eaton v. Evans, 204 F.3d 1094, 1097, 53 USPQ2d 1696 (Fed. Cir. 2000).

[95] *Eaton*, 204 F.3d at 1097, 53 USPQ2d 1696; Cooper v. Goldfarb, 154 F.3d 1321, 1327, 47 USPQ2d 1896 (Fed. Cir. 1998); *Dow Chem. Co.*, 267 F.3d at 1341, 60 USPQ2d 1519.

[96] Creative Compounds, LLC v. Starmark Labs., 651 F.3d 1303, 1312, 99 USPQ2d 1168 (Fed. Cir. 2011) (internal quotation omitted).

[97] *Dow Chem. Co.*, 267 F.3d at 1341, 60 USPQ2d 1519.

[98] Burroughs Wellcome Co. v. Barr Labs., Inc., 40 F.3d 1223, 1228–30, 32 USPQ2d 1915 (Fed. Cir. 1994), *cert. denied*, 516 U.S. 1070 (1996).

[99] *Mahurkar*, 79 F.3d at 1578, 38 USPQ2d 1288.

[100] For a detailed discussion of conception and reduction to practice, as well as abandonment, suppression and concealment, *see generally* MPEP §2138, *available at* http://www.uspto.gov/web/offices/pac/mpep/mpep.htm. See Chapter 2, §III.D.10 for further discussion of interference proceedings.

prove that an issued patent is invalid under Section 102(g).[101] To prevail, the patent challenger must present clear and convincing evidence (a) that the patented invention was made in the United States by a prior inventor[102] and (b) rebutting any evidence that creates a genuine issue of material fact that the prior inventor abandoned, suppressed, or concealed the invention.[103] The prior inventor must invent *in this country*, thus conception by a foreign party and reduction to practice in the United States by another will not satisfy Section 102(g).[104]

In both interferences and infringement lawsuits, an alleged prior inventor's oral testimony requires corroboration.[105] The sufficiency of the corroboration is based on the totality of the circumstances, including the interest of a corroborating witness in the outcome of the proceeding.[106] Even if the alleged prior inventor is not interested in the outcome of the proceeding, the corroboration rule applies.[107] Oral testimony by an interested party requires documentary corroboration.[108] The standard of proof required to corroborate a reduction to practice is more

---

[101] *See, e.g.*, Union Carbide Chems. & Plastics Tech. Corp. v. Shell Oil Corp., 308 F.3d 1167, 1189–90, 64 USPQ2d 1545 (Fed. Cir. 2002); *Dow Chem. Co.*, 267 F.3d 1334, 60 USPQ2d 1519.

[102] *Dow Chem. Co.*, 267 F.3d at 1339, 60 USPQ2d 1519.

[103] Apotex USA, Inc. v. v. Merck & Co., 254 F.3d 1031, 1037–38, 59 USPQ2d 1139 (Fed. Cir. 2001). Rebuttal evidence is not limited to activities that occurred in the United States. *Id.* at 1036. The first inventor's failure to file a patent application is not, by itself, evidence sufficient to create a genuine issue of material fact of abandonment, suppression, or concealment. *Id.* at 1039.

[104] Solvay S.A. v. Honeywell Int'l, Inc., 622 F.3d 1367, 1376–77, 96 USPQ2d 1870 (Fed. Cir. 2010).

[105] Adenta GmbH v. OrthoArm, Inc., 501 F.3d 1364, 1371–72, 84 USPQ2d 1428 (Fed. Cir. 2007); Slip Track Sys., Inc. v. Metal Lite, Inc., 304 F.3d 1256, 1263, 64 USPQ2d 1423 (Fed. Cir. 2002); Finnigan Corp. v. United States Int'l Trade Comm'n, 180 F.3d 1354, 1366–69, 51 USPQ2d 1001 (Fed. Cir. 1999). While the corroboration rule usually arises in the context of priority disputes under §102(g), the rule is not limited to those situations. *Finnigan Corp.*, 180 F.3d at 1367–68, 51 USPQ2d 1001; *see, e.g.*, Lacks Indus. v. McKechnie Vehicle Components USA, 322 F.3d 1335, 1349–51, 66 USPQ2d 1083 (Fed. Cir. 2003) (corroboration in 102(b) context); *see also Union Carbide Chems. & Plastics Tech. Corp.*, 308 F.3d at 1189, 64 USPQ2d 1545.

[106] Adenta GmbH v. OrthoArm, Inc., 501 F.3d 1364, 84 USPQ2d 1428 (Fed. Cir. 2007); *Finnigan Corp.*, 180 F.3d at 1368–69, 51 USPQ2d 1001; *see, e.g.*, *Lacks Indus.*, 322 F.3d at 1350–51, 66 USPQ2d 1083. For a list of potentially useful factors to determine the corroborative sufficiency of a witness's testimony, see Juicy Whip, Inc. v. Orange Bang, Inc., 292 F.3d 728, 741, 63 USPQ2d 1251 (Fed. Cir.), *cert. denied*, 537 U.S. 1019 (2002).

[107] *Finnigan Corp.*, 180 F.3d at 1367–69, 51 USPQ2d 1001.

[108] *Lacks Indus.*, 322 F.3d at 1350, 66 USPQ2d 1083. Corroboration is not required if physical evidence is used to prove invention. *Slip Track Sys., Inc.*, 304 F.3d at 1263, 64 USPQ2d 1423. Documentary or physical evidence that was not made contemporaneously with the alleged prior invention, however, may be no more reliable than oral testimony. *See, e.g., Juicy Whip, Inc.*, 292 F.3d at 743, 63 USPQ2d 1251.

stringent than the standard of proof required to corroborate a conception.[109]

D. Nonobvious

A new and useful product or process is not patentable if it would have been "obvious" to persons skilled in the art when the invention was made. The requirement of "non-obvious subject matter," 35 U.S.C. §103, was added to the patent statute in 1952 to codify the judicially created requirement of "invention."[110]

Section 103(a) states, in pertinent part:

> A patent may not be obtained . . . if the differences between the subject matter sought to be patented and the prior art are such that the subject matter as a whole would have been obvious at the time the invention was made to a person having ordinary skill in the art to which said subject matter pertains. Patentability shall not be negatived by the manner in which the invention was made.[111]

The requirement of "invention" arose from the Supreme Court's 1851 opinion in *Hotchkiss v. Greenwood*.[112] The patent in *Hotchkiss* covered an improved doorknob design, using ceramic knobs instead of the wood and metal knobs known in the art. The Court ruled the patent invalid because the improvement lacked the skill and ingenuity that characterizes a patentable invention. According to the Court, this was the work of a skillful mechanic, not an inventor. Subsequent cases applied lack of invention as grounds for invalidity until Congress enacted Section 103.[113]

---

[109] Singh v. Brake, 222 F.3d 1362, 1369–70, 55 USPQ2d 1673 (Fed. Cir. 2000).

[110] Graham v. John Deere Co., 383 U.S. 1, 10–17, 148 USPQ 459 (1966). Congress amended §103 in 1984 (adding what is now subsection (c)) and 1995 (adding what is now subsection (b)).

[111] The Leahy-Smith America Invents Act changes "at the time of the invention" to "before the effective filing date of the claimed invention." *See* Pub.L. 112-29, H.R. 1229 (2011), sec. 3(c). This will conform section 103 to the new definition of prior art in section 102 when that definition takes effect in 2013. See §III of this chapter.

[112] 52 U.S. (11 How.) 248 (1851).

[113] For a review of the "invention" requirement, and the drafting of § 103, and judicial response to that statute in the initial decades after its enactment, *see* George M. Sirilla, *35 U.S.C. §103: From Hotchkiss to Hand to Rich, The Obvious Patent Law Hall-of-Famers*, 32 J. MARSHALL L. REV. 437 (1999).

1. The Statutory Framework

Section 103(a) focuses on "subject matter sought to be patented" and whether "the subject matter as a whole" would have been obvious in view of the pertinent prior art. Because "the subject matter sought to be patented" is defined by the claims of the invention, the test focuses on the nonobviousness of the entire claim, rather than on any one claim element.[114] In litigation, the words of the claim must be construed by the court before evaluating nonobviousness.[115]

Unlike the provisions of Section 102, which focus on the activities of real people—e.g., "the applicant for patent" and "others" in Section 102(a)—nonobviousness is assessed from the viewpoint of a "person having ordinary skill in the art." This is a hypothetical person, who is presumed to know all of the prior art, but whose thinking about the art reflects the conventional wisdom of those in the art at the time the invention was made.[116]

Obviousness is assessed "at the time the invention was made." This means that using hindsight must be avoided.[117] Although it is difficult, the decision maker must (1) step back in time to the moment just before the invention was made and (2) consider the issue from the viewpoint of a hypothetical person who does not know the invention.[118] Then, in light of all the

---

[114]Panduit Corp. v. Dennison Mfg. Co., 810 F.2d 1561, 1576, 1 USPQ2d 1593 (Fed. Cir.), cert. denied, 481 U.S. 1052 (1987).

[115]See Chapter 5 for further discussion of claim construction.

[116]KSR Int'l v. Teleflex, Inc., 550 U.S. 398, 420, 82 USPQ2d 1385 (2007). An inventor is presumed to have greater than ordinary skill in the art. Standard Oil Co. v. American Cyanamid Co., 774 F.2d 448, 454, 227 USPQ 293 (Fed. Cir. 1985); Amgen Inc. v. F. Hoffmann-La Roche, Ltd., 580 F.3d 1340, 1363, 92 USPQ2d 1289 (Fed. Cir. 2009).

[117]See, e.g., Ortho-McNeil Pharm., Inc. v. Mylan Labs., Inc., 520 F.3d 1358, 1364–65, 86 USPQ2d 1196 (Fed. Cir. 2008); W. L. Gore & Assocs., Inc., 721 F.2d at 1551, 220 USPQ 303. By its nature, hindsight devalues two things: the discovery and the path to the discovery. Before the problem is solved, the would-be inventor who undertakes the task of finding a solution to a technological problem does not know how to succeed. Once the problem is solved and the solution is disclosed, however, all know that the problem can be solved and one way to solve it. See generally Tom Arnold, Future Considerations—Views of a Private Practitioner, in NONOBVIOUSNESS—THE ULTIMATE CONDITION OF PATENTABILITY 8:1, 3–5 (John F. Witherspoon ed., 1980).

[118]W. L. Gore & Assocs., Inc., 721 F.2d at 1553, 220 USPQ 303; see e.g., Ecolochem Inc. v. Southern Cal. Edison Co., 227 F.3d 1361, 1371, 56 USPQ2d 1065 (Fed. Cir. 2000), cert. denied, 532 U.S. 974 (2001); Tokai Corp. v. Easton Enterprises Inc., 632 F.3d 1358, 1378, 97 USPQ2d 1673 (Fed. Cir. 2011).

relevant facts, the decision maker must determine, as a matter of law, whether the differences between the claimed invention and the prior art are such that the claimed invention as a whole would have been obvious at *that* time to *that* hypothetical person.[119]

The last sentence of Section 103(a) provides that "[p]atentability shall not be negatived by the manner in which the invention was made." Thus, a nonobvious invention can arise from systematic experimentation as well as from a "flash of creative genius."[120]

2. The Relevant Factual Determinations

The ultimate decision regarding nonobviousness is a question of law, but that decision is based on the totality of the evidence, which includes specific factual determinations.[121] To hold an issued patent invalid for obviousness, there must be clear and convincing evidence supporting that conclusion.[122]

The Supreme Court's 1966 decision in *Graham v. John Deere Co.* requires determining as issues of fact (1) the scope and content of the prior art, (2) the differences between the prior art and the claims at issue, and (3) the level of ordinary skill in the pertinent art.[123] The decision maker may also determine (4) which, if any, "secondary considerations" provide objective evidence about whether the claimed invention was obvious when made, outside of the context of the contentions in litigation.[124] The Supreme Court reaffirmed this factual framework in its 2007 decision in *KSR International Co. v. Teleflex, Inc.*[125]

---

[119] *Panduit Corp.*, 810 F.2d at 1566–68, 1 USPQ2d 1593.

[120] Graham v. John Deere Co., 383 U.S. 1, 15, 148 USPQ 459 (1966).

[121] *Id.* at 17, 148 USPQ 459.

[122] *See, e.g.*, PharmaStem Therapeutics Inc. v. ViaCell Inc., 491 F.3d 1342, 1360, 83 USPQ2d 1289 (Fed. Cir. 2007), *cert. denied,* 552 U.S. 1258 (2008); Polaroid Corp. v. Eastman Kodak Co., 789 F.2d 1556, 1558, 229 USPQ 561 (Fed. Cir.), *cert. denied,* 479 U.S. 850 (1986). During prosecution, if the examiner initially presents sufficient evidence for a prima facie showing of obviousness, the burden shifts to the applicant to counter by, for example, producing evidence of secondary considerations; then the ultimate decision is made from the entire record using a preponderance standard. *In re* Oetiker, 977 F.2d 1443, 1446, 24 USPQ2d 1443 (Fed. Cir. 1992).

[123] 383 U.S. 1, 17–18, 148 USPQ 459 (1966).

[124] *See Graham*, 383 U.S. at 17, 148 USPQ 459.

[125] 550 U.S. 398, 406, 82 USPQ2d 1385 (2007).

Having made these factual determinations, obviousness or non-obviousness is determined as a matter of law. The Federal Circuit developed a body of law to prevent the use of hindsight, which asks whether the prior art would have taught or suggested the claimed invention or whether it would have motivated the person of ordinary skill to make that invention. In *KSR*, the Supreme Court referred to this as "a useful insight" and added other factual pointers, such as commercial motivation and a reasonable expectation of success that may shed light on the ultimate determination.[126] These are discussed in §I.D.2.e. of this chapter[127]

a. *A Determination of the Scope and Content of the Prior Art*

The prior art relevant to nonobviousness includes art that is the same as the invention's art and those arts that logically relate to the inventor's concern.[128] For example, if one wishes to stack cheese slices so that they are easily separated, then the pertinent arts would include the cheese arts, the sliced food manufacturing and packing industry art, and any art concerned with stacking flexible materials.[129] Case law has developed

---

[126] *KSR Int'l*, 550 U.S. at 417–421, 82 USPQ2d 1385; Star Scientific, Inc. v. R. J. Reynolds Tobacco Co., No. 2010-1183, slip op. at 16–18, 99 USPQ2d 1924 (Fed. Cir. August 26, 2011); Ortho-McNeil Pharm., Inc. v. Mylan Labs., Inc., 520 F.3d 1358, 1364–65, 86 USPQ2d 1196 (Fed. Cir. 2008).

[127] The PTO has published guidelines for patent examiners, synthesizing the PTO's understanding of the law of obviousness as it has evolved since *KSR* in 2007. The most recent revision was in September 2010. *See* MPEP §2141, *available at* http://www.uspto.gov/web/offices/pac/mpep/mpep.htm.

[128] *KSR*, 550 U.S. at 420–21, 82 USPQ2d 1385; *In re* Klein, 647 F.3d 1343, 1348, 98 USPQ2d 1991 (Fed. Cir. 2011); Innovention Toys, LLC v. MGA Entertainment, Inc., 637 F.3d 1314, 1321–22, 98 USPQ2d 1013 (Fed. Cir. 2011). *In re* Clay, 966 F.2d 656, 658–60, 23 USPQ2d 1058 (Fed. Cir. 1992); *see also* Ruiz v. A. B. Chance Co., 234 F.3d 654, 664, 57 USPQ2d 1161 (Fed. Cir. 2000) ("The scope of the prior art includes art that is 'reasonably pertinent to the particular problem with which the invention was involved' "). While the scope and content of the prior art may be ascertained by examining the particular problem the inventor was trying to solve, it is improper to define the problem in terms of the solution. Monarch Knitting Mach. v. Sulzer Morat GmbH, 139 F.3d 877, 881–83, 45 USPQ2d 1977 (Fed. Cir. 1998).

[129] L.D. Schreiber Cheese Co. v. Clearfield Cheese Co., 540 F. Supp. 1128, 214 USPQ 285 (W.D. Pa. 1982), *aff'd without op.*, 716 F.2d 891 (3d Cir. 1983).

within particular technical fields that may further help to identify the relevant art.[130]

Considerable debate has surrounded the prior art relevant to nonobviousness.[131] However, it is now accepted that that prior art includes material established by the novelty subsections of 35 U.S.C. §102 (i.e., (a), (e), and (g)), namely:

1. printed publications or patents from anywhere in the world that were published or issued before the applicant's date of invention;
2. prior use or prior knowledge that occurred in the United States before the applicant's date of invention;
3. a U.S. patent application by a different inventive entity that subsequently issued and was filed before the applicant's date of invention; and
4. another's invention that was made in the United States and that was not abandoned, suppressed, or concealed before the invention date of the invention in question.

Material defined by 35 U.S.C. §102(b) (discussed in this chapter, §II.B.1) also is considered prior art relevant to the issue of nonobviousness.[132] For example, a printed publication from anywhere in the world that was published more than one year before the U.S. application date at issue can be used to show obviousness.

Since 1997, material defined by 35 U.S.C. §102(f) (discussed in this chapter, §II.B.4) is also considered prior art relevant to the issue of nonobviousness. Thus, for example, information disclosed in confidence to an inventor that inspired the invention

---

[130] See, e.g., Eisai Co. v. Dr. Reddy's Labs., Ltd., 533 F.3d 1353, 1357–58, 87 USPQ2d 1452 (Fed. Cir. 2008) (looking for structural similarity of lead compounds in chemical cases); Muni-auction, Inc. v. Thomson Corp., 532 F.3d 1318, 1326–27, 87 USPQ2d 1350 (Fed. Cir. 2008) (finding substitution of Web browsers for older computer network obvious); Leapfrog Enters. v. Fisher-Price, Inc., 485 F.3d 1157, 1160–61, 82 USPQ2d 1687 (Fed. Cir. 2007) ("Applying modern electronics to older mechanical devices has been commonplace in recent years").

[131] See, e.g., In re Bass, 474 F.2d 1276, 177 USPQ 178 (C.C.P.A. 1973) (Rich, J. and Baldwin, J.); Donald S. Chisum, Sources of Prior Art in Patent Law, 52 WASH. L. REV. 1 (1976).

[132] In re Kaslow, 707 F.2d 1366, 217 USPQ 1089 (Fed. Cir. 1983).

can be used to show obviousness.[133] Additionally, prior art may be created by admission.[134]

A reference need not work to qualify as prior art. Even a reference that discloses an inoperative device is prior art for all that it teaches.[135]

The express and implied teachings of the relevant prior art are determined from the perspective of the hypothetical person with ordinary skill at the time just before the claimed invention was made.[136] When a piece of prior art is analyzed, it must be understood in its entirety.[137] The collective prior art may contain conflicting teachings, pointing toward and teaching away from the claimed invention under consideration.[138]

Section 103(c) excludes certain categories of activities from the relevant prior art for inventors employed by the same company and for companies engaged in joint research projects. Section 103(c)(1) applies to inventions "owned by the same person or subject to an obligation of assignment to the same person." Section 103(c)(2) relates to inventions "made by or on behalf of parties to a joint research agreement that was in effect on or before the date the claimed invention was made."

---

[133] Oddz On Prods. Inc. v. Just Toys Inc., 122 F.3d 1396, 1401–04, 43 USPQ2d 1641 (Fed. Cir. 1997).

[134] Riverwood Int'l Corp. v. R. A. Jones & Co., 324 F.3d 1346, 1354–55, 66 USPQ2d 1331 (Fed. Cir. 2003). One's own work, however, cannot be prior art by virtue of admission alone. Id.

[135] See, e.g., Geo M. Martin Co. v. Alliance Machine Systems Int'l, 618 F.3d 1294, 3102–03, 96 USPQ2d 1212 (Fed. Cir. 2010); Amgen Inc. v. Hoechst Marion Roussel, Inc., 314 F.3d 1313, 1330, 1357, 65 USPQ2d 1385 (Fed. Cir. 2003).

[136] Merck & Co. v. Biocraft Labs., Inc., 874 F.2d 804, 807, 10 USPQ2d 1843 (Fed. Cir.), cert. denied, 493 U.S. 975 (1989).

[137] See, e.g., U.S. v. Adams, 383 U.S. 39, 52, 148 USPQ 479 (1966); W. L. Gore & Assocs., Inc. v. Garlock, Inc., 721 F.2d 1540, 1550–51, 220 USPQ 303 (Fed. Cir. 1983), cert. denied, 469 U.S. 851 (1984). A reference may be said to teach away when a person of ordinary skill, upon reading the reference, would be discouraged from following the path set out in the reference, or would be led in a direction divergent from the path that was taken by the inventor of the patent in suit. Ricoh Co. v. Quanta Computer Inc., 550 F.3d 1325, 1332–33, 89 USPQ2d 1577 (Fed. Cir. 2008) (finding no teach-away), cert. denied, 129 S. Ct. 2864 (2009).

[138] See, e.g., Crocs, Inc. v. U.S. Int'l Trade Comm'n, 598 F.3d 1294, 1308–10, 93 USPQ2d 1777 (Fed. Cir. 2010); Source Search Technologies, LLC v. LendingTree LLC, 588 F.3d 1063, 92 USPQ2d 1907 (Fed. Cir. 2009); In re Icon Health & Fitness, Inc., 496 F.3d 1374, 1381–82, 83 USPQ2d 1746 (Fed. Cir. 2007); In re Young, 927 F.2d 588, 591–92, 18 USPQ2d 1089 (Fed. Cir. 1991).

b. A Determination of the Differences Between the Prior Art and the Claims at Issue

In contrast to the requirement in an anticipation analysis that all elements of the claimed invention must be present in a single prior art reference (discussed in this chapter, §I.C), the nonobviousness determination does not require strict identity.[139] Obviousness can be shown where it would have been obvious to modify a single piece of prior art,[140] or to combine the teachings of multiple pieces of prior art, to arrive at the claimed invention at the time that invention was made.[141] An obviousness analysis may also include consideration of the logic, judgment and common sense of a person of ordinary skill in the art even if not expressed in a prior art reference or expert opinion.[142]

Examining the specific differences between the prior art and the claims at issue may help to determine whether the claimed invention would have been obvious to a hypothetical person with ordinary skill in the pertinent art.[143] Examining only these differences, however, can mislead the decision maker into believing that the differences are the invention.[144] The claimed invention must be considered *as a whole* when deciding nonobviousness under Section 103.[145]

---

[139] *In re* Foster, 343 F.2d 980, 145 USPQ 166 (C.C.P.A. 1965), *cert. denied*, 383 U.S. 966, 149 USPQ 906 (1966); *see, e.g.*, Beckson Marine, Inc. v. NFM, Inc., 292 F.3d 718, 726, 63 USPQ2d 1031 (Fed. Cir. 2002) (prior art "need not anticipate the invention to serve as prior art").

[140] SIBIA Neurosciences Inc. v. Cadus Pharm. Corp., 225 F.3d 1349, 1356, 55 USPQ2d 1927 (Fed. Cir. 2000); B.F. Goodrich Co. v. Aircraft Braking Sys., 72 F.3d 1577, 1582–83, 37 USPQ2d 1314 (Fed. Cir. 1996).

[141] *In re* Shaffer, 229 F.2d 476, 479, 108 USPQ 326 (C.C.P.A. 1956) ("It is too well settled for citation that references may be combined for the purpose of showing that a claim is unpatentable").

[142] *See, e.g.*, Wyers v. Master Lock Co., 616 F.3d 1231, 1238–45, 95 USPQ2d 1525 (Fed. Cir. 2010), *cert. denied*, 131 S. Ct. 1531 (2011); Perfect Web Tech., Inc. v. InfoUSA, Inc., 587 F.3d 1324,1329–30, 92 USPQ2d 1849 (Fed. Cir. 2009).

[143] *See, e.g., In re* Huang, 100 F.3d 135, 138, 40 USPQ2d 1685 (Fed. Cir. 1996).

[144] Jones v. Hardy, 727 F.2d 1524, 220 USPQ 1021 (Fed. Cir. 1984).

[145] Ruiz v. A. B. Chance Co., 357 F.3d 1270, 1275, 69 USPQ2d 1686 (Fed. Cir. 2004); Para-Ordnance Mfg. v. SGS Imps. Int'l Inc., 73 F.3d 1085, 1087, 37 USPQ2d 1237 (Fed. Cir. 1995), *cert. denied*, 519 U.S. 822 (1996).

c. A Determination of the Level of Ordinary Skill in the Pertinent Art

The decision maker is required to determine the level of ordinary skill in the pertinent art at the time the invention was made.[146] What is or would have been obvious to a jury, a judge, a layperson, or a genius matters not at all. What is relevant is what would have been obvious to Section 103's hypothetical person of ordinary skill in the art.[147]

Among the factors that may be considered when determining the level of ordinary skill in the pertinent art are: (a) the types of problems encountered in the art, (b) the prior art solutions to those problems, (c) the rapidity with which innovations are made, (d) the sophistication of the technology, (e) the educational level of the inventor, and (f) the educational level of active workers in the field.[148]

d. A Determination of Which, if Any, Secondary Considerations Merit Attention

Facts that can help focus the decision maker's attention on the circumstances surrounding the origin of the claimed invention have been collectively characterized by the Supreme Court as "secondary considerations."[149] Some regional circuits took these secondary considerations into account only in close cases, while other regional circuits required that they always be applied.[150] The Federal Circuit resolved this ambiguity, requir-

---

[146] Ruiz, 234 F.3d at 666–67, 57 USPQ2d 1161; Kloster Speedsteel AB v. Crucible Inc., 793 F.2d 1565, 230 USPQ 81, modified in part, 231 USPQ 160 (Fed. Cir. 1986), cert. denied, 479 U.S. 1034 (1987).

[147] Innovention Toys, LLC, 637 F.3d at 1321–22, 98 USPQ2d 1013; Okajima v. Bourdeau, 261 F.3d 1350, 1354–55, 59 USPQ2d 1795 (Fed. Cir. 2001), cert. denied, 534 U.S. 1128 (2002); Ryko Mfg. Co. v. Nu-Star Inc., 950 F.2d 714, 718–19, 21 USPQ2d 1053 (Fed. Cir. 1991).

[148] Envtl. Designs v. Union Oil Co. of Cal., 713 F.2d 693, 218 USPQ 865 (Fed. Cir. 1983), cert. denied, 464 U.S. 1043, 224 USPQ 520 (1984); see, e.g., Micro Motion Inc. v. Exac Corp., 741 F. Supp. 1426, 1434–35, 16 USPQ2d 1001 (N.D. Cal. 1990). In any given case, one or more factors may predominate, and not all factors may be present. Ruiz, 234 F.3d at 666–67, 57 USPQ2d 1161; In re GPAC Inc., 57 F.3d 1573, 1579, 35 USPQ2d 1116 (Fed. Cir. 1995).

[149] Graham, 383 U.S. at 17–18, 148 USPQ 459; KSR Int'l, 550 U.S. at 406–7, 82 USPQ2d 1385.

[150] See, e.g., Medical Lab. Automation v. Labcon Inc., 670 F.2d 671, 211 USPQ 1145, 213 USPQ 537 (7th Cir. 1981); Nickola v. Peterson, 580 F.2d 898, 198 USPQ 385 (6th Cir. 1978), cert. denied, 440 U.S. 961, 201 USPQ 959 (1979).

ing that secondary considerations be considered before deciding the nonobviousness issue.[151]

Secondary considerations may help the decision-maker avoid the use of hindsight. These considerations tend to focus attention on economic and motivational issues rather than technical issues and are therefore more susceptible to judicial treatment than are the highly technical facts often present in patent litigation.[152]

A court must provide reasons for discounting evidence of secondary considerations.[153] One common reason for doing so is that the secondary considerations cannot outweigh a clear showing that the prior art in fact would have taught or suggested the invention.[154] A second common reason is that the patent owner is required to show a nexus between the claimed invention and the alleged objective evidence of non-obviousness. For example, where a party contends that an invention is nonobvious because a product embodying the claimed invention enjoyed commercial success, the patent owner must also show that the commercial success related to the patented features of the product.[155]

Evidence of secondary considerations may demonstrate obviousness as well as nonobviousness. For example, in *KSR*, the Supreme Court observed:

---

[151] *See, e.g., Ortho-McNeil Pharm., Inc.,* 520 F.3d at 1365, 86 USPQ2d 1196 ("[T]his evidence is not just a cumulative or confirmatory part of the obviousness calculus but constitutes independent evidence of nonobviousness."); Ruiz v. A. B. Chance Co., 234 F.3d 654, 667, 57 USPQ2d 1161 (Fed. Cir. 2000); Richardson-Vicks Inc. v. Upjohn Co., 122 F.3d 1476, 1483, 44 USPQ2d 1181 (Fed. Cir. 1997); Stratoflex Inc. v. Aeroquip Corp., 713 F.2d 1530, 1538–39, 218 USPQ 871 (Fed. Cir. 1983).

[152] *Graham,* 383 U.S. at 36, 148 USPQ 459; *Crocs, Inc.,* 598 F.3d at 1310–11, 93 USPQ2d 1777.

[153] Pro-Mold & Tool Co. v. Great Lakes Plastics, 75 F.3d 1568, 1573, 37 USPQ2d 1626 (Fed. Cir. 1996).

[154] Anderson's-Black Rock, Inc. v. Pavement Salvage Co., 396 U.S. 57, 61, 163 USPQ 673 (1969); *see, e.g.,* Wyers v. Master Lock Co., 616 F.3d 1231, 1245–46, 95 USPQ2d 1525 (Fed. Cir. 2010); Sundance Inc., v. DeMonte Fabricating Ltd., 550 F.3d 1356, 1368, 89 USPQ2d 1535 (Fed. Cir. 2008) and cases cited therein.

[155] *See, e.g., Geo. M. Martin Co.,* 618 F.3d at 1304–06, 96 USPQ2d 1212 (finding no nexus); *Wyers,* 616 F.3d at 1245–46, 95 USPQ2d 1525; Media Technologies Licensing, LLC v. Upper Deck Co., 596 F.3d 1334, 1338–40, 93 USPQ2d 1911 (Fed. Cir.), *cert. denied,* 131 S. Ct. 305 (2010); Rolls-Royce, PLC v. United Technologies Corporation, 603 F.3d 1325, 1340, 95 USPQ2d 1097 (Fed. Cir. 2010) (finding nexus); *see also* Hybritech, Inc. v. Monoclonal Antibodies, Inc., 802 F.2d 1367, 1382–83, 231 USPQ 81 (Fed. Cir. 1986) (considering the effect of marketing on commercial success).

"When there is a design need or market pressure to solve a problem and there are a finite number of identified, predictable solutions, a person of ordinary skill has good reasons to pursue the known options within his or her technical grasp. If this leads to the anticipated success, it is likely the product not of innovation but of ordinary skill and common sense."[156]

One secondary consideration is long-felt but unsolved need.[157] For example, when air pollution control devices could remove 97 percent of sulfur dioxide emitted into the air by smokestacks, there was still a desire for even greater sulfur removal. A method found to remove 99.5 percent of the sulfur[158] appears to be a nonobvious invention because, had it been obvious to solve the long-felt need for greater sulfur removal, more than one person likely would have devised that method.[159]

Another secondary consideration is commercial success. A commercially successful product or process appears to be a nonobvious invention because, had it been obvious to create this commercial success, more than one person likely would have created it.[160] Sales figures alone may be sufficient evidence of commercial success.[161] Some additional secondary considerations are

---

[156] *KSR Int'l.*, 550 U.S. at 421, 82 USPQ2d 1385.

[157] *See, e.g.*, Procter & Gamble Co. v. Teva Pharms USA, Inc., 566 F.3d 989, 998, 90 USPQ2d 1947 (Fed. Cir. 2009). *See generally* Monarch Knitting Mach. Corp. v. Sulzer Morat GmbH, 139 F.3d 877, 883–84, 45 USPQ2d 1977 (Fed. Cir. 1998) ("The relevant secondary consideration is 'long-felt *but unsolved need*,' not long-felt need in isolation"). In contrast to long-felt need is a "shortly-felt requirement." Ecolochem Inc. v. Southern Cal. Edison Co., 227 F.3d 1361, 1376–77, 56 USPQ2d 1065 (Fed. Cir. 2000), *cert. denied*, 532 U.S. 974 (2001).

[158] Envtl. Designs v. Union Oil Co. of Cal., 713 F.2d 693, 218 USPQ 865 (Fed. Cir. 1983), *cert. denied*, 464 U.S. 1043, 224 USPQ 520 (1984).

[159] *See generally* Note, *Subtests of "Nonobviousness": A Nontechnical Approach to Patent Validity*, 112 U. PA. L. REV. 1169 (1964), *reprinted in* NONOBVIOUSNESS—THE ULTIMATE CONDITION OF PATENTABILITY (John F. Witherspoon ed., 1980).

[160] *See, e.g.*, Symbol Techs. Inc. v. Opticon Inc., 935 F.2d 1569, 1578–79, 19 USPQ2d 1241 (Fed. Cir. 1991). Commercial success of an infringing product can be evidence of the commercial success of the claimed invention. Brown & Williamson Tobacco Corp. v. Philip Morris Inc., 229 F.3d 1120, 1130, 56 USPQ2d 1456 (Fed. Cir. 2000).

[161] Tec Air Inc. v. Denso Mfg. Mich. Inc., 192 F.3d 1353, 1360–61, 52 USPQ2d 1294 (Fed. Cir. 1999). Sales figures plus market data may provide stronger evidence of commercial success. *Id.*; *see, e.g.*, Ruiz v. A. B. Chance Co., 234 F.3d 654, 668, 57 USPQ2d 1161 (Fed. Cir. 2000).

failed efforts of others,[162] copying by others,[163] praise for the invention,[164] unexpected results,[165] disbelief of experts,[166] general skepticism of those in the art,[167] commercial acquiescence,[168] and simultaneous development.[169] Two or more of these secondary considerations may appear together. For example, if there is a long-felt but unsolved need, failed efforts of others and commercial success may well exist.

3. Weighing the Evidence to Reach the Ultimate Conclusion of Law

The Supreme Court in *Graham,* having laid out the requisite factual framework for analyzing nonobviousness, declined to instruct courts on how to perform the final step, applying the facts to the statutory standard. The Court recognized that, although there would be "difficulties" in applying this test, the law was amenable to case-by-case development.[170] In *KSR,* the Supreme Court again refused to provide detailed guidance as to how courts should take the final step in the analysis. Rather, *KSR* described the Supreme Court's jurisprudence as "an

---

[162] *See, e.g.,* Advanced Display Sys. v. Kent State Univ., 212 F.3d 1272, 1284–85, 54 USPQ2d 1673 (Fed. Cir. 2000), *cert. denied,* 532 U.S. 904 (2001).

[163] *Advanced Display Sys.,* 212 F.3d at 1285–86, 54 USPQ2d 1673; Specialty Composites v. Cabot Corp., 845 F.2d 981, 991, 6 USPQ2d 1601 (Fed. Cir. 1988). Copying by itself is equivocal evidence of nonobviousness because copying could have occurred out of a lack of concern for patents. *Ecolochem Inc.,* 227 F.3d at 1380, 56 USPQ2d 1065.

[164] Interconnect Planning Corp. v. Feil, 774 F.2d 1132, 227 USPQ 543 (Fed. Cir. 1985); Corning Glass Works v. Sumitomo Elec. U.S.A. Inc., 671 F. Supp. 1369, 1376–77, 5 USPQ2d 1545 (S.D.N.Y. 1987), *aff'd,* 868 F.2d 1251, 9 USPQ2d 1962 (Fed. Cir. 1989).

[165] Lindemann Maschinenfabrik v. American Hoist & Derrick, 730 F.2d 1452, 221 USPQ 481 (Fed. Cir. 1984).

[166] United States v. Adams, 383 U.S. 39, 148 USPQ 479 (1966).

[167] *See, e.g.,* Pressure Products Medical Supplies, Inc. v. Greatbatch Ltd., 599 F.3d 1308, 1319 (Fed. Cir. 2010); Monarch Knitting Mach. v. Sulzer Morat GmbH, 139 F.3d 877, 885, 45 USPQ2d 1977 (Fed. Cir. 1998). A more probative form of skepticism is prior art that teaches away from the path taken by the inventor. *Id.; Ecolochem Inc.,* 227 F.3d at 1379–80, 56 USPQ2d 1065.

[168] EWP Corp. v. Reliance Universal Inc., 755 F.2d 898, 225 USPQ 20 (Fed. Cir.), *cert. denied,* 474 U.S. 843 (1985).

[169] Ecolochem Inc. v. Southern Cal. Edison Co., 227 F.3d 1361, 1379, 56 USPQ2d 1065 (Fed. Cir. 2000), *cert. denied,* 532 U.S. 974 (2001); Hybritech Inc. v. Monoclonal Antibodies Inc., 802 F.2d 1367, 1380 n.4, 231 USPQ 81 (Fed. Cir. 1986), *cert. denied,* 480 U.S. 947 (1987).

[170] *Graham,* 383 U.S. at 18, 148 USPQ 459.

expansive and flexible approach": "*Graham* sets forth a broad inquiry and invites courts, where appropriate, to look at any secondary considerations that would prove instructive."[171]

In *KSR*, the Supreme Court summarized its jurisprudence on the ultimate question of obviousness as follows:

> When a work is available in one field of endeavor, design incentives and other market forces can prompt variations of it, either in the same field or a different one. If a person of ordinary skill can implement a predictable variation, §103 likely bars its patentability. For the same reason, if a technique has been used to improve one device, and a person of ordinary skill in the art would recognize that it would improve similar devices in the same way, using the technique is obvious unless its actual application is beyond his or her skill.[172]

The Court recognized that "[f]ollowing these principles may be more difficult in other cases than it is here because the claimed subject matter may involve more than the simple substitution of one known element for another or the mere application of a known technique to a piece of prior art ready for the improvement."[173]

KSR explored three types of arguments that had been advanced in the case law on the issue of obviousness. These were (1) the Federal Circuit's requirement of finding "teaching, suggestion or motivation" in the prior art to make the claimed invention ("the TSM test"); (2) the role of the person of ordinary skill in combining prior art references that were directed to problems other than those solved by the patent in suit; and (3) whether an invention can be proved obvious by showing that the claimed advance in the art would have been "obvious to try."

---

[171] *KSR, Int'l,* 550 U.S. at 415, 82 USPQ2d 1385.

[172] *Id.* at 417, 82 USPQ2d 1385.

[173] *Id.; see, e.g.,* Rothman v. Target Corp., 556 F.3d 1310, 1319-21, 89 USPQ2d 1897 (Fed. Cir.) (predictable art), *cert. denied,* 130 S. Ct. 626 (2009); Sanofi-Synthelabo v. Apotex, Inc., 550 F.3d. 1075, 1085–90, 89 USPQ2d 1370 (Fed. Cir. 2008) (unpredictable art), *cert. denied,* 130 S. Ct. 493 (2009).

Teaching, suggestion, and motivation: *KSR* overruled the Federal Circuit's requirement that, to find obviousness, there *must* be teaching, suggestion, or motivation in the art to make the claimed invention. The Supreme Court found the TSM test "a useful insight."

> Helpful insights, however, need not become rigid and mandatory formulas; and when it is so applied, the TSM test is incompatible with our precedents. The obviousness analysis cannot be confined by a formalistic conception of the words teaching, suggestion, and motivation, or by overemphasis on the importance of published articles and the explicit content of issued patents. The diversity of inventive pursuits and of modern technology counsels against limiting the analysis in this way. In many fields it may be that there is little discussion of obvious techniques or combinations, and it often may be the case that market demand, rather than scientific literature, will drive design trends.[174]

However, *KSR* also reaffirmed the importance of determining obviousness without hindsight, and, in dicta, suggested that a "flexible" approach to the factors of teaching, suggestion, and motivation would conform to the Supreme Court's jurisprudence.[175] In the wake of *KSR*, the Federal Circuit has reaffirmed the usefulness of the TSM test.[176] Where the test is applied, evidence of teaching, suggestion, or motivation may be found expressly in a prior art reference itself,[177] or it can also be found elsewhere.[178] The relevant evidence may also come from the knowledge of one with ordinary skill, or the nature of the

---

[174] *KSR, Int'l,* 550 U.S. at 419, 82 USPQ2d 1385.

[175] *Id.,* 550 U.S. at 421–22, 82 USPQ2d 1385.

[176] *See, e.g.,* Takeda Chem. Indus. v. Alphapharma Pty., Ltd., 492 F.3d 1350, 1356–57, 83 USPQ2d 1169 (Fed. Cir. 2007), *cert. denied,* 128 S. Ct. 1739 (2008); Commonwealth Sci. & Indus. Research Org. v. Buffalo Tech. (USA), Inc., 542 F.3d 1363, 1375–76, 88 USPQ2d 1564 (Fed. Cir. 2008); Star Scientific, Inc. v. R. J. Reynolds Tobacco Co., No. 2010-1183, slip op. at 17, 99 USPQ 1924 (Fed. Cir. Aug. 26, 2011).

[177] *See* Princeton Biochemicals Inc. v. Beckman Coulter Inc., 411 F.3d 1332, 1338, 75 USPQ2d 1051 (Fed. Cir. 2005).

[178] *See id.;* McGinley v. Franklin Sports, Inc., 262 F.3d 1339, 1351, 60 USPQ2d 1001 (Fed. Cir. 2001).

problem to be solved.[179] Motivation to combine based on the nature of the problem to be solved is " 'particularly relevant with simpler mechanical technologies.' "[180]

Evidence of motivation need not be documentary.[181] The motivation, teaching, or suggestion may be implicit.[182] Prior art can "teach away" from its combination with another source.[183] The presence or absence of teaching, suggestion, or motivation is an issue of fact.[184]

With respect to the quantum of proof necessary to sustain a conclusion of obviousness, the Federal Circuit has stated that the mere fact that the prior art can be modified does not make the modification obvious unless the prior art suggests the desirability of the modification.[185]

The meaning of "ordinary skill": As discussed earlier in this section, the person of ordinary skill is presumed to be knowledgeable of all of the prior art but to be guided by the conventional wisdom in the field. This is by contrast to inventors, who as a class are believed to have "above ordinary" skill or insight. In *KSR*, the Supreme Court addressed the extent to which a person of ordinary skill could be expected to combine teachings from "interrelated" references:

> Often, it will be necessary for a court to look to interrelated teachings of multiple patents; the effects of demands known to the design community or present in the marketplace; and the back-

---

[179] *Princeton Biochemicals,* 411 F.3d at 1338, 75 USPQ2d 1051; Akamai Techs., Inc. v. Cable & Wireless Internet Servs., Inc., 344 F.3d 1186, 1196, 68 USPQ2d 1186 (Fed. Cir. 2003); *Beckson Marine, Inc.,* 292 F.3d at 727–28, 63 USPQ2d 1031.

[180] Tokai Corp. v. Easton Enters., Inc., 632 F.3d 1358, 1371, 97 USPQ2d 1673 (Fed. Cir. 2011) (quoting Ruiz v. A. B. Chance Co., 357 F.3d 1270, 1276 (Fed. Cir. 2004)).

[181] Novo Nordisk A/S v. Becton Dickinson & Co., 304 F.3d 1216, 1219, 64 USPQ2d 1524 (Fed. Cir. 2002).

[182] *In re* Kotzab, 217 F.3d 1365, 1370, 55 USPQ2d 1313 (Fed. Cir. 2000) ("The test for an implicit showing is what the combined teachings, knowledge of one of ordinary skill in the art, and the nature of the problem to be solved as a whole would have suggested to those of ordinary skill in the art").

[183] *See, e.g.,* Winner Int'l Royalty Corp. v. Wang, 202 F.3d 1340, 1349–50, 53 USPQ2d 1580 (Fed. Cir.), cert. denied, 530 U.S. 1238 (2000). If combining prior art would produce a seemingly inoperative device, that art teaches away from that combination. *McGinley,* 262 F.3d at 1353–55, 60 USPQ2d 1001.

[184] *Novo Nordisk A/S,* 304 F.3d at 1219, 64 USPQ2d 1524.

[185] Cordis Corp. v. Medtronic AVE, Inc., 511 F.3d 1157, 1172, 85 USPQ2d 1427 (Fed. Cir. 2008).

ground knowledge possessed by a person having ordinary skill in the art, all in order to determine whether there was an apparent reason to combine the known elements in the fashion claimed by the patent at issue. To facilitate review, this analysis should be made explicit. As our precedents make clear, however, the analysis need not seek out precise teachings directed to the specific subject matter of the challenged claim, for a court can take account of the inferences and creative steps that a person of ordinary skill in the art would employ.[186]

Similarly, in applying this principle to the *KSR* facts, the Court stated:

Common sense teaches, however, that familiar items may have obvious uses beyond their primary purposes, and in many cases a person of ordinary skill will be able to fit the teachings of multiple patents together like pieces of a puzzle. . . . A person of ordinary skill is also a person of ordinary creativity, not an automaton.[187]

To facilitate appellate review, a court must provide an explicit analysis of its reasons for ruling on nonobviousness.[188] Mere conclusory statements that the fact finder is relying on "common sense," without more, are insufficient.[189]

Obvious to try: In the appeal that led to the *KSR* decision, the Federal Circuit had rejected the argument that the claimed invention would have been obvious to try "because '[o]bvious to try' has long been held not to constitute obviousness."[190] The Supreme Court rejected this "constricted analysis," and set

---

[186] *KSR, Int'l,* 550 U.S. at 418, 82 USPQ2d 1385 (citation omitted).

[187] *Id.* at 420–21, 82 USPQ2d 1385. Post-*KSR* decisions applying this principle include *Wyers,* 616 F.3d at 1239–40, 95 USPQ2d 1525; Ball Aerosol & Specialty Container, Inc. v. Limited Brands, Inc., 555 F.3d 984, 992-93, 89 USPQ2d 1870 (Fed. Cir. 2009), and Perfect Web Technologies, Inc. v. InfoUSA, Inc., 587 F.3d 1324, 1330, 92 USPQ2d 1849 (Fed. Cir. 2009).

[188] *KSR,* 550 U.S. at 417–18, 82 USPQ2d 1385; *In re* Lee, 277 F.3d 1338, 1342, 61 USPQ2d 1430 (Fed. Cir. 2002).

[189] TriMed, Inc. v. Stryker Corp., 608 F.3d 1333, 1342–43, 95 USPQ2d 1577 (Fed. Cir. 2010); *In re Lee,* 277 F.3d at 1344, 61 USPQ2d 1430.

[190] *KSR, Int'l,* 550 U.S. at 414, 82 USPQ2d 1385.

forth the following test for when a claimed invention might be invalid for obviousness because it was obvious to try:

> When there is a design need or market pressure to solve a problem and there are a finite number of identified, predictable solutions, a person of ordinary skill has good reason to pursue the known options within his or her technical grasp. If this leads to the anticipated success, it is likely the product not of innovation but of ordinary skill and common sense. In that instance the fact that a combination was obvious to try might show that it was obvious under §103.[191]

Following *KSR*, the Federal Circuit has elaborated on this standard, based on its 1988 decision in *In re O'Farrell*. The "obvious to try" analysis remains improper where

> what would have been "obvious to try" would have been to vary all parameters or try each of numerous possible choices until one possibly arrived at a successful result, where the prior art gave either no indication of which parameters were critical or no direction as to which of many possible choices is likely to be successful.[192]

It is also improper where

> what was "obvious to try" was to explore a new technology or general approach that seemed to be a promising field of experimentation, where the prior art gave only general guidance as to the particular form of the claimed invention or how to achieve it.[193]

Within the parameters framed by *KSR* and *Kubin,* a series of fact-intensive decisions, often involving divided panels of the Federal Circuit, have turned on (1) the number and complexity of the choices available to the person of ordinary skill when the invention was made, and (2) whether or not there

---

[191] *Id.* at 421, 82 USPQ2d 1385.
[192] *In re* Kubin, 561 F.3d 1351, 1359–61, 90 USPQ2d 1417 (Fed. Cir. 2009), citing *In re* O'Farrell, 853 F.2d 894, 903, 7 USPQ2d 1673 (Fed. Cir. 1988).
[193] *Id.*

was a "reasonable expectation of success based on those finite choices.[194]

4. Double Patenting

35 U.S.C. §101 provides that an inventor who makes a new and useful invention may obtain "a patent" on that invention. The doctrine forbidding "double patenting" arises from the notion that "a patent" means "one patent."

Courts have distinguished between two situations: "statutory" double patenting and "obviousness-type" double patenting. Statutory double patenting occurs when the second patent seeks protection for the same invention as an earlier-issued patent, thereby violating the one-patent provision of §101. Obviousness-type double patenting is a judicially created doctrine that bars the issue of a second patent whose claims are "so alike" those of an already issued patent. In both situations, the purpose of the rules is to prevent "unjustified timewise extension of the right to exclude."[195]

The Federal Circuit has explained the differences between the analysis of obviousness under 35 U.S.C. §103 and that of obviousness-type double patenting:

> In general, the obviousness analysis applies to double patenting, except for three distinctions. First, statutory obviousness compares claimed subject matter to the prior art, while non-statutory double patenting compares claims in an earlier patent to claims in a later

---

[194] *See, e.g.,* Abbott Labs. v. Sandoz, Inc., 544 F.3d 1341, 1351, 89 USPQ2d 1161 (Fed. Cir. 2008) (not obvious to try); *Sanofi-Synthelabo,* 550 F.3d. at 1085–90, 89 USPQ2d 1370 (not obvious to try); Bayer Schering Pharma. AG v. Barr Labs., Inc., 575 F.3d 1341, 1346–50, 91 USPQ2d 1569 (Fed. Cir. 2009) (obvious to try), *cert. denied,* 130 S. Ct. 2404 (2010); *In re Kubin,* 561 F.3d at 1360–61, 90 USPQ2d 1417 (obvious to try); *Rolls-Royce, PLC,* 603 F.3d. at 1339, 95 USPQ2d 1097 (not obvious to try); *Media Technologies Licensing, LLC,* 596 F.3d at 1337–38, 93 USPQ2d 1911 (obvious to try).

[195] Takeda Pharmaceutical Co. v. Doll, 561 F.3d 1372, 1375, 90 USPQ2d 1496 (Fed. Cir. 2009). For example, a claim directed to a process for making a product is not patentably distinct from an earlier patent directed to the product unless the product can also be made by other processes that are "materially different" so that the scope of the two claims are "patentably distinct." *Id.* at 1375–76, 90 USPQ2d 1496.

patent or application. Second, double patenting does not require inquiry into a motivation to modify the prior art. Finally, double patenting does not require inquiry into objective criteria suggesting non-obviousness.[196]

There are, however, situations in which the PTO requires a patent applicant to prosecute claims directed to related inventions in multiple applications. Under 35 U.S.C. §121, "[i]f two or more independent and distinct inventions are claimed in one application, the [PTO] may require the application to be restricted to one of the inventions." One or more "divisional" applications may be filed to claim other "independent and distinct" inventions.[197] A second patent application filed at the instruction of the PTO may not be used as "prior art" for purposes of asserting double patenting.[198] Thus, a threshold inquiry where obviousness type double patenting is asserted as a defense is whether or not the §121 "safe harbor" applies.[199]

II. THE REQUIREMENTS OF PATENTABILITY

A. Originality

A patent will not be granted for a patentable invention unless the named inventor is an original inventor.[200] An original inventor is one who conceived the invention on his or her

---

[196] Procter & Gamble Co. v. Teva Pharms. USA, Inc. 566 F.3d 989, 999, 90 USPQ2d 1947 (Fed. Cir. 2009) (internal citations omitted); *see also* Amgen Inc. v. F. Hoffmann-La Roche Ltd., 580 F.3d 1340, 1358–63, 92 USPQ2d 1289 (Fed. Cir. 2009); Sun Pharm. Indus., Ltd. v. Eli Lilly & Co., 611 F.3d 1381, 95 USPQ2d 1797 (Fed. Cir. 2010), *cert. denied,* 131 S. Ct. 2445 (2011); Pfizer, Inc. v. Teva Pharms. USA, Inc., 518 F.3d 1353, 1362–65, 86 USPQ2d 1001 (Fed. Cir. 2008); Geneva Pharms., Inc. v. GlaxoSmithKline PLC, 349 F.3d 1373, 1382-86, 68 USPQ2d 1865 (Fed. Cir. 2003).

[197] 35 U.S.C. §121; 37 C.F.R. §§ 1.141–1.146.

[198] 35 U.S.C. §121; *see, e.g.,* Boehringer Ingelheim Int'l GmbH v. Barr Labs., Inc., 592 F.3d 1340, 1350–54, 93 USPQ2d 1417 (Fed. Cir. 2010).

[199] *See generally Boehringer Ingelheim Int'l GmbH,* 592 F.3d 1340, 93 USPQ2d 1417; Oddz On Prods. Inc. v. Just Toys Inc., 122 F.3d 1396, 43 USPQ2d 1641 (Fed. Cir. 1997).

[200] 35 U.S.C. §102(f); *see, e.g., Oddz On Prods. Inc.,* 122 F.3d 1396, 43 USPQ2d 1641.

own.[201] If more than one person contributed to the conception of the invention, they are joint inventors.[202] The inventor or inventors named on an issued patent are presumed to be the true and only inventors.[203] An error regarding the named inventor or inventors can be corrected in an issued patent, provided the error occurred without deceptive intent on the part of the nonjoined inventor or inventors.[204]

B. Statutory Bars

An inventor who does not promptly seek a patent runs the risk of losing the right to obtain a patent. An inventor loses the right to obtain a patent if one of the events set forth in 35 U.S.C. §102(b), (c), or (d) occurs.

---

[201] O'Reilly v. Morse, 56 U.S. (15 How.) 62 (1853). Proving that a purported inventor derived an invention from another requires clear and convincing evidence of (1) prior conception of the invention by another and (2) communication of that prior conception to the named inventor. Gambro Lundia AB v. Baxter Healthcare Corp. 110 F.3d 1573, 1576–78, 42 USPQ2d 1378 (Fed. Cir. 1997). The communication must be sufficient to enable one of ordinary skill to make and use the invention. *Gambro*, 110 F.3d at 1576–78, 42 USPQ2d 1378. If a purported inventor derived information from another that, when combined with other prior art makes the invention obvious, then the invention is unpatentable by that purported inventor under 35 U.S.C. §103. *Oddz On Prods. Inc.*, 122 F.3d at 1403–04, 43 USPQ2d 1641.

[202] 35 U.S.C. §116; Vanderbilt Univ. v. ICOS Corp., 601 F.3d 1297, 1302-03, 94 USPQ2d 1481 (Fed. Cir. 2010), *cert. denied*, 131 S. Ct. 1043 (2011); Kimberly-Clark Corp. v. Procter & Gamble Distrib. Co., 973 F.2d 911, 915–17, 23 USPQ2d 1921 (Fed. Cir. 1992); *Burroughs Wellcome Co.*, 40 F.3d at 1227–29, 32 USPQ2d 1915. Thompson v. Haynes, 305 F.3d 1369, 1384, 64 USPQ2d 1650 (Fed. Cir. 2002); Acromed Corp. v. Sofamor Danek Group, Inc., 253 F.3d 1371, 1379–81, 59 USPQ2d 1130 (Fed. Cir. 2001).

[203] *Vanderbilt Univ.*, 601 F.3d at 1305-08, 94 USPQ2d 1481; Board of Educ. v. American Bioscience, 333 F.3d 1330, 1337, 67 USPQ2d 1252 (Fed. Cir. 2003); *Acromed Corp.*, 253 F.3d at 1379, 59 USPQ2d 1130.

[204] 35 U.S.C. §256; Stark v. Advanced Magnetics Inc., 119 F.3d 1551, 43 USPQ2d 1321 (Fed. Cir. 1997); *see also* Frank's Casing Crew & Rental Tools v. PMR Techs., Ltd., 292 F.3d 1363, 1377, 63 USPQ2d 1065 (Fed. Cir. 2002). Correcting inventorship before the patent issues requires lack of deceptive intent on the part of both the misjoined and the non-joined persons. 35 U.S.C.A. §116 (2001); *Stark*, 119 F.3d 1551, 43 USPQ2d 1321. To sue under §256, one need not have potential ownership in the patent. Chou v. University of Chi., 254 F.3d 1347, 1356–59, 59 USPQ2d 1257 (Fed. Cir. 2001). District courts lack the authority to change the order in which the inventors are listed. Fina Tech., Inc. v. Ewen, 265 F.3d 1325, 1327–28, 60 USPQ2d 1314 (Fed. Cir. 2001). If inventorship is properly corrected under PTO regulations, the correction is presumed to be valid. Winbond Elec. Corp. v. United States Int'l Trade Comm'n, 262 F.3d 1363, 1371–72, 60 USPQ2d 1029 (Fed. Cir. 2001).

1. Section 102(b)

Pursuant to Section 102(b), an inventor loses his or her right to obtain a patent if

the invention was patented or described in a printed publication in this or a foreign country or in public use or on sale in this country, more than one year prior to the date of the application for patent in the United States.

The Section 102(b) items or events that can bar the issuance of a patent if they occur more than one year before the application date are: domestic or foreign patents, domestic or foreign publications, domestic public use of the invention, and the invention being on sale domestically. These items and events can arise through either the acts of the inventor or the acts of others.

"[T]he invention." The statutory bars set forth in Section 102(b) all refer to "the invention." This primarily refers to the inventor's conception, rather than a physical embodiment of that idea and it refers to a conception that is complete, not just substantially complete.[205] Reduction to practice usually provides the best evidence that an invention is complete, but such evidence is not necessary in every case.[206]

As with novelty determinations, when deciding whether a Section 102(b) bar has arisen, the subject matter of the barring activity must be compared with the invention as claimed.[207] If the subject matter of the barring activity contains each element of the claimed invention, a Section 102(b) bar may have

---

[205] Pfaff v. Wells Elecs. Inc., 525 U.S. 55, 60, 66, 48 USPQ2d 1641 (1998); Space Sys./Loral, Inc. v. Lockheed Martin Corp., 271 F.3d 1076, 1080, 60 USPQ2d 1861 (Fed. Cir. 2001).

[206] *Pfaff*, 525 U.S. at 66, 48 USPQ2d 1641; *Space Sys./Loral, Inc.*, 271 F.3d at 1080, 60 USPQ2d 1861.

[207] Orion IP, LLC v. Hyundai Motor America, 605 F.3d 967, 974, 95 USPQ2d 1297 (Fed. Cir. 2010); Dana Corp. v. American Axle & Mfg., Inc., 279 F.3d 1372, 1375–76, 61 USPQ2d 1609 (Fed. Cir. 2002) ("[A] court may not invalidate the claims of a patent without construing the disputed limitations of the claims and applying them to the allegedly invalidating acts").

arisen.[208] If the subject matter of the barring activity does *not* contain each element of the claimed invention and thus there is no Section 102(b) bar, the subject matter can still be used to show that the claimed invention does not meet the nonobviousness condition of patentability.[209]

"[T]he invention was patented or described in a printed publication in this or a foreign country . . . more than one year prior to the date of the application for patent in the United States." The words of Section 102(b) dealing with patents and publications (i.e., "patented or described in a printed publication in this or a foreign country") are identical to the words used in Section 102(a). The words have been interpreted the same way for purposes of both sections.[210]

"[T]he invention was . . . in public use . . . in this country, more than one year prior to the date of the application for patent in the United States." "The proper test for the public use prong of the §102(b) statutory bar is whether the purported use: (1) was accessible to the public; or (2) was commercially exploited."[211]

The purpose of the public use bar is to prevent the inventor from exploiting the invention commercially while delaying the filing of a patent application.[212] For this reason, in contrast to use under Section 102(a), the use of the claimed invention

---

[208] *See generally Dana Corp.,* 279 F.3d at 1375–76, 61 USPQ2d 1609; Scaltech Inc. v. Retec/Tetra, L.L.C., 178 F.3d 1378, 1383–84, 51 USPQ2d 1055 (Fed. Cir. 1999). When a claim covers several embodiments, a §102(b) bar may arise if the subject matter of the barring activity is one of those embodiments. *Scaltech, Inc.,* 269 F.3d at 1330, 60 USPQ2d 1687.

[209] See this chapter, §I.D.2.a. Such a situation is sometimes referred to as a §102(b)/103 rejection. *See, e.g., In re* Corcoran, 640 F.2d 1331, 1333, 208 USPQ 867 (C.C.P.A. 1981). The Federal Circuit has suggested that obviousness is part of the §102(b) inquiry. *See, e.g.,* Allen Eng'g Corp. v. Bartell Indus., 299 F.3d 1336, 1352, 63 USPQ2d 1769 (Fed. Cir. 2002); *Netscape Commc'ns Corp.,* 295 F.3d at 1321, 63 USPQ2d 1580.

[210] *See* MPEP §2128, *available at* http://www.uspto.gov/web/offices/pac/mpep/mpep.htm. *Orion IP, LLC,* 605 F.3d at 974, 95 USPQ2d 1297 (Fed. Cir. 2010); *Finisar Corp.,* 523 F.3d at 1334, 86 USPQ2d 1609.

[211] Invitrogen Corp. v. Biocrest Mfg., L.P., 424 F.3d 1374, 1380, 76 USPQ2d 1741 (Fed. Cir. 2005). *See generally* MPEP §2133(a), *available at* http://www.uspto.gov/web/offices/pac/mpep/mpep.htm.

[212] Pfaff v. Wells Elecs., Inc., 525 U.S. 55, 64–65, 48 USPQ2d 1641 (1998).

need not be publicly accessible.[213] For example, under Section 102(b), a part of the internal mechanism of a safe is publicly used when the safe is used by the public even though nobody can see the safe's internal parts.[214] Similarly, if an inventor practices a patentable process in complete secrecy but sells goods made by that process, the inventor's use may be a public use under Section 102(b).[215] If, however, the secret commercial use is by someone other than the inventor, and the inventor does not know of or consent to it, the secret commercial use usually will not create a Section 102(b) bar.[216]

A public use does not create a Section 102(b) bar when the primary purpose for the use is experimental.[217] This is because some inventions can only be tested adequately in public.[218] For example, if an inventor who has invented road pavement tests that pavement on a road used by the public, that use will not be deemed a public use under Section 102(b).[219]

A patent challenger has the burden of proving public use.[220] However, if the patent challenger makes a prima facie case of public use, the patent owner must present convincing evidence to counter that showing.[221] Experimental use is one

---

[213] Egbert v. Lippmann, 104 U.S. 333 (1881); Minnesota Mining & Mfg. Co. v. Chemque, Inc., 303 F.3d 1294, 1307, 64 USPQ2d 1270 (Fed. Cir. 2002), *cert. dismissed*, 538 U.S. 972 (2003).

[214] Hall v. Macneale, 107 U.S. 90 (1883).

[215] Metallizing Eng'g Co. v. Kenyon Bearing & Auto Parts Co., 153 F.2d 516, 68 USPQ 54 (2d Cir.), *cert. denied*, 328 U.S. 840, 69 USPQ 631 (1946).

[216] W. L. Gore & Assocs. v. Garlock Inc., 721 F.2d 1540, 1549–50, 220 USPQ 303 (Fed. Cir. 1983), *cert. denied*, 469 U.S. 851 (1984).

[217] Clock Spring L.P. v. Wrapmaster, Inc., 560 F.3d 1317, 1326–28, 90 USPQ2d 1212 (Fed. Cir. 2009); Eli Lilly & Co. v. Zenith Goldline Pharms., Inc., 471 F.3d 1369, 1380–81, 81 USPQ2d 1324 (Fed. Cir. 2006), *cert. denied sub nom.* Teva Pharms. USA, Inc. v. Eli Lilly & Co., 128 S. Ct. 146 (2007), and *cert. denied sub nom.* Dr. Reddy's Labs, Ltd. v. Eli Lilly & Co., 128 S. Ct. 288 (2007); Netscape Commc'ns Corp. v. Konrad, 295 F.3d 1315, 1321–23, 63 USPQ2d 1580 (Fed. Cir. 2002). Experimental use ends with an actual reduction to practice. New Railhead Mfg., L.L.C. v. Vermeer Mfg. Co., 298 F.3d 1290, 1297–99, 63 USPQ2d 1843 (Fed. Cir. 2002), *cert. denied*, 537 U.S. 1232 (2003).

[218] Elizabeth v. Pavement Co., 97 U.S. 126, 134 (1878).

[219] *Id.*

[220] T.P. Lab., Inc. v. Professional Positioners Inc., 724 F.2d 965, 220 USPQ 577 (Fed. Cir.), *cert. denied*, 469 U.S. 826, 224 USPQ 616 (1984). Prior to the mid-1980s, after the patent challenger presented evidence of public use, the burden shifted to the patent owner to present evidence to show that the use was experimental.

[221] Lough v. Brunswick Corp., 86 F.3d 1113, 1120, 39 USPQ2d 1100 (Fed. Cir. 1996), *cert. denied*, 522 U.S. 806 (1997); *T.P. Lab. Inc.*, 724 F.2d at 971, 220 USPQ 577.

type of evidence to counter a prima facie case of public use. Evidence relating to experimental use includes: length of the test period, whether payment was received for the product, agreements as to confidentiality, who conducted the tests, the extent of the inventor's control over the testing, how many tests were conducted, whether records were kept, and the length of the testing period in relation to tests of similar products.[222]

Experimental use is determined through an objective test; subjective evidence of the inventor regarding experimental use carries little weight.[223]

Experimental public use by someone other than the inventor is an invalidating public use if the use is by a person whom the inventor does not control.[224]

"[T]he invention was . . . on sale in this country, more than one year prior to the date of the application for patent in the United States." To establish an on-sale bar: (1) the invention must be the subject of a commercial offer for sale, and (2) the invention must be ready for patenting.[225]

The commercial-offer-for-sale condition is met only by an offer that another party can make into a binding contract by simple acceptance.[226] Determining whether such an offer was made is informed by a federal common law of contract based on the Uniform Commercial Code and the state and federal decisions interpreting their version of that code.[227] The offer for sale must

---

[222] *Clock Spring, L.P.*, 560 F.3d at 1326–27, 90 USPQ2d 1212.

[223] Electromotive Div. of Gen. Motors Corp. v. Transportation Sys. Div. of Gen. Elec. Co., 417 F.3d 1203, 1212, 75 USPQ2d 1650 (Fed. Cir. 2005); *Lough*, 86 F.3d at 1120, 39 USPQ2d 1100.

[224] Baxter Int'l Inc. v. Cobe Labs. Inc., 88 F.3d 1054, 1059–60, 39 USPQ2d 1437 (Fed. Cir. 1996).

[225] Pfaff v. Wells Elecs. Inc., 525 U.S. 55, 67–68, 48 USPQ2d 1641 (1998). *See generally* MPEP §2133.03(b), *available at* http://www.uspto.gov/web/offices/pac/mpep/mpep.htm; Brasseler U.S.A. I, L.P. v. Stryker Sales Corp., 182 F.3d 888, 890, 51 USPQ2d 1470 (Fed. Cir. 1999).

[226] Linear Tech. Corp. v. Micrel, Inc., 275 F.3d 1040, 1050–52, 61 USPQ2d 1225 (Fed. Cir. 2001), *cert. denied*, 538 U.S. 1052 (2003); Scaltech, Inc. v. Retec/Tetra, L.L.C., 269 F.3d 1321, 1328, 60 USPQ2d 1687 (Fed. Cir. 2001); Group One, Ltd. v. Hallmark Cards, Inc., 254 F.3d 1041, 1047–48, 59 USPQ2d 1121 (Fed. Cir. 2001), *cert. denied*, 534 U.S. 1127 (2002).

[227] *Linear Tech. Corp.*, 275 F.3d at 1048, 61 USPQ2d 1225; *Group One Ltd.*, 254 F.3d at 1047–48, 59 USPQ2d 1121. Without more, providing product samples to prospective customers is not a commercial offer for sale. Minnesota Mining Mfg. Co. v. Chemque, Inc., 303 F.3d 1294, 1308, 64 USPQ2d 1270 (Fed. Cir. 2002), *cert. dismissed*, 538 U.S. 972 (2003).

take place between two separate entities,[228] and there is no exception to the on-sale bar for joint development[229] or suppliers.[230]

With respect to a method patent, performing the method for consideration constitutes placing the method on sale. This would include sale of product made by a patented method.[231]

An invention may not be offered for sale before its conception date. However, if an earlier offer to sell the invention has been made and that offer remains open, the on-sale bar can apply from the date of conception.[232]

The Supreme Court identified at least two ways of satisfying the ready-for-patenting condition: (a) proof of a reduction to practice, or (b) proof of drawings or descriptions of the invention that are sufficiently specific to enable one skilled in the art to practice the invention.[233] An invention cannot be ready for patenting before an enabling disclosure can be made.[234] An unappreciated reduction to practice can meet the ready-for-patenting condition.[235]

The on-sale bar does not require a public sale, i.e., a sale "to the trade."[236] For example, a commercial sale under a secrecy agreement will raise a Section 102(b) on-sale bar.[237] An offer to sell any patent rights that an inventor may obtain as a result of his or her invention does not raise the on-sale bar.[238] Similarly, an offer of a license under a patent does not raise the on-sale

---

[228] Netscape Commc'ns Corp. v. Konrad, 295 F.3d 1315, 1324, 63 USPQ2d 1580 (Fed. Cir. 2002).

[229] *Brasseler U.S.A. I, L.P.*, 182 F.3d at 890–91, 51 USPQ2d 1470.

[230] Special Devices, Inc. v. OEA, Inc., 270 F.3d 1353, 1355-58, 60 USPQ2d 1537 (Fed. Cir. 2001).

[231] Plumtree Software, Inc. v. Datamize, LLC, 473 F.3d 1152, 1162-64, 81 USPQ2d 1251 (Fed. Cir. 2006); Elan Corp. v. Andrx Pharms., Inc., 366 F.3d 1336, 1341, 70 USPQ2d 1722 (Fed. Cir. 2004).

[232] August Tech. Corp. v. Camtek, Ltd., No. 2010-1458, 99 USPQ2d 1766 (Fed. Cir. August 22, 2011).

[233] Pfaff v. Wells Elecs. Inc., 525 U.S. 55, 67–68, 48 USPQ2d 1641 (1998).

[234] Space Systems/Loral, Inc. v. Lockheed Martin Corp., 271 F.3d 1076, 1080, 60 USPQ2d 1861 (Fed. Cir. 2001).

[235] Abbott Labs. v. Geneva Pharms., 182 F.3d 1315, 1318–19, 51 USPQ2d 1307 (Fed. Cir. 1999), *cert. denied*, 528 U.S. 1078 (2000).

[236] Brasseler U.S.A. I, L.P. v. Stryker Sales Corp., 182 F.3d 888, 891, 51 USPQ2d 1470 (Fed. Cir. 1999).

[237] *See, e.g.*, Hobbs v. United States Atomic Energy Comm'n, 451 F.2d 849, 171 USPQ 713 (5th Cir. 1971).

[238] Moleculon Research Corp. v. CBS Inc., 793 F.2d 1261, 229 USPQ 805 (Fed. Cir. 1986), *cert. denied*, 479 U.S. 1030 (1987).

bar.[239] Further, an actual license, by itself, does not raise the on-sale bar,[240] although the license or lease of a product or device may trigger the bar.[241]

Sales made primarily for a bona fide experimental purpose rather than for commercial exploitation do not raise a Section 102(b) on-sale bar.[242]

"[M]ore than one year prior to the date of the application for patent in the United States." The reference point for Section 102(b) is the patent application date; to bar a patent, items or events must exist or occur more than one year before the application date.[243] The date that is exactly one year before the application date is known as the "critical date."

In effect, Section 102(b) creates a one-year, risk-free period during which the inventor may perfect the invention, decide if the invention is worth patenting, prepare a patent application, and market the invention.[244] No act of the inventor or anyone else during the risk-free period gives rise to a Section 102(b) bar. But, if the inventor waits over a year after invention to apply for a patent, there is a risk of a Section 102(b) bar.

2. Section 102(c)

An inventor loses the right to obtain a patent if he or she abandons the invention. The abandonment concept under 35 U.S.C. §102(c) is different from Section 102(g)'s "abandoned, suppressed, or concealed" concept.[245] When Section 102(g)

---

[239] *In re* Kollar, 286 F.3d 1326, 1331–32, 62 USPQ2d 1425 (Fed. Cir. 2002).

[240] *Id.* at 1329–34. *See generally* Group One, Ltd. v. Hallmark Cards, Inc., 254 F.3d 1041, 1052–53, 59 USPQ2d 1121 (Fed. Cir. 2001), *cert. denied,* 534 U.S. 1127 (2002) (Lourie, J., additional remarks).

[241] Minton v. National Ass'n of Sec. Dealers, Inc., 336 F.3d 1373, 1378, 67 USPQ2d 1614 (Fed. Cir. 2003).

[242] *Pfaff,* 525 U.S. at 67, 48 USPQ2d 1641 (1998); *Eli Lilly & Co.* 471 F.3d at 1380–81, 81 USPQ2d 1324; EZ Dock v. Schafer Sys., Inc., 276 F.3d 1347, 1351–58, 61 USPQ2d 1289 (Fed. Cir. 2002); *see generally* MPEP §2133.03(e), *available at* http://www.uspto.gov/web/offices/pac/mpep/mpep.htm.

[243] For the history of the one-year grace period, see *Pfaff,* 525 U.S. at 63–66, 48 USPQ2d 1641; Scaltech, Inc. v. Retec/Tetra, L.L.C., 269 F.3d 1321, 1327, 60 USPQ2d 1687 (Fed. Cir. 2001).

[244] *See generally* General Elec. Co. v. United States, 654 F.2d 55 (Ct. Cl. 1981); Gould Inc. v. United States, 579 F.2d 571, 198 USPQ 156 (Ct. Cl. 1978).

[245] 2 DONALD S. CHISUM, CHISUM ON PATENTS §6.03 (2010).

applies, an inventor's right to a patent is subordinated to a second inventor's right to a patent. When Section 102(c) applies, an inventor loses his or her right to a patent altogether.

Decisions under Section 102(c) are rare. For Section 102(c) to apply, an inventor must intend to abandon his or her invention.[246] The inventor's intent can be express, or it can be implied from a long and unexcused delay in filing a patent application.[247] Abandoning a patent application (discussed in Chapter 2, §III.D.7) does not by itself constitute Section 102(c) abandonment.[248]

3. Section 102(d)

An inventor loses his or her right to obtain a U.S. patent if (1) the inventor applied for a patent or an inventor's certificate on the invention in a foreign country more than 12 months before his or her U.S. filing date, and (2) the invention was patented or the subject of an inventor's certificate prior to the U.S. filing date.[249]

An invention is patented within the meaning of Section 102(d) when it confers legal rights. Section 102(d), unlike Section 102(a), does not require that the patent be publicly available. Section 102(d) encourages inventors to file applications promptly in the United States.[250]

4. Section 102(f)

Under 35 U.S.C. §102(f), a person is not entitled to a patent if he or she is not the true inventor.[251] Section 102(f)

---

[246]Paul T. Meiklejohn, *Abandonment Under §102(c) and Forfeiture,* 20 IDEA 227 (1978).

[247]*Id.;* Electric Storage Battery Co. v. Shimadzu, 307 U.S. 5, 41 USPQ 155 (1939).

[248] *See generally* MPEP §2134, *available at* http://www.uspto.gov/web/offices/pac/mpep/mpep.htm.

[249]35 U.S.C. §102(d); *see generally* MPEP §2135.

[250]Bayer AG v. Schein Pharms., Inc., 301 F.3d 1306, 1312–13, 64 USPQ2d 1001 (Fed. Cir. 2002); *In re* Kathawala, 9 F.3d 942, 947, 28 USPQ2d 1785 (Fed. Cir. 1993). The foreign application must have been filed by the U.S. applicant or someone acting on his behalf. Boston Scientific Scimed, Inc. v. Medtronic Vascular, Inc., 497 F.3d 1293, 1297–98, 83 USPQ2d 1669 (Fed. Cir. 2007).

[251] *See generally* MPEP §2137, *available at* http://www.uspto.gov/web/offices/pac/mpep/mpep.htm.

prevents a person from getting a patent on inventions that were developed by someone else and "derived" from the "true" inventor. In order for Section 102(f) to apply, it must be shown that (1) someone other than the claimed inventor conceived of the invention before the claimed inventor, and (2) that the prior conception was communicated to the alleged inventor.[252]

C. Disclosure

A patent has been described as a contract between an inventor and the government. In consideration for receiving the right to exclude others from making, using, offering for sale, selling, or importing the invention for a specified period of time, the inventor must disclose his or her invention.[253] As noted earlier, the specification may be in any format (see Chapter 2, §III.B.1), but it must (1) describe the invention sought to be patented, (2) enable one skilled in the pertinent art to make or carry out the invention, (3) enable one skilled in the pertinent art to use the invention, and (4) set forth the best mode of carrying out the invention contemplated by the inventor.[254]

If the specification does not fulfill each of the four requirements above, the inventor must add new matter to the specification. Adding new matter causes the inventor to lose the original filing date, which, in turn, might cause an inventor to lose the right to obtain a patent because of prior art published, patented, or that otherwise became available during the intervening time, or because a statutory time bar arose.[255] Based on the same rationale, under 35 U.S.C. §120, a sufficient disclosure is also

---

[252]Eaton Corp. v. Rockwell Int'l Corp., 323 F.3d 1332, 1344–45, 66 USPQ2d 1271 (Fed. Cir. 2003); Gambro Lundia AB v. Baxter Healthcare Corp., 110 F.3d 1573, 1575–78, 42 USPQ2d 1378 (Fed. Cir. 1997); Price v. Symsek, 988 F.2d 1187, 1190, 26 USPQ2d 1031 (Fed. Cir. 1993). The communication must be sufficient to allow one of ordinary skill in the art to construct and successfully operate the invention. *Gambra Lundia AB*, 110 F.3d at 1577–78, 42 USPQ2d 1378.

[253]Festo Corp. v. Shoketsu Kinzoku Kogyo Kabushiki Co., 535 U.S. 722, 736, 62 USPQ2d 1705 (2002); MPEP §2162, *available at* http://www.uspto.gov/web/offices/pac/mpep/mpep .htm.

[254]35 U.S.C. §112, ¶1.

[255]Anascape, Ltd. v. Nintendo of America, 601 F.3d 1333, 1341–42, 94 USPQ2d 1627 (Fed. Cir. 2010) (Gajarsa, J. concurring); Reiffin v. Microsoft Corp. 214 F.3d 1342, 1345–46, 54 USPQ2d 1915 (Fed. Cir. 2000).

necessary to claim priority to an earlier-filed U.S. patent application.[256] Not surprisingly, therefore, when the sufficiency of a disclosure is challenged, inventors try to show that the specification fulfills the four requirements above.

1. Description of the Invention Sought to Be Patented

The inventor must describe in the specification the invention covered by the claims. This requirement to describe the invention is separate and distinct from the enablement requirement:

> [A] separate requirement to describe one's invention is basic to patent law. Every patent must describe an invention. It is part of the *quid pro quo* of a patent; one describes an invention, and, if the law's other requirements are met, one obtains a patent. The specification must then, of course, describe how to make and use the invention (*i.e.*, enable it), but that is a different task. A description of the claimed invention allows the United States Patent and Trademark Office ("PTO") to examine applications effectively; courts to understand the invention, determine compliance with the statute, and to construe the claims; and the public to understand and improve upon the invention and to avoid the claimed boundaries of the patentee's exclusive rights.[257]

Although it is not necessary for the specification to describe word for word what is in the claims, the specification and drawings must reasonably convey to those skilled in the art that the inventor was in possession, at the time the specification was filed, of what is in the claims. In its 2010 en banc decision in *Ariad Pharmaceuticals, Inc. v. Eli Lilly Co.*, the court elaborated that "possession" means possession as evidenced by disclosure:

> The term "possession," however, has never been very enlightening. It implies that as long as one can produce records documenting a written description of a claimed invention, one can show possession. But the hallmark of written description is disclosure. Thus,

---

[256] *See, e.g.,* Vas-Cath Inc. v. Mahurkar, 935 F.2d 1555, 1559, 19 USPQ2d 1111 (Fed. Cir. 1991).
[257] Ariad Pharms., Inc. v. Eli Lilly & Co., 598 F.3d 1336, 1343–48, 94 USPQ2d 1161 (Fed. Cir. 2010) (en banc), *Id.*

"possession as shown in the disclosure" is a more complete formulation. Yet whatever the specific articulation, the test requires an objective inquiry into the four corners of the specification from the perspective of a person of ordinary skill in the art. Based on that inquiry, the specification must describe an invention understandable to that skilled artisan and show that the inventor actually invented the invention claimed.[258]

Written description issues arise in two primary contexts. First, there is the issue of whether the disclosure of a limited number of embodiments is sufficient to support broader claims, either original claims or claims as amended during prosecution.[259] Second, where the patent at issue is a continuation of an earlier application, the issue is whether the claims of the continuation are entitled to the priority date of a parent application. By statute, this determination turns on whether the subject matter of the continuation claims was adequately disclosed in the parent.[260]

Because the claims are an integral part of the specification, whatever is described in the original claims as filed in the PTO may suffice to satisfy the written description requirement, provided that those claims were adequately supported by the remainder of the specification.[261] Reference in the specification to a deposit in a public depository is an adequate description of the

---

[258] *Ariad Pharms.*, 598 F.3d at 1351, 94 USPQ2d 1161; *see also Moba, B.V.*, 325 F.3d at 1320–21, 66 USPQ2d 1429; Purdue Pharma L.P. v. Faulding Inc., 230 F.3d 1320, 1323, 1328–29, 56 USPQ2d 1481 (Fed. Cir. 2000). Proof of actual possession without an adequate description in the specification is not sufficient. *Enzo Biochem, Inc.*, 323 F.3d at 969, 63 USPQ2d 1609, 1618.

[259] *See, e.g., Ariad Pharms., Inc.* 598 F.3d at 1354–58, 94 USPQ2d 1161; Crown Packaging Tech., Inc. v. Ball Metal Beverage Container Corp., 635 F.3d 1373, 1380–83, 98 USPQ2d 1244 (Fed. Cir. 2011); Centocor Ortho Biotech, Inc. v. Abbott Labs., 636 F.3d. 1341, 1348, 97 USPQ2d 1870 (Fed. Cir. 2011); LizardTech, Inc. v. Earth Res. Mapping, Inc., 424 F.3d 1336, 1344–46, 76 USPQ2d 1724 (Fed. Cir. 2005); University of Rochester v. G. D. Searle & Co., 358 F.3d 916, 927–28, 69 USPQ2d 1886 (Fed. Cir.), *cert. denied*, 543 U.S. 1015 (2004); Regents of Univ. of Cal. v. Eli Lilly & Co., 119 F.3d 1559, 1566–69, 43 USPQ2d 1398 (Fed. Cir. 1997), *cert. denied*, 523 U.S. 1089 (1998); *In re* Wallach, 378 F.3d 1330, 1334 (Fed. Cir. 2004). In the context of claims amended in a reissue application, see Revolution Eyewear, Inc. v. Aspex Eyewear, Inc., 563 F.3d 1358, 1366–67, 90 USPQ2d 1733 (Fed. Cir. 2009).

[260] 35 U.S.C. §120; Lockwood v. American Airlines Inc., 107 F.3d 1565, 1571–72, 41 USPQ2d 1961 (Fed. Cir. 1997); Vas-Cath Inc. v. Mahurkar, 935 F.2d 1555, 19 USPQ2d 1111 (Fed. Cir. 1991); *see, e.g., Anascape, Ltd.*, 601 F.3d at 1337–40, 94 USPQ2d 1627; PowerOasis, Inc. v. T-Mobile USA, Inc., 522 F.3d 1299, 1305–10, 86 USPQ2d 1385 (Fed. Cir. 2008).

[261] *Ariad Pharms., Inc.*, 598 F.3d at 1349, 94 USPQ2d 1161.

deposited biological material.[262] Depending on the circumstances, drawings may provide an adequate written description.[263]

In *Ariad Pharmaceuticals, Inc.,* the Federal Circuit emphasized that the written description inquiry is fact-intensive:

> The law must be applied to each invention at the time it enters the patent process, for each patented advance has a novel relationship with the state of the art from which it emerges. Thus, we do not try here to predict and adjudicate all the factual scenarios to which the written description requirement could be applied. Nor do we set out any bright-line rules governing, for example, the number of species that must be disclosed to describe a genus claim, as this number necessarily changes with each invention, and it changes with progress in a field.[264]

The court summarized the controlling principles as follows:

> There are, however, a few broad principles that hold true across all cases. We have made clear that the written description requirement does not demand either examples or an actual reduction to practice; a constructive reduction to practice that in a definite way identifies the claimed invention can satisfy the written description requirement. Conversely, we have repeatedly stated that actual "possession" or reduction to practice outside of the specification is not enough. Rather, as stated above, it is the specification itself that must demonstrate possession. And while the description requirement does not demand any particular form of disclosure, or that the specification recite the claimed invention *in haec verba,* a description that merely renders the invention obvious does not satisfy the requirement.[265]

The PTO has published detailed guidelines relating to the written description requirement, outlining recurring factual patterns.[266]

---

[262] *Enzo Biochem, Inc.,* 323 F.3d at 965, 63 USPQ2d 1609, 1618. Functional descriptions of genetic material might satisfy the written-description requirement. *Id.* at 964, 63 USPQ2d 1609; *Amgen Inc.,* 314 F.3d at 1332, 65 USPQ2d 1385.

[263] *See, e.g., Vas-Cath Inc.,* 935 F.2d at 1564–65, 19 USPQ2d 1111 (Fed. Cir. 1991); Bradford Co. v. Conteyor North America, Inc., 603 F.3d 1262, 1268–69, 94 USPQ2d 1917 (Fed. Cir. 2010).

[264] *Ariad Pharms., Inc.,* 598 F.3d at 1351–52, 94 USPQ2d 1161.

[265] *Id.* at 1352 (citations omitted).

[266] *See* MPEP § 2163, *available at* http://www.uspto.gov/web/offices/pac/mpep/mpep.htm.

2. Enabling One Skilled in the Pertinent Art to Make or Carry Out the Invention

In addition to describing the invention, as set forth in the previous section, the disclosure of a patent must enable one skilled in the pertinent art to make the claimed product or carry out the claimed process without undue experimentation.[267]

The enablement requirement applies to the invention as claimed. Thus, a patent applicant who obtains broad claims must be prepared to defend the proposition that the full scope of those claims has been enabled.[268]

Three questions arise in determining whether the inventor's specification enables one skilled in the pertinent art to make or carry out the invention without undue experimentation: (a) How much does the Section 112 hypothetical person skilled in the pertinent art know? (b) At what point in time must the specification be enabling? (c) What is undue experimentation?[269]

How much does the Section 112 hypothetical person skilled in the pertinent art know? What the Section 112 hypothetical person knows usually can be left out of the specification.[270] The Section 112 hypothetical person is presumed to know only what is generally and reasonably available to the U.S. public.[271] The Section 112 hypothetical person is not presumed to know as much as the earlier discussed Section 103 hypothetical person, who is presumed to know all the prior art relevant to the nonobvious determination, including some material not publicly available.[272] The knowledge of the Section 112 hypothetical person, however, cannot be used to supply the patentable aspects of

---

[267] *See, e.g.,* Alza Corp. v. Andrx Pharms, LLC, 603 F.3d 935, 940–41, 94 USPQ2d 1823 (Fed. Cir. 2010); Enzo Biochem Inc. v. Calgene Inc., 188 F.3d 1362, 1371, 52 USPQ2d 1129 (Fed. Cir. 1999).

[268] Auto. Techs. Int'l Inc. v. BMW of N. Am., Inc., 501 F.3d 1274, 1285, 84 USPQ2d 1108 (Fed. Cir. 2007); Liebel-Flarsheim Co. v. Medrad, Inc., 481 F.3d 1371, 1380, 82 USPQ2d 1113 (Fed. Cir. 2007).

[269] *See generally* MPEP §2164, *available at* http://www.uspto.gov/web/offices/pac/mpep/mpep.htm.

[270] *In re* Buchner, 929 F.2d, 660, 661, 18 USPQ2d 1331 (Fed. Cir. 1991); Hybritech, Inc. v. Monoclonal Antibodies, Inc., 802 F.2d 1367, 1384, 231 USPQ 81 (Fed. Cir. 1986), *cert. denied,* 480 U.S. 947 (1987).

[271] *In re* Howarth, 654 F.2d 103, 210 USPQ 689 (C.C.P.A. 1981).

[272] 3 DONALD S. CHISUM, CHISUM ON PATENTS §7.03[2] (2010).

an invention.[273] For example, when the claimed invention is the application of unpredictable technology in an early stage of development, an enabling disclosure must provide a specific teaching, not a starting point for further research.[274]

At what point in time must the specification be enabling? The specification must be enabling when it is filed.[275] Therefore, if the specification is enabling only in light of something that happens after filing, then it does not satisfy Section 112.[276] A major exception to the requirement that the specification be enabling when filed is allowed when the specification indicates that the inventor can and will make the specification enabling when a patent is granted.[277] For example, if the invention requires using a trade secret that cannot be disclosed, such as a microorganism, Section 112 is satisfied if the inventor agrees to make the trade secret available to the public at the time the patent issues.

What is undue experimentation? A specification that requires some experimentation to make or carry out the invention can be enabling.[278] For example, if carrying out a process requires adjusting a parameter depending on the altitude at which the process is carried out, Section 112 would be satisfied even though some experimentation might be necessary to determine what the parameter should be for a particular altitude.

A specification is not enabling if it requires a level of experimentation that is unreasonable under the circumstances.[279]

---

[273] Genentech Inc. v. Novo Nordisk A/S, 108 F.3d 1361, 1366–68, 42 USPQ2d 1001 (Fed. Cir.), *cert. denied*, 522 U.S. 963 (1997).

[274] *Id.*

[275] Chiron Corp. v. Genentech, Inc., 363 F.3d 1247, 1254, 70 USPQ2d 1321 (Fed. Cir. 2004), *cert. denied*, 543 U.S. 1050 (2005); Union Carbide Chem. & Plastic Tech v. Shell Oil, 308 F.3d 1167, 1185, 64 USPQ2d 1545 (Fed. Cir. 2002).

[276] *See, e.g.,* Gould v. Quigg, 822 F.2d 1074, 1078, 3 USPQ2d 1302 (Fed. Cir. 1987).

[277] *In re* Wands, 858 F.2d 731, 8 USPQ2d 1400 (Fed. Cir. 1988); *In re* Lundak, 773 F.2d 1216, 227 USPQ 90 (Fed. Cir. 1985).

[278] Moba, B.V. v. Diamond Automation, Inc., 325 F.3d 1306, 1321, 66 USPQ2d 1429 (Fed. Cir.), *cert. denied*, 540 U.S. 982 (2003); National Recovery v. Magnetic Separation Sys., 166 F.3d 1190, 1197, 49 USPQ2d 1671 (Fed. Cir. 1999).

[279] *Ex parte* Forman, 230 USPQ 546 (B.P.A.I.); *see, e.g.,* Adang v. Fischhoff, 286 F.3d 1346, 1355–58, 62 USPQ2d 1504 (Fed. Cir. 2002) (undue experimentation required). For a list of illustrative, nonmandatory factors that may be considered in determining whether a specification would require undue experimentation, see *Enzo Biochem Inc.*, 188 F.3d at 1371, 52 USPQ2d 1129.

For example, if the invention requires the use of a computer doing X and the inventor does not supply the computer program that causes the computer to do X, Section 112 would not be satisfied if programming a computer to do X would require years of effort.[280]

3. Enabling One Skilled in the Pertinent Art to Use the Invention

The Section 112 requirement that the specification enable one skilled in the pertinent art to use the invention incorporates the utility condition of patentability (discussed in this chapter, §I.B).[281] Thus, an invention that does not satisfy the utility condition because the invention does not work will not satisfy Section 112's enable-to-use requirement.[282] On the other hand, the fact that an invention satisfies the utility condition does not mean it will satisfy the enable-to-use requirement. For example, a compound may be useful if it restores hair growth, but if the patent applicant claims the way the compound restores hair growth, then enabling one to use this compound requires a disclosure of actual observation that the compound works that way or a disclosure from which one of ordinary skill would necessarily conclude that it works that way.[283]

4. Best Mode Contemplated by the Inventor

The inventor must disclose in the specification the best mode of carrying out the claimed invention contemplated by

---

[280]White Consol. Indus. v. Vega Servo-Control, 713 F.2d 788, 790–92, 218 USPQ 961 (Fed. Cir. 1983). *See also* Northern Telecom, Inc. v. Datapoint Corp., 908 F.2d 931, 941–43, 15 USPQ2d 1321 (Fed. Cir.), *cert. denied*, 498 U.S. 920 (1990).

[281]*In re* Fisher, 421 F.3d 1365, 1378–79, 76 USPQ2d 1225 (Fed. Cir. 2005). *See, e.g., In re* '318 Patent Infringement Litig. 583 F.3d 1317, 1327, 92 USPQ2d 1385 (Fed. Cir. 2009).

[282]*Fisher,* 421 F.3d at 1378–79, 76 USPQ2d 1225.

[283]Ortho-McNeil Pharm., Inc. v. Mylan Labs., Inc., 520 F.3d 1358, 1365, 86 USPQ2d 1196 (Fed. Cir. 2008); *In re* Cortright, 165 F.3d 1353, 49 USPQ2d 1464 (Fed. Cir. 1999). A claim to using this compound to restore hair growth was enabled by examples that disclosed the amount of compound to apply and the amount of time to apply it. *Id.*

the inventor at the time of filing.[284] The purpose of the best mode requirement is to keep an inventor from concealing from the public preferred embodiments that the inventor has conceived.[285] Thus, for example, if the inventor knows or believes that a claimed method is best when run at seven degrees Fahrenheit, then the inventor must disclose this.

There are two factual issues involved in determining whether the best mode requirement was met: (1) Did the inventor have a best mode of practicing the claimed invention at the time the invention was filed (a subjective determination) and, if so, (2) was that best mode disclosed in sufficient detail to allow one with ordinary skill to practice the invention without undue experimentation (an objective determination).[286] The first inquiry is satisfied if the inventor believed that the disclosed mode was the best mode, even if it was not the best mode in reality.[287] The best mode contemplated at the time of filing must be disclosed even if further testing to perfect the invention is ongoing.[288]

For the second inquiry, disclosure of particular manufacturing procedures is not necessarily required,[289] and disclosing the function of software is generally sufficient when software must be

---

[284] *See generally* MPEP §2165, *available at* http://www.uspto.gov/web/offices/pac/mpep/mpep.htm; Zygo Corp. v. Wyko Corp., 79 F.3d 1563, 1566–68, 38 USPQ2d 1281 (Fed. Cir. 1996); Glaxo Inc. v. Novopharm Ltd., 52 F.3d 1043, 1049–52, 34 USPQ2d 1565 (Fed. Cir.), *cert. denied*, 516 U.S. 988 (1995). If the named inventors are subsequently corrected, the best mode requirement applies to the corrected inventors. Pannu v. Iolab Corp., 155 F.3d 1344, 1351 n.5, 47 USPQ2d 1657 (Fed. Cir. 1998). Only the best mode of practicing the *claimed* invention needs to be disclosed. Cardiac Pacemakers, Inc. v. St. Jude Med., Inc., 381 F.3d 1371, 1379, 72 USPQ2d 1333 (Fed. Cir. 2004), *cert. denied*, 544 U.S. 1032 (2005).

[285] Bayer AG v. Schein Pharms., Inc., 301 F.3d 1306, 1316, 64 USPQ2d 1001 (Fed. Cir. 2002); United States Gypsum Co. v. National Gypsum Co., 74 F.3d 1209, 1215, 37 USPQ2d 1388 (Fed. Cir. 1996).

[286] High Concrete Structures, Inc. v. New Enter. Stone & Lime Co., 377 F.3d 1379, 1382–83, 71 USPQ2d 1948 (Fed. Cir. 2004); *Bayer AG*, 301 F.3d at 1320, 64 USPQ2d 1001; *Eli Lilly & Co.*, 251 F.3d at 963, 58 USPQ2d 1865; Robotic Vision Sys. v. View Eng'g Inc., 112 F.3d 1163, 1165, 42 USPQ2d 1619 (Fed. Cir. 1997). Of course, prior to answering these questions, the first task is to determine the *claimed* invention, i.e., to construe the claims at issue. *Bayer AG*, 301 F.3d at 1320, 64 USPQ2d 1001. For further discussion of claim construction, see Chapter 5.

[287] *See, e.g.*, Engel Indus., Inc. v. Lockformer Co., 946 F.2d 1528, 1531–33, 20 USPQ2d 1300 (Fed. Cir. 1991).

[288] *See* Wellman, Inc. v. Eastman Chem. Co., 642 F.3d 1355, 1362, 98 USPQ2d 1505 (Fed. Cir. 2011).

[289] Teleflex, Inc. v. Ficosa N. Am. Corp., 299 F.3d 1313, 1331–32, 63 USPQ2d 1374 (Fed. Cir. 2002); *United States Gypsum Co.*, 74 F.3d at 1213, 37 USPQ2d 1388.

disclosed.[290] Preferred subject matter that is unclaimed, but novel and involved in the best mode of carrying out the claimed invention, must be disclosed.[291] Preferred subject matter that is not novel, but is a part of the claimed invention, must be disclosed.[292] As a result, an inventor may be required to disclose preferred subject matter without any right to exclude others from using the subject matter other than in the context of the claimed invention.[293] It may be necessary to update the best mode disclosure under certain circumstances.[294]

Under the Leahy-Smith America Invents Act, the requirement that the patent applicant disclose the best mode is retained for purposes of proceedings in the PTO. However, the failure to disclose the best mode is eliminated as an invalidity defense in patent litigation. This provision applies to all infringement actions commenced on or after September 16, 2011.[295]

D. Definite Claims

Because others look to the patent's claims to determine what cannot be done without the patent owner's permission,[296] 35 U.S.C. §112, ¶2 requires that the claims must "particularly point out and distinctly claim the invention."[297] Section 112, ¶2 also requires that the issued claim must set forth what the applicant regards as his or her invention.[298]

---

[290] *Robotic Vision Sys.*, 112 F.3d at 1166, 42 USPQ2d 1619; Fonar Corp. v. General Elec. Co., 107 F.3d 1543, 1549, 41 USPQ2d 1801 (Fed. Cir.), *cert. denied*, 522 U.S. 908 (1997).

[291] Eli Lilly & Co. v. Barr Labs., Inc., 251 F.3d 955, 964–67, 58 USPQ2d 1869 (Fed. Cir. 2001); *see also Bayer AG*, 301 F.3d at 1322, 64 USPQ2d 1001.

[292] Ajinomoto Co. v. Int'l Trade Comm'n, 597 F.3d 1267, 1274, 94 USPQ2d 1055 (Fed. Cir. 2010) ("[B]est mode . . . applies to . . . all [claim] limitations, not just the novel ones"); *see Bayer AG*, 301 F.3d at 1316–30, 1323–28, 64 USPQ2d 1001 (no best mode violation where unclaimed, undisclosed process did not materially affect the claimed product).

[293] *See Ajinomoto Co.*, 597 F.3d at 1274–75, 94 USPQ2d 1055 (Fed. Cir. 2010).

[294] *See* Applied Materials v. Advanced Semiconductor Materials, 98 F.3d 1563, 1575–84, 40 USPQ2d 1481 (Fed. Cir. 1996), *cert. denied*, 520 U.S. 1230 (1997); Transco Prods. Inc. v. Performance Contracting Inc., 38 F.3d 551, 32 USPQ2d 1077 (Fed. Cir. 1994), *cert. denied*, 513 U.S. 1151 (1995).

[295] *See* Leahy-Smith America Invents Act, Pub.L. 112-29, H.R. 1249 (2011), sec. 15, amending 35 U.S.C. §282.

[296] Athletic Alternatives Inc. v. Prince Mfg. Inc., 73 F.3d 1573, 1581, 37 USPQ2d 1365 (Fed. Cir. 1996).

[297] 35 U.S.C. §112, ¶2; Halliburton Energy Servs., Inc. v. M-I LLC, 514 F.3d 1244, 1249, 85 USPQ2d 1654 (Fed. Cir. 2008).

[298] Solomon v. Kimberly-Clark Corp., 216 F.3d 1372, 1377–80, 55 USPQ2d 1279 (Fed. Cir. 2000).

An issued claim is sufficiently definite if, when read in light of the specification, it reasonably apprises one of ordinary skill in the art of the scope of the invention.[299] The statutory requirement does not mean that claims must be as precise or specific as possible.[300]

With respect to claims that describe an invention in terms of its function, definiteness turns on whether the patent complies with 35 U.S.C. §112, ¶6. That section permits functional claiming language, but limits the scope of the claim element to the structure disclosed in the specification for performing the claimed function, and equivalents thereof. If the specification does not sufficiently identify structure to perform the claimed function, then the claim is invalid for indefiniteness.[301] For example, the disclosure that a claimed function may be performed by a programmed computer or software without disclosure of the program itself, may not suffice.[302]

A claim may describe a product by the way that it is made (a "product-by-process" claim).[303] However, a single claim that

---

[299] *See generally* MPEP §§ 2171–73, *available at* http://www.uspto.gov/web/offices/pac/mpep/mpep.htm; Halliburton Energy Servs., Inc. v. M-I LLC, 514 F.3d 1244, 85 USPQ2d 1654 (Fed. Cir. 2008); Amgen Inc. v. Chugai Pharm. Co., 927 F.2d 1200, 1217–18, 18 USPQ2d 1016 (Fed. Cir.), *cert. denied*, 502 U.S. 856 (1991). If a claim meets the enablement requirements, it is not indefinite if some experimentation is necessary to determine the *scope* of the claim. Exxon Research & Eng'g Co. v. United States, 265 F.3d 1371, 1378–80, 60 USPQ2d 1272 (Fed. Cir. 2001); *see also* Capon v. Eshhar, 418 F.3d 1349, 1360, 76 USPQ2d 1078 (Fed. Cir. 2005).

[300] PPG Indus. v. Guardian Indus. Corp., 156 F.3d 1351, 1355, 48 USPQ2d 1351 (Fed. Cir. 1998); Oakley, Inc. v. Sunglass Hut Int'l, 316 F.3d 1331, 1341, 65 USPQ2d 1321 (Fed. Cir. 2003).

[301] *In re* Donaldson Co., 16 F.3d 1189, 1195, 29 USPQ2d 1845 (Fed. Cir. 1994) (en banc); Default Proof Credit Card Sys., Inc. v. Home Depot, U.S.A., Inc., 412 F.3d 1291, 1298, 75 USPQ2d 1116 (Fed. Cir. 2005); *see generally* MPEP §2181, *available at* http://www.uspto.gov/web/offices/pac/mpep/mpep.htm. An invention claimed as a means for performing a function without more (a "single means") claim is indefinite, because it inherently seeks to claim all means of performing that function. Section 112 ¶6 only applies where an element of the claim, as opposed to the entire claim, is set forth in "means" language. *In re* Hyatt, 708 F.2d 712,714–15,218 USPQ 195 (Fed. Cir. 1983).

[302] Blackboard, Inc. v. Desrie2Learn Inc., 574 F.3d 1371, 1382-85 (Fed. Cir. 2009); Aristocrat Techs. Austl. Pty. Ltd. v. International Game Tech. 521 F.3d 1328, 1331, 86 USPQ2d 1235 (Fed. Cir.), *cert. denied*, 555 U.S. 1070 (2008). Net MoneyIN, Inc. v. VeriSign, Inc., 545 F.3d 1359, 1367, 88 USPQ2d 1751 (Fed. Cir. 2008).

[303] *In re* Luck, 476 F.2d 650, 177 USPQ 523 (C.C.P.A. 1973); Abbott Labs. v. Sandoz, Inc., 566 F.3d 1282, 1291-94, 90 USPQ2d 1769 (Fed. Cir. 2009) (en banc) ("process" limitations are substantive, such that infringement requires a finding that the product is made by the claimed process), *cert. denied sub nom.* Astellas Pharma, Inc. v. Lupin Ltd., 130 S. Ct. 1052 (2010).

combines product elements and process elements describing how the product is to be used is indefinite.[304]

A claim is not necessarily indefinite if it contains words of "degree,"[305] is susceptible to both a broad and a narrow meaning,[306] the parties disagree on the meaning of the claim,[307] construing the claim is difficult,[308] the claim covers some inoperable embodiments,[309] or the claim has a drafting error that has multiple reasonable and possible corrections.[310]

A claim is indefinite only if it is not amenable to claim construction or is "insolubly ambiguous."[311]

III. Changes to the Law of Validity Under the Leahy-Smith America Invents Act

A. "Effective Filing Date"

As discussed in §I.C. of this chapter, under the current patent statute, there are essentially two temporal triggers for public use, sale, patenting or publication to become "prior art": the date of "invention" by the applicant for patent and the statutory

---

[304] IPXL Holdings, LLC v. Amazon.com, Inc., 430 F.3d 1377, 1383–84,77 USPQ2d 1140 (Fed. Cir. 2005); Rembrandt Data Technologies, LP v. AOL, LLC, 641 F.3d. 1331, 98 USPQ2d 1393 (Fed. Cir. 2011).

[305] Young v. Lumenis, Inc., 492 F.3d 1336, 1345–46, 83 USPQ2d 1191 (Fed. Cir. 2007).

[306] Digital Biometrics Inc. v. Identix Inc., 149 F.3d 1335, 1344, 47 USPQ2d 1418 (Fed. Cir. 1998).

[307] North Am. Vaccine v. American Cyanamid Co., 7 F.3d 1571, 1579, 28 USPQ2d 1333 (Fed. Cir. 1993), *cert. denied,* 511 U.S. 1069 (1994).

[308] Datamize, LLC v. Plumtree Software, Inc., 417 F.3d 1342, 1347, 75 USPQ2d 1801 (Fed. Cir. 2005); Bancorp Servs., LLC v. Hartford Life Ins. Co., 359 F.3d 1367, 1372, 69 USPQ2d 1996 (Fed. Cir. 2004); *Exxon Research & Eng'g Co.,* 265 F.3d at 1375, 60 USPQ2d 1272.

[309] *Id.* at 1382 (inoperable embodiments is an enablement issue). For more on inoperable embodiments, see generally *Crown Operations, Int'l Ltd. v. Solutia Inc.,* 289 F.3d 1367, 1380–81, 62 USPQ2d 1917 (Fed. Cir. 2002).

[310] CBT Flint Partners, LLC. v. Return Path, Inc., 654 F.3d 1353, 1358–59, 99 USPQ2d 1610 (Fed. Cir. 2011).

[311] Enzo Biochem, Inc. v. Applera Corp., 599 F.3d 1325, 1332–36, 94 USPQ2d 1321 (Fed. Cir. 2010), *cert. denied,* No. 10-426, 2011 WL 2437054 (U.S. 2011); *Halliburton Energy Servs., Inc.,* 514 F.3d at 1250, 85 USPQ2d 1654; *Datamize, LLC,* 417 F.3d at 1347–48, 75 USPQ2d 1801.

bar date, one year before the filing of the application for patent. This is commonly called a "first to invent" system.

The Leahy Smith America Invents Act will, in time, shift the "first to invent" system of determining patent validity to one based on the "first inventor to file" an application for patent.

New 35 U.S.C. §100(i) defines the reference date—the "effective filing date"—as follows:

> (i) (1) The term "effective filing date" for a claimed invention or an application for patent means—
>
>   (A) if subparagraph (B) does not apply, the actual filing date of the patent or the application for the patent containing a claim to the invention; or
>
>   (B) the filing date of the earliest application for which the patent or application is entitled, as to such invention, to a right of priority under section 119, 365(a), or 365(b) or to the benefit of an earlier filing date under section 120, 121 or 365(c).
>
> (2) The effective filing date for a claimed invention in an application for reissue or reissued patent shall be determined by deeming the claim to the invention to have been contained in the patent for which reissue was sought.[312]

Thus, the presumptive priority date will be the filing date of the patent application, unless the patent applicants can demonstrate that they are entitled to the benefit of the filing date of an earlier application. The entitlement to an earlier filing date is analyzed on a claim-by-claim basis.[313]

---

[312] Leahy-Smith America Invents Act, Pub.L. 112-29, H.R. 1249 (2011), sec. 3, amending 35 U.S.C. §100.

[313] See generally this chapter, §II.C., which discusses issues of adequacy of disclosure relating to the applicability of 35 U.S.C. §119 and 120. 35 U.S.C. §365 contains parallel provisions for international applications filed under the Patent Cooperation Treaty.

B. Novelty Under the New §102

The full text of revised 35 U.S.C. §102 is set forth in the Addendum to this chapter.

Under Section 102(a)(1), an invention is not novel if "the claimed invention was patented, described in a printed publication, or in public use, on sale or otherwise available to the public before the effective filing date of the claimed invention." The act thus retains the categories of acts that might defeat novelty from the old Section 102(a) and (b), but changes the reference date to the effective filing date for that claim.[314]

The statute removes all geographical limitations on where the prior acts occurred. It is no longer necessary that prior "public use" or "on sale" activity be "in the United States." However, the statute codifies the requirement that, for an act to defeat novelty, the information must have been "available to the public."[315]

Under Section 102(a)(2), a patent or a published patent application has the prior art date of its effective filing date, provided that it names "another inventor."[316] The concept of who is "another inventor" is discussed in the context of the current 35 U.S.C. §102(e), in this chapter, §I.C.2.

C. Statutory Bar: The Revised One-Year Grace Period for the Inventor's Own Work

The current version of 35 U.S.C. §102(b) provides a one-year grace period based on the acts of either the inventor or a third party, as described in this chapter, §II.B.1.

The amended statute continues the grace period in Section 102(b), but only for information that was disclosed by "the

---

[314] Leahy-Smith America Invents Act, Pub.L. 112-29, H.R. 1249 (2011), sec. 3, amending 35 U.S.C. §102.

[315] *Id.; see also* H.R. Rep. No. 112-98 (2011), at 42–43.

[316] Leahy-Smith America Invents Act, Pub.L. 112-29, H.R. 1249 (2011), sec. 3, amending 35 U.S.C. §102(a).

inventor or joint inventor or another who obtained the subject matter directly or indirectly from the inventor or joint inventor."[317]

With respect to disclosures by third parties in patents and patent applications, Section 102(b)(2)(A) and (B) exclude from the prior art information that was "obtained ... directly or indirectly from the inventor or joint inventor" of the patent at issue, or if inventors had previously triggered the one-year grace period by disclosing the information themselves.[318]

Finally, Section 102(b)(2)(C) excludes from the prior art information that was disclosed in a patent application that, on the effective date of the patent at issue, was "owned by the same person or subject to an obligation of assignment to the same person."[319] This continues the statutory exemption for co-workers within a research organization, as set forth in the current Section 103(c)(1).

D. Joint Development Work

In addition to the grace period provided for the work of the inventors and their co-workers, the revised Section 102(c) excludes from the prior art those disclosures made by the parties to a joint research agreement that was in effect as of the effective filing date of the claimed invention. This is done by treating the parties to such an agreement as if their work was under common ownership, for purposes of revised Section 102(b)(2)(C). The purpose of these provisions, first added by the CREATE Act of 2004, is to promote joint research activity.[320]

---

[317]Leahy-Smith America Invents Act, Pub.L. 112-29, H.R. 1249 (2011), sec. 3, amending 35 U.S.C. §102(b).

[318]*Id.*

[319]*Id.*

[320]Leahy-Smith America Invents Act, Pub.L. 112-29, H.R. 1249 (2011), sec. 3, amending 35 U.S.C. §102(c); *see also* H.R. Rep. No. 112-98 (2011) at 43. For the CREATE Act of 2004, *see* P.L. 108-453, 118 Stat. 3596, amending then-current 35 U.S.C. §103(c), and 70 Fed. Reg. 54259 (2005).

E. Derivation

Under the current Section 102(f), a person loses the right to a patent if "he did not himself invent the subject matter sought to be patented." The law of "derivation" is discussed in this chapter, §II.B.4.

Under the Smith-Leahy America Invents Act, contests as to priority of inventorship, e.g., interference practice in the PTO or the defense of prior invention under 35 U.S.C. §102(g), are eliminated. However, the act provides two avenues to contest whether the work of an alleged prior inventor was, in fact, "derived from the inventor" of a patent in issue. One avenue is to file a civil action to decide contested allegations of derivation.[321] The second avenue is by bringing a "derivation proceeding" in the PTO.[322]

F. Other Changes

When the new validity provisions take effect, conforming amendments will be made to the remainder of the patent statute. For example, under the current statute, nonobviousness was tested "at the time the invention was made." Under the new statute, the same test will be applied "before the effective filing date of the claimed invention."[323] Provisions relating to inventions made abroad or made in outer space will be abrogated.

As noted earlier in this chapter, §II.C.4, the requirement that the inventor disclose the best mode of practicing the invention is maintained, but a failure to do so is no longer available

---

[321] Leahy-Smith America Invents Act, Pub.L. 112-29, H.R. 1249 (2011), sec. 3, amending 35 U.S.C. §291 ("Derived Patents").

[322] *Id.*, sec. 3, amending 35 U.S.C. §135 ("Derivation Proceedings").

[323] *Id.*, sec. 3. The act also changes the last sentence of 35 U.S.C. §103(a) to read that "Invention shall not be *negated* by the manner in which the invention was made" (emphasis supplied), instead of the formulation that said that invention would not be "negatived." *Id.*, amending 35 U.S.C. §103(a). The House Report states that no substantive change was intended by this particular amendment. H.R. Rep. No. 112-98 (2011) at 43 n.21.

as a defense in litigation. This provision, unlike the changes to Section 102, took effect with the enactment of the America Invents Act on September 16, 2011.[324]

Also immediately effective is a provision that places within the prior art "any strategy for reducing, avoiding or deferring tax liability." Thus, for purposes of determining patentability, a claim directed to such a strategy "shall be deemed insufficient to differentiate a claimed invention" from the art.[325]

G. Effective Date of the "First Inventor to File" Amendments: March 16, 2013

Except for the two provisions noted at the end of the previous section, the new validity provisions will take effect on March 16, 2013, 18 months after the effective date of the act, and will apply to applications that have an "effective filing date" on or after March 16, 2013. Because of the delay inherent in patent prosecution, such patents are unlikely to issue before 2014 at the earliest.

Because the new validity provisions do not affect patents already issued, or that will issue on applications with an effective filing date before March 16, 2013, the currently existing validity provisions will continue to apply for decades to come. A first step in any analysis of patent validity will be to determine which set of statutory provisions applies.

---

[324] Leahy-Smith America Invents Act, Pub.L. 112-29, H.R. 1249 (2011), sec. 15.
[325] *Id.*, sec. 14.

ADDENDUM TO CHAPTER 4

The following is the text of the version of 35 U.S.C. §§102 and 103 that is currently in effect and that will continue to apply to all patent claims with an effective filing date earlier than March 16, 2013:

35 U.S.C. § 102. Conditions for patentability; novelty and loss of right to patent

A person shall be entitled to a patent unless—

(a) the invention was known or used by others in this country, or patented or described in a printed publication in this or a foreign country, before the invention thereof by the applicant for patent, or

(b) the invention was patented or described in a printed publication in this or a foreign country or in public use or on sale in this country, more than one year prior to the date of the application for patent in the United States, or

(c) he has abandoned the invention, or

(d) the invention was first patented or caused to be patented, or was the subject of an inventor's certificate, by the applicant or his legal representatives or assigns in a foreign country prior to the date of the application for patent in this country on an application for patent or inventor's certificate filed more than twelve months before the filing of the application in the United States, or

(e) the invention was described in (1) an application for patent, published under section 122(b), by another filed in the United States before the invention by the applicant for patent or (2) a patent granted on an application for patent by another filed in the United States before the invention by the applicant for patent, except that an international application filed under the treaty defined in section 351(a) shall have the effects for the purposes of this subsection of an application filed in the United States only if the international application designated the United States and was published under Article 21(2) of such treaty in the English language; or

(f) he did not himself invent the subject matter sought to be patented, or

(g)(1) during the course of an interference conducted under <u>section 135</u> or <u>section 291</u>, another inventor involved therein establishes, to the extent permitted in <u>section 104</u>, that before such person's invention thereof the invention was made by such other inventor and not abandoned, suppressed, or concealed, or

(2) before such person's invention thereof, the invention was made in this country by another inventor who had not abandoned, suppressed, or concealed it. In determining priority of invention under this subsection, there shall be considered not only the respective dates of conception and reduction to practice of the invention, but also the reasonable diligence of one who was first to conceive and last to reduce to practice, from a time prior to conception by the other.

35 U.S.C. § 103. Conditions for patentability; non-obvious subject matter

(a) A patent may not be obtained though the invention is not identically disclosed or described as set forth in <u>section 102</u> of this title, if the differences between the subject matter sought to be patented and the prior art are such that the subject matter as a whole would have been obvious at the time the invention was made to a person having ordinary skill in the art to which said subject matter pertains. Patentability shall not be negatived by the manner in which the invention was made.

(b)(1) Notwithstanding subsection (a), and upon timely election by the applicant for patent to proceed under this subsection, a biotechnological process using or resulting in a composition of matter that is novel under section 102 and nonobvious under subsection (a) of this section shall be considered nonobvious if—

(A) claims to the process and the composition of matter are contained in either the same application for patent or in separate applications having the same effective filing date; and

(B) the composition of matter, and the process at the time it was invented, were owned by the same person or subject to an obligation of assignment to the same person.

(2) A patent issued on a process under paragraph (1)—

(A) shall also contain the claims to the composition of matter used in or made by that process, or

(B) shall, if such composition of matter is claimed in another patent, be set to expire on the same date as such other patent, notwithstanding section 154.

(3) For purposes of paragraph (1), the term "biotechnological process" means—

(A) a process of genetically altering or otherwise inducing a single- or multi-celled organism to—

    (i) express an exogenous nucleotide sequence,

    (ii) inhibit, eliminate, augment, or alter expression of an endogenous nucleotide sequence, or

    (iii) express a specific physiological characteristic not naturally associated with said organism;

(B) cell fusion procedures yielding a cell line that expresses a specific protein, such as a monoclonal antibody; and

(C) a method of using a product produced by a process defined by subparagraph (A) or (B), or a combination of subparagraphs (A) and (B).

(c)(1) Subject matter developed by another person, which qualifies as prior art only under one or more of subsections (e), (f), and (g) of section 102 of this title, shall not preclude patentability under this section where the subject matter and the claimed invention were, at the time the claimed invention was made, owned by the same person or subject to an obligation of assignment to the same person.

(2) For purposes of this subsection, subject matter developed by another person and a claimed invention shall be deemed to have been owned by the same person or subject to an obligation of assignment to the same person if—

(A) the claimed invention was made by or on behalf of parties to a joint research agreement that was in effect on or before the date the claimed invention was made;

(B) the claimed invention was made as a result of activities undertaken within the scope of the joint research agreement; and

(C) The application for patent for the claimed invention discloses or is amended to disclose the names of the parties to the joint research agreement.

(3) For purposes of paragraph (2), the term "joint research agreement" means a written contract, grant, or cooperative agreement entered into by two or more persons or entities for the performance of experimental, developmental, or research work in the field of the claimed invention.

The following is the text of amended 35 U.S.C. §§100(i), 102, and 103, which bear on the determination of validity under the Smith-Leahy America Invents Act. These provisions will apply to patent claims that have an effective filing date on or after March 16, 2013:

[35 U.S.C. § 100 (i)]

"(i)(1) The term 'effective filing date' for a claimed invention in a patent or application for patent means—

"(A) if subparagraph (B) does not apply, the actual filing date of the patent or the application for the patent containing a claim to the invention; or

"(B) the filing date of the earliest application for which the patent or application is entitled, as to such invention, to a right of priority under section 119, 365(a), or 365(b) or to the benefit of an earlier filing date under section 120, 121, or 365(c).

"(2) The effective filing date for a claimed invention in an application for reissue or reissued patent shall be determined by deeming the claim to the invention to have been contained in the patent for which reissue was sought.

35 U.S.C. § 102. Conditions for patentability; novelty

"(a) NOVELTY; PRIOR ART.—A person shall be entitled to a patent unless—

"(1) the claimed invention was patented, described in a printed publication, or in public use, on sale, or otherwise available to the public before the effective filing date of the claimed invention; or

"(2) the claimed invention was described in a patent issued under section 151, or in an application for patent published or deemed published under section 122(b), in which the patent or application, as the case may be, names another inventor and was effectively filed before the effective filing date of the claimed invention.

"(b) EXCEPTIONS.—

"(1) DISCLOSURES MADE 1 YEAR OR LESS BEFORE THE EFFECTIVE FILING DATE OF THE CLAIMED INVENTION.—A disclosure made 1 year or less before the effective filing date of a claimed invention shall not be prior art to the claimed invention under subsection (a)(1) if—

"(A) the disclosure was made by the inventor or joint inventor or by another who obtained the subject matter disclosed directly or indirectly from the inventor or a joint inventor; or

"(B) the subject matter disclosed had, before such disclosure, been publicly disclosed by the inventor or a joint inventor or another who obtained the subject matter disclosed directly or indirectly from the inventor or a joint inventor.

"(2) DISCLOSURES APPEARING IN APPLICA-
TIONS AND PATENTS.—A disclosure shall not
be prior art to a claimed invention under subsection (a)(2) if—

"(A) the subject matter disclosed was obtained
directly or indirectly from the inventor or
a joint inventor;

"(B) the subject matter disclosed had, before
such subject matter was effectively filed
under subsection (a)(2), been publicly disclosed by the inventor or a joint inventor or
another who obtained the subject matter
disclosed directly or indirectly from the
inventor or a joint inventor; or

"(C) the subject matter disclosed and the
claimed invention, not later than the effective filing date of the claimed invention,
were owned by the same person or subject
to an obligation of assignment to the same
person.

"(c) COMMON OWNERSHIP UNDER JOINT RESEARCH
AGREEMENTS.—Subject matter disclosed and a
claimed invention shall be deemed to have been owned
by the same person or subject to an obligation of assignment to the same person in applying the provisions of
subsection (b)(2)(C) if—

"(1) the subject matter disclosed was developed and
the claimed invention was made by, or on behalf
of, 1 or more parties to a joint research agreement that was in effect on or before the effective
filing date of the claimed invention;

"(2) the claimed invention was made as a result of
activities undertaken within the scope of the
joint research agreement; and

"(3) the application for patent for the claimed invention discloses or is amended to disclose the names
of the parties to the joint research agreement.

"(d) PATENTS AND PUBLISHED APPLICATIONS
EFFECTIVE AS PRIOR ART.—For purposes of deter-

mining whether a patent or application for patent is prior art to a claimed invention under subsection (a)(2), such patent or application shall be considered to have been effectively filed, with respect to any subject matter described in the patent or application—

"(1) if paragraph (2) does not apply, as of the actual filing date of the patent or the application for patent; or

"(2) if the patent or application for patent is entitled to claim a right of priority under section 119, 365(a), or 365(b), or to claim the benefit of an earlier filing date under section 120, 121, or 365(c), based upon 1 or more prior filed applications for patent, as of the filing date of the earliest such application that describes the subject matter."

35 U.S.C. § 103. Conditions for patentability; non-obvious subject matter

"A patent for a claimed invention may not be obtained, notwithstanding that the claimed invention is not identically disclosed as set forth in section 102, if the differences between the claimed invention and the prior art are such that the claimed invention as a whole would have been obvious before the effective filing date of the claimed invention to a person having ordinary skill in the art to which the claimed invention pertains. Patentability shall not be negated by the manner in which the invention was made."

CHAPTER 5

CLAIM CONSTRUCTION

I. THE CONTROLLING COURT DECISIONS

The claims of a patent are a description, in words, of the subject matter that applicants for patent regard as their invention. If the patent issues, the PTO awards exclusive rights for the invention, i.e., that which has been claimed.[1] The interpretation of the words or phrases in patent claims is called claim construction.

Claim construction is the linchpin of analyzing most disputes about the validity or infringement of a patent. It is the first step in determining whether the patent, if challenged, satisfies the conditions and requirements of patentability (discussed in Chapter 4) and in determining whether the patent is infringed (discussed in Chapter 6).[2] Given the importance of claim construction, resolution of claim construction issues may resolve the entire dispute between the parties. Under principles of stare decisis, a patent claim, once construed authoritatively by the courts, may also provide guidance as to how that claim should be construed in subsequent cases.[3]

---

[1] 35 U.S.C. §112, ¶2; 35 U.S.C. §154; Phillips v. AWH Corp., 415 F.3d 1303, 1312, 75 USPQ2d 1321 (Fed. Cir. 2005), cert. denied, 546 U.S. 1170 (2006). See also Chapter 4, §II.D.

[2] 35 U.S.C. §271; Markman v. Westview Instruments, Inc., 517 U.S. 370, 373–74, 38 USPQ2d 1461 (1996); see also Chapter 6, §I.C.

[3] Markman, 517 U.S. at 390–91, 38 USPQ2d 1461. A district court will generally consider a claim construction decided in an earlier litigation, but the second court is not compelled to reach the same conclusions. Nilssen v. Motorola, Inc., 80 F. Supp. 2d 921, 924 n.4 (N.D. Ill. 2000); Texas Instruments, Inc. v. Linear Tech. Corp., 182 F. Supp. 2d 580, 589 (E.D. Tex. 2002); Kollmorgen Corp. v. Yaskawa Elec. Corp., 147 F. Supp. 2d 464, 468 (W.D. Va. 2001); KX Indus., L.P. v. PUR Water Purification Prods., Inc., 108 F. Supp. 2d 380 (D. Del. 2000), aff'd, 18 F. App'x 871 (Fed. Cir. 2001). Under conventional principles of collateral estoppel, a court is more likely to apply an earlier construction asserted against a party to the earlier litigation. See, e.g., Mycogen Plant Sci. v. Monsanto Co., 252 F.3d 1306, 1310–11, 58 USPQ2d 1891 (Fed. Cir. 2001); Abbott Labs. v. Dey, L.P., 110 F. Supp. 2d 667, 669–74, 55 USPQ2d 1728 (N.D. Ill. 2000). Where the earlier action terminated short of a final decision, for example, in a settlement after

Before the mid-1990s, there was a division of authority as to whether claim construction was an issue to be resolved by the court as a matter of law or by the finder of fact, which could be either court or jury. In 1995, in *Markman v. Westview Instruments, Inc.*, a divided Federal Circuit decided en banc that claim construction was purely an issue of law, to be decided by the court, and that the Seventh Amendment did not bar courts from treating claim construction as such in cases tried to a jury.[4] In 1996, a unanimous Supreme Court affirmed, but on a different rationale. The Supreme Court found that history and precedent provided "no clear answers" to the constitutional question, and decided based on "functional considerations . . . in the choice between judge and jury to define terms of art."[5] The Court wrote:

> The construction of written instruments is one of those things that judges often do and are likely to do better than jurors unburdened by training in exegesis. Patent construction in particular "is a special occupation, requiring, like all others, special training and practice. The judge, from his training and discipline, is more likely to give a proper interpretation to such instruments than a jury; and he is, therefore, more likely to be right, in performing such a duty, than a jury can be expected to be." Parker v. Hulme, 18 F. Cas., at 1140.[6]

The Supreme Court recognized that claim construction is a task with "evidentiary underpinnings," which might include the resolution of conflicting testimony from experts as to the meaning of claim terms. Nevertheless, the Court stated that "[i]n the main, we expect, any credibility determinations will be subsumed within the necessarily sophisticated analysis of the whole document, required by the standard construction rule that a

---

claim construction, issue preclusion may not be appropriate. Pfizer, Inc. v. Teva Pharms. USA, Inc., 429 F.3d 1364, 1376, 77 USPQ2d 1257 (Fed. Cir. 2005); Dana v. E.S. Originals, Inc., 342 F.3d 1320, 69 USPQ2d 1138 (Fed. Cir. 2003); R.F. Del., Inc. v. Pacific Keystone Techs., Inc., 326 F.3d 1255, 1260–62, 66 USPQ2d 1593 (Fed. Cir. 2003).

[4] 52 F.3d 967, 979, 983–88, 34 USPQ2d 1321 (Fed. Cir. 1995) (en banc), *aff'd*, 517 U.S. 370, 38 USPQ2d 1461 (1996).

[5] *Markman*, 517 U.S. at 388, 38 USPQ2d 1461.

[6] *Id.* at 388–89, 38 USPQ2d 1461; for empirical research regarding claim construction rulings on appeal during 1996–2003, see Kimberly A. Moore, *Markman Eight Years Later: Is Claim Construction More Predictable?*, 9 LEWIS & CLARK L. REV. 231, 233 (2005).

term can be defined only in a way that comports with the instrument as a whole."[7]

In the years following *Markman,* claim construction has been a discrete issue addressed in most appellate decisions in patent cases. A split in authority arose in the early 2000s as to the relative weight to be accorded to the various types of evidence relevant to claim construction, including intrinsic evidence, i.e., the patent itself and its prosecution history, and extrinsic evidence, i.e., dictionaries, technical treatises and testimony from fact and expert witnesses. In 2005, the Federal Circuit's en banc decision in *Phillips v. AWH Corp.* established a comprehensive methodology for claim construction, establishing an evidentiary hierarchy to be followed by courts considering claim construction issues.[8]

Claim construction is reviewed on appeal as a question of law, nominally without deference to the decision of the district court.[9]

II. COMPREHENSIVE CLAIM CONSTRUCTION METHODOLOGY

Many of the issues that arise in claim construction have a history that began long before modern style claims developed.[10] In modern patent claiming practice, which is described as periph-

---

[7] *Markman,* 517 U.S. at 389–90, 38 USPQ2d 1461.

[8] 415 F.3d 1303, 75 USPQ2d 1321 (Fed. Cir. 2005), *cert. denied,* 546 U.S. 1170 (2006).

[9] Arlington Indus., Inc. v. Bridgeport Fittings, Inc., 632 F.3d 1246, 1252–53, 97 USPQ2d 1811 (Fed. Cir. 2011); Cybor Corp. v. FAS Techs., Inc., 138 F.3d 1448, 1456, 46 USPQ2d 1169 (Fed. Cir. 1998). *But see id.* at 1462–63, 46 USPQ2d 1169 (Plager and Bryson, J.J., concurring). The degree of deference due to, and accorded to, claim construction decisions of the district courts has been a controversial issue in the published decisions of the Federal Circuit; *see id.* at 1463–66, 46 USPQ2d 1169 (Mayer, C.J., dissenting), 138 F.3d at 1473–78, 46 USPQ2d 1169 (Rader, J., dissenting), and 138 F.3d at 1478–81, 46 USPQ2d 1169 (Newman, J., additional views); *Phillips,* 415 F.3d at 1328, 75 USPQ2d 1321 (majority opinion) and 415 F.3d at 1330–35, 75 USPQ2d 1321 (Mayer, J., dissenting), 75 USPQ 2d 1321; Amgen Inc. v. Hoechst Marion Roussel, Inc., 469 F.3d 1039, 80 USPQ2d 1944 (Fed. Cir. 2006) (order on petition for rehearing en banc).

[10] The complex history of the evolution of modern patent claims (which involved the actions and reactions of applicants, the federal courts, the Patent Office, and the Congress) is beyond the scope of this monograph. For a thorough review, see Karl B. Lutz, *Evolution of the Claims of U.S. Patents* [in three parts], 20 J. PAT. & TRADEMARK OFF. SOC'Y 134, 377, 457 (1938); *see also* RIDSDALE ELLIS, PATENT CLAIMS §§1–10 (1949); Warren T. Jessup, *The Doctrine of Equivalents,* 54 J. PAT. & TRADEMARK OFF. SOC'Y 248, 252–62 (1972); ANTHONY W. DELLER, PATENT CLAIMS §§1–11 (2d ed. 1971).

eral claiming,[11] the claims define the metes and bounds of a patented invention in the same way that a deed to property describes the borders between adjacent tracts of land.[12]

Because modern claims define the scope of the patented invention, interpreting the words used in a claim explains the scope of the claim.[13] Thus, claim construction can be described in various ways. For example, it has been described as giving the language of the claims its meaning,[14] as determining the scope of the claims,[15] and as determining both the meaning and scope of the claims.[16]

---

[11] Before 1900, applicants generally practiced central claiming. In central claiming, a narrow claim that used reference characters to point out an embodiment of the invention was set forth and a phrase (such as "substantially as described") was added at the end of the claim to refer back to the specification. Initially, the courts allowed referring back phrases to be used to enlarge the literal narrowness of the claim. When the courts stopped allowing such phrases to enlarge the claims (thus, limiting claims to their narrow literal language), the practice of central claiming was abandoned and the practice of peripheral claiming came to dominate. One characteristic of the difference between central claiming and peripheral claiming is the number of claims. It was common to have only one or two claims under central claiming, but common to have numerous claims under peripheral claiming. Regarding central versus peripheral claiming, see RIDSDALE ELLIS, PATENT CLAIMS §§4–9 (1949); Warren T. Jessup, *The Doctrine of Equivalents*, 54 J. PAT. & TRADEMARK OFF. SOC'Y 248, 264–67 (1972); ANTHONY W. DELLER, PATENT CLAIMS §§5–11 (2d ed. 1971). In 1997, the Supreme Court noted that the change from central to peripheral claiming was "not of statutory origin." Warner-Jenkinson v. Hilton Davis Chem. Co., 520 U.S. 17, 27 n.4, 41 USPQ2d 1865 (1997). Central claiming survives today only in design patents, where a claim to an ornamental design is made by reference to the drawings of the patent. Claim construction, i.e., a description in words of the inventive aspects of the design, is permitted, but not required, with respect to design patents. Egyptian Goddess, Inc. v. Swisa, Inc., 543 F.3d 665, 679–81, 88 USPQ2d 1658 (Fed. Cir. 2008) (en banc), *cert. denied*, 129 S. Ct. 1917 (2009).

[12] See generally Chapter 4, §II.D. *See also* Innova/Pure Water, Inc. v. Safari Water Filtration Sys., Inc., 381 F.3d 1111, 1115, 72 USPQ2d 1001 (Fed. Cir. 2004); Johnson & Johnston Assocs. v. R.E. Serv., 285 F.3d 1046, 1052, 62 USPQ2d 1225 (Fed. Cir. 2002).

[13] *See generally* O2 Micro Int'l Ltd. v. Beyond Innovation Tech. Co., 521 F.3d 1351, 1362–63, 86 USPQ2d 1304 (Fed. Cir. 2008); Gart v. Logitech, Inc., 254 F.3d 1334, 1339, 59 USPQ2d 1290 (Fed. Cir. 2001), *cert. denied*, 534 U.S. 1114 (2002). Thus, whether amendments made during reexamination proceedings enlarged the scope of the claim is a claim construction issue. Predicate Logic Inc. v. Distributive Software Inc., 544 F.3d 1298, 1302, 88 USPQ2d 1526 (Fed. Cir. 2008); Creo Prods., Inc. v. Presstek, Inc., 305 F.3d 1337, 1344, 64 USPQ2d 1385 (Fed. Cir. 2002).

[14] *See, e.g.*, American Piledriving Equip. Inc. v. Geoquip Inc., 637 F.3d 1324, 1331–32, 98 USPQ2d 1001 (Fed. Cir. 2011); Invitrogen Corp. v. Clontech Labs., Inc., 429 F.3d 1052, 1076–77, 77 USPQ2d 1161 (Fed. Cir. 2005); *see also* Dow Chem. Co. v. Sumitomo Chem. Co., 257 F.3d 1364, 1372, 59 USPQ2d 1609 (Fed. Cir. 2001) ("legally operative meaning").

[15] *See, e.g.*, Abbott Labs. v. Sandoz Inc., 544 F.3d 1341, 1358, 89 USPQ2d 1161 (Fed. Cir. 2008); Lockheed Martin Corp. v. Space Sys./Loral, Inc., 324 F.3d 1308, 1318, 66 USPQ2d 1282 (Fed. Cir. 2003); Interactive Gift Express, Inc. v. Compuserve Inc., 256 F.3d 1323, 1330, 59 USPQ2d 1401 (Fed. Cir. 2001); Pitney Bowes v. Hewlett-Packard Co., 182 F.3d 1298, 1304, 51 USPQ2d 1161 (Fed. Cir. 1999).

[16] *See, e.g.*, *O2 Micro Int'l Ltd.* 521 F.3d at 1360–61, 86 USPQ2d 1304; Prima Tek II, L.L.C. v. Polypap, S.A.R.L., 318 F.3d 1143, 1148, 65 USPQ2d 1818 (Fed. Cir. 2003); Cybor Corp. v. FAS Techs., 138 F.3d 1448, 1454, 46 USPQ2d 1169 (Fed. Cir. 1998) (en banc).

Determining the meaning and scope of a claim has been described as ascertaining its true and proper meaning.[17] Because such a description could give the mistaken impression that the words in a patent claim have a universally correct meaning,[18] it is perhaps more useful to describe claim construction as determining the acquired meaning of claim language. Such a description is consistent with the Supreme Court's 1996 holding that "judges, not jurors, are the better suited to find the acquired meaning of patent terms."[19] In all events, the goal is to construe claim terms as they would have been understood by a person of ordinary skill in the art at the time of the invention,[20] unless the patent applicant has clearly and unambiguously redefined the terms in the patent specification or prosecution history.[21]

Regardless of how claim construction is described, it centers on the words actually used in the claims.[22] Judges cannot add or subtract words from the claims,[23] and they cannot rewrite

---

[17] E-Pass Tech. Inc. v. 3Com Corp., 473 F.3d 1213, 1219; 81 USPQ2d 1385 (Fed. Cir. 2007) ("proper meaning"); Middleton, Inc. v. Minnesota Mining & Mfg. Co., 311 F.3d 1384, 1387, 65 USPQ2d 1138 (Fed. Cir. 2002) ("proper meaning"); Phillips v. AWH Corp., 415 F.3d 1303, 1313, 75 USPQ2d 1321 (Fed. Cir. 2005), *cert. denied*, 546 U.S. 1170 (2006) ("true meaning"); *Cybor Corp.*, 138 F.3d at 1454 n.3, 46 USPQ2d 1169 ("true meaning"); *see also* CCS Fitness, Inc. v. Brunswick Corp., 288 F.3d 1359, 1365, 62 USPQ2d 1658 (Fed. Cir. 2002) ("correct scope and meaning").

[18] Words in a patent do not have a universally correct meaning. Two examples are: (1) different words in a patent may have the same meaning, and (2) the same word in a patent may have different meanings. Regarding (1), *see* Hologic Inc. v. SenoRx Inc., 639 F.3d 1329, 1336–38, 97 USPQ2d 1974 (Fed. Cir. 2011). Regarding (2), *see* Haemonetics Corp. v. Baxter Healthcare Corp., 607 F.3d 776, 95 USPQ2d 1556 (Fed. Cir. 2010); Pitney Bowes v. Hewlett-Packard Co., 182 F.3d 1298, 1310–11, 51 USPQ2d 1161 (Fed. Cir. 1999). *See generally* PIN/NIP, Inc. v. Platte Chem. Co., 304 F.3d 1235, 1244, 64 USPQ2d 1344 (Fed. Cir. 2002).

[19] Markman v. Westview Instruments, Inc., 517 U.S. 370, 388, 38 USPQ2d 1461 (1996). Similarly, claim construction can be described as giving an "appropriate meaning." *See, e.g.*, Riles v. Shell Exploration & Prod. Co., 298 F.3d 1302, 1310, 63 USPQ2d 1819 (Fed. Cir. 2002).

[20] *See, e.g.*, PSN Ill., LLC v. Ivoclar Vivadent, Inc., 525 F.3d 1159, 1164–65, 86 USPQ2d 1892 (Fed. Cir. 2008), *cert. denied*, 129 S. Ct. 647 (2008).

[21] *See, e.g.*, Honeywell Int'l Inc. v. Universal Avionics Sys. Corp., 493 F.3d 1358, 1361, 83 USPQ2d 1425 (Fed. Cir. 2007); Chamberlain Group, Inc. v. Lear Corp., 516 F.3d 1331, 1337, 86 USPQ2d 1104 (Fed. Cir. 2008).

[22] Z4 Techs., Inc. v. Microsoft Corp., 507 F.3d 1340, 1347–48, 85 USPQ2d 1340 (Fed. Cir. 2007), *cert. dismissed*, 128 S. Ct. 2107 (2008); MBO Labs. Inc. v. Becton Dickinson & Co., 474 F.3d 1323, 1329, 1331, 81 USPQ2d 1661 (Fed. Cir. 2007) (there must be " 'a textual reference in the actual language of the claim with which to associate a proffered claim construction' ") (citation omitted); Renishaw PLC v. Marposs Societa' per Azioni, 158 F.3d 1243, 1248, 48 USPQ2d 1117 (Fed. Cir. 1998) ("a claim must explicitly recite a term in need of definition before a definition may enter the claim"). *See generally* Telemac Cellular Corp. v. Topp Telecom, Inc., 247 F.3d 1316, 1324, 58 USPQ2d 1545 (Fed. Cir. 2001) ("a construction that flies in the face of the express language of the claims is not preferred").

[23] *See, e.g.*, Callicrate v. Wadsworth Mfg., Inc., 427 F.3d 1361, 1369, 77 USPQ2d 1041 (Fed. Cir. 2005); Novo Indus., L.P. v. Micro Molds Corp., 350 F.3d 1348, 1354, 69 USPQ2d 1128 (Fed.

the claims.[24] Claim construction begins and ends with the actual words of the claims.[25] Between the beginning and the end of claim construction, though, more than just the words of the claims are consulted.

A. Determining the Acquired Meaning of Claim Language

1. Not All Sources of Meaning Are Treated Equally

Generally, only the claim language that is in dispute needs to be construed.[26]

The Federal Circuit's en banc decision in *Phillips v. AWH Corp.* established a hierarchy of the evidence that can be relied on to determine the acquired meaning of a claim term.[27] *Phillips* did not overrule pre-2005 claim construction decisions, but rather instructed courts as to the relative weight to be accorded to the various types of evidence that had previously been found to be relevant.[28]

Cir. 2003) ("a district court can . . . only [correct an error in a patent by interpretation of the patent where no certificate of correction has been issued] if (1) the correction is not subject to reasonable debate based on consideration of the claim language and the specification and (2) the prosecution history does not suggest a different interpretation of the claims").

[24] Rembrandt Data Techs., LP v. AOL, LLC, 641 F.3d 1331, 1340–41, 98 USPQ2d 1393 (Fed. Cir. 2011); Inventio AG v. Thyssenkrupp Elevator Ams. Corp., 649 F.3d 1350, 1359–61, 99 USPQ2d 1112 (Fed. Cir. 2011); SmithKline Beecham Corp. v. Apotex Corp., 403 F.3d 1331, 1339–40, 74 USPQ2d 1398 (Fed. Cir. 2005), *cert. denied,* 547 U.S. 1218 (2006). *But see* Pause Tech. LLC v. TiVo Inc., 419 F.3d 1326, 1333, 76 USPQ2d 1110 (Fed. Cir. 2005) ("However, in clarifying the meaning of claim terms, courts are free to use words that do not appear in the claim so long as 'the resulting claim interpretation . . . accord[s] with the words chosen by the patentee to stake out the boundary of the claimed property' ") (citation omitted).

[25] Scanner Techs. Corp. v. ICOS Vision Sys. Corp., N.V., 365 F.3d 1299, 1303, 70 USPQ2d 1900 (Fed. Cir. 2004); *Renishaw PLC,* 158 F.3d at 1248, 48 USPQ2d 1117; *see also* Prima Tek II, L.L.C. v. Polypap, S.A.R.L., 318 F.3d 1143, 1148, 65 USPQ2d 1818 (Fed. Cir. 2003).

[26] O2 Micro Int'l Ltd. v. Beyond Innovation Tech. Co., 521 F.3d 1351, 1360–63, 86 USPQ2d 1304 (Fed. Cir. 2008); Vanderlande Indus. Nederland BV v. ITC, 366 F.3d 1311, 1322–23, 70 USPQ2d 1696 (Fed. Cir. 2004). It may be that one issue is dispositive. *See generally* Ballard Med. Prods. v. Allegiance Healthcare Corp., 268 F.3d 1352, 1358, 60 USPQ2d 1493 (Fed. Cir. 2001). Also, to resolve the dispute, it may not be necessary to ascertain the full extent of the claim language. *See, e.g.,* Pickholtz v. Rainbow Techs., Inc., 284 F.3d 1365, 1374, 62 USPQ2d 1340 (Fed. Cir. 2002). However, to provide necessary context, it may sometimes be necessary for the court to construe terms that are not in dispute. Amgen Inc. v. Hoechst Marion Roussel, Inc., 314 F.3d 1313, 1353, 65 USPQ2d 1385 (Fed. Cir. 2003).

[27] 415 F.3d 1303, 75 USPQ2d 1321 (Fed. Cir. 2005), *cert. denied,* 546 U.S. 1170 (2006).

[28] MBO Labs Inc. v. Becton Dickinson & Co., 474 F.3d 1323, 1329, 81 USPQ2d 1661 (Fed. Cir. 2007).

Words in a claim can potentially acquire meaning from various sources.[29] For example, the words can acquire meaning from (1) the ordinary use of the English language; (2) the customary use by a group (e.g., a trade, professional, scientific, or technological group); or (3) the particular use within the patent or its prosecution history. In certain circumstances, the words in a claim can acquire meaning from other sources.

The Federal Circuit refers to the patent and its prosecution history as intrinsic evidence.[30] Evidence that is external to the patent and its prosecution history (e.g., dictionaries, treatises, expert and inventor testimony) is referred to as extrinsic evidence.[31]

As set forth in *Phillips,* intrinsic evidence is preferred over extrinsic evidence.[32] The first focus is the claim term itself, and the context in which it is used. "Because claim terms are normally used consistently throughout the patent, the usage of a term in one claim can often illuminate the meaning of the same term in other claims." For example, the presence of a limitation in a dependent claim gives rise to the presumption that the same limitation is not present in an independent claim.[33]

---

[29] Vitronics Corp. v. Conceptronic, 90 F.3d 1576, 1582, 39 USPQ2d 1573 (Fed. Cir. 1996). Additionally, one or more of these sources may show that a word in a claim has *not* acquired a certain meaning. See this chapter, §II.B.

[30] Abbott Labs. v. Sandoz, Inc., 566 F.3d 1282, 1288–89, 90 USPQ2d 1769 (Fed. Cir. 2009), *cert. denied,* 130 S. Ct. 1052 (2010); V-Formation, Inc. v. Benetton Group SPA, 401 F.3d 1307, 1311, 74 USPQ2d 1042 (Fed. Cir. 2005). Prior art cited in the prosecution history is considered intrinsic evidence. Tate Access Floors v. Interface Architectural Res., Inc., 279 F.3d 1357, 1371 n.4, 61 USPQ2d 1647 (Fed. Cir. 2002).

[31] Zodiac Pool Care v. Hoffinger Indus., 206 F.3d 1408, 1414, 54 USPQ2d 1141 (Fed. Cir. 2000); Pitney Bowes v. Hewlett-Packard Co., 182 F.3d 1298, 1308–09, 51 USPQ2d 1161 (Fed. Cir.); Markman v. Westview Instruments, Inc., 52 F.3d 967, 980, 34 USPQ2d 1321 (Fed. Cir. 1995) (en banc), *aff'd,* 517 U.S. 370, 38 USPQ2d 1461 (1996).

[32] Intrinsic evidence has an elevated status because that evidence is the public record of the patent owner's right to exclude others from practicing the patented invention, and the public is entitled to rely on the public record to ascertain the scope of the patented invention. Hologic, Inc. v. SenoRx Inc., 639 F.3d 1329, 97 USPQ2d 1974 (Fed. Cir. 2011); *Vitronics Corp.,* 90 F.3d at 1583, 39 USPQ2d 1573. It might be unfair to use an obvious error in the prosecution history when construing the claims. *See, e.g.,* Storage Tech. Corp. v. Cisco Sys., Inc., 329 F.3d 823, 832, 66 USPQ2d 1545 (Fed. Cir. 2003); Rambus Inc. v. Infineon Techs. AG, 318 F.3d 1081, 1090, 65 USPQ2d 1705 (Fed. Cir.), *cert. denied,* 540 U.S. 874 (2003). *But see* Springs Window Fashions v. Novo Indus., 323 F.3d 989, 995–96, 65 USPQ2d 1826 (Fed. Cir. 2003); Viskase Corp. v. American Nat'l Can Co., 261 F.3d 1316, 1322, 59 USPQ2d 1823 (Fed. Cir. 2001).

[33] Phillips v. AWH Corp., 415 F.3d 1303, 1314–15, 75 USPQ2d 1321 (Fed. Cir. 2005), *cert. denied,* 546 U.S. 1170 (2006); the doctrine of "claim differentiation" is discussed in this chapter, §II.A.3.d.

After the claim terms themselves, the patent specification is the most important guide to the meaning of a term.[34] " 'The descriptive part of the specification aids in ascertaining the scope and meaning of the claims inasmuch as the words of the claims must be based on the description. . . .' . . . The close kinship between the written description and the claims is enforced by the statutory requirement that the specification describe the invention in 'full, clear, concise, and exact terms.' 35 U.S.C. §112, para.1."[35]

The patent's prosecution history also may be important to claim construction, because it "provides evidence of how the PTO and the inventor understood the patent" and, further, may indicate "whether the inventor limited the invention in the course of prosecution, making the claim scope narrower than it would otherwise be."[36]

Extrinsic evidence may be useful for claim construction, because it may inform the court how those skilled in the art understand a particular term outside of the context of the litigation-based positions of the parties. But the Federal Circuit deems extrinsic evidence less reliable than intrinsic evidence, because extrinsic evidence is divorced from the context of the interchange between the inventor and the PTO examiner that gave rise to the particular patent claims at issue.[37]

2. Ordinary or Customary Meaning

A claim term is generally given its ordinary and customary meaning, defined as "the meaning that the term would have to a person of ordinary skill in the art in question at the time of the invention, i.e., as of the effective filing date of the patent application."[38]

---

[34] *Phillips*, 415 F.3d at 1315, 75 USPQ2d 1321; *see also* Arlington Indus., Inc. v. Bridgeport Fittings, Inc., 632 F.3d 1246, 1253, 97 USPQ2d 1811 (Fed. Cir. 2011).

[35] *Phillips, 415 F.3d* at 1315–16, 75 USPQ2d 1321 (internal citations omitted).

[36] *Id.* at 1317, 75 USPQ2d 1321.

[37] *Id.* at 1317–19, 75 USPQ2d 1321.

[38] *Phillips*, 415 F.3d at 1312–13, 75 USPQ2d 1321; American Piledriving Equip. Inc. v. Geoquip Inc., 637 F.3d 1324, 1331–32, 98 USPQ2d 1001 (Fed. Cir. 2011).

In those cases where the ordinary meaning of a claim term as understood by a person of ordinary skill in the art is readily apparent even to laypersons, the ordinary meaning becomes the acquired meaning of the term.[39] In many cases, however, determining the meaning of a claim term as understood by a person of ordinary skill in the art requires an examination of terms that have a particular meaning in a field of art.[40] Because the words in a claim were not intended to be considered in a vacuum but rather in the context of the art and in the context of the intrinsic evidence, the particular use of those words in the patent cannot be ignored.[41] Also, because of the nature of language, the linguistic scope of the ordinary meaning may not be coextensive with the scope of the patented invention.[42]

3. The Particular Use of Claim Language in the Intrinsic Evidence

a. The Applicant as Lexicographer

Patent law allows a patent applicant to be a lexicographer.[43] In other words, the patent applicant is free (1) to create

---

[39] *Phillips*, 415 F.3d at 1314, 75 USPQ2d 1321; Callicrate v. Wadsworth Mfg., Inc., 427 F.3d 1361, 1367–68, 77 USPQ2d 1041 (Fed. Cir. 2005) ("The straightforward mechanical technology and understandable claim language give that meaning to this term"). However, a court is required to construe even words with an ordinary meaning if, in the context of the patent, the meaning of such terms is disputed. O2 Micro Int'l Ltd. v. Beyond Innovation Tech. Co., 521 F.3d 1351, 1360–63, 86 USPQ2d 1304 (Fed. Cir. 2008).

[40] *Phillips*, 415 F.3d at 1314, 75 USPQ2d 1321.

[41] Fuji Photo Film Co. v. U.S. Int'l Trade Comm'n, 386 F.3d 1095, 1098–99, 72 USPQ2d 1769 (Fed. Cir. 2004); Toro Co. v. White Consol. Indus., 199 F.3d 1295, 1301, 53 USPQ2d 1065 (Fed. Cir. 1999); Renishaw PLC v. Marposs Societa' per Azioni, 158 F.3d 1243, 1250, 48 USPQ2d 1117 (Fed. Cir. 1998); Vitronics Corp. v. Conceptronic, 90 F.3d 1576, 1582, 39 USPQ2d 1573 (Fed. Cir. 1996); Markman v. Westview Instruments, Inc., 52 F.3d 967, 979, 34 USPQ2d 1321 (Fed. Cir. 1995) (en banc), aff'd, 517 U.S. 370, 38 USPQ2d 1461 (1996); see, e.g., Arlington Indus., Inc. v. Bridgeport Fittings, Inc., 632 F.3d 1246, 1254, 97 USPQ2d 1811 (Fed. Cir. 2011) (use of a term can define that term "by implication"); Pitney Bowes v. Hewlett-Packard Co., 182 F.3d 1298, 1311, 51 USPQ2d 1161 (Fed. Cir. 1999) (same word has different meaning depending on the context).

[42] *Renishaw PLC*, 158 F.3d at 1250, 48 USPQ2d 1117 ("Ultimately, the interpretation to be given a term can only be determined and confirmed with a full understanding of what the inventor actually invented and intended to envelop with the claim").

[43] *Phillips*, 415 F.3d at 1315–16, 75 USPQ2d 1321; see also Honeywell Int'l, Inc. v. Universal Avionics Sys. Corp., 493 F.3d 1358, 1361, 83 USPQ2d 1425 (Fed. Cir. 2007); Renishaw PLC, 158 F.3d at 1249, 48 USPQ2d 1117; Vitronics Corp. v. Conceptronic, 90 F.3d 1576, 1582, 39 USPQ2d 1573 (Fed. Cir. 1996); Markman, 52 F.3d at 980, 34 USPQ2d 1321.

a new word; (2) to assign any meaning he or she wants to a word without regard to the ordinary or accustomed usage of that word; or (3) to modify a word's ordinary or accustomed meaning (by, for example, disclaiming a portion of its ordinary meaning).[44] It is always necessary to check whether the applicant has acted as lexicographer.[45]

The only requirement the applicant must meet as lexicographer is that the special meaning must appear with reasonable clarity and precision in the patent or its prosecution history.[46] If the special meaning of claim language is reasonably clear and precise, the court's role in claim construction is to pronounce that meaning as the acquired meaning of the word used in the claim.[47]

---

[44] Sinorgchem Co., Shandong v. U.S. Int'l Trade Comm'n, 511 F.3d 1132, 1135–38 (Fed. Cir. 2008); 3M Innovative Props. Co. v. Avery Dennison Corp., 350 F.3d 1365, 1371, 1374, 69 USPQ2d 1050 (Fed. Cir. 2003); *cert. denied*, 542 U.S. 920 (2004); *see, e.g.,* Honeywell Inc. v. Victor Co. of Japan, Ltd., 298 F.3d 1317, 1323–24, 63 USPQ2d 1904 (Fed. Cir. 2002); Augustine Med. v. Gaymar Indus., 181 F.3d 1291, 1298, 50 USPQ2d 1900 (Fed. Cir. 1999). The applicant can even use words in a way that differs from the customary meaning in patent law. *See generally* KCJ v. Kinetic Concepts, 223 F.3d 1351, 1356, 55 USPQ2d 1835 (Fed. Cir. 2000).

[45] Astrazeneca AB v. Mutual Pharm. Co., Inc., 384 F.3d 1333, 1339–41, 72 USPQ2d 1726 (Fed. Cir. 2004); Interactive Gift Express, Inc. v. Compuserve Inc., 256 F.3d 1323, 1336, 59 USPQ2d 1401 (Fed. Cir. 2001); John D. Watts v. XL Sys., 232 F.3d 877, 883, 56 USPQ2d 1836 (Fed. Cir. 2000) (even if the claim terms were clear on their face, the court "must consult the specification to determine if the patentee redefined any of those terms"); *Vitronics Corp.,* 90 F.3d at 1582, 39 USPQ2d 1573 (definition can be express or implied); *see, e.g.,* Middleton, Inc. v. Minnesota Mining & Mfg. Co., 311 F.3d 1384, 1388, 65 USPQ2d 1138 (Fed. Cir. 2002). *See generally* Gart v. Logitech, Inc., 254 F.3d 1334, 1341, 59 USPQ2d 1290 (Fed. Cir. 2001), *cert. denied,* 534 U.S. 1114 (2002); Biovail Corp. v. Andrx Pharms., Inc., 239 F.3d 1297, 1300–01, 57 USPQ2d 1813 (Fed. Cir. 2001).

[46] *Honeywell Int'l Inc.,* 493 F.3d at 1361, 83 USPQ2d 1425; Boss Control, Inc. v. Bombardier, Inc., 410 F.3d 1372, 1376–79 (Fed. Cir. 2005); *Astrazeneca AB,* 384 F.3d at 1339–41, 72 USPQ2d 1726; Renishaw PLC v. Marposs Societa' per Azioni, 158 F.3d 1243, 1249, 48 USPQ2d 1117 (Fed. Cir. 1998). The special meaning may be explicitly set forth in the patent or its prosecution history, or it may be implicit therein. Rambus Inc. v. Infineon Techs. AG, 318 F.3d 1081, 1088, 65 USPQ2d 1705 (Fed. Cir.), *cert. denied,* 540 U.S. 874 (2003); *see also* Invitrogen Corp. v. Biocrest Mfg., L.P., 327 F.3d 1364, 1367, 66 USPQ2d 1631 (Fed. Cir. 2003). *But see* Mycogen Plant Sci. v. Monsanto Co., 243 F.3d 1316, 1327–28, 58 USPQ2d 1030 (Fed. Cir. 2001) (special meaning must be "explicit"). Generally, the varied use of a term shows that the term has a broad, not a limited, meaning. Prima Tek II, L.L.C. v. Polypap, S.A.R.L., 318 F.3d 1143, 1151, 65 USPQ2d 1818 (Fed. Cir. 2003). When determining if a statement was lexicographic, " 'it is important to determine whether the statement was designed to define the claim term or to describe a preferred embodiment.' " LG Elec. Inc. v. Bizcom Elec. Inc., 453 F.3d 1364, 1374, 79 USPQ2d 1443 (Fed. Cir. 2006).

[47] *See, e.g.,* Phillips v. AWH Corp., 415 F.3d 1303, 1316, 75 USPQ2d 1321 (Fed. Cir. 2005), *cert. denied,* 546 U.S. 1170 (2006) ("the inventor's lexicography governs"); Voice Techs. Group v. VMC Sys., 164 F.3d 605, 613–14, 49 USPQ2d 1333 (Fed. Cir. 1999) ("When the meaning of a term as used in a patent is clear, that is the meaning that must be applied in the construction of the claim").

The test for determining if a special meaning is reasonably clear and precise is whether the patent or its prosecution history puts one of ordinary skill in the relevant art, or a reasonable competitor, on notice that the applicant intended to so specially define the claim language.[48]

b. Reading Claims in the Context of the Intrinsic Evidence

As discussed above, the Federal Circuit's en banc decision in *Phillips* mandates that claim language be interpreted whenever possible in the context of the evidence intrinsic to the prosecution of the patent at issue. This evidence consists of the patent claims themselves, the specification of the patent and the prosecution history of the patent, in that order.[49]

The appropriate starting point is always the particular use in the claim containing the language at issue. The context in which a term is used in the claim can be instructive.[50]

---

[48] OrthoMcNeil Pharm. v. Caraco Pharm. Labs., Ltd., 476 F.3d 1321, 1327–28, 81 USPQ2d 1427 (Fed. Cir. 2007); *see also* Union Carbide Chems. & Plastic Tech. Corp. v. Shell Oil Co., 308 F.3d 1167, 1177–78, 64 USPQ2d 1545 (Fed. Cir. 2002); Bell Atl. Network Servs. v. Covad Commc'ns, 262 F.3d 1258, 1268, 59 USPQ2d 1865 (Fed. Cir. 2001); Multiform Desiccants Inc. v. Medzam Ltd., 133 F.3d 1473, 1477–78, 45 USPQ2d 1429 (Fed. Cir. 1998) (broad definition, which was added during prosecution but was not coextensive with disclosure in patent, was excluded as source of meaning). For words with a common meaning, it may be necessary for the applicant to clearly point out how the term in the patent differs from conventional understanding. Apple Computer v. Articulate Sys., 234 F.3d 14, 21 n.5, 57 USPQ2d 1057 (Fed. Cir. 2000).

[49] *Phillips*, 415 F.3d at 1312–17, 75 USPQ2d 1321. Also potentially relevant is the particular use of a word in other written documents such as related patents or their prosecution histories. *See generally* Microsoft Corp. v. Multi-Tech Sys., Inc., 357 F.3d 1340, 1347–50, 69 USPQ2d 1815 (Fed. Cir.), *cert. denied*, 543 U.S. 821 (2004); Goldenberg v. Cytogen, Inc., 373 F.3d 1158, 1166–68, 71 USPQ2d 1255 (Fed. Cir. 2004). *See also* Verizon Servs. Corp. v. Vonage Holdings Corp., 503 F.3d 1295, 1306–07, 84 USPQ2d 1609 (Fed. Cir. 2007). *But see* Ventana Med. Sys., Inc. v. Biogenix Labs., Inc., 473 F.3d 1173, 1182–84, 81 USPQ2d 1314 (Fed. Cir. 2006).

[50] *Phillips*, 415 F.3d at 1314, 75 USPQ2d 1321; Pfizer, Inc. v. Teva Pharms. USA, Inc., 429 F.3d 1364, 1373, 77 USPQ2d 1257 (Fed. Cir. 2005); *Pause Tech. LLC*, 419 F.3d at 1330–31, 76 USPQ2d 1110; American Piledriving Equip. Inc. v. Geoquip Inc., 637 F.3d 1324, 1332–33, 98 USPQ2d 1001 (Fed. Cir. 2011); Pause Tech. LLC v. TiVo Inc., 419 F.3d 1326, 1331, 76 USPQ2d 1110 (Fed. Cir. 2005); *Interactive Gift Express, Inc.*, 256 F.3d at 1336–37, 59 USPQ2d 1401; Pitney Bowes v. Hewlett-Packard Co., 182 F.3d 1298, 1305, 51 USPQ2d 1161 (Fed. Cir. 1999) (consulting preamble and body of claim).

While the claim term must be read in the context of the entire patent,[51] it is improper to read limitations from the specification into the claim term.[52] A recurring dispute in claim construction, and a frequent source of reversal by the Federal Circuit, arises where the court reads features of one or more disclosed embodiments into claims that are drafted more broadly.[53] It is sometimes a fine line that separates proper from improper reliance on the specification.[54]

For some patents, the scope of the claimed invention might not be any different from the embodiment, or embodiments, disclosed in the intrinsic evidence, where the patentee has demonstrated a clear intention to limit claim scope. For example, when the preferred embodiment is described in the specification as the invention itself or, conversely, when the specification makes clear that the invention includes or does not include particular features, claim elements may be interpreted in accordance with such statements.[55]

---

[51] *See generally Phillips*, 415 F.3d at 1313, 75 USPQ2d 1321 ("the person of ordinary skill in the art is deemed to read the claim . . . in the context of the entire patent"); American Piledriving Equip. Inc. v. Geoquip Inc., 637 F.3d 1324, 1333, 98 USPQ2d 1001 (Fed. Cir. 2011) ("the specification . . . is always highly relevant to the claim construction analysis") (internal citations omitted); Nystrom v. Trex Co., 424 F.3d 1136, 1142–44, 76 USPQ2d 1481 (Fed. Cir. 2005), *cert. denied*, 547 U.S. 1055 (2006); Georgia-Pacific Corp. v. United States Gypsum Co., 195 F.3d 1322, 1332, 52 USPQ2d 1590 (Fed. Cir. 1999) ("The specification of the patent in suit is the best guide to the meaning of a disputed term"), *cert. denied*, 531 U.S. 816 (2000). *But see* Tivo Inc. v. Echostar Commc'ns Corp., 516 F.3d 1290, 1300–01, 85 USPQ2d 1801 (Fed. Cir. 2008) (description of specific features in the patent disclosure as "the invention" may limit the claims).

[52] *Phillips*, 415 F.3d at 1323–24, 75 USPQ2d 1321; *see, e.g.,* Callicrate v. Wadsworth Mfg., Inc., 427 F.3d 1361, 1368, 77 USPQ2d 1041 (Fed. Cir. 2005); JVW Enters., Inc. v. Interact Accessories, Inc., 424 F.3d 1324, 1335, 76 USPQ2d 1641 (Fed. Cir. 2005). *See generally* Toro Co. v. White Consol. Indus., Inc., 266 F.3d 1367, 1371, 60 USPQ2d 1437 (Fed. Cir. 2001).

[53] *See, e.g.,* Arlington Indus., Inc. v. Bridgeport Fittings, Inc., 632 F.3d 1246, 1254, 97 USPQ2d 1811 (Fed. Cir. 2011); Interactive Gift Express, Inc. v. Compuserve Inc., 256 F.3d 1323, 1338–39, 59 USPQ2d 1401 (Fed. Cir. 2001); *see also In re* Omeprazole Patent Litig., 483 F.3d 1364, 1372, 82 USPQ2d 1643 (Fed. Cir. 2007); Bio-Technology Gen. Corp. v. Duramed Pharms., 325 F.3d 1356, 1362, 66 USPQ2d 1360 (Fed. Cir. 2003).

[54] *Arlington Indus.*, 632 F.3d at 1255, 97 USPQ2d 1811; Bell Atl. Network Servs. v. Covad Commc'ns, 262 F.3d 1258, 1270, 59 USPQ2d 1865 (Fed. Cir. 2001).

[55] *See, e.g.,* Trading Techs. Int'l, Inc. v. eSpeed, Inc., 595 F.3d 1340, 1353, 93 USPQ2d 1805 (Fed. Cir. 2010); Edwards Lifesciences, LLC v. Cook, Inc., 582 F3d 1322, 1329, 92 USPQ2d 1599 (Fed. Cir. 2009); Terlep v. Brinkmann Corp., 418 F.3d 1379, 1383–84, 76 USPQ2d 1053 (Fed. Cir. 2005); Norian Corp. v. Stryker Corp., 432 F.3d 1356, 1359–60, 77 USPQ2d 1242 (Fed. Cir. 2005).

More generally, however, an inventor is permitted to claim an invention more broadly than the specific embodiments disclosed in the specification. As the Federal Circuit stated in *Phillips*:

> To avoid importing limitations from the specification into the claims, it is important to keep in mind that the purposes of the specification are to teach and enable those of skill in the art to make and use the invention and to provide a best mode for doing so. . . . Much of the time, upon reading the specification in that context, it will become clear whether the patentee is setting out specific examples of the invention to accomplish those goals, or whether the patentee intends for the claims and the embodiments in the specification to be strictly coextensive.[56]

This general rule applies even where the inventor has disclosed only a single illustrative embodiment of the invention.[57]

The patent's prosecution history should also be considered in determining the acquired meaning of a claim term. As the Federal Circuit stated in *Phillips*, "the prosecution history can often inform the meaning of the claim language by demonstrating how the inventor understood the invention and whether the inventor limited the invention in the course of prosecution, making the claim scope narrower than it would otherwise be."[58] However, for amendments made during the prosecution of a patent to limit claim scope, such limitations must be clear and unambiguous.[59]

---

[56] *Phillips*, 415 F.3d at 1323, 75 USPQ2d 1321.

[57] *See, e.g.*, Liebel-Flarsheim Co. v. Medrad, Inc., 358 F.3d 898, 905, 69 USPQ2d 1801 (Fed. Cir.), *cert. denied*, 543 U.S. 925 (2004). *But see Arlington Indus., Inc.*, 632 F.3d at 1258, 97 USPQ2d 1811 (Lourie, J., dissenting) ("But in construing the claims we should avail ourselves of the knowledge we glean from the patent specification to see what the inventors disclosed as their invention. The bottom line in claim construction should be that the claims should not mean more than what the specification indicates, one way or the other, the inventors invented")

[58] *Phillips*, 415 F.3d at 1317, 75 USPQ2d 1321; *see also, e.g.*, Computer Docking Station Corp. v. Dell, Inc., 519 F.3d 1366, 1374–75, 86 USPQ2d 1129 (Fed. Cir. 2008); Nystrom v. Trex Co., 424 F.3d 1136, 1142, 1144, 76 USPQ2d 1481 (Fed. Cir. 2005), *cert. denied*, 547 U.S. 1055 (2006).

[59] *See, e.g.*, Purdue Pharma, L.P. v. Endo Pharms., Inc., 438 F.3d 1123, 1136, 77 USPQ2d 1767 (Fed. Cir. 2006); Microsoft Corp. v. Multi-Tech Sys., Inc., 357 F.3d 1340, 1349, 69 USPQ2d 1815 (Fed. Cir.), *cert. denied*, 543 U.S. 821 (2004); Cordis Corp. v. Medtronic AVE, Inc., 339 F.3d 1352, 1358–62, 67 USPQ2d 1876 (Fed. Cir. 2003), *cert. denied*, 540 U.S. 1213 (2004).

When the intrinsic evidence is not clear as to the metes and bounds of the invention that was patented, there are certain guideposts, or general rules of patent construction, discussed in §II.A.3.d of this chapter, that may be helpful.

c. Resorting to Extrinsic Evidence

Extrinsic evidence may always be used to educate the court with respect to the underlying technology, to allow the court to interpret the claims as they would have been understood by a person of ordinary skill in the art.[60] However, extrinsic evidence may not be used as a source of the acquired meaning of a claim term unless the intrinsic evidence is not sufficient for determining the acquired meaning. Put another way, a claim definition supported by intrinsic evidence will trump a definition suggested, however strongly, by extrinsic evidence.[61] Extrinsic evidence includes dictionaries, treatises, expert testimony, publications, and inventor testimony.[62]

Among relevant extrinsic evidence, extrinsic evidence that is publicly accessible prior to the trial (e.g., prior art) is deemed more objective and reliable than opinion testimony.[63] While opinion testimony on claim construction should be treated with the "utmost caution,"[64] it may be relevant to the extent that it

---

[60] See, e.g., Phillips, 415 F.3d at 1317–19, 75 USPQ2d 1321; Aqua-Aerobic Sys. v. Aerators, 211 F.3d 1241, 1244–45, 54 USPQ2d 1566 (Fed. Cir. 2000); Pitney Bowes v. Hewlett-Packard Co., 182 F.3d 1298, 1308, 51 USPQ2d 1161 (Fed. Cir. 1999).

[61] See generally Phillips, 415 F.3d at 1317–24, 75 USPQ2d 1303; LB Plastics, Inc. v. Amerimax Home Prods., Inc. 499 F.3d 1303, 1308, 84 USPQ2d 1341 (Fed. Cir. 2007); Pfizer, Inc. v. Teva Pharms. USA, Inc., 429 F.3d 1364, 1374–75, 77 USPQ2d 1257 (Fed. Cir. 2005); Vitronics Corp. v. Conceptronic, 90 F.3d 1576, 1585, 39 USPQ2d 1573 (Fed. Cir. 1996). See generally Verve, LLC v. Crane Cams, Inc., 311 F.3d 1116, 1119–20, 65 USPQ2d 1051 (Fed. Cir. 2002). Of course, the court can receive (and consider) evidence that it does not ultimately rely on.

[62] Phillips, 415 F.3d at 1318, 75 USPQ2d 1321; Pfizer, Inc., 429 F.3d at 1374–75, 75 USPQ2d 1801; see also Chamberlain Group Inc. v. Lear Corp., 516 F.3d 1331, 1335, 86 USPQ2d 1104 (Fed. Cir. 2008); Pickholtz v. Rainbow Techs., Inc., 284 F.3d 1365, 1373, 62 USPQ2d 1340 (Fed. Cir. 2002).

[63] Vitronics Corp., 90 F.3d at 1585, 39 USPQ2d 1573; see also Arthur A. Collins v. Northern Telecom Ltd., 216 F.3d 1042, 1044–45, 55 USPQ2d 1143 (Fed. Cir. 2000) (prior art).

[64] Vitronics Corp., 90 F.3d at 1585, 39 USPQ2d 1573; Symantec Corp. v. Computer Assocs. Int'l, 522 F.3d 1279, 1290–91, 86 USPQ2d 1449 (Fed. Cir. 2008).

tends to show an established meaning of a term to persons skilled in the art.[65] An inventor's communication to his or her patent attorney before the patent was filed may have some relevance.[66] There is the possibility that, even after considering extrinsic evidence (and the guideposts discussed in the next section), the court may decide the patent is so unclear that it is invalid for indefiniteness.[67]

d. Potentially Useful Claim Construction Guideposts

The Federal Circuit has recognized certain guideposts that may help a court with claim construction problems.[68] These guideposts, which are also known as canons of construction, are not immutable rules.[69] Nonetheless, the court may find them helpful in determining the acquired meaning of claim language.[70]

---

[65] *See, e.g.,* Markman v. Westview Instruments, Inc., 52 F.3d 967, 983, 34 USPQ2d 1321 (Fed. Cir. 1999); *Phillips,* 415 F.3d at 1318, 75 USPQ2d 1321; Gen. Protecht Group, Inc. v. Int'l Trade Comm'n, 619 F.3d 1303, 1310, 96 USPQ2d 1292 (Fed. Cir. 2010); Spansion Inc. v. Int'l Trade Comm'n., 629 F.3d 1331, 97 USPQ2d 1417, 1425 (Fed. Cir. 2010); Datamize, LLC v. Plumtree Software, Inc., 417 F.3d 1342, 1348, 75 USPQ2d 1801 (Fed. Cir. 2005).

[66] Howmedica Osteonics Corp. v. Wright Med. Tech. Inc., 540 F.3d 1337, 1346, 88 USPQ2d 1129 (Fed. Cir. 2008); Netword, LLC v. Centraal Corp., 242 F.3d 1347, 1355, 58 USPQ2d 1076 (Fed. Cir. 2001) (attorney-client privilege not asserted).

[67] *See generally* Datamize, LLC v. Plumtree Software, Inc., 417 F.3d 1342, 75 USPQ2d 1801 (Fed. Cir. 2005). *See, e.g.,* Amgen Inc. v. Hoechst Marion Roussel, Inc., 314 F.3d 1313, 1342, 65 USPQ2d 1385 (Fed. Cir. 2003); *see also* Personalized Media Commc'ns v. United States Int'l Trade Comm'n, 161 F.3d 696, 705, 48 USPQ2d 1880 (Fed. Cir. 1998) ("A determination of claim indefiniteness is a legal conclusion that is drawn from the court's performance of its duty as the construer of patent claims"). See also Chapter 4, §II.D.

[68] Silicon Graphics Inc. v. ATI Tech. Inc., 607 F.3d 784, 789, 95 USPQ2d 1417 (Fed. Cir. 2010); Renishaw PLC v. Marposs Societa' per Azioni, 158 F.3d 1243, 1248, 48 USPQ2d 1117 (Fed. Cir. 1998).

[69] Bristol-Myers Squibb Co. v. Ben Venue Labs., Inc., 246 F.3d 1368, 1376, 58 USPQ2d 1508 (Fed. Cir. 2001); IMS Tech. v. Haas Automation, 206 F.3d 1422, 1432, 54 USPQ2d 1129 (Fed. Cir.), *cert. dismissed,* 530 U.S. 1299 (2000); *Renishaw PLC,* 158 F.3d at 1248, 48 USPQ2d 1117. *See generally* Fantasy Sports Props., Inc. v. SportsLine.com, 287 F.3d 1108, 1115–16, 62 USPQ2d 1564 (Fed. Cir. 2002).

[70] *See, e.g.,* Arlington Indus., Inc. v. Bridgeport Fittings, Inc., 632 F.3d 1246, 1254, 97 USPQ2d 1811 (Fed. Cir. 2011); Karlin Tech. v. Surgical Dynamics, 177 F.3d 968, 972, 50 USPQ2d 1465 (Fed. Cir. 1999).

The guideposts provide that:

1. ordinarily, each claim in a patent has a different scope;[71] ordinarily, a dependent claim has a narrower scope than the claim from which it depends;[72] and, ordinarily, an independent claim has a broader scope than a claim that depends from it.[73] These generalizations are referred to as the doctrine of claim differentiation. The doctrine does not apply where the intrinsic evidence leads to a different conclusion;[74]

2. ordinarily, claims are not limited to the preferred embodiment disclosed in the specification;[75]

3. ordinarily, different words in a patent have different meanings;[76]

---

[71] *Arlington Indus., Inc.*, 632 F.3d at 1254, 97 USPQ2d 1811; *In re* Cruciferous Sprout Litig., 301 F.3d 1343, 1348–49, 64 USPQ2d 1202 (Fed. Cir. 2002), *cert. denied*, 538 U.S. 907 (2003). *See generally* Creo Prods., Inc. v. Presstek, Inc., 305 F.3d 1337, 1345, 1349–50, 64 USPQ2d 1385 (Fed. Cir. 2002); Xerox Corp. v. 3Com Corp., 267 F.3d 1361, 1366, 60 USPQ2d 1526 (Fed. Cir. 2001); TurboCare Div. of Demag Delaval v. General Elec., 264 F.3d 1111, 1123, 60 USPQ2d 1017 (Fed. Cir. 2001).

[72] Phillips v. AWH Corp., 415 F.3d 1303, 1315, 75 USPQ2d 1321 (Fed. Cir. 2005), *cert. denied*, 546 U.S. 1170 (2006); Innova/Pure Water, Inc. v. Safari Water Filtration Sys., Inc., 381 F.3d 1111, 1123, 72 USPQ2d 1001 (Fed. Cir. 2004); AK Steel Corp. v. Sollac, 344 F.3d 1234, 1242, 68 USPQ2d 1280 (Fed. Cir. 2003).

[73] Acumed LLC v. Stryker Corp., 483 F.3d 800, 805–06, 82 USPQ2d 1481 (Fed. Cir.), *cert. denied*, 552 U.S. 1022 (2007); Liebel-Flarsheim Co. v. Medrad, Inc., 358 F.3d 898, 909–10, 69 USPQ2d 1801 (Fed. Cir.), *cert. denied*, 543 U.S. 925 (2004); *AK Steel Corp.*, 344 F.3d at 1242, 68 USPQ2d 1280.

[74] *See, e.g.*, Regents of Univ. of Cal. v. Dakocytomation Cal., Inc., 517 F.3d 1364, 1376–77, 85 USPQ2d 1929 (Fed. Cir. 2008); Nystrom v. Trex Co., 424 F.3d 1136, 1143, 76 USPQ2d 1481 (Fed. Cir. 2005), *cert. denied*, 547 U.S. 1055 (2006).

[75] *Phillips*, 415 F.3d at 1323, 75 USPQ2d 1321; Innogenetics, N.V. v. Abbott Labs., 512 F.3d 1363, 1370, 85 USPQ2d 1641 (Fed. Cir. 2008) ("as is well established, an applicant is not required to describe in the specification every conceivable and possible future embodiment of his invention"); Home Diagnostics, Inc. v. LifeScan, Inc., 381 F.3d 1352, 1357 (Fed. Cir. 2004); Interactive Gift Express, Inc. v. Compuserve Inc., 256 F.3d 1323, 1341, 59 USPQ2d 1401 (Fed. Cir. 2001); Electra Instrument v. O.U.R. Scientific Int'l, 214 F.3d 1302, 1308, 54 USPQ2d 1910 (Fed. Cir. 2000) (correct construction excluded preferred embodiment); IMS Tech. v. Haas Automation, 206 F.3d 1422, 1433–34, 54 USPQ2d 1129 (Fed. Cir.), *cert. dismissed*, 530 U.S. 1299 (2000).

[76] *Innova/Pure Water, Inc.*, 381 F.3d at 1119–20; CAE Screenplates v. Heinrich Fiedler GmbH, 224 F.3d 1308, 1317, 55 USPQ2d 1804 (Fed. Cir. 2000); *see also* Power Mosfet Techs., L.L.C. v. Siemens AG, 378 F.3d 1396, 1409–10, 72 USPQ2d 1129 (Fed. Cir. 2004); Pickholtz v. Rainbow Techs., Inc., 284 F.3d 1365, 1373, 62 USPQ2d 1340 (Fed. Cir. 2002) (different words were synonyms). *See generally* Rambus Inc. v. Infineon Techs. AG, 318 F.3d 1081, 1089 n.4, 65 USPQ2d 1705 (Fed. Cir.), *cert. denied*, 540 U.S. 874 (2003). *But see* Nystrom v. Trex Co., 424 F.3d 1136, 1143, 76 USPQ2d 1481 (Fed. Cir. 2005), *cert. denied*, 547 U.S. 1055 (2006) ("Different terms or phrases in separate claims may be construed to cover the same subject matter where the written description and prosecution history indicate that such a reading of the terms or phrases is proper").

4. ordinarily, the same word in a patent has the same meaning;[77]

5. ordinarily, the meaning should align with the purpose of the patented invention;[78]

6. ordinarily, general descriptive terms are given their full meaning;[79]

7. ordinarily, absent broadening language, numerical ranges are construed exactly as written;[80]

8. ordinarily, absent recitation of order, steps of a method are not construed to have a particular order;[81]

---

[77] *Phillips*, 415 F.3d at 1314, 75 USPQ2d 1321; American Piledriving Equip. Inc. v. Geoquip Inc., 637 F.3d 1324, 1332–33, 98 USPQ2d 1001 (Fed. Cir. 2011); Callicrate v. Wadsworth Mfg., Inc., 427 F.3d 1361, 1371–72, 77 USPQ2d 1041 (Fed. Cir. 2005); Frank's Casing Crew & Rental Tools, Inc. v. Weatherford Int'l, Inc., 389 F.3d 1370, 1377–78, 73 USPQ2d 1065 (Fed. Cir. 2004). *See generally* Dayco Prods., Inc. v. Total Containment, Inc., 258 F.3d 1317, 1326, 59 USPQ2d 1489 (Fed. Cir. 2001) (same words in multiple patents from same parent application). *But see* Haemonetics Corp. v. Baxter Healthcare Corp., 607 F.3d 776, 782, 95 USPQ2d 1556 (Fed. Cir. 2010) (different use of the same term in different embodiments clearly shown by the intrinsic evidence); Computer Docking Station Corp. v. Dell, Inc., 519 F.3d 1366, 86 USPQ2d 1129 (Fed. Cir. 2008) (preamble may use words differently than the body of the claim).

[78] *In re* Gabapentin Patent Litig., 503 F.3d 1254, 1263, 84 USPQ2d 1651 (Fed. Cir. 2007); Innovad Inc. v. Microsoft Corp., 260 F.3d 1326, 1332–33, 59 USPQ2d 1676 (Fed. Cir. 2001); Purdue Pharma L.P. v. Boehringer Ingelheim GmbH, 237 F.3d 1359, 1364, 57 USPQ2d 1647 (Fed. Cir. 2001); *see also* Apple Computer v. Articulate Sys., 234 F.3d 14, 25, 57 USPQ2d 1057 (Fed. Cir. 2000); Hockerson-Halberstadt v. Avia Group Int'l, 222 F.3d 951, 956, 55 USPQ2d 1487 (Fed. Cir. 2000). Functional limitations, however, generally should not be read into purely structural claims. Schwing GmbH v. Putzmeister Aktiengesellschaft, 305 F.3d 1318, 1324–25, 64 USPQ2d 1641 (Fed. Cir. 2002).

[79] Innova/Pure Water, Inc. v. Safari Water Filtration Sys., Inc., 381 F.3d 1111, 1118, 1120, 72 USPQ2d 1001 (Fed. Cir. 2004); Akamai Tech. Inc. v. Cable & Wireless Internet Servs. Inc., 344 F.3d 1186, 1194, 68 USPQ2d 1186 (Fed. Cir. 2003); *see also* Invitrogen Corp. v. Biocrest Mfg., L.P., 327 F.3d 1364, 1370–71, 66 USPQ2d 1631 (Fed. Cir. 2003); RF Del., Inc. v. Pacific Keystone Techs., 326 F.3d 1255, 1263, 66 USPQ2d 1593 (Fed. Cir. 2003). Terms of approximation are given their full meaning unless clearly limited by intrinsic evidence. Playtex Prods., Inc. v. Procter & Gamble Co., 400 F.3d 901, 907–08, 73 USPQ2d 2010 (Fed. Cir. 2005) ("substantially" and "generally"); Liquid Dynamics Corp. v. Vaughan Co., 355 F.3d 1361, 1368, 69 USPQ2d 1595 (Fed. Cir. 2004) (citing Anchor Wall Sys., Inc. v. Rockwood Retaining Walls, Inc., 340 F.3d 1298, 1310–11, 67 USPQ2d 1865 (Fed. Cir. 2003) ("generally" and "substantially" are descriptive terms commonly used " 'to avoid a strict numerical boundary to the specified parameter' ")). *But see* OrthoMcNeil Pharm. v. Caraco Pharm. Labs., Ltd., 476 F.3d 1321, 1326–28, 81 USPQ2d 1427 (Fed. Cir. 2007) ("about" as it relates to claimed ratios should be construed narrowly because the patentee could have claimed broader numerical ranges).

[80] Jeneric/Pentron v. Dillon Co., 205 F.3d 1377, 1381, 54 USPQ2d 1086 (Fed. Cir. 2000).

[81] Combined Sys., Inc. v. Defense Tech. Corp. of Am., 350 F.3d 1207, 1211–12, 68 USPQ2d 1933 (Fed. Cir. 2003) (particular order required); Altiris, Inc. v. Symantec Corp., 318 F.3d 1363, 1369–71, 65 USPQ2d 1865 (Fed. Cir. 2003) (no order required); Interactive Gift Express, Inc. v. Compuserve Inc., 256 F.3d 1323, 1342–44, 59 USPQ2d 1401 (Fed. Cir. 2001) (no order required).

9. absent highly persuasive evidentiary support, a construction should literally read on the preferred embodiment;[82] and

10. where two alternative claim constructions are equally plausible based on the intrinsic evidence, claims should be construed so as to preserve their validity.[83]

B. Determining that a Meaning Has Not Been Acquired

Disputed claim language need be construed "only to the extent necessary to resolve the controversy."[84] Because a determination that disputed claim language has *not* acquired a certain meaning may resolve the controversy between the litigants, a court's claim construction ruling may only need to pronounce that a certain meaning has not been acquired. For example, if the party that bears the burden of proof cannot prevail unless a certain meaning has been acquired, then the court's determination that the disputed claim language has not acquired that meaning can resolve the controversy.[85] Even if such a determination does

---

[82] Cytologix Corp. v. Ventana Med. Sys., Inc., 424 F.3d 1168, 1175, 76 USPQ2d 1592 (Fed. Cir. 2005); Nellcor Puritan Bennett, Inc. v. Masimo Corp., 402 F.3d 1364, 1368–69, 74 USPQ2d 1351 (Fed. Cir. 2005); *Interactive Gift Express, Inc.*, 256 F.3d at 1343, 59 USPQ2d 1401; Vitronics Corp. v. Conceptronic, 90 F.3d 1576, 1583–84, 39 USPQ2d 1573 (Fed. Cir. 1996). *See generally* Abbott Labs. v. TorPharm, Inc., 300 F.3d 1367, 1372, 63 USPQ2d 1929 (Fed. Cir. 2002); Smith & Nephew Inc. v. Ethicon Inc., 276 F.3d 1304, 1309–10, 61 USPQ2d 1065 (Fed. Cir. 2001). *But see* North Am. Container, Inc. v. Plastipak Packaging, Inc., 415 F.3d 1335, 1346, 75 USPQ2d 1545 (Fed. Cir. 2005).

[83] *Phillips*, 415 F.3d at 1327–28; Energizer Holdings, Inc. v. United States Int'l Trade Comm'n, 435 F.3d 1366, 77 USPQ2d 1625 (Fed. Cir. 2006) (to avoid invalidity on indefiniteness grounds); Datamize, LLC v. Plumtree Software, Inc., 417 F.3d 1342, 1347–48, 75 USPQ2d 1801 (Fed. Cir. 2005); Liebel-Flarsheim Co. v. Medrad, Inc., 358 F.3d 898, 911, 69 USPQ2d 1801 (Fed. Cir.) ("unless the court concludes, after applying all the available tools of claim construction, that the claim is still ambiguous, the axiom regarding the construction to preserve the validity of the claim does not apply"), *cert. denied*, 543 U.S. 925 (2004). A claim that is susceptible of only one reasonable construction, though, cannot be construed differently to preserve validity. *Apple Computer*, 234 F.3d at 24, 57 USPQ2d 1057; Electra Instrument v. O.U.R. Scientific Int'l, 214 F.3d 1302, 1309, 54 USPQ2d 1910 (Fed. Cir. 2000).

[84] Vivid Techs. v. American Sci. & Eng'g, 200 F.3d 795, 803, 53 USPQ2d 1289 (Fed. Cir. 1999); *see, e.g.*, Network LLC v. Centraal Corp., 242 F.3d 1347, 1353, 58 USPQ2d 1076 (Fed. Cir. 2001); Biovail Corp. v. Andrx Pharms., Inc., 239 F.3d 1297, 1301, 57 USPQ2d 1813 (Fed. Cir. 2001).

[85] *See, e.g.*, Every Penny Counts Inc. v. American Express Co., 563 F.3d 1378, 1381–82, 90 USPQ2d 1851 (Fed. Cir. 2009) (infringement issue resolved), *cert. denied*, 130 S. Ct. 565 (2009).

not end the controversy, the court may nonetheless find it useful to disqualify a proposed construction.[86] Further, even if a proposed construction is not disqualified in its entirety, it has become quite common for a court to determine if some portion of the full scope of a claim term's proposed meaning is not within the acquired meaning.[87]

One or more of the sources of meaning may show that a word in a claim has *not* acquired a certain meaning. For example, a specific meaning may

1. have been clearly and unambiguously disclaimed or disavowed in the intrinsic evidence;[88]
2. have been disclaimed or disavowed in the extrinsic evidence;[89]

---

[86] *See, e.g.,* Lacks Indus. v. McKechnie Vehicle Components USA, 322 F.3d 1335, 1342, 1343–44, 66 USPQ2d 1083 (Fed. Cir. 2003); Renishaw PLC v. Marposs Societa' per Azioni, 158 F.3d 1243, 1251, 48 USPQ2d 1117 (Fed. Cir. 1998).

[87] This determination can occur in many different situations. For example, it can occur when checking if the applicant has acted as a lexicographer, when checking that the proposed meaning is consistent with the particular use of that word in the intrinsic evidence, and when resolving ambiguity by comparison to the scope of the patented invention.

[88] Elbex Video, Ltd. v. Sensormatic Elecs. Corp., 508 F.3d 1366, 1371–73, 85 USPQ2d 1137 (Fed. Cir. 2007) (no "clear and unmistakable surrender"); Gillespie v. Dywidag Sys. Int'l, USA, 501 F.3d 1285, 1290–91, 84 USPQ2d 1051 (Fed. Cir. 2007) (disclaimed); Sorenson v. United States Int'l Trade Comm'n, 427 F.3d 1375, 1378–81, 77 USPQ2d 1083 (Fed. Cir. 2005) (no "clear and unambiguous disavowal"); Salazar v. Procter & Gamble Co., 414 F.3d 1342, 1344–48, 75 USPQ2d 1369 (Fed. Cir. 2005) (no "clear and unambiguous disavowal" attributed to applicant's silence regarding examiner's statement of reasons for allowance); Cordis Corp. v. Medtronic AVE, Inc., 339 F.3d 1352, 1358, 1361, 1363, 67 USPQ2d 1876 (Fed. Cir. 2003) (no "clear and unambiguous disavowal"), *cert. denied,* 540 U.S. 1213 (2004); Omega Eng'g, Inc. v. Raytek Corp., 334 F.3d 1314, 1324–25, 1328, 1333–35, 67 USPQ2d 1321 (Fed. Cir. 2003) (disavowed); Apex Inc. v. Raritan Computer, Inc., 325 F.3d 1364, 1377, 66 USPQ2d 1444 (Fed. Cir.) (no clear disavowal), *cert. denied,* 540 U.S. 1073 (2003); Northrop Grumman Corp. v. Intel Corp., 325 F.3d 1346, 1354–56, 66 USPQ2d 1341 (Fed. Cir. 2003) ("no clear disclaimer"); Rambus Inc. v. Infineon Techs. AG, 318 F.3d 1081, 1094–95, 65 USPQ2d 1705 (Fed. Cir. 2003) (no "clear disclaimer or disavowal of claim scope"), *cert. denied,* 540 U.S. 874 (2003); LNP Eng'g Plastics v. Miller Waste Mills, 275 F.3d 1347, 1355–56, 61 USPQ2d 1193 (Fed. Cir. 2001) (no disclaimer during reexamination); Ballard Med. Prods. v. Allegiance Healthcare Corp., 268 F.3d 1352, 1359–61, 60 USPQ2d 1493 (Fed. Cir. 2001) (disclaimed in means-plus-function context).

[89] Nystrom v. Trex Co., 424 F.3d 1136, 1145–46, 76 USPQ2d 1481 (Fed. Cir. 2005), *cert. denied,* 547 U.S. 1055 (2006).

3. be inconsistent with the claim at issue[90] or other intrinsic evidence;[91] or

4. be the subject of a waiver or of judicial estoppel.[92]

III. ANCILLARY PROCEDURAL MATTERS

A. Judicial Education

A patent is both a legal and a technical document.[93] Additionally, the patent's prosecution history has both legal and technological content.[94] To the extent that a patent contains technical information, it is addressed not to lawyers or laypersons, but to a person skilled in the art to which the patent pertains.[95]

---

[90] *See, e.g.*, Waner v. Ford Motor Co., 331 F.3d 851, 855, 66 USPQ2d 1943 (Fed. Cir. 2003), *cert. denied*, 540 U.S. 1105 (2004); *Lacks Indus.*, 322 F.3d at 1343–44, 66 USPQ2d 1083; Ecolab, Inc. v. Paraclipse, Inc., 285 F.3d 1362, 1371, 62 USPQ2d 1349 (Fed. Cir. 2002) ("black matte surface" excluded); Interactive Gift Express, Inc. v. Compuserve Inc., 256 F.3d 1323, 1336, 59 USPQ2d 1401 (Fed. Cir. 2001) ("material object").

[91] *See, e.g.*, Masco Corp. v. United States, 303 F.3d 1316, 1325–26, 64 USPQ2d 1182 (Fed. Cir. 2002); *Ecolab, Inc.*, 285 F.3d at 1371–72, 62 USPQ2d 1349 ("vertical surface" excluded based on prosecution history); Kustom Signals, Inc. v. Applied Concepts, Inc., 264 F.3d 1326, 1331–32, 60 USPQ2d 1135 (Fed. Cir. 2001), *cert. denied*, 535 U.S. 986 (2002); Georgia-Pacific Corp. v. United States Gypsum Co., 195 F.3d 1322, 1332, 52 USPQ2d 1590 (Fed. Cir. 1999), *cert. denied*, 531 U.S. 816 (2000).

[92] SuperGuide Corp. v. DirecTV Enters., Inc., 358 F.3d 870, 889–90, 69 USPQ2d 1865 (Fed. Cir. 2004); *Interactive Gift Express, Inc.*, 256 F.3d at 1344–49, 59 USPQ2d 1401. The doctrine of waiver precludes a party from adopting a new claim construction on appeal. *Id.* A party may, however, offer new arguments (based on evidence of record) for its old construction. *Id.* The doctrine of judicial estoppel precludes a party from changing its claim construction on appeal from the construction it successfully presented at trial. *Id.*; SanDisk Corp. v. Memorex Prods., Inc., 415 F.3d 1278, 1290–92, 75 USPQ2d 1475 (Fed. Cir. 2005) ("[T]he equities do not favor applying judicial estoppel to prevent claim construction arguments from evolving after preliminary injunction"), *cert. denied*, 546 U.S. 1076 (2005). *See generally* Inverness Med. Switz. GmbH v. Warner Lambert Co., 309 F.3d 1373, 1380–81, 64 USPQ2d 1933 (Fed. Cir. 2002) (no waiver); Tegal Corp. v. Tokyo Electron Am., Inc., 257 F.3d 1331, 1343, 1344, 59 USPQ2d 1385 (Fed. Cir. 2001) (waiver), *cert. denied*, 535 U.S. 927 (2002).

[93] Nilssen v. Osram Sylvania Inc., 504 F.3d 1223, 1235, 84 USPQ2d 1811 (Fed. Cir. 2007), *cert. denied*, 554 U.S. 903 (2008); Pitney Bowes v. Hewlett-Packard, 182 F.3d 1298, 1309, 51 USPQ2d 1161 (Fed. Cir. 1999).

[94] Multiform Desiccants v. Medzam, Ltd., 133 F.3d 1473, 1477, 45 USPQ2d 1429 (Fed. Cir. 1998).

[95] *Phillips*, 415 F.3d at 1312–13, 75 USPQ 2d 1321. The Federal Circuit has also stated that the language in a patent is supposed to provide notice to "competitors" about the scope of a claimed invention. Markman v. Westview Instruments, Inc., 52 F.3d 967, 978–79, 34 USPQ2d 1321 (Fed. Cir. 1995) (en banc), *aff'd*, 517 U.S. 370, 38 USPQ2d 1461 (1996).

Accordingly, as discussed in this chapter, §II.A.3.c, although extrinsic evidence has inherent limitations, the court may, in its discretion, consult extrinsic evidence for help in understanding the technical aspects of the intrinsic evidence.[96] Moreover, although dictionaries, treatises, and the like are characterized as extrinsic evidence to aid the court, courts may consult extrinsic sources regardless of whether they have been introduced into evidence by the parties.[97]

As with most matters in civil litigation, the process of identifying and focusing on both the technical and legal issues that will be presented to the court begins with the parties, as part of the pretrial preparation of an action. Whether governed by a local rule that dictates the timing of events or not, the parties will, at some point in discovery, exchange: (1) claim terms that each side believes need to be construed; (2) preliminary claim constructions proposed by each side; and (3) an identification of the evidence, intrinsic and extrinsic, that each side intends to rely on to support its proposed construction.[98] Based on these exchanges, the parties can identify the claim constructions about which they can agree, and those that need to be resolved by the court.

Whenever the disputed issues are presented to the district court, the court has several options for coming to grips with the underlying technology. Some courts require the parties to prepare a technology tutorial, separate and apart from a hearing on the disputed claim terms. Such a tutorial may take many

---

[96]Phillips v. AWH Corp., 415 F.3d 1303, 1317–19, 75 USPQ 2d 1321 (Fed. Cir. 2005), *cert. denied,* 546 U.S. 1170 (2006); *Markman,* 52 F.3d at 980–81 34 USPQ2d 1321; Vitronics Corp. v. Conceptronic, 90 F.3d 1576, 1584 n.6, 39 USPQ2d 1573 (Fed. Cir. 1996); *see also* Apex Inc. v. Raritan Computer, Inc., 325 F.3d 1364, 1371, 1374, 66 USPQ2d 1444 (Fed. Cir.), *cert. denied,* 540 U.S. 1073 (2003); Gart v. Logitech, Inc., 254 F.3d 1334, 1340, 59 USPQ2d 1290 (Fed. Cir. 2001), *cert. denied,* 534 U.S. 1114 (2002); Hockerson-Halberstadt v. Avia Group Int'l, 222 F.3d 951, 955, 55 USPQ2d 1487 (Fed. Cir. 2000) ("a court may receive extrinsic evidence to educate itself about the underlying technology"); *Pitney Bowes,* 182 F.3d at 1308–09, 51 USPQ2d 1161.

[97] Texas Digital Sys., Inc. v. Telegenix, Inc., 308 F.3d 1193, 1203, 64 USPQ2d 1812 (Fed. Cir. 2002), *cert. denied,* 538 U.S. 1058 (2003); *see also* Boehringer Ingelheim Vetmedica, Inc. v. Schering-Plough Corp., 320 F.3d 1339, 1346, 65 USPQ2d 1961 (Fed. Cir. 2003).

[98] *See, e.g.,* N.D. Cal. Patent Local Rules 4-1–4-3 (2010).

forms, including written submissions, video submissions, and live argument, with or without witnesses.[99]

In addition, or as an alternative, Federal Rules of Evidence, Rule 706 permits the appointment of an independent court-appointed technical expert.[100] Finally, to aid it in understanding the technical aspects of the evidence, the court can seek the assistance of an independent advisor.[101] There are advantages and disadvantages to each approach.[102]

B. Time and Context for Claim Construction Ruling

Absent a local rule to the contrary,[103] a judge has complete discretion regarding when to make his or her claim construction ruling, with one exception.[104] The exception is that, in a case where the right to trial by jury has not been waived, the

---

[99] For an example of such an order from the District of Delaware, see http://www.ded. uscourts.gov/LPSmain.htm > "Forms" > "Form Scheduling Order—Patent," ¶ 9. For a further discussion of technology tutorials, see The Sedona Conference, Report on the *Markman* Process (WG5) (Kenneth C. Bass III ed., Nov. 2010 version), at 3, available at http://www.these donaconference.org/dltForm?did=Markman_Process.pdf; and MENELL ET AL., PATENT CASE MANAGEMENT JUDICIAL GUIDE (Federal Judicial Center, 2009), at 5-14–5-15.

[100] *See, e.g.,* Rohm & Haas Co. v. Lonza, 997 F. Supp. 635, 638 n.1 (E.D. Pa. 1998); Genentech, Inc. v. Boehringer Mannheim GmbH, 989 F. Supp. 359, 361 (D. Mass. 1997). *See generally* JOE S. CECIL & THOMAS E. WILLGING, COURT-APPOINTED EXPERTS: DEFINING THE ROLE OF EXPERTS APPOINTED UNDER FEDERAL RULE OF EVIDENCE 706 (1993); MANUAL FOR COMPLEX LITIGATION (FOURTH) §11.51 (2004). For the important differences between a Rule 706 expert and a special master, see 9 JAMES W. MOORE ET AL., MOORE'S FEDERAL PRACTICE §53.02[3]–[4] (3d ed. 2008).

[101] *See, e.g.,* TechSearch, L.L.C. v. Intel Corp., 286 F.3d 1360, 1376–81, 62 USPQ2d 1449 (Fed. Cir.), *cert. denied,* 537 U.S. 995 (2002); *see also* MediaCom Corp. v. Rates Tech., 4 F. Supp. 2d 17, 29–30, 35–38 (D. Mass. 1998), which includes an example of an order (and undertaking) for the engagement of a technical advisor. *See also* Si-Hung Choy, *Comment: Judicial Education After* Markman v. Westview Instruments, Inc.: *The Use of Court-Appointed Experts,* 47 UCLA L. REV. 1423, 1429 (2000). The Federal Circuit can appoint technical assistants pursuant to 28 U.S.C.A. §715(c)–(d).

[102] *See* MENELL ET AL., PATENT CASE MANAGEMENT JUDICIAL GUIDE (Federal Judicial Center, 2009), at 5-12–5-18.

[103] *See, e.g.,* N.D. Cal. Patent Local Rule 4 (2010); E.D. Tex. Local Civil Rules, Appendix M, Patent Rule 4 (2011). Several other jurisdictions have adopted (or are currently considering) local patent rules for claim construction proceedings based at least in part on the Northern California and Eastern Texas models. For example, the District of New Jersey, which is the forum for a substantial number of patent infringement actions involving the pharmaceutical industry based on the Hatch-Waxman Act, 21 U.S.C. §355, has adopted local patent rules tailored to particular procedural issues presented in such actions. D. N.J. Local Rule 9-3.3.6 (2011).

[104] Cytologix Corp. v. Ventana Med. Sys., Inc., 424 F.3d 1168, 1172–73, 76 USPQ2d 1592 (Fed. Cir. 2005); Sofamor Danek Group v. DePuy-Motech, 74 F.3d 1216, 1221, 37 USPQ2d 1529 (Fed. Cir. 1996).

judge should complete the claim construction before giving the jury its final instructions because the jurors should know the claim construction to apply in their deliberations.[105] Regardless of when the ruling is made, the judge should set forth an express construction of the material claim terms in dispute, to facilitate review on appeal.[106]

Courts and commentators have expressed a wide range of opinions concerning the best time for claim construction and the best procedural context.[107] Jurisdictions that have adopted local patent rules generally favor claim construction earlier in the action, following a mandatory exchange of contentions by the parties, but before the close of fact discovery.[108] A standing order used in the District of Delaware provides for claim construction after the close of fact discovery and expert discovery, but before the filing of dispositive motions.[109] Claim construction can also be addressed as part of the dispositive motion process.[110]

---

[105] Sulzer Textil A.G. v. Picanol N.V., 358 F.3d 1356, 1366–68, 69 USPQ2d 1961 (Fed. Cir. 2004); Hewlett-Packard Co. v. Mustek Sys., Inc., 340 F.3d 1314, 1320–21, 67 USPQ2d 1825 (Fed. Cir. 2003). Regarding whether a party whose contrary claim construction position is on record must object to the jury instruction, *see generally Ecolab, Inc. v. Paraclipse, Inc.*, 285 F.3d 1362, 1369–70, 62 USPQ2d 1349 (Fed. Cir. 2002). Regarding whether an erroneous instruction warrants a new trial, *see generally id.* at 1374–76, 62 USPQ2d 1349; *Cardiac Pacemakers, Inc. v. St. Jude Med., Inc.*, 381 F.3d 1371, 1382–83, 72 USPQ2d 1333 (Fed. Cir. 2004), *cert. denied*, 544 U.S. 1032 (2005); *Arlington Indus., Inc. v. Bridgeport Fittings, Inc.*, 345 F.3d 1318, 3125, 68 USPQ2d 1439 (Fed. Cir. 2003) (erroneous jury instruction regarding claim interpretation is grounds for a new trial). Regarding clarifying claim construction upon a question from a deliberating jury, see generally *MacNeill Eng'g Co. v. Trisport, Ltd.*, 126 F. Supp. 2d 51, 61–69 (D. Mass. 2001).

[106] AFG Indus., Inc. v. Cardinal IG Co., 239 F.3d 1239, 1247, 57 USPQ2d 1776 (Fed. Cir. 2001).

[107] *See, e.g.*, MANUAL FOR COMPLEX LITIGATION (FOURTH) §33.223 (2004); The Sedona Conference, Report on the *Markman* Process (WG5) (Kenneth C. Bass III ed., Nov. 2010 version), at 5 and Appendices A and B, *available at* http://www.thesedonaconference.org/dltForm?did=Markman_Process.pdf (proposing different timing depending upon the complexity of the action); MENELL ET AL., PATENT CASE MANAGEMENT JUDICIAL GUIDE (Federal Judicial Center, 2009), at 5-4–5-5 (favoring claim construction in the middle of fact discovery).

[108] *See, e.g.*, N.D. Cal. Patent Local Rules 4-1–4-6 (2010); E.D. Tex. Patent Rules 4-1–4-6 (2011).

[109] Delaware Form Order, http://www.ded.uscourts.gov/LPSmain.htm > "Forms" > "Form Scheduling Order—Patent," ¶ 9.

[110] *See, e.g.*, MediaCom Corp. v. Rates Tech., 4 F. Supp. 2d 17, 20–24 (D. Mass. 1998). However, this same judge, writing several years later, suggested that the better practice was to hold a claim construction hearing before any hearing on dispositive motions, and independent of that hearing. Amgen Inc. v. Hoechst Marion Roussel, Inc., 126 F. Supp. 2d 69, 80, 57 USPQ2d 1449 (D. Mass. 2001), *aff'd in part, rev'd in part*, 314 F.3d 1313, 65 USPQ2d 1385 (Fed. Cir. 2003).

Because each case is unique, the optimal time for claim construction will vary from case to case.[111] In some cases (e.g., where the technology is simple and the parties can easily identify the disputed claim language that will resolve their dispute), this moment may come early.[112] In other cases (e.g., where the technology is complex or the dispositive claim language disputes cannot easily be identified), this moment may come late.[113] In the authors' experience, waiting until fact and expert discovery are substantially complete allows the court the advantage of addressing claim construction after the parties have identified and explored the issues that are truly in dispute, and allows the court to better consider those issues in the context in which they will arise either in dispositive motions or at trial. However, the local rules enacted in the Northern District of California and the Eastern District of Texas, which mandate a claim construction ruling early in an action, sometimes serve to focus the parties' subsequent discovery efforts and, in theory, may resolve enough of the disputed issues to promote early resolution of the action.

Intertwined with the timing of the claim construction ruling is the issue of whether the parties will be allowed to amend their theories of the case after the court's ruling.[114] Because the claim

---

[111] *See generally* Vivid Techs. v. American Sci. & Eng'g, 200 F.3d 795, 803, 53 USPQ2d 1289 (Fed. Cir. 1999) ("[T]he stage at which the claims are construed may vary with the issues, their complexity, the potentially dispositive nature of the construction, and other considerations of the particular case").

[112] *See, e.g.,* Aspex Eyewear, Inc. v. E'Lite Optik, Inc., No. 3:98-CV-2996-D, 2001 U.S. Dist. LEXIS 2088, at *4–7 (N.D. Tex. Feb. 27, 2001). *But see* William F. Lee & Anita K. Krug, *Still Adjusting to* Markman: *A Prescription for the Timing of Claim Construction Hearings,* 13 HARV. J.L. & TECH. 55, 80 (1999) (arguing that, even in cases where the claims can be construed early, late claim construction may be more desirable).

[113] *See also* Embrex v. Service Eng'g Corp., 1998 U.S. Dist. LEXIS 15143, at *6 (E.D.N.C. June 22, 1998), *aff'd,* 216 F.3d 1343, 55 USPQ2d 1161 (Fed. Cir. 2000) (because "the issues involved . . . are extremely technical and complicated," claim construction set for conclusion of all evidence in a jury trial).

[114] The Northern District of California patent local rules were amended in 2008 to eliminate post-claim construction amendments of right to infringement and validity contentions. Such amendments now require a timely motion showing good cause. N.D. Cal. Patent Local Rule 3-6 (2010). By contrast, the local rule of the Eastern District of Texas permits amendment without leave, but within specified time intervals following the entry of a claim construction order. E.D. Tex. Local Civil Rules, Appendix M, Patent Rule 3-6 (2008). *See generally* Loral Fairchild Corp. v. Victor Co. of Japan, 911 F. Supp. 76, 79 (E.D.N.Y. 1996), where Federal Circuit Judge Rader, sitting by designation, stated: "With most aspects of trial hinging on [the claim construction] determination . . . a conscientious court will generally endeavor to make this ruling before trial."

construction ruling can " 'change[] the rules of the game' "[115] and thus render previously irrelevant arguments very relevant,[116] there is, generally, nothing improper in a party's amending its contentions and expert reports after a claim construction ruling.[117] Under the facts of a particular case, however, it may be appropriate to preclude a party from such amendments.[118]

The claim construction ruling can be made in a number of different contexts, including the resolution of (1) a motion for a preliminary injunction;[119] (2) a motion for summary judgment regarding infringement or invalidity;[120] (3) a motion for judgment as a matter of law;[121] or (4) requests for jury instructions.[122] A ruling on claim construction can also be freestanding, i.e., unconnected to a request for other relief.[123] A 2008

---

[115] Lexion Med., LLC v. Northgate Techs., Inc., 641 F.3d 1352, 1358–59, 98 USPQ2d 1388 (Fed. Cir. 2011); Asyst Techs., Inc. v. Emtrak Inc., 544 F.3d 1310, 1317, 88 USPQ2d 1623 (Fed. Cir. 2008) (citation omitted).

[116] Becton Dickinson & Co. v. Syntron Bioresearch, 51 USPQ2d 1722, 1734 (S.D. Cal. 1998); see also Lexion Med., LLC, 641 F. 3d 1352, 1359; Johns Hopkins Univ. v. CellPro, Inc., 152 F.3d 1342,1357, 47 USPQ2d 1705 (Fed. Cir. 1998).

[117] Lexion Med., LLC, 641 F.3d at 1358–59, 98 USPQ2d 1388; Becton Dickinson & Co., 51 USPQ2d at 1734. The Northern District of California patent local rules expressly state that a claim construction ruling may provide the good cause required to permit amendment of a party's contentions. See N.D. Cal. Patent Local Rule 3-6 (2008).

[118] Compare, e.g., Becton Dickinson & Co., 51 USPQ2d at 1734–37 (neither Fed. R. Civ. P. 26(e), nor judicial estoppel justified precluding the plaintiff's amendments), with Loral Fairchild Corp., 911 F. Supp. at 79 (plaintiff precluded from changing its theory of liability by Rule 26(e) and by judicial estoppel). See also Rambus, Inc. v. Infineon Techs. AG, 145 F. Supp. 2d 721, 730–32, 60 USPQ2d 1385 (E.D. Va. 2001) (with claim construction after expert discovery, expert should have offered opinions in the alternative); Itron, Inc. v. Benghiat, No. 99-501 (JRT/FLN), 2001 U.S. Dist. LEXIS 23230, at *3–5 (D. Minn. Dec. 21, 2001) (supplemental expert report permitted). See generally Genentech v. Amgen, Inc., 289 F.3d 761, 773–74, 62 USPQ2d 1640 (Fed. Cir. 2002) (preclusion because of noncompliance with local rule).

[119] See, e.g., Purdue Pharma L.P. v. Boehringer Ingelheim GmbH, 237 F.3d 1359, 1364–65, 57 USPQ2d 1647 (Fed. Cir. 2001).

[120] See, e.g., MediaCom Corp. v. Rates Tech., 4 F. Supp. 2d 17, 22–23 (D. Mass. 1998); McNulty v. Taser Int'l Inc., 61 USPQ2d 1937, 1941 (C.D. Cal. 2002).

[121] See, e.g., York Prods. v. Central Tractor Farm & Family Ctr., 99 F.3d 1568, 40 USPQ2d 1619 (Fed. Cir. 1996); Vitronics Corp. v. Conceptronic, 90 F.3d 1576, 39 USPQ2d 1573 (Fed. Cir. 1996).

[122] See generally Patent Litigation in the District of Delaware: The Judges' Perspective, 18 DEL. LAW. 6, 9 (Winter 2000/2001) (Judge McKelvie: "I look at claim construction as determining what the jury instruction is going to be").

[123] See, e.g., Aspex Eyewear, Inc. v. E'Lite Optik, Inc., No. 3:98-CV-2996-D, 2001 U.S. Dist. LEXIS 2088 (N.D. Tex. Feb. 27, 2001); Caterpillar v. Detroit Diesel Corp., 961 F. Supp. 1249, 1256–60, 41 USPQ2d 1876 (N.D. Ind. 1996). Occasionally, courts specifically treat their early freestanding claim construction ruling as nonconclusive. See, e.g., Thomson Consumer Elecs. v. Innovatron, S.A., 43 F. Supp. 2d 26, 29 (D.D.C. 1999); see also Vivid Techs. v. American Sci. & Eng'g, 997 F. Supp. 93 (D. Mass. 1997), aff'd, 200 F.3d 795, 53 USPQ2d 1289 (Fed. Cir. 1999).

survey of the practices of federal judges found that the most common practice is to have a separate claim construction process and to issue a separate claim construction ruling.[124]

IV. SELECTED SUBSTANTIVE ISSUES IN CLAIM CONSTRUCTION

In addition to a standard (nonstatutory) introductory phrase,[125] most claims have three parts: (1) a preamble; (2) transitional language; and (3) a body.[126] Using a ceiling fan as an example,[127] a claim with these three parts could be:

I claim: A ceiling fan comprising:

    (a)   a motor having a rod extending outwardly,
    (b)   three blades disposed from the rod, and
    (c)   a cord coupled to the motor for switching the motor on and off.

In this example, "A ceiling fan" is the preamble, "comprising" is the transitional language, and (a) through (c) make up the body. One way of thinking about the body of a claim is that it usually contains all the elements of the claimed invention.[128] Another way of thinking about the body of a claim is that it generally contains all the limitations on the scope of the claim.[129]

---

[124] Rebecca N. Eyre et al., *Patent Claim Construction: A Survey of Federal District Judges* (Federal Judicial Center, 2008), at 14, available at http://www.fjc.gov/public/pdf.nsf/lookup/patclaim.pdf/$file/patclaim.pdf.

[125] Examples of standard introductory phrases are: "I (or we) claim" or "The invention claimed is." MPEP §608.01(m) (8th ed. 2001, rev. July 2008). Another example is: "What is claimed is." JEFFREY G. SHELDON, HOW TO WRITE A PATENT APPLICATION §6.3.2 (1999). See also Chapter 2, §III.B.1.

[126] *See generally* JEFFREY G. SHELDON, HOW TO WRITE A PATENT APPLICATION §6.3 (1999); ROBERT C. FABER, LANDIS ON MECHANICS OF PATENT CLAIM DRAFTING §§4A–9 (5th ed. 2003).

[127] *See* Markman v. Westview Instruments, Inc., 517 U.S. 370, 374 n.1, 38 USPQ2d 1461 (1996).

[128] *See generally* 5A DONALD S. CHISUM, CHISUM ON PATENTS §18.03[4][a] (2007).

[129] *See, e.g.*, American Med. Sys., Inc. v. Biolitec, Inc., 618 F.3d 1354, 1359, 96 USPQ2d 1652 (Fed. Cir. 2010).

A. Potential Relevance of the Preamble to the Scope of the Claim

The preamble is an introductory statement that precedes the body of the claim.[130] A preamble can serve a variety of purposes,[131] including summarizing the type of invention or identifying the function of the invention.[132] The preamble has the import that the claim as a whole suggests for it.[133]

Although the preamble is always part of the claim, it might not be relevant to the scope of the claim.[134] Generally, the preamble is relevant to the scope of the claim (and thus relevant to claim construction) if (1) the preamble is a limitation on the claimed invention, or (2) the preamble is necessary to give life, meaning, and vitality to the body of the claim.[135] In determining whether the preamble is relevant to claim construction, courts review the body of the claim,[136] but they may also review the entirety of the patent[137] and the prosecution history[138] to

---

[130] Corning Glass Works v. Sumitomo Elec., U.S.A., 868 F.2d 1251, 1257, 9 USPQ2d 1962 (Fed. Cir. 1989); JEFFREY G. SHELDON, HOW TO WRITE A PATENT APPLICATION §6.3.3.1 (1999).

[131] C. R. Bard v. M3 Sys., 157 F.3d 1340, 1350, 48 USPQ2d 1225 (Fed. Cir. 1998), cert. denied, 526 U.S. 1130 (1999).

[132] JEFFREY G. SHELDON, HOW TO WRITE A PATENT APPLICATION §6.3.3.1 (1999); see, e.g., American Med. Sys., Inc., 618 F.3d 1354, 1360, 96 USPQ2d 1652 (Fed. Cir. 2010) (preamble term set forth description of overall process claimed).

[133] See generally American. Med. Sys., Inc., 618 F.3d at 1360, 96 USPQ2d 1652 (Fed. Cir. 2010); Storage Tech. Corp. v. Cisco Sys., Inc., 329 F.3d 823, 831, 66 USPQ2d 1545 (Fed. Cir. 2003).

[134] Pitney Bowes v. Hewlett-Packard Co., 182 F.3d 1298, 1305, 51 USPQ2d 1161 (Fed. Cir. 1999); see also American. Med. Sys., Inc., 618 F.3d at 1359, 96 USPQ2d 1652.

[135] Symantec Corp. v. Computer Assocs. Int'l, Inc., 522 F.3d 1279, 86 USPQ2d 1449 (Fed. Cir. 2008); NTP, Inc. v. Research In Motion, Ltd., 418 F.3d 1282, 1305–06, 75 USPQ2d 1763 (Fed. Cir. 2005), cert. denied, 546 U.S. 1157 (2006); Pitney Bowes, 182 F.3d at 1305, 51 USPQ2d 1161; see also Catalina Mktg. Int'l v. Coolsavings.com, 289 F.3d 801, 808–10, 62 USPQ2d 1781 (Fed. Cir. 2002) see, e.g., Bristol-Myers Squibb Co. v. Ben Venue Labs., Inc., 246 F.3d 1368, 1375, 58 USPQ2d 1508 (Fed. Cir. 2001) (not a limitation); Karsten Mfg. Corp. v. Cleveland Golf Co., 242 F.3d 1376, 1380, 58 USPQ2d 1286 (Fed. Cir. 2001) (limitation).

[136] Altiris, Inc. v. Symantec Corp., 318 F.3d 1363, 1371–72, 65 USPQ2d 1865 (Fed. Cir. 2003); see, e.g., STX, LLC v. Brine, 211 F.3d 588, 591, 54 USPQ2d 1347 (Fed. Cir. 2000) (the body of the claim "was a self-contained description that could stand alone").

[137] Symantec Corp. v. Computer Assocs. Int'l, 522 F.3d 1279, 1288–90, 86 USPQ2d 1449 (Fed. Cir. 2008); Bicon Inc. v. Straumann Co., 441 F.3d 945, 951–52, 78 USPQ2d 1267 (Fed. Cir. 2006).

[138] See, e.g., MBO Labs., Inc. v. Becton Dickinson & Co., 474 F.3d 1323, 1329–30, 81 USPQ2d 1661 (Fed. Cir. 2007); Glaxo Wellcome, Inc. v. Impax Labs., 356 F.3d 1348, 1353, 69 USPQ2d 1705 (Fed. Cir. 2004); In re Cruciferous Sprout Litig., 301 F.3d 1343, 1347–48, 64 USPQ2d 1202 (Fed. Cir. 2002), cert. denied, 538 U.S. 907 (2003).

gain an understanding of what the inventors actually invented and intended to encompass by the claim.[139]

Regarding the preamble as limitation, the preamble may[140] or may not[141] be a limitation on the claimed invention.[142] For example, if the applicant uses both the preamble *and* the body of the claim to define the subject matter of the claimed invention, then the court will recognize the preamble as a limitation on the claimed invention.[143] The preamble is not a limitation when it is used only to state a purpose or intended use for the invention and the structurally complete invention is defined in the body of the claim.[144]

For example, the preamble may be relevant because it explains a limitation in the body of the claim.[145] In the ceiling

---

[139] *In re* Cruciferous Sprout Litig., 301 F.3d at 1345, 64 USPQ2d 1202; *Catalina Mktg. Int'l*, 289 F.3d at 808, 62 USPQ2d 1781; *see, e.g.*, Cordis Corp. v. Medtronic AVE, Inc., 511 F.3d 1157, 1179–80, 85 USPQ2d 1427 (Fed. Cir. 2008), *cert. denied*, 129 S. Ct. 201 (2008); Corning Glass Works v. Sumitomo Elec., U.S.A., 868 F.2d 1251, 1257, 9 USPQ2d 1962 (Fed. Cir. 1989).

[140] *See, e.g.*, Poly-America, L.P. v. GSE Lining Tech., 383 F.3d 1303,1309–10, 72 USPQ2d 1685 (Fed. Cir. 2004); Invitrogen Corp. v. Biocrest Mfg., L.P., 327 F.3d 1364, 1370, 66 USPQ2d 1631 (Fed. Cir. 2003); Tegal Corp. v. Tokyo Electron Am., Inc., 257 F.3d 1331, 1344, 59 USPQ2d 1385 (Fed. Cir. 2001), *cert. denied*, 535 U.S. 927 (2002).

[141] *See, e.g.*, Intirtool, Ltd. v. Texar Corp., 369 F.3d 1289, 1293–96, 70 USPQ2d 1780 (Fed. Cir. 2004); *STX, LLC*, 211 F.3d at 591, 54 USPQ2d 1347.

[142] *See generally* American Med. Sys., Inc. v. Biolitec, Inc., 618 F.3d 1354, 1358, 96 USPQ2d 1652 (Fed. Cir. 2010) ("Whether to treat a preamble term as a claim limitation is determined on the facts of each case in light of the claim as a whole and the invention described in the patent") (internal citations omitted); Computer Docking Station Corp. v. Dell, Inc., 519 F.3d 1366, 1375, 86 USPQ2d 1129 (Fed. Cir. 2008) ("In considering whether a preamble limits a claim, the preamble is analyzed to ascertain whether it states a necessary and defining aspect of the invention, or is simply an introduction to the general field of the claim") (internal citations omitted).

[143] *American Med. Sys., Inc.*, Inc., 618 F.3d at 1360-61; 96 USPQ2d 1652; NTP, Inc. v. Research In Motion, Ltd., 418 F.3d 1282, 1305–06, 75 USPQ2d 1763 (Fed. Cir. 2005), *cert. denied*, 546 U.S. 1157 (2006). A special form of claim known as a Jepson-type claim allows the applicant to recite in the preamble all the conventional or known elements or steps of the claimed invention. *See, e.g.*, *In re* Glatt Air Techniques Inc., 630 F.3d 1026, 1027–28, 97 USPQ2d 1661 (Fed. Cir. 2011). In a Jepson-type claim, the preamble is a limitation. Howmedica Osteonics Corp. v. Wright Med. Tech. Inc., 540 F.3d 1337, 1344, 88 USPQ2d 1129 (Fed. Cir. 2008).

[144] *Symantec Corp.*, 522 F.3d at 1288–89, 86 USPQ2d 1449; *Intirtool, Ltd.*, 369 F.3d at 1293–96, 70 USPQ2d 1780 ("body of the claim 'describes a structurally complete invention such that deletion of the preamble phrase does not affect the structure or steps of the claimed invention' ") (citation omitted); STX, LLC v. Brine, 211 F.3d 588, 591, 54 USPQ2d 1347 (Fed. Cir. 2000); *see, e.g.*, Altiris, Inc. v. Symantec Corp., 318 F.3d 1363, 1371–72, 65 USPQ2d 1865 (Fed. Cir. 2003) (preamble recited purpose); Embrex v. Service Eng'g Corp., 216 F.3d 1343, 1347–48, 55 USPQ2d 1161 (Fed. Cir. 2000) (preamble describes the purpose of the invention); *see also* Purdue Pharma L.P. v. Boehringer Ingelheim GmbH, 98 F. Supp. 2d 362, 376–77, 55 USPQ2d 1168 (S.D.N.Y. 2000) (the preambles "merely set forth an intended use or benefit"), *aff'd*, 237 F.3d 1359, 57 USPQ2d 1647 (Fed. Cir. 2001).

[145] *See, e.g.*, Pitney Bowes v. Hewlett-Packard Co., 182 F.3d 1298, 1305–06, 51 USPQ2d 1161 (Fed. Cir. 1999).

fan example, because the elements (a) through (c) could be read to describe a standing fan (or possibly even a boat's motor), a court might recognize the preamble ("A ceiling fan") as necessary to give life, meaning, and vitality to the body of the claim.

B. Transitional Language

Most claims require transitional language between the preamble and the body of the claim.[146] Certain transitional language has customary meaning in patent law.[147] For example, the word "comprising" means including the elements that follow in the body but not excluding additional, unrecited elements.[148] Claims that use "comprising" or "comprised of" are referred to as open claims.[149] In the ceiling fan example, the transitional language is "comprising," which means that a ceiling fan with elements (a) through (c) *and* light bulbs is within the literal scope of the claim.[150]

---

[146] ROBERT C. FABER, LANDIS ON MECHANICS OF PATENT CLAIM DRAFTING §7 (5th ed. 2003).

[147] If the applicant acts as a lexicographer, these words and phrases can acquire a different meaning. See this chapter, §II.A.2.

[148] CIAS, Inc. v. Alliance Gaming Corp., 504 F.3d 1356, 1359–61, 84 USPQ2d 1737 (Fed. Cir. 2007), *cert. denied,* 128 S. Ct. 2080 (2008); Free Motion Fitness, Inc. v. Cybex Int'l, Inc., 423 F.3d 1343, 1347, 76 USPQ2d 1432 (Fed. Cir. 2005); Gillette Co. v. Energizer Holdings, Inc., 405 F.3d 1367, 1371–72, 74 USPQ2d 1586 (Fed. Cir. 2005); Power Mosfet Techs., L.L.C. v. Siemens AG, 378 F.3d 1396, 1409, 72 USPQ2d 1129 (Fed. Cir. 2004) (" 'Comprising,' while permitting additional elements not required by a claim, does not remove the limitations that are present"); Invitrogen Corp. v. Biocrest Mfg., L.P., 327 F.3d 1364, 1368, 66 USPQ2d 1631 (Fed. Cir. 2003) (method claim). *See generally* Smith & Nephew Inc. v. Ethicon Inc., 276 F.3d 1304, 1311, 61 USPQ2d 1065 (Fed. Cir. 2001); Innovad Inc. v. Microsoft Corp., 260 F.3d 1326, 1333, 59 USPQ2d 1676 (Fed. Cir. 2001); Georgia-Pacific Corp. v. United States Gypsum Co., 195 F.3d 1322, 1327–28, 52 USPQ2d 1590 (Fed. Cir. 1999), *cert. denied,* 531 U.S. 816 (2000). Among other words having the same customary meaning are "including" and "wherein." ROBERT C. FABER, LANDIS ON MECHANICS OF PATENT CLAIM DRAFTING §7 (4th ed. 1999); *see also* SanDisk Corp. v. Memorex Prods., Inc., 415 F.3d 1278, 1284, 75 USPQ2d 1475 (Fed. Cir.), *cert. denied,* 546 U.S. 1076 (2005); Mars, Inc. v. H. J. Heinz Co., L.P., 377 F.3d 1369, 1375–76, 71 USPQ2d 1837 (Fed. Cir. 2004) ("[t]he MPEP specifically provides that [t]he transitional term 'comprising,' . . . is synonymous with 'including,' 'containing,' or 'characterized by' ").

[149] *See generally Gillette Co.,* 405 F.3d at 1371–72, 74 USPQ2d 1586; *Free Motion Fitness, Inc.,* 423 F.3d at 1350–51, 76 USPQ2d 1432. *See also* ROBERT C. FABER, LANDIS ON MECHANICS OF PATENT CLAIM DRAFTING §7 (4th ed. 1999).

[150] Similarly, such a ceiling fan with *four* blades attached to the rod would also be within the literal scope of the claim. *See, e.g.,* Tate Access Floors v. Maxcess Techs., 222 F.3d 958, 970, 55 USPQ2d 1513 (Fed. Cir. 2000).

The transitional phrase "consisting of" yields a claim of more limited scope.[151] "Consisting of" basically means including only the elements that follow in the body and no more.[152] Claims that use "consisting of" are referred to as closed claims.[153] Thus, if the ceiling fan claim had used "consisting of" as its transitional language, then a ceiling fan with elements (a) through (c) and light bulbs would *not* be within the literal scope of the claim.[154]

C.　Elements Expressed in Means-Plus-Function Form

Pursuant to 35 U.S.C. §112, paragraph 6, a claim element can be expressed as a means for performing a specified function without reciting the structure or material that performs the claimed function.[155] For example, element (c) of the ceiling fan claim, which is expressed as "a cord coupled to the motor for switching the motor on and off," could be written instead functionally as "means for switching the motor on and off."[156]

---

[151] *See generally Georgia-Pacific Corp.*, 195 F.3d at 1327–28, 52 USPQ2d 1590.

[152] Immunocept LLC v. Fullbright & Jaworski LLP, 504 F.3d 1281, 1283–84, 85 USPQ2d 1085 (Fed. Cir. 2007); Norian Corp. v. Stryker Corp., 363 F.3d 1321, 1331–32, 70 UPSQ2d 1508 (Fed. Cir. 2004); ROBERT C. FABER, LANDIS ON MECHANICS OF PATENT CLAIM DRAFTING §8 (4th ed. 1999).

[153] CIAS, Inc. v. Alliance Gaming Corp., 504 F.3d 1356, 1361–62, 84 USPQ2d 1737 (Fed. Cir. 2007), *cert. denied*, 553 U.S. 1018 (2008); Norian Corp. v. Stryker Corp, 432 F.3d 1356, 1359, 77 USPQ2d 1242 (Fed. Cir. 2005).

[154] Occupying a middle ground between open and closed claims are claims using the transitional phrase "consisting essentially of." PPG Indus. v. Guardian Indus. Corp, 156 F.3d 1351,1354, 48 USPQ2d 1351 (Fed. Cir. 1998). The phrase "[c]onsisting essentially of" limits the scope of the claim to the recited elements and additional unrecited elements that do not materially affect the basic and novel characteristics of the claimed invention. MPEP §2111.03 (8th ed. 2001, rev. July 2008); *see also* W. E. Hall Co., Inc. v. Atlanta Corrugating, LLC, 370 F.3d 1343, 1353–54, 71 USPQ2d 1135 (Fed. Cir. 2004); Crystal Semiconductor Corp. v. TriTech Microelectronics Int'l, 246 F.3d 1336, 1348, 1350–51, 57 USPQ2d 1953 (Fed. Cir. 2001) ("having" transition phrase).

[155] 35 U.S.C.A. §112, ¶6 (2001). Before the enactment of the Patent Act of 1952, claims elements expressed in functional language were held invalid because, in theory, they covered any possible way to perform the claimed function. O'Reilly v. Morse, 56 U.S. (15 How.) 62, 112, 13, 118–20 (1853); Halliburton Oil Well Cementing Co. v. Walker, 329 U.S. 1, 12–14, 71 USPQ 175 (1946). *See generally* Warner-Jenkinson Co. v. Hilton Davis Chem. Co., 520 U.S. 17, 27–28, 41 USPQ2d 1865 (1997). For a thorough review of the history of this statutory provision, see Rudolph P. Hofmann, Jr. & Edward F. Heller III, *The Rosetta Stone for the Doctrine of Means-Plus-Function Patent Claims*, 23 RUTGERS COMPUTER & TECH. L.J. 227, 272–79 (1997).

[156] Section 112, paragraph 6 also allows claim elements to be expressed in step-plus-function form. Masco Corp. v. United States, 303 F.3d 1316, 1326–28, 64 USPQ2d 1182 (Fed. Cir. 2002). *See generally* Apex Inc. v. Raritan Computer, Inc., 325 F.3d 1364, 1371, 66 USPQ2d 1444 (Fed. Cir.), *cert. denied*, 540 U.S. 1073 (2003).

Whether an element of a claim is in means-plus-function form is a claim construction question.[157] Use of the term "means" creates a presumption that the element is to be construed in accordance with Section 112, paragraph 6.[158] This presumption may be rebutted, however, when the claim element recites sufficiently definite structure or material to perform the claimed function.[159] Absence of the term "means" creates a presumption that the element is not to be construed in accordance with Section 112, paragraph 6.[160] However, this presumption may be rebutted when the claim element does not recite sufficiently definite structure or material to perform the claimed function.[161] In determining whether these presumptions have been rebutted by a preponderance of the evidence,[162] the court may examine the intrinsic evidence and any relevant extrinsic evidence.[163]

Two claim construction questions arise with elements expressed in means-plus-function form:[164] (1) What is the func-

---

[157] Inventio AG v. Thyssenkrupp Elevator Am. Corp., 649 F.3d 1350, 1356, 99 USPQ2d 1112, 1116–17, (Fed. Cir. 2011); Kemco Sales v. Control Papers Co., 208 F.3d 1352, 1360, 54 USPQ2d 1308 (Fed. Cir. 2000).

[158] Rembrandt Data Techs., LP v. AOL, LLC, 641 F.3d 1331, 1340–41, 98 USPQ2d 1393 (Fed. Cir. 2011); Inventio AG, 649 F.3d at 1356, 99 USPQ2d 1112.

[159] Phillips v. AWH Corp., 415 F.3d 1303, 1311, 75 USPQ2d 1321 (Fed. Cir. 2005); see also Rembrandt Data Techs., 641 F.3d at 1340–41, 98 USPQ2d 1394; Callicrate v. Wadsworth Mfg., Inc., 427 F.3d 1361, 1368, 77 USPQ2d 1041 (Fed. Cir. 2005). Thus, a claim element that uses the term "means" and does not specify any structure or material for performing the recited function will be construed in accordance with §112, ¶6. TI Group Auto. Sys. (N. Am.), Inc. v. VDO N. Am., L.L.C., 375 F.3d 1126, 1135, 71 USPQ2d 1328 (Fed. Cir. 2004), cert. denied, 543 U.S. 1147 (2005); BBA Nonwovens Simpsonville v. Superior Nonwovens, 303 F.3d 1332, 1343, 64 USPQ2d 1257 (Fed. Cir. 2002). This presumption may also be rebutted when the claim element recites no function corresponding to the means. Apex Inc., 325 F.3d at 1372, 66 USPQ2d 1444.

[160] Inventio AG, 649 F.3d at 1356, 99 USPQ2d 1112, John D. Watts v. XL Sys., 232 F.3d 877, 880, 56 USPQ2d 1836 (Fed. Cir. 2000). Absence of the term "step for" also creates a presumption that the element is not to be construed in accordance with §112, ¶6. Cardiac Pacemakers, Inc. v. St. Jude Med., Inc., 381 F.3d 1371, 1381–82, 72 USPQ2d 1333 (Fed. Cir. 2004) (a method claim reciting " 'the method comprises the steps of' " does not trigger the application of §112, ¶6 absent the specific language " 'step for' "), cert. denied, 544 U.S. 1032 (2005).

[161] Inventio AG, 649 F.3d at 1356, 99 USPQ2d 1112, John D. Watts, 232 F.3d at 880–81.

[162] Apex Inc., 325 F.3d at 1372, 66 USPQ2d 1444 cert. denied, 540 U.S. 1073 (2003).

[163] Inventio AG, 649 F.3d at 1356, 99 USPQ2d 1112 (Fed. Cir. 2011); see, e.g., CCS Fitness, Inc. v. Brunswick Corp., 288 F.3d 1359,1369–70, 62 USPQ2d 1658 (Fed. Cir. 2002).

[164] See generally JVW Enters., Inc. v. Interact Accessories, Inc., 424 F.3d 1324, 1330–32, 76 USPQ2d 1641 (Fed. Cir. 2005); Northrop Grumman Corp. v. Intel Corp., 325 F.3d 1346, 1350, 66 USPQ2d 1341 (Fed. Cir. 2003).

tion claimed in that element?[165] and (2) What structure or material disclosed in the specification performs the function claimed in that element?[166] Once these questions are answered, the means-plus-function claim element can be construed in accordance with Section 112, paragraph 6.[167]

---

[165] *JVW Enters., Inc.*, 424 F.3d at 1330–32, 76 USPQ2d 1641; Omega Eng'g, Inc. v. Raytek Corp., 334 F.3d 1314, 1321–23, 1328, 1332, 67 USPQ2d 1321 (Fed. Cir. 2003); Multiform Desiccants v. Medzam, Ltd., 133 F.3d 1473, 1479, 45 USPQ2d 1429 (Fed. Cir. 1998) ("[T]he first step in interpretation of the claim is determination of the meaning of the words used to describe the claimed function, if such meaning is in dispute"). There can be more than one function. *See, e.g., Northrop Grumman Corp.*, 325 F.3d at 1350, 66 USPQ2d 1341. When identifying the function, it is important not to improperly broaden or improperly narrow that function. Cardiac Pacemakers, Inc. v. St. Jude Med., Inc., 296 F.3d 1106, 63 USPQ2d 1725 (Fed. Cir. 2002); *see, e.g.,* Lockheed Martin Corp. v. Space Sys./Loral, Inc., 324 F.3d 1308, 1319, 66 USPQ2d 1282 (Fed. Cir. 2003) (improper broadening); *see also* Creo Prods., Inc. v. Presstek, Inc., 305 F.3d 1337, 1346, 64 USPQ2d 1385 (Fed. Cir. 2002); Generation II Orthotics v. Medical Tech., 263 F.3d 1356, 1363–67, 59 USPQ2d 1919 (Fed. Cir. 2001).

[166] *See, e.g.,* Aristocrat Techs. Austl. Pty. Ltd. v. International Game Tech., 521 F.3d 1328, 1333–37, 86 USPQ2d 1235 (Fed. Cir. 2008), *cert. denied,* 129 S. Ct. 754 (2008); Callicrate v. Wadsworth Mfg., Inc., 427 F.3d 1361, 1369, 77 USPQ2d 1041 (Fed. Cir. 2005). *See generally* Tehrani v. Hamilton Med., Inc., 331 F.3d 1355, 1362, 67 USPQ2d 1015 (Fed. Cir. 2003). The prosecution history may be consulted to answer the question. *See, e.g.,* Cross Med. Prod. Inc. v. Medtronics Sofamor Danek Inc., 424 F.3d 1293, 76 USPQ2d 1662 (Fed. Cir. 2005); Overhead Door Corp. v. Chamberlain Group, Inc., 194 F.3d 1261, 1272–73, 52 USPQ2d 1321 (Fed. Cir. 1999) (reissue proceedings). There might only be one structure or material disclosed in the specification that performs the claimed function. *See, e.g.,* Cortland Line Co. v. Orvis Co., 203 F.3d 1351, 1357, 53 USPQ2d 1734 (Fed. Cir. 2000). Structure or material disclosed in the specification that performs the claimed function is referred to as "corresponding" structure or material. *See, e.g., Overhead Door Corp.*, 194 F.3d at 1271–72, 52 USPQ2d 1321. Structure is only "corresponding" if the structure is clearly linked by the specification or prosecution history to the specified function. *JVW Enters., Inc.*, 424 F.3d at 1330–32, 76 UPSQ2d 1641; Medical Instrumentation & Diagnostics Corp. v. Elekta AB, 344 F.3d 1205, 1210–1219, 68 USPQ2d 1263 (Fed. Cir. 2003) ("The requirement that structure must be clearly linked or associated with the claimed function is the quid pro quo for the convenience of claiming in functional terms"), *cert. denied,* 541 U.S. 959 (2004); Medtronic, Inc. v. Advanced Cardiovascular, 248 F.3d 1303, 1311–15, 58 USPQ2d 1607 (Fed. Cir. 2001) (that the structure is capable of performing the function is not sufficient). Additional aspects of the structure that are unrelated to the recited function are not "corresponding." *Aristocrat Techs. Austl. Pty. Ltd.*, 521 F.3d at 1333–34, 86 USPQ2d 1235; *see, e.g., Northrop Grumman Corp.*, 325 F.3d at 1352–54, 66 USPQ2d 1341. Whether structure is corresponding is determined from the perspective of one with ordinary skill in the art.

[167] *Cross Med. Prod. Inc.*, 424 F.3d at 1306–09, 76 USPQ2d 1662. Ordinary principles of claim construction are used to construe the meaning of the words used in a means-plus-function format. *Lockheed Martin Corp.*, 324 F.3d at 1319, 66 USPQ2d 1282; *Cardiac Pacemakers, Inc.*, 296 F.3d at 1113, 63 USPQ2d 1725; *see, e.g.,* Ballard Med. Prods. v. Allegiance Healthcare Corp., 268 F.3d 1352, 1359–62, 60 USPQ2d 1493 (Fed. Cir. 2001) (explicit disavowal); Globetrotter Software, Inc. v. Elan Computer Group, 236 F.3d 1363, 1368–69, 57 USPQ2d 1542 (Fed. Cir. 2001) (examining the intrinsic evidence). *See generally Generation II Orthotics,* 263 F.3d at 1365–67, 59 USPQ2d 1919. Not all claim language found in a means-plus-function claim element is construed in accordance with §112, ¶6. *See, e.g.,* IMS Tech. v. Haas Automation, 206 F.3d 1422, 1432, 54 USPQ2d 1129 (Fed. Cir.), *cert. dismissed,* 530 U.S. 1299 (2000); *Multiform Desiccants,* 133 F.3d at 1479–80, 45 USPQ2d 1429.

If the specification does not disclose sufficient structure to perform a claimed function, the claim may be invalid for indefiniteness.[168]

Means-plus-function claim elements are not construed literally, i.e., the acquired meaning of the element is not any and all means for performing the specified function. Instead, claim elements expressed in means-plus-function form are construed more narrowly.[169] Specifically, such claim elements are construed to cover (1) the structure or material disclosed in the patent's specification that perform the claimed function, and (2) equivalents of that disclosed structure or material.[170] Thus, for example, if element (c) of the ceiling fan claim was written as "means for switching the motor on and off" and the only structure disclosed in the specification that switched the motor on and off was a cord, then the means-plus-function claim element would be construed to cover (1) that cord, and (2) equivalents of that cord.

Determining whether a particular means for performing the recited function is a Section 112, paragraph 6 equivalent has not been treated as a claim construction issue.[171] For example, determining whether a product accused of literal infringement has structure that is equivalent to the structure disclosed in the patent for performing the recited function in a means-plus-function claim element (i.e., the corresponding structure) is a question of fact.[172]

---

[168] *Cardiac Pacemakers, Inc.*, 296 F.3d at 1113–19, 63 USPQ2d 1725; *see also Aristocrat Techs. Austl. Pty. Ltd.*, 521 F.3d at 1333–37, 86 USPQ2d 1235.

[169] *See generally* Nomos Corp. v. BrainLAB USA, Inc., 357 F.3d 1364, 1367–69, 69 USPQ2d 1853 (Fed. Cir. 2004); *Ballard Med. Prods.*, 268 F.3d at 1362, 60 USPQ2d 1493.

[170] *See, e.g.,* Versa Corp. v. Ag-Bag Int'l Ltd., 392 F.3d 1325, 1329, 73 USPQ2d 1191 (Fed. Cir. 2004); *IMS Tech.*, 206 F.3d at 1432, 54 USPQ2d 1129. When the patent discloses alternative structures for performing the recited function, the proper claim construction identifies all the structures. TI Group Auto. Sys. (N. Am.), Inc. v. VDO N. Am., L.L.C., 375 F.3d 1126, 1137, 71 USPQ2d 1328 (Fed. Cir. 2004), *cert. denied*, 543 U.S. 1147 (2005); *Creo Prods., Inc.*, 305 F.3d at 1345, 1346, 64 USPQ2d 1385. If an applicant explicitly disavows that a particular structure is within the scope of the invention, then that disavowed structure will not be covered by the means-plus-function claim. *See Ballard Med. Prods.*, 268 F.3d at 1359–62, 60 USPQ2d 1493.

[171] Identifying equivalents without identifying the corresponding structure is an error. Texas Digital Sys., Inc. v. Telegenix, Inc., 308 F.3d 1193, 1213, 64 USPQ2d 1812 (Fed. Cir. 2002), *cert. denied*, 538 U.S. 1058 (2003).

[172] See Chapter 6, §I.C.1.

CHAPTER 6

INFRINGEMENT

I. CLAIMS OF INFRINGEMENT

Subject to certain statutory exceptions, discussed in this chapter, infringement occurs when (1) someone (2) without authority (3) makes, uses, offers to sell, sells, or imports (4) any patented invention (5) within the United States, its territories, or its possessions (6) during the term of the patent.[1] For purposes of infringement, a patented invention is defined by a patent claim—and the elements of that claim—as set forth in the issued patent.[2]

Direct infringement, defined in 35 U.S.C. §271(a), occurs when one party makes, uses, offers to sell, sells, or imports each element of a patented invention.[3] Indirect infringement, defined in §271(b) and (c) can occur when a party aids or abets direct infringement by others.[4]

The party asserting infringement bears the burden of proof, by a preponderance of the evidence.[5]

A. Someone

A direct infringer may practice each element of the patent claim alone or through others based on vicarious liability.[6] If the direct infringer is a corporation, the corporate officers can be personally liable if the corporate veil can be pierced.[7]

---

[1] 35 U.S.C. §271(a).

[2] Markman v. Westview Instruments, Inc., 517 U.S. 370, 373–74, 38 USPQ2d 1461 (1996). See Chapter 2, §III.B for a general discussion of the contents of a patent, including claims. Claim construction and claim elements are discussed in Chapter 5.

[3] Southwall Techs., Inc. v. Cardinal IG Co., 54 F.3d 1570, 1575, 34 USPQ2d 1673 (Fed. Cir.), cert. denied, 516 U.S. 987 (1995); see, e.g., Contech Stormwater Solutions, Inc. v. Baysaver Techs., Inc., 310 F. App'x 404, 408 (Fed. Cir. 2009) (no infringement where one element not found in accused product).

[4] Global-Tech Appliances Inc. v. SEB S.A., 131 S. Ct. 2060, 98 USPQ2d 1665, 1668–71 (2011); see also Hewlett-Packard Co. v. Bausch & Lomb Inc., 909 F.2d 1464, 1468–69, 15 USPQ2d 1525 (Fed. Cir. 1990).

[5] Seal-Flex Inc. v. Athletic Track & Court Constr., 172 F.3d 836, 84, 50 USPQ2d 1225 (Fed. Cir. 1999); SSIH Equip. S.A. v. United States Int'l Trade Comm'n, 718 F.2d 365, 376, 218 USPQ 678 (Fed. Cir. 1983).

[6] BMC Ress., Inc. v. Paymentech, L.P., 498 F.3d 1373, 1379, 84 USPQ2d 1545 (Fed. Cir. 2007); see, e.g., Centillion Data Sys., LLC v. Qwest Commc'ns Int'l, Inc., 631 F.3d 1279, 1286–87, 97 USPQ2d 1697 (Fed. Cir. 2011) (no vicarious liability); Cross Med. Prods. v. Medtronic Sofamor Danek, Inc., 424 F.3d 1293, 1310–12, 76 USPQ2d 1662 (Fed. Cir. 2005) (no vicarious liability); Clear with Computers, LLC v. Hyundai Motor Am., Inc., No. 6:09-cv-479, 2011 WL 2436535, at *3–4 (E.D. Tex. June 14, 2011) (vicarious liability).

[7] Al-Site Corp. v. VSI Int'l Inc., 174 F.3d 1308, 1331, 50 USPQ2d 1161 (Fed. Cir. 1999); see, e.g., Wordtech Syss., Inc v. Integrated Networks Solutions, Inc., 609 F.3d 1308, 1314–15, 95 USPQ2d 1619 (Fed. Cir. 2010) (improper jury instructions on officer liability for corporation's infringement).

Whether a patent claim may be "jointly" directly infringed currently turns on whether the claim is directed to a system or a method. The issue arises because a claim may be directed to a collection of instrumentalities (an "apparatus" or "system" claim), not all of which are controlled by the same party. For example, a "system for wireless communication" may include a handheld device, owned and operated by an individual, and computer and switching equipment, owned and operated by a communications service provider. For such a system, the direct infringer is the person who "put the invention into service, i.e., control[s] the system as a whole and obtain[s] benefit from it." Thus, the owner of the handheld device can be the person who has infringed, even though he or she does not own or control each element of the system.[8]

With respect to a method patent, however, direct infringement requires that a single entity perform each of the claimed steps of the method, unless the defendant has exercised direction or control over the other alleged joint infringers.[9] The issue of joint infringement ("divided infringement") of method claims is currently before the Federal Circuit for en banc review.[10]

A state, or an arm of the state, such as a state agency or university, can invoke Eleventh Amendment sovereign immunity as a defense to patent infringement.[11] This immunity can be waived. Waiver in one action generally does not extend to a separate action.[12] Federal Circuit law, rather than state law, governs whether there has been an Eleventh Amendment waiver.[13]

Before 2011, a patent owner could, and often did, sue multiple defendants in a single action on the grounds that each of

---

[8] *Centillion Data Sys., LLC,* 631 F.3d at 1283–86, 97 USPQ2d 1697; NTP, Inc. v. Research in Motion, Ltd., 418 F.3d 1282, 1317, 75 USPQ2d 1763 (Fed. Cir. 2005).

[9] BMC Res., Inc., 498 F.3d at 1380–81, 84 USPQ2d 1545.

[10] McKesson Techs. Inc. v. Epic Sys. Corp., No. 2010–1291, 2011 WL 2173401, at *1 (Fed. Cir. May 26, 2011); Akamai Techs., Inc. v. MIT, Nos. 2009–1372, –1380, –1416, –1417, 2011 WL 1518909, at *1 (Fed. Cir. Apr. 20, 2011).

[11] Florida Prepaid Postsecondary Educ. Expense Bd. v. College Sav. Bank, 527 U.S. 627, 630, 51 USPQ2d 1081 (1999).

[12] Biomedical Patent Mgmt. Corp. v. California, 505 F.3d 1328, 1339, 85 USPQ2d 1074 (Fed. Cir. 2007); *see, e.g.,* Vas-Cath, Inc. v. Curators of Univ. of Mo., 473 F.3d 1376, 1383–84, 81 USPQ2d 1524 (Fed. Cir. 2007) (waiver in appeal phase found in view of waiver in proceeding below); A123 Sys., Inc. v. Hydro-Quebec, 626 F.3d 1213, 1219–20, 97 USPQ2d 1257 (Fed. Cir. 2010) (no waiver despite waiver in separate suit involving same parties, same patent).

[13] *Biomedical Patent Mgmt. Corp.,* 505 F.3d. at 1334, 85 USPQ2d 1074.

them infringed the same patent, even if their activities were otherwise unrelated. Permissive joinder was governed by Rule 20(b), Federal Rules of Civil Procedure. For actions filed after September 16, 2011, the joinder of accused infringers is governed by 35 U.S.C. §299. Other than cases where the right to relief is asserted against the parties jointly or severally, joinder requires a showing that the alleged acts of infringement relate to "the same accused product or process" such that "questions of fact common to all defendants . . . will arise in the action."[14]

B. Without Authority

By statute, a patent has the attributes of personal property.[15] This includes the right to license others to practice the patented invention. A licensee who is acting within the scope of the license does not infringe the licensed patent.[16] For example, if a license allows company A to make and sell a patented item east of the Mississippi River, then company A does not infringe when it sells the item east of the Mississippi River, but it does infringe when it sells the item west of the Mississippi River. Licenses are interpreted based on ordinary principles of state contract law.[17]

A doctrine of implied license has been judicially created based on the concept that patent rights in an item are "exhausted" after an authorized sale. More specifically, the first authorized,

---

[14]Leahy-Smith America Invents Act, Pub.L. 112-29, H.R. 1249 (2011), sec. 19, adding 35 U.S.C. §299, and setting effective date as date of enactment of the statute. The new statute does not apply to lawsuits in which the acts of alleged infringement are the filing of Abbreviated New Drug Applications by multiple parties each seeking approval of the Food and Drug Administration to market generic copies of a patented pharmaceutical before the expiration of the patents alleged to cover that drug. *Id.* (new rules apply to all civil actions "other than one in which an act of infringement under section 271(e)(2) has been pled").

[15]35 U.S.C. §261 (2001).

[16]*See, e.g.,* Intel Corp. v. VIA Techs., Inc., 319 F.3d 1357, 1361–62, 65 USPQ2d 1934 (Fed. Cir. 2003). "The right to 'make, use and sell' a product inherently includes the right to have it made by a third party, absent a clear indication of intent to the contrary." CoreBrace LLC, v. Star Seismic LLC, 566 F.3d 1069, 1072–73, 91 USPQ2d 1209 (Fed. Cir. 2009).

[17]Power Lift, Inc. v. Weatherford Nipple-Up Sys., Inc., 871 F.2d 1082, 1085, 10 USPQ2d 1464 (Fed. Cir. 1989); *see, e.g.,* Imation Corp. v. Koninklijke Philips Elec. N.V., 586 F.3d 980, 985, 92 USPQ2d 1664 (Fed. Cir. 2009) (applying New York law to interpret license); *Corebrace LLC,* 566 F.3d at 1072–75, 91 USPQ2d 1209 (applying Utah law to interpret license).

unconditional sale of an item in the United States that embodies a patented invention terminates the patent owner's rights in that item.[18] After such a sale, the buyer is impliedly authorized to repair, use, modify, and resell the purchased item, free from further claims under the patent laws by the seller.[19] Thus, continuing the illustration above, if company B bought the patented item from company A east of the Mississippi River, then company B can repair the item and sell it east or west of the Mississippi River. For purposes of the exhaustion doctrine, an item embodies the patented invention if it has the essential features of the invention and its reasonable and intended use is to practice the invention.[20] Express conditions accompanying the sale or license of a patented item are generally upheld, in which case the exhaustion doctrine does not apply.[21]

The authorized sale of a *nonpatented* item that is used to practice a patented invention also may create an implied license. Such license may arise if the nonpatented item sold has no non-infringing use, the scope of the implied license encompasses the patented invention, and the circumstances of the sale plainly indicate that the grant of a license should be implied.[22] Other grounds for an implied license include an express agreement that implies a license or acts of the patent owner that create a legal

---

[18] Quanta Computer, Inc. v. LG Elecs., Inc., 553 U.S. 617, 637, 86 USPQ2d 1673 (2008); *see, e.g.*, TransCore, LP v. Electronic Transaction Consultants Corp., 563 F.3d 1271, 1274–77, 90 USPQ2d 1372 (Fed. Cir. 2009) (authorized sale based on covenant not to sue); Tessera, Inc. v. International Trade Comm'n, 98 USPQ2d 1868, 1876–78 (Fed. Cir. 2011) (authorized sale despite licensee's later breach of payment terms); Fujifilm Corp. v. Benun, 605 F.3d 1366, 1371–72, 95 USPQ2d 1985 (Fed. Cir.) (no exhaustion for sale outside the United States) *cert. denied*, 131 S. Ct. 829 (2010).

[19] *See* Jazz Photo Corp. v. United States Int'l Trade Comm'n, 264 F.3d 1094, 1102–1105, 59 USPQ2d 1907 (Fed. Cir. 2001) (distinguishing permissible repair from impermissible reconstruction), *cert. denied*, 536 U.S. 950 (2002).

[20] *Quanta Computer, Inc.*, 553 U.S. at 631–32, 86 USPQ2d 1673.

[21] Princo Corp. v. International Trade Comm'n, 616 F.3d 1318, 1328, 96 USPQ2d 1233 (Fed. Cir. 2010), *cert. denied*, 179 L. Ed. 2d 1209 (2011); *see, e.g.*, Monsanto Co. v. Scruggs, 459 F.3d 1328, 1335–36, 79 USPQ2d 1813 (Fed. Cir. 2006) (no exhaustion given, inter alia, license condition that accompanied sale).

[22] Met-Coil Sys. Corp. v. Korners Unlimited Inc., 803 F.2d 684, 686, 231 USPQ 474 (Fed. Cir. 1986); *see, e.g.*, Glass Equip. Dev. Inc. v. Besten Inc., 174 F.3d 1337, 1342, 50 USPQ2d 1300 (Fed. Cir. 1999) (insufficient evidence of no noninfringing uses); Monsanto Co. v. Scruggs, 459 F.3d 1328, 1336, 79 USPQ2d 1813 (Fed. Cir. 2006), *cert. denied*, 549 U.S. 1342 (2007) (circumstances of sale did not imply a license). In certain circumstances, the license term may extend beyond the life of the nonpatented item. Carborundum Co. v. Molten Metal Equip. Innovations, 72 F.3d 872, 878–80, 37 USPQ2d 1169 (Fed. Cir. 1995).

or equitable estoppel-like limitation on the right to sue.[23] An implied license based on legal estoppel may be found where a patentee licensed a right, received consideration, and then tries to take back the granted right.[24] An implied license based on equitable estoppel principles may be found, for example, where a party knows of a patent and the patentee objects to the party's infringement, but the patentee delays in seeking relief and thereby misleads the infringer into believing the patentee does not object.[25]

The burden of proving an implied license is on the party asserting it.[26]

A statutory "safe harbor" under 35 U.S.C. §271(e)(1) provides limited authorization to practice a patented invention for uses reasonably related to meeting the reporting requirements of federal food and drug laws, e.g., the development of new pharmaceuticals or generic forms of an existing drug.[27]

C. Makes, Uses, Offers to Sell, Sells, or Imports

In the context of patent law, "makes" means creating an operable assembly of the patented invention;[28] "uses" means

---

[23] *See, e.g.,* Jacobs v. Nintendo of America, Inc., 370 F.3d 1097, 1100, 71 USPQ2d 1055 (Fed. Cir. 2004) (implied license based on settlement agreement); Zenith Elecs. Corp. v. PDI Commc'n Sys., 522 F.3d 1348, 1360–62, 86 USPQ2d 1513 (Fed. Cir. 2008) (implied license based on express license); *TransCore, LP,* 563 F.3d at 1278–80, 90 USPQ2d 1372 (implied license by legal estoppel); Wang Labs., Inc. v. Mitsubishi Elecs. of Am., 103 F.3d 1571, 1580–82, 41 USPQ2d 1263 (Fed. Cir.), *cert. denied,* 522 U.S. 818 (1997) (implied license by equitable estoppel).

[24] *TransCore, LP,* 563 F.3d at 1279, 90 USPQ2d 1372 (quoting Wang Labs., Inc., 103 F.3d at 1581, 41 USPQ2d 1263); General Protecht Group, Inc. v. Leviton Mfg. Co., 651 F.3d 1355, 1361–62, 99 USPQ2d 1275 (Fed. Cir. 2011) (where parent patent was licensed for accused product, implied license under continuation of parent patent is presumed, absent evidence of mutual intent to the contrary).

[25] *Wang Labs., Inc.,* 103 F.3d at 1580–82, 41 USPQ2d 1263.

[26] *Carborundum Co.,* 72 F.3d at 878, 37 USPQ2d 1169.

[27] Merck KgaA v. Integra Lifesciences I, Ltd., 545 U.S. 193, 205–08, 74 USPQ2d 1801 (2005). Section 271(e)(1) has been construed to cover certain medical devices for which FDA approval is required. Eli Lilly & Co. v. Medtronic Inc., 496 U.S. 661, 15 USPQ2d 1121 (1990). The safe harbor does not apply to a device that is not subject to FDA approval, even if the device is used exclusively for investigations related to FDA submissions. Proveris Sci. Corp. v. Innovasystems, Inc., 536 F.3d 1256, 1264–66, 87 USPQ2d 1602 (Fed. Cir. 2008). The safe harbor applies to process patents in actions under Section 337 of the Tariff Act if the imported product is used for purposes within the §271(e)(1) exception. Amgen Inc. v. United States Int'l Trade Comm'n, 565 F.3d 846, 851–52, 90 USPQ2d 1842 (Fed. Cir. 2009).

[28] Deepsouth Packing Co. v. Laitram Corp., 406 U.S. 518, 529 (1972); *see, e.g.,* Centillion Data Sys., LLC v. Qwest Commc'ns Int'l, 631 F.3d 1279, 1288, 97 USPQ2d 1697 (Fed. Cir. 2011). Regarding whether a composition with a transitory existence can be infringing, see generally *Novartis Corp. v. Ben Venue Labs, Inc.,* 271 F.3d 1043, 1049 n.5, 60 USPQ2d 1836 (Fed. Cir. 2001).

something other than mere possession[29] or nonprofit, experimental use;[30] and "sells" means more than just the transfer of tangible property.[31] "Offers to sell" is interpreted according to its ordinary meaning in contract law.[32]

1. *Direct Infringement*

Direct infringement occurs when one party makes, uses, offers to sell, sells, or imports each element of a patented invention.[33] Circumstantial evidence can be sufficient to prove direct infringement.[34] In certain cases, evidence that an industry standard directly infringes a claim, and that the accused product conforms to that standard, can be sufficient to prove direct infringement.[35] For a claim with a functional limitation, the patent owner need not have actually tested the accused device if infringement can be proved otherwise.[36]

In the Process Patent Amendments Act of 1988, with subsequent amendment,[37] Congress expanded the rights conferred

---

[29] *See, e.g., Centillion Data Sys., LLC,* 631 F.3d at 1284, 97 USPQ2d 1697 (use of system claim occurs when a party "control[s] the system as a whole and obtain[s] benefit from it"); Medical Solutions, Inc. v. C Change Surgical LLC, 541 F.3d 1136, 1141, 88 USPQ2d 1275 (Fed. Cir. 2008) (not a use to merely display at trade show). Testing is a use that may be infringing. Waymark Corp. v. Porta Sys. Corp., 245 F.3d 1364, 1366–67, 58 USPQ2d 1456 (Fed. Cir. 2001).

[30] 35 U.S.C. §271(e)(1) creates an exception for experimentation related to submissions to the FDA. *See Merck KgaA,* 545 U.S. at 195, 74 USPQ2d 1801. Outside of this statutory exception, the experimental use defense is very narrow. Madey v. Duke Univ., 307 F.3d 1351, 1361–63, 64 USPQ2d 1737 (Fed. Cir. 2002), *cert. denied,* 539 U.S. 958 (2003); *see, e.g.,* Monsanto Co. v. E.I. DuPont de Nemours & Co., No. 4:09-cv-686, 2010 WL 3039210, at *10 (E.D. Mo. July 30, 2010) (no experimental use).

[31] *See, e.g.,* Transocean Offshore Deepwater Drilling, Inc. v. Maersk Contractors USA, Inc., 617 F.3d 1296, 1310–11, 96 USPQ2d 1104 (Fed. Cir. 2010) (sale based on contract, with schematics, to sell infringing product).

[32] Rotec Indus. v. Mitsubishi Corp., 215 F.3d 1246, 1255, 55 USPQ2d 1001 (Fed. Cir. 2000). *But see* 3D Sys. Inc. v. Aarotech Lab. Inc., 160 F.3d 1373, 1378–79, 48 USPQ2d 1773 (Fed. Cir. 1998) (declining to apply state contract law or federal on-sale bar law under §102(b) to decide whether an offer to sell under §271(a) took place).

[33] 35 U.S.C. §271(a).

[34] Vita-Mix Corp. v. Basic Holding, Inc., 581 F.3d 1317, 1326, 92 USPQ2d 1340 (Fed. Cir. 2009); Lucent Techs., Inc. v. Gateway, Inc., 580 F.3d 1301, 1318, 92 USPQ2d 1555 (Fed. Cir. 2009), *cert. denied,* 130 S. Ct. 3324 (2010); Moleculon Research Corp. v. CBS, Inc., 793 F.2d 1261, 1272, 229 USPQ 805 (Fed. Cir. 1986), *cert. denied,* 479 U.S. 1030 (1987).

[35] Fujitsu Ltd. v. Netgear, Inc., 620 F.3d 1321, 1327, 96 USPQ2d 1742 (Fed. Cir. 2010).

[36] Martek Biosciences Corp. v. Nutrinova Inc., 579 F.3d 1363, 1373–74, 92 USPQ2d 1148 (Fed. Cir. 2009).

[37] 35 U.S.C. §154. For a review of the legislative history, see *Eli Lilly & Co. v. Am. Cyanamid Co.,* 82 F.3d 1568, 38 USPQ2d 1705 (Fed. Cir. 1996); *see also* Novo Nordisk of N. Am. v. Genentech Inc., 77 F.3d 1364, 1367, 37 USPQ2d 1773 (Fed. Cir. 1996).

by a patent to include the right to exclude the use, offer for sale, sale, or import of *products* made by a patented *process*.[38] A product will be deemed not made by the patented process if it is materially changed by subsequent processes or if it becomes a trivial and nonessential component of another product.[39] A product will be rebuttably presumed to be made by a patented process if there is a substantial likelihood it was made by the process and the patent owner undertook reasonable efforts to determine the process used.[40] There are many statutory limitations on the damages available for violation of this process-patent right and many detailed conditions.[41]

By statute, it is also an act of infringement to submit an application to the Food and Drug Administration (FDA) for expedited approval of a generic drug.[42] This permits any patent infringement claim relating to the proposed generic to be adjudicated during the pendency of the application for FDA approval, even though no commercial use, sale, or offer for sale of the proposed generic has taken place.[43] Infringement is tested with reference to "the product likely to be sold following FDA approval."[44]

---

[38] Such use, sale, offer to sell, or importation may make one liable as an infringer. 35 U.S.C.A. §271(g) (2001); *see, e.g.,* Bayer AG v. Housey Pharms., Inc., 340 F.3d 1367 (Fed. Cir. 2003) (statute is limited to physical goods that are manufactured, not information); Ajinomoto Co. v. Archer-Daniels-Midland Co., 228 F.3d 1338, 1347–48, 56 USPQ2d 1332 (Fed. Cir. 2000), *cert. denied,* 532 U.S. 1019 (2001) (statute can apply even if the practice of a process abroad is authorized).

[39] 35 U.S.C.A. §271(g) (2001); Biotec Biologische Naturverpackungen v. Biocorp, 249 F.3d 1341, 1351–52, 58 USPQ2d 1737 (Fed. Cir. 2001); Amgen Inc. v. F. Hoffmann-La Roche Ltd., 580 F.3d 1340, 1379, 92 USPQ2d 1289 (Fed. Cir. 2009) ("Materiality is context-dependent").

[40] 35 U.S.C.A. §295 (2001); *Novo Nordisk of N. Am.,* 77 F.3d at 1368 n.6, 37 USPQ2d 1773.

[41] *See, e.g.,* 35 U.S.C.A. §§271(g) and 287(b) (2001); Kinik Co. v. United States Int'l Trade Comm'n, 362 F.3d 1359, 1361–63, 70 USPQ2d 1300 (Fed. Cir. 2004) (defenses available under §271(g) do not apply to actions under 19 U.S.C. §1337(a)(1)(B)(ii)).

[42] 35 U.S.C. §271(e)(2).

[43] 21 U.S.C. §355(j); *see* Eli Lilly & Co. v. Medtronic Inc., 496 U.S. 661, 678, 15 USPQ2d 1121 (1990); Allergan, Inc. v. Alcon Labs., Inc., 324 F.3d 1322, 1326–27, 66 USPQ2d 1225 (Fed. Cir.), cert. denied, 540 U.S. 1048 (2003); Warner-Lambert Co. v. Apotex Corp., 316 F.3d 1348, 1354–62, 65 USPQ2d 1481 (Fed. Cir. 2003) (no claim for relief where defendant's application for FDA approval is directed to a use not covered by the patent in suit). An Abbreviated New Drug Application (ANDA) filer who is not sued for infringement under §271(e)(2) within the 45-day period provided by statute may seek declaratory judgment of noninfringement. 21 U.S.C §355(j)(5)(C); 35 U.S.C. §271(e)(5); Caraco Pharm. Labs., Ltd. v. Forest Labs., Inc. 527 F.3d 1278, 1283, 86 USPQ2d 1289 (Fed. Cir. 2008).

[44] Abbott Labs. v. TorPharm, Inc., 300 F.3d 1367, 1568, 63 USPQ2d 1929 (Fed. Cir. 2002); Glaxo Inc., v. Novopharm Ltd., 110 F.3d 1562, 1568, 42 USPQ2d 1257 (Fed. Cir. 1997).

2. Indirect Infringement

Indirect infringement can occur when a party aids or abets direct infringement by others.[45]

A party can be liable for indirect infringement by actively inducing infringement.[46] The party must have specific, knowing intent to encourage infringement, as opposed to intent merely to cause acts that are later found to infringe.[47] Intent may be proven through circumstantial evidence.[48] Deliberate indifference to a known risk that a patent exists can satisfy this intent requirement.[49]

Liability for inducement also requires that the person alleged to have been induced is directly infringing a patent claim. For example, a person who sells gold and instructs the buyer in how to use the gold to directly infringe a patented invention can be

---

[45] *See generally* Hewlett-Packard Co. v. Bausch & Lomb Inc., 909 F.2d 1464, 1468–69, 15 USPQ2d 1525 (Fed. Cir. 1990). There is no liability for aiding and abetting that occurred before a patent's issuance. National Presto Indus. Inc. v. West Bend Co., 76 F.3d 1185, 1194–96, 37 USPQ2d 1685 (Fed. Cir. 1996).

[46] 35 U.S.C. §271(b); *see, e.g.,* Forest Labs. v. IVAX Pharms., Inc., 501 F.3d 1263, 1272, 84 USPQ2d 1099 (Fed. Cir. 2007) (inducement); Mikkelsen Graphic Eng'g Inc. v. Zund Am., Inc., No. 07-c-391, 2011 WL 1330782, at *11 (E.D. Wis. Apr. 7, 2011) (no inducement). Active inducement requires an affirmative act. Tegal Corp. v. Tokyo Electron Co., 248 F.3d 1376, 1378–79, 58 USPQ2d 1791 (Fed. Cir. 2001).

[47] DSU Med. Corp. v. JMS Co., 471 F.3d 1293, 1304–06, 81 USPQ2d 1238 (Fed. Cir. 2006); Global-Tech Appliances Inc. v. SEB S.A., 131 S. Ct. 2060, 98 USPQ2d 1665, 1668 (2011); *see, e.g.,* AstraZeneca LP v. Apotex, Inc., 633 F.3d 1042, 1059–61, 97 USPQ2d 1029 (Fed. Cir. 2010) (inducement based on product label); nCube Corp. v. Seachange Int'l, Inc. 436 F.3d 1317, 1324–25, 77 USPQ2d 1481 (Fed. Cir. 2006) (no inducement if no knowledge of directly infringing acts).

[48] Symantec Corp. v. Computer Assocs. Int'l, Inc., 522 F.3d 1279, 1293, 86 USPQ2d 1449 (Fed. Cir. 2008); Liquid Dynamics Corp. v. Vaughan Co., 449 F.3d 1209, 1219–20, 79 USPQ2d 1094 (Fed. Cir.), *cert. denied,* 549 U.S. 1032 (2006). In a copyright case that adopted the patent law concept of inducement, the Supreme Court addressed the evidence that can support an inference of intent to induce infringement. Metro-Goldwyn-Mayer Studios Inc. v. Grokster, Ltd., 545 U.S. 913, 75 USPQ2d 1001 (2005). The classic case of direct evidence of inducing is advertising or solicitation that sends a message designed to stimulate others to infringe. Advertising that is not sent may nonetheless be used to show a party's intent. Mere knowledge of infringing potential or knowledge of actual infringing use by a third party are not sufficient to show intent if a product has noninfringing uses. Also insufficient to show intent are ordinary acts incident to product distribution (e.g., offering technical support or product updates). Other evidence of intent, which may not be sufficient on its own, may be relevant. For example, failure to take affirmative steps to prevent infringement may support an inference of intent to induce infringement. *Id.* Intent to induce infringement will not be found if the alleged inducer had no knowledge of the directly infringing acts. nCube Corp. v. Seachange Int'l, Inc. 436 F.3d 1317, 1324–25, 77 USPQ2d 1481 (Fed. Cir. 2006).

[49] *Global-Tech Appliances, Inc.,* 131 S. Ct. at 2068–72, 98 USPQ2d at 1671–73.

liable for inducement.[50] Corporate officers who act culpably can be liable for inducing their corporation's direct infringement, regardless of whether the corporate veil is pierced.[51]

Under the rule of contributory infringement, a seller also is liable for indirect infringement if:

1. the seller sells a component of a patented machine, manufacture, combination or composition, or a material or apparatus for use in practicing a patented process;
2. the item sold constitutes a material part of the invention;
3. the seller knows that the item sold is especially made or especially adapted for use in an infringement of a patent; and
4. the item sold is not a staple article or commodity of commerce suitable for substantial noninfringing use.[52]

In addition, the buyer must be a direct infringer.[53] For example, if a patented invention is the mechanical combination of parts A and B, a person who merely sells part B would not be liable as a direct infringer; however, if part B is sold to someone who combines part B with part A (direct infringement), the seller can be liable as a contributory infringer.

As with active inducement of infringement, liability for contributory infringement requires a certain level of knowledge; that is, the seller of the material part must know that the item sold is especially made or especially adapted for use in a product

[50] Dynacore Holdings Corp. v. U.S. Philips Corp., 363 F.3d 1263, 1274, 70 USPQ2d 1369 (Fed. Cir. 2004).

[51] Hoover Group Inc. v. Custom Metalcraft Inc., 84 F.3d 1408, 1412, 38 USPQ2d 1860 (Fed. Cir. 1996); see, e.g., Power Lift Inc. v. Lang Tools Inc., 774 F.2d 478, 481, 227 USPQ 435 (Fed. Cir. 1985) (officer liable for inducing corporation); Wordtech Syss., Inc v. Integrated Networks Solutions, Inc., 609 F.3d 1308, 1315–16, 95 USPQ2d 1619 (Fed. Cir. 2010) (improper jury instructions on officer liability for inducement).

[52] 35 U.S.C. §271(c); Golden Blount, Inc. v. Robert H. Peterson Co., 365 F.3d 1054, 1065, 70 USPQ2d 1624 (Fed. Cir. 2004); see, e.g., Lucent Techs., Inc. v. Gateway, Inc., 580 F.3d 1301, 1320–21, 92 USPQ2d 1555 (Fed. Cir. 2009) (affirming verdict of contributory infringement), cert. denied, 130 S. Ct. 3324 (2010); Ricoh Co. v. Quanta Computer Inc., 550 F.3d 1325, 1336–40, 89 USPQ2d 1577 (Fed. Cir. 2008) (reversing summary judgment of no contributory infringement), cert. denied, 129 S. Ct. 2864 (2009).

[53] Aro Mfg. Co. v. Convertible Top Replacement Co., 365 U.S. 336, 341, 128 USPQ 354, (1961); DSU Med. Corp. v. JMS Co., 471 F.3d 1293, 1303, 81 USPQ2d 1238 (Fed. Cir. 2006); Sage Prods. Inc. v. Devon Indus., Inc., 126 F.3d 1420, 1429, 44 USPQ2d 1103 (Fed. Cir. 1997).

or process that infringes a patent.[54] Contributory infringement also requires that the item sold not be suitable for substantial noninfringing use.[55] Thus, for example, a mere seller of gold will not be liable even if the seller knows the buyer is using the gold to infringe a patent, because gold is suitable for substantial non-infringing uses.

D. The Patented Invention

Infringement generally exists if any one of a patent's claims covers the alleged infringer's product or process.[56] Determining whether a patent claim covers the alleged infringer's product or process involves two steps.[57] First, the court must interpret, as a matter of law, what the words in the claim mean.[58] Second, applying this construction of the claim terms, the finder of fact must determine, as a matter of fact, if the claim covers the alleged infringer's product or process.[59] For patent infringement, each

---

[54] *See* Global-Tech Appliances, Inc. v. SEB S.A., 131 S. Ct. 2060, 2064–69, 98 USPQ2d 1665, 1668–71 (2011); Aro Mfg. Co. v. Convertible Top Replacement Co., 377 U.S. 476, 488, 141 USPQ 681 (1964). For example, a letter from the patent owner to the seller of the material part that gives notice of the patent and alleges infringement can satisfy this knowledge requirement; Fujitsu Ltd. v. Netgear Inc., 620 F.3d 1321, 1329–30, 96 USPQ2d 1742 (Fed. Cir. 2010).

[55] *See, e.g., Fujitsu Ltd.*, 620 F.3d at 1330–31 (ability to turn off infringing feature is not a noninfringing use); Cross Med. Prods., Inc. v. Medtronic Sofamor Danek, Inc., 424 F.3d 1293, 1314, 76 USPQ2d 1662 (Fed. Cir. 2005) (reversing summary judgment of infringement in light of possible noninfringing uses).

[56] Markman v. Westview Instruments Inc., 517 U.S. 370, 374, 38 USPQ2d 1461 (1996). Regarding the difference in infringement analysis of product claims and process claims, see generally *Amgen Inc. v. Hoechst Marion Roussel, Inc.*, 314 F.3d 1313, 1346–47, 65 USPQ2d 1385 (Fed. Cir. 2003). For infringement actions brought under 35 U.S.C. §271(e)(2), a proposed generic drug infringes if the generic, if approved, would infringe a claim of the patent in suit. Abbott Labs. v. TorPharm, Inc., 300 F.3d 1367, 1373, 63 USPQ2d 1929 (Fed. Cir. 2002).

[57] *See generally* Desper Prods. Inc. v. QSound Labs Inc., 157 F.3d 1325, 1332, 48 USPQ2d 1088 (Fed. Cir. 1998); Interactive Pictures v. Infinite Pictures, 274 F.3d 1371, 1376, 61 USPQ2d 1152 (Fed. Cir. 2001), *cert. denied*, 537 U.S. 825 (2002).

[58] *Markman*, 517 U.S. at 374, 38 USPQ2d 1461. For further discussion of claim construction, see Chapter 5.

[59] *Markman*, 517 U.S. at 374, 38 USPQ2d 1461. A court's findings of fact pursuant to Fed. R. Civ. P. 52(a) must be more than bald conclusions. Golden Blount, Inc. v. Robert H. Peterson Co., 365 F.3d 1054, 1060–61, 70 USPQ2d 1624 (Fed. Cir. 2004). Infringement of a design patent, directed to the ornamental features of an object, is determined by a different test—whether an ordinary observer would find that the accused device embodies the patented design or any colorable imitation thereof. Egyptian Goddess, Inc. v. Swisa, Inc., 543 F.3d 665, 678, 88 USPQ2d 1658 (Fed. Cir. 2008) (en banc); *see, e.g.,* Crocs, Inc. v. International Trade Comm'n, 598 F.3d 1294, 1303–07, 93 USPQ2d 1777 (Fed. Cir. 2010) (infringement of design patent); Richardson v. Stanley Works, Inc., 597 F.3d 1288, 1295–96, 93 USPQ2d 1937 (Fed. Cir. 2010) (no infringement of design patent).

element of the patent claim must be found in the accused product or process, either literally or by a substantial equivalent.[60] If a single element is not present, there can be no infringement.[61]

1. Literal Infringement

Generally, a claim is literally infringed if each properly construed claim element reads on the accused product or process.[62] Thus, for example, if a claim is for a three-bladed ceiling fan with the blades attached to a solid rod that connects to a motor, then the claim literally reads on (a) a copy of the three-bladed ceiling fan with blades attached to a solid rod that connects to a motor, and (b) some improved fans, such as a three-bladed ceiling fan with blades attached to a solid rod that connects to a motor and that also has a cord for switching the fan on and off.[63] Each element of the claim is found in both infringing fans. In contrast, this claim would not literally read on a three-bladed ceiling fan with blades attached to a hollow rod that connects to a motor. The solid-rod claim element is not found in this other fan.

---

[60] SmithKline Diagnostics v. Helena Labs. Corp., 859 F.2d 878, 889, 8 USPQ2d 1468 (Fed. Cir. 1988); Warner-Jenkinson Co. v. Hilton Davis Chem. Co., 520 U.S. 17, 28–30, 41 USPQ2d 1865 (1997). (Fed. Cir. 2003). A judicially created exception to the all-elements rule, the reverse doctrine of equivalents, is discussed in this chapter, §I.D.2.

[61] Mas-Hamilton Group v. LaGard Inc., 156 F.3d 1206, 1211, 48 USPQ2d 1010 (Fed. Cir. 1998); Wavetronix LLC v. EIS Elec. Integrated Sys., 573 F.3d 1343, 1360, 91 USPQ2d 1468 (Fed. Cir. 2009) (doctrine of equivalents cannot be applied so as to vitiate a claim element).

[62] Allen Eng'g Corp. v. Bartell Indus., 299 F.3d 1336, 1345, 63 USPQ2d 1769 (Fed. Cir. 2002); see, e.g., QR Spex, Inc. v. Motorola Inc., 588 F. Supp. 2d 1240, 1250 (C.D. Cal. 2008) (no literal infringement); Ormco Corp. v. Align Tech., Inc., 609 F. Supp. 2d 1057, 1064–67 (C.D. Cal. 2009) (literal infringement for some of the asserted claims). A claim need only read on part of an accused product for infringement. SunTiger Inc. v. Scientific Research Funding Group, 189 F.3d 1327, 1336, 51 USPQ2d 1811 (Fed. Cir. 1999). Even if all claim elements are found literally, there may be no literal infringement based on the reverse doctrine of equivalents; see §I.D.2 of this chapter. Claims expressed in product-by-process language read on products made by the identical process. Atlantic Thermoplastics Co. v. Faytex Corp., 970 F.2d 834, 23 USPQ2d 1481 (Fed. Cir. 1992). The process terms of such claims serve as substantive limitations in determining infringement. Abbott Labs. v. Sandoz, Inc., 566 F.3d 1282, 1291–95, 90 USPQ2d 1769 (Fed. Cir. 2009), cert. denied sub nom. Astellas Pharma, Inc. v. Lupin Ltd., 130 S. Ct. 1052 (2010).

[63] Whether improvements or modification to an accused device avoids infringement depends on the relevant facts. Glaxo Wellcome, Inc. v. Andrx Pharms., 344 F.3d 1226, 1233–34, 68 USPQ2d 1302 (Fed. Cir. 2003).

For a claim element expressed in means-plus-function language,[64] literal infringement occurs when the accused product either (a) uses a means that is *identical* to the means disclosed in the patent's specification to perform the *identical* function of the claim element, or (b) uses a means that is *structurally equivalent* to the means disclosed in the patent's specification to perform the *identical* function of the claim element.[65] Thus, for example, if a claim is for a ceiling fan with a means for switching the fan on and off and the specification describes only a cord for switching the fan on and off, then the claim would cover only (a) a ceiling fan with a means for switching the fan on and off that is identical to the disclosed cord, and (b) ceiling fans with a means for switching the fan on and off that is equivalent to the disclosed cord. Determining whether another means (e.g., a remote-control unit for switching the fan on and off) is equivalent is a question of fact.[66]

2. Infringement Under the Doctrine of Equivalents

The doctrine of equivalents, which has existed since 1853,[67] allows a court or jury to find infringement when an accused

---

[64] See Chapter 5, §IV.C for further discussion of means-plus-function claims.

[65] Lockheed Martin Corp. v. Space Sys./Loral, Inc., 324 F.3d 1308, 1320, 66 USPQ2d 1282 (Fed. Cir. 2003); 35 U.S.C. §112, ¶6; see, e.g., Frank's Casing Crew & Rental Tools, Inc. v. Weatherford Int'l, Inc., 389 F.3d 1370, 1378, 73 USPQ2d 1065 (Fed. Cir. 2004) (different means); Hewlett-Packard Co. v. Mustek Sys., Inc., 340 F.3d 1314, 1321, 67 USPQ2d 1825 (Fed. Cir. 2003) (different function). Regarding step-plus-function claim elements in method claims, see generally O.I. Corp. v. Tekmar Co., 115 F.3d 1576, 1582–83, 42 USPQ2d 1777 (Fed. Cir. 1997).

[66] Odetics Inc. v. Storage Tech. Corp., 185 F.3d 1259, 1268–69, 51 USPQ2d 1225 (Fed. Cir. 1999). The test for statutory equivalence of a means-plus-function claim under 35 U.S.C. §112, ¶6 is whether the accused means is insubstantially different from the means for performing the claimed function that is disclosed in the patent specification. WMS Gaming Inc. v. International Game Tech., 184 F.3d 1339, 1351, 51 USPQ2d 1385 (Fed. Cir. 1999); Overhead Door Corp. v. Chamberlain Group Inc., 194 F.3d 1261, 1273, 52 USPQ2d 1321 (Fed. Cir. 1999). One way to find statutory equivalence is if the accused means performs the (1) identical claimed function (2) in substantially the same way (3) to achieve substantially the same result as the means disclosed in the patent's specification. Odetics Inc. v. Storage Tech. Corp., 185 F.3d 1259, 1267, 51 USPQ2d 1225 (Fed. Cir. 1999); Hearing Components, Inc. v. Shure Inc., 600 F.3d 1357, 1370, 94 USPQ2d 1385 (Fed. Cir. 2010). If the disclosed structure is of little importance to the claimed invention, the range of equivalents may be broader. IMS Tech. Inc. v. Haas Automation, Inc., 206 F.3d 1422, 1436, 54 USPQ2d 1129 (Fed. Cir.), cert. dismissed, 530 U.S. 1299 (2000); Uniloc USA, Inc. v. Microsoft Corp., 632 F.3d 1292, 1304–05, 98 USPQ2d 1203 (Fed. Cir. 2011). To support a claim of literal infringement, the equivalent means must have been available at the time the patent issued. Al-Site Corp. v. VSI Int'l Inc., 174 F.3d 1308, 1320, 50 USPQ2d 1161 (Fed. Cir. 1999).

[67] Winans v. Denmead, 56 U.S. (15 How.) 330 (1853). See generally Warner-Jenkinson Co. v. Hilton Davis Chem. Co., 520 U.S. 17, 41 USPQ2d 1865 (1997).

product or process is the substantial equivalent of the patented invention.[68] The doctrine is not applied to the invention as a whole; it is applied to the individual elements of the claimed invention.[69] Intent plays no role in the application of the doctrine.[70] Equivalence is a question of fact that is decided by the trier of fact.[71] Equivalence is determined at the time of infringement.[72]

The essential inquiry underlying the doctrine of equivalents is whether the accused product or process contains each element either as claimed or as an equivalent to the element.[73] The doctrine, which requires an element-by-element inquiry, cannot be used to eliminate completely any claim element.[74] The test for whether an element in the alleged infringer's prod-

---

[68]Festo Corp. v. Shoketsu Kinzoku Kogyo Kabushiki Co., 535 U.S. 722, 732, 62 USPQ2d 1705 (2002) ("The scope of a patent is not limited to its literal terms but instead embraces all equivalents to the claims described"); *Warner-Jenkinson Co.,* 520 U.S. at 34, 41 USPQ2d 1865; *see, e.g.,* Corning Glass Works v. Sumitomo Elec. U.S.A. Inc., 868 F.2d 1251, 1257–62, 9 USPQ2d 1962 (Fed. Cir. 1989) (infringement); Sage Prods. Inc. v. Devon Indus. Inc., 126 F.3d 1420, 1424, 44 USPQ2d 1103 (Fed. Cir. 1997) (no infringement).

[69] *Warner-Jenkinson Co.,* 520 U.S. at 29, 41 USPQ2d 1865; Kahn v. General Motors Corp., 135 F.3d 1472, 1478, 45 USPQ2d 1608 (Fed. Cir.), *cert. denied,* 525 U.S. 875 (1998). This application puts a premium on thoughtful patent claim drafting. *Sage Prods. Inc.,* 126 F.3d at 1425, 44 USPQ2d 1103.

[70] *Warner-Jenkinson Co.,* 520 U.S. at 36, 41 USPQ2d 1865; Moore, U.S.A. v. Standard Register Co., 229 F.3d 1091, 1107, 56 USPQ2d 1225 (Fed. Cir. 2000), *cert. denied,* 532 U.S. 1008 (2001).

[71]Graver Tank & Mfg. Co. v. Linde Air Prods. Co., 339 U.S. 605, 609, 85 USPQ 328 (1950). *See generally* Warner-Jenkinson Co., 520 U.S. at 37–39, 41 USPQ2d 1865 (1997) (guidance regarding jury's role in deciding doctrine of equivalents issue). Generalized testimony as to equivalence is insufficient to support infringement under the doctrine of equivalents. *See generally* Hewlett-Packard Co. v. Mustek Sys., Inc., 340 F.3d 1314, 1322–23, 67 USPQ2d 1825 (Fed. Cir. 2003); PC Connector Solutions LLC v. SmartDisk Corp., 406 F.3d 1359, 1364, 74 USPQ2d 1698 (Fed. Cir. 2005).

[72] *Warner-Jenkinson Co.,* 520 U.S. at 37, 41 USPQ2d 1865.

[73] *Id.* at 40, 41 USPQ2d 1865; KCJ Corp. v. Kinetic Concepts, 223 F.3d 1351, 1359, 55 USPQ2d 1835 (Fed. Cir. 2000). For a process claim, each step must be performed either as claimed or by an equivalent step. Canton Bio-Med. v. Integrated Liner Techs., 216 F.3d 1367, 1369–70, 55 USPQ2d 1378 (Fed. Cir. 2000). Determining equivalence under the doctrine of equivalents is different from determining statutory equivalence in the context of means-plus-function claims. *See generally* Odetics Inc. v. Storage Tech. Corp., 185 F.3d 1259, 1267, 51 USPQ2d 1225 (Fed. Cir. 1999).

[74] *Warner-Jenkinson Co.,* 520 U.S. at 40, 41 USPQ2d 1865; *see, e.g.,* Trading Techs. Int'l, Inc. v. eSpeed, Inc., 595 F.3d 1340, 1355–56, 93 USPQ2d 1805 (Fed. Cir. 2010) (element would be vitiated); Depuy Spine, Inc. v. Medtronic Sofamor Danek, Inc., 469 F.3d 1005, 1017–19, 80 USPQ2d 1865 (Fed. Cir. 2006), *cert. denied,* 552 U.S. 940 (2007) (element would not be vitiated). This limitation on the doctrine of equivalents is a question of law. *Trading Techs. Int'l, Inc.,* 595 F.3d at 1355, 93 USPQ2d 1805. One-to-one correspondence is not required; e.g., two components of an accused product may serve as an equivalent of one claim element. Ethicon Endo-Surgery Inc. v. United States Surgical Corp., 149 F.3d 1309, 1320, 47 USPQ2d 1272 (Fed. Cir. 1998); Wavetronix LLC v. EIS Elec. Integrated Sys., 573 F.3d 1343, 1361, 91 USPQ2d 1468 (Fed. Cir. 2009).

uct or process is equivalent to a claimed element is whether the differences between the two are insubstantial to one of ordinary skill in the art.[75] One way to determine if an element in the accused product or process is equivalent to a claimed element is the function-way-result test.

Pursuant to this test, an element in an accused product or process is equivalent to a claimed element if the accused element performs substantially the same function in substantially the same way to accomplish substantially the same result as the claimed element.[76] Therefore, continuing the patented three-bladed ceiling fan illustration, in an accused ceiling fan with blades attached to a hollow rod that connects to a motor, the hollow-rod element would be an equivalent to the claimed solid-rod element if the hollow rod performs substantially the same function, in substantially the same way, and for substantially the same purpose as the solid-rod element. Similarly, if the accused ceiling fan uses a remote-control unit to turn the fan on and off, the remote-control element would be an equivalent to the claimed cord element if the differences between the remote-control unit and the cord were insubstantial to one of ordinary skill in the art.

Claims written in means-plus-function form can be infringed under the doctrine of equivalents.[77] Also, claims where the alleged

---

[75] Amgen Inc. v. F. Hoffmann-La Roche, Ltd., 580 F.3d 1340, 1382, 92 USPQ2d 1289 (Fed. Cir. 2009); see Warner-Jenkinson Co., 520 U.S. at 40, 41 USPQ2d 1865. Known interchangeability of substitutes for a claimed element, as well as independent experimentation by the accused infringer, may be probative. Id. at 36; Multiform Desiccants Inc. v. Medzam, Ltd., 133 F.3d 1473, 1480–81, 45 USPQ2d 1429 (Fed. Cir. 1998).

[76] Graver Tank & Mfg. Co. v. Linde Air Prods. Co., 339 U.S. 605, 608, 85 USPQ 328 (1950); see, e.g., V-Formation Inc. v. Benetton Group SpA, 401 F.3d 1307, 1313, 74 USPQ2d 1042 (Fed. Cir. 2005) (applying function-way-result test to affirm noninfringement); Crown Packaging Tech., Inc. v. Rexam Beverage Can Co., 559 F.3d 1308, 1312–15, 90 USPQ2d 1186 (Fed. Cir. 2009) (applying function-way-result test to reverse noninfringement).

[77] The equivalence test for means-plus-function claims is whether the differences between the elements of the accused product or process and the claim elements—as shown in the corresponding means in the specification—are insubstantial. Mas-Hamilton Group v. LaGard Inc., 156 F.3d 1206, 1212, 48 USPQ2d 1010 (Fed. Cir. 1998). The function-way-result test may be used to determine if the differences are insubstantial. Id; see, e.g., Stumbo v. Eastern Outdoors, Inc., 508 F.3d 1358, 1364, 85 USPQ2d 1275 (Fed. Cir. 2007); Interactive Pictures v. Infinite Pictures, 274 F.3d 1371, 1381–84, 61 USPQ2d 1152 (Fed. Cir. 2001), cert. denied, 537 U.S. 825 (2002) (infringement); Ballard Med. v. Allegiance Healthcare Corp., 268 F.3d 1352, 1363, 60 USPQ2d 1493 (Fed. Cir. 2001) (no infringement). If a proposed equivalent existed before the patent was filed, the doctrine of equivalents analysis for a means-plus-function element is the same as the literal infringement analysis for that element. Frank's Casing Crew & Rental Tools, Inc. v. Weatherford Int'l, Inc., 389 F.3d 1370, 1379, 73 USPQ2d 1065 (Fed. Cir. 2004).

equivalent is separately patented can be infringed under the doctrine of equivalents.[78]

Two major legal limitations apply to using the doctrine of equivalents to allow a patent owner a broader right to exclude than is given by the literal language of the claims.[79] First, a patent owner cannot use the doctrine to cover subject matter that encompasses, or "ensnares," the prior art.[80] Thus, pioneer inventions, ones that mark a significant step forward in an art, often are entitled to a broad range of equivalents, while inventions in a crowded field are frequently restricted to a narrow range of equivalents, if any.[81]

---

[78] Siemens Med. Solutions USA, Inc. v. Saint-Gobain Ceramics & Plastics, Inc., 637 F.3d 1269, 1278–79, 1283, 97 USPQ2d 1897 (Fed. Cir. 2011) (no heightened evidentiary standard where equivalent is separately patented).

[79] See generally Wilson Sporting Goods v. David Geoffrey & Assocs., 904 F.2d 677, 683–85, 14 USPQ2d 1942 (Fed. Cir.), cert. denied, 498 U.S. 992 (1990). There are other limitations. For example, if the patent expressly identifies a role for a claim element, then there is no equivalent in an accused product or process that does not substantially perform that role. Hoffer v. Microsoft Corp., 405 F.3d 1326, 1330, 74 USPQ2d 1481 (Fed. Cir. 2005), cert. denied, 546 U.S. 1131 (2006); K-2 Corp. v. Salomon S. A., 191 F.3d 1356, 1367, 52 USPQ2d 1001 (Fed. Cir. 1999); Sage Prods. Inc. v. Devon Indus., Inc., 126 F.3d 1420, 1429, 44 USPQ2d 1103 (Fed. Cir. 1997). Also, as a matter of law, a patent owner cannot rely on the doctrine of equivalents with respect to disclosed-but-unclaimed subject matter. Johnson & Johnston Assocs. v. R.E. Servs., 285 F.3d 1046, 62 USPQ2d 1225 (Fed. Cir. 2002) (en banc). For this disclosure-dedication rule to apply, the disclosure must be of such specificity that one of ordinary skill in the art could identify the disclosed-but-unclaimed subject matter. Toro Co. v. White Consol. Indus., Inc., 383 F.3d 1326, 1332–34, 72 USPQ2d 1449 (Fed. Cir. 2004), cert. denied, 544 U.S. 948 (2005) (patent drafter's intent is not a factor); PSC Computer Prods., Inc. v. Foxconn Int'l, Inc., 355 F.3d 1353, 1357–61, 69 USPQ2d 1460 (Fed. Cir. 2004). Further, the clear disavowal of specific subject matter in the specification precludes the application of the doctrine of equivalents to that subject matter. AstraZeneca AB v. Mutual Pharm. Co., Inc., 384 F.3d 1333, 1342, 72 USPQ2d 1726 (Fed. Cir. 2004).

[80] Wilson Sporting Goods, 904 F.2d at 683, 14 USPQ2d 1942, cert. denied, 498 U.S. 992 (1990); see, e.g., Marquip Inc. v. Fosber Am. Inc., 198 F.3d 1363, 1367–68, 53 USPQ2d 1015 (Fed. Cir. 1999) (equivalent ensnares prior art); DePuy Spine, Inc. v. Medtronic Sofamor Danek, Inc., 567 F.3d 1314, 1322–29, 90 USPQ2d 1865 (Fed. Cir. 2009) (no ensnarement). Thus, if an accused infringer is practicing the prior art, then there can be no infringement under the doctrine of equivalents. See Sextant Avionique, S. A. v. Analog Devices Inc., 172 F.3d 817, 827, 49 USPQ2d 1865 (Fed. Cir. 1999). Determining if the prior art limits a particular scope of equivalents is a question of law. DePuy Spine, Inc., 567 F.3d at 1324, 90 USPQ2d 1865.

[81] See generally Abbott Labs. v. Dey, L. P., 287 F.3d 1097, 1105, 62 USPQ2d 1545 (Fed. Cir.), cert. denied, 537 U.S. 1039 (2002); Augustine Med. Inc. v. Gaymar Indus. Inc., 181 F.3d 1291, 1301–02, 50 USPQ2d 1900 (Fed. Cir. 1999). One way to determine if prior art restricts the range of equivalents is to craft a hypothetical claim that would literally read on the accused product or process and then determine if that hypothetical claim would have been patentable. If the hypothetical claim is patentable, then the prior art is not a bar to applying the doctrine of equivalents. If the hypothetical claim is not patentable, however, then finding infringement under the doctrine of equivalents is not proper. Abbott Labs., 287 F.3d at 1105–07, 62 USPQ2d 1545; see, e.g., Interactive Pictures v. Infinite Pictures, 274 F.3d 1371, 61 USPQ2d 1152 (Fed. Cir. 2001) cert. denied, 537 U.S. 825 (2002) (hypothetical claim is patentable), Ultra-Tex Surfaces Inc. v. Hill Bros. Chem. Co., 204 F.3d 1360, 1364–65, 53 USPQ2d 1892 (Fed. Cir. 2000) (hypothetical

Second, a patent owner can be estopped from benefiting from the doctrine of equivalents due to prosecution history estoppel (formerly known as file wrapper estoppel); that is, something an applicant gave up during the patent's prosecution to obtain allowance of the patent cannot be recaptured by the doctrine of equivalents.[82] For example, if the original patent application for a ceiling fan had claims directed to three-bladed ceiling fans with either a hollow or a solid rod and the applicant narrowed those claims by amendment to cover only solid-rod, three-bladed ceiling fans in light of hollow-rod prior art, then the patent owner would be estopped from claiming that hollow-rod, three-bladed ceiling fans infringe under the doctrine of equivalents.

The first step in a prosecution history estoppel analysis is to identify the claim elements that are allegedly met by equivalents; the analysis does not apply to elements that are literally infringed.[83] The next step is to determine if those elements have been amended in a way that creates prosecution history estoppel.[84]

A narrowing amendment made for *any* reason related to the statutory conditions and requirements for patentability can create prosecution history estoppel as to the amended claim element.[85] Voluntary amendments—e.g., ones that were not

---

claim is not patentable). The hypothetical claim cannot be narrower than the actual claim. Streamfeeder, LLC v. Sure-Feed Systems, Inc., 175 F.3d 974, 983, 50 USPQ2d 1515 (Fed. Cir. 1999). The patent owner has the burden of proving that the hypothetical claim does not literally read on the prior art. *Id.* at 982–83, 50 USPQ2d 1515.

[82]Warner-Jenkinson Co. v. Hilton Davis Chem. Co., 520 U.S. 17, 30, 41 USPQ2d 1865 (1997); Regents of Univ. of Cal. v. DakoCytomation Cal., Inc., 517 F.3d 1364, 1378, 85 USPQ2d 1929 (Fed. Cir. 2008); *see, e.g.,* L.B. Plastics, Inc. v. Amerimax Home Prods., 499 F.3d 1303, 1309–10, 84 USPQ2d 1341 (Fed. Cir. 2007) (estoppel based on criticism of prior art in patent specification). Whether prosecution history estoppel applies is a question of law. Bai v. L&L Wings Inc., 160 F.3d 1350, 1354, 48 USPQ2d 1674 (Fed. Cir. 1998).

[83]*Abbott Labs.,* 287 F.3d at 1103, 62 USPQ2d 1545; *see, e.g.,* Ericsson, Inc. v. Harris Corp., 352 F.3d 1369, 1375, 69 USPQ2d 1109 (Fed. Cir. 2003).

[84]*Abbott Labs.,* 287 F.3d at 1103, 62 USPQ2d 1545.

[85]Festo Corp. v. Shoketsu Kinzoku Kogyo Kabushiki Co., 535 U.S. 722, 736, 62 USPQ2d 1705 (2002); *see, e.g.,* Pioneer Magnetics, Inc. v. Micro Linear Corp., 330 F.3d 1352, 1356, 66 USPQ2d 1859 (Fed. Cir. 2003) (amendment related to patentability). Narrowing amendments include those that change existing claim limitations or add new claim limitations. Honeywell Int'l, Inc. v. Hamilton Sundstrand Corp., 370 F.3d 1131, 1139–41, 71 USPQ2d 1065 (Fed. Cir. 2004) (en banc), *cert. denied,* 545 U.S. 1127 (2005). Narrowing amendments also include rewriting a dependent claim into independent form, when combined with canceling the original independent claim. *Id.* at 1141–44, 71 USPQ2d 1065; Felix v. American Honda Motor Co., 562 F.3d 1167, 1183–84, 90 USPQ2d 1524 (Fed. Cir. 2009). Amendments that do *not* narrow the

required by the PTO or made in response to a rejection by the PTO—can create prosecution history estoppel.[86] If the prosecution history does not provide a reason for the amendment, then it is presumed that the reason for the amendment was related to patentability, and prosecution history estoppel applies.[87] The patent owner may rebut the presumption,[88] and has the burden to show the reason for the amendment.[89] The court decides, as a matter of law[90] and from the viewpoint of one skilled in the art,[91] if the reason is sufficient to overcome prosecution history estoppel.[92]

When a claim amendment gives rise to prosecution history estoppel, there is a presumption that application of the doctrine of equivalents is completely barred, i.e., there is no range of equivalents available for the amended claim element. The patent owner can overcome the presumption of a complete bar by showing that one skilled in the art could not reasonably be expected to have drafted a claim that would have literally encompassed the alleged equivalent.[93]

---

literal scope of the original claim do not create prosecution history estoppel. *See, e.g.,* Primos, Inc. v. Hunter's Specialties, Inc., 451 F.3d 841, 849, 79 USPQ2d 1129 (Fed. Cir. 2006).

[86] Pioneer Magnetics, Inc., 330 F.3d. 1352, 1357, 66 USPQ2d 1859 (3d. Cir. 2003).

[87] Warner-Jenkinson Co. v. Hilton Davis Chem. Co., 520 U.S. 17, 33, 41 USPQ2d 1865 (1997); Insituform Techs. v. Cat Contracting, 161 F.3d 688, 692, 48 USPQ2d 1610 (Fed. Cir. 1998), *cert. denied,* 526 U.S. 1018 (1999); Hilton Davis Chem. Co. v. Warner-Jenkinson Co., 114 F.3d 1161, 1163, 43 USPQ2d 1152 (Fed. Cir. 1997).

[88] Sextant Avionique, S.A. v. Analog Devices Inc., 172 F.3d 817, 828, 49 USPQ2d 1865 (Fed. Cir. 1999).

[89] *Warner-Jenkinson Co.,* 520 U.S. at 33, 41 USPQ2d 1865. The patent owner must base his or her argument solely upon the public record. *Pioneer Magnetics, Inc.,* 330 F.3d at 1356, 66 USPQ2d 1859.

[90] K-2 Corp. v. Salomon S. A., 191 F.3d 1356, 1368, 1369, 52 USPQ2d 1001 (Fed. Cir. 1999); Loral Fairchild Corp. v. Sony Corp., 181 F.3d 1313, 1323, 50 USPQ2d 1865 (Fed. Cir. 1999), *cert. denied,* 528 U.S. 1075 (2000).

[91] Merck & Co. v. Mylan Pharms. Inc., 190 F.3d 1335, 1340, 51 USPQ2d 1954 (Fed. Cir. 1999). If issues of patent practice are relevant, then experience in patent law and prosecution is presumed. *Id.*

[92] Warner-Jenkinson Co. v. Hilton Davis Chem. Co., 520 U.S. 17, 33, 41 USPQ2d 1865 (1997); Hilton Davis Chem. Co. v. Warner-Jenkinson Co., 114 F.3d 1161, 1163, 43 USPQ2d 1152 (Fed. Cir. 1997). The process to decide the reason for an amendment and whether that reason is sufficient to overcome prosecution history estoppel is left to the court's discretion. *Id.; see, e.g.,* Bai v. L&L Wings Inc., 160 F.3d 1350, 1355–56, 48 USPQ2d 1674 (Fed. Cir. 1998) (reason for the amendment was clear from the prosecution record, and patent owner's arguments to the contrary were unpersuasive). Whether an amendment was necessary to obtain allowance is irrelevant. *Id.* at 1356, 48 USPQ2d 1674.

[93] Festo Corp. v. Shoketsu Kinzoku Kogyo Kabushiki Co., 535 U.S. 722, 740–41, 62 USPQ2d 1705 (2002).

Situations in which the patent owner might be able to make such a showing include:

> [t]he equivalent may have been unforeseeable at the time of application; the rationale underlying the amendment may bear no more than a tangential relation to the equivalent in question; or there may be some other reason suggesting that the patentee could not reasonably be expected to have described the insubstantial substitute in question.[94]

These three situations are discussed in detail in the Federal Circuit's decision in *Festo Corp. v. Shoketsu Kinzoku Kogyo Kabushiki Co.* following remand by the Supreme Court.[95] An equivalent was foreseeable if, at the time of the amendment, it was known in the technical field of the pre-amendment claim, whether or not it was known to the inventor of the patent in suit.[96]

An equivalent will be deemed tangentially related to an amendment, rather than directly relevant, only in very limited circumstances.[97]

In addition to amendment-based prosecution history estoppel, there can also be argument-based prosecution history estoppel.[98]

---

[94] *Festo Corp.*, 535 U.S. at 740–41, 62 USPQ2d 1705. Festo Corp. v. Shoketsu Kinzoku Kogyo Kabushiki Co., 344 F.3d 1359, 1368–70, 68 USPQ2d 1321 (Fed. Cir. 2003), *cert. denied*, 541 U.S. 988 (2004).

[95] *Festo Corp.*, 344 F.3d at 1368–70, 68 USPQ2d 1321.

[96] Festo Corp. v. Shoketsu Kinzoku Kogyo Kabushiki Co., 493 F.3d 1368, 1382, 83 USPQ2d 1385 (Fed. Cir. 2007), *cert. denied*, 553 U.S. 1093 (2008).

[97] Cross Med. Prods., Inc. v. Medtronic Sofamor Danek, Inc., 480 F.3d 1335, 1342–44 82 USPQ2d 1065 (Fed. Cir. 2007); *see, e.g.*, Chimie v. PPG Indus., Inc., 402 F.3d 1371, 1382–83, 74 USPQ2d 1321 (Fed. Cir. 2005) (presumption of complete bar not rebutted); Insituform Techs. Inc. v. CAT Contracting Inc., 385 F.3d 1360, 1368–71, 72 USPQ2d 1870 (Fed. Cir. 2004) (presumption rebutted); Glaxo Wellcome, Inc. v. Impax Labs., Inc., 356 F.3d 1348, 1353–56, 69 USPQ2d 1705 (Fed. Cir. 2004) (presumption not rebutted).

[98] Unmistakable assertions made to the Patent Office in support of patentability may give rise to estoppel. Conoco, Inc. v. Energy & Envtl. Int'l, Inc., 460 F.3d 1349, 1364, 79 USPQ2d 1801 (Fed. Cir. 2006); *see, e.g.*, Cordis Corp. v. Medtronic AVE, Inc., 339 F.3d 1352, 1363, 67 USPQ2d 1876 (Fed. Cir. 2003), *cert. denied*, 540 U.S. 1213 (2004) (no argument-based estoppel); CAE Screenplates v. Heinrich Fiedler GmbH, 224 F.3d 1308, 1319, 55 USPQ2d 1804 (Fed. Cir. 2000) (argument-based estoppel). Claims allowed not due to any particular argument, however, are not estopped by argument. Fiskars Inc. v. Hunt Mfg. Co., 221 F.3d 1318, 1322–23, 55 USPQ2d 1569 (Fed. Cir. 2000), *cert. denied*, 532 U.S. 972 (2001). Disputing an examiner's statement during prosecution,

Absent an unmistakable indication to the contrary, subject matter surrendered by amendment to one claim is surrendered for all other claims containing the amended term.[99] An estoppel arising in the prosecution history of one patent application can apply to a related application.[100]

In addition to the judicially created doctrine of equivalents, there is a judicially created reverse doctrine of equivalents. The reverse doctrine of equivalents, which is a question of fact,[101] allows a court to find no infringement even though each element of the patent's claim literally reads on the accused product or process.[102] The test for the reverse doctrine of equivalents is whether the apparently literally infringing product or process is so far changed in principle that it performs the same or similar function in a substantially different way.[103]

E. Within the United States, Its Territories, or Its Possessions

The patent owner's right to exclude is, with one exception, in force throughout the United States, its territories, and its possessions.[104] Infringement of product claims by an imported

---

without more, usually will not give rise to argument-based prosecution history estoppel. Dow Chem. Co. v. Sumitomo Chem. Co., Ltd., 257 F.3d 1364, 1382, 59 USPQ2d 1609 (Fed. Cir. 2001).

[99] Glaxo Wellcome, Inc. v. Impax Labs., Inc., 356 F.3d 1348, 1356–57, 69 USPQ2d 1705 (Fed. Cir. 2004); *Felix*, 562 F.3d at 1183, 90 USPQ2d 1524.

[100] *See, e.g.,* Elkay Mfg. Co. v. Ebco Mfg. Co., 192 F.3d 973, 981, 52 USPQ2d 1109 (Fed. Cir. 1999), *cert. denied,* 529 U.S. 1066 (2000). *See generally* Biogen, Inc. v. Berlex Labs., Inc., 318 F.3d 1132, 1141, 1142–43, 65 USPQ2d 1809 (Fed. Cir. 2003).

[101] Roche Palo Alto LLC v. Apotex, Inc., 531 F.3d 1372, 1377, 87 USPQ2d 1308 (Fed. Cir. 2008); Polaroid Corp. v. Eastman Kodak Co., 789 F.2d 1556, 1573, 229 USPQ 561 (Fed. Cir.), *cert. denied,* 479 U.S. 850 (1986). *But see* Amgen Inc. v. Hoechst Marion Roussel, Inc., 314 F.3d 1313, 1351, 65 USPQ2d 1385 (Fed. Cir. 2003) (reverse doctrine of equivalents is equitable in nature).

[102] SRI Int'l v. Matsushita Elec. Corp. of Am., 775 F.2d 1107, 1125, 227 USPQ 577 (Fed. Cir. 1985); Monsanto Co. v. Mycogen Plant Sci. Inc., 61 F. Supp. 2d 133, 185–88 (D. Del. 1999).

[103] Graver Tank & Mfg. Co. v. Linde Air Prods. Co., 339 U.S. 605, 608–09, 85 USPQ 328 (1950); *see, e.g.,* Monsanto Co. v. Mycogen Plant Science, Inc., 61 F. Supp. 2d 133, 185–88 (D. Del. 1999) (insufficient evidence to support reverse doctrine of equivalents); Scripps Clinic & Research Found. v. Genentech Inc., 927 F.2d 1565, 1581, 18 USPQ2d 1001 (Fed. Cir. 1991) (reversing summary judgment of infringement in view of possible reverse doctrine of equivalents). The principle of the patent claim is determined in light of intrinsic evidence. *Roche Palo Alto LLC,* 531 F.3d at 1378, 87 USPQ2d 1308.

[104] *See* 35 U.S.C. §§100(c), 154. *See generally* Johns Hopkins Univ. v. CellPro Inc., 152 F.3d 1342, 1365–68, 47 USPQ2d 1705 (Fed. Cir. 1998). Accordingly, manufacture outside the United

product is determined by reference to the form of the product in the United States. Whether infringement by offering for sale is within the United States is determined by the location of the contemplated sale.[105]

The one exception is that the use of a patented invention on a vessel, aircraft, or vehicle of any foreign country that enters the United States temporarily or accidentally is not an infringement, provided that (1) the foreign country provides similar privileges to U.S. vessels, aircraft, or vehicles; and (2) the patented invention is used exclusively for the needs of the vessel, aircraft, or vehicle, and is not sold in or used for the manufacture of anything to be sold in or exported from the United States.[106]

Indirect infringers do not escape liability by performing their acts outside the United States, its territories, and its possessions. If an act of direct infringement occurs within the United States, its territories, or its possessions, those who aided and abetted the direct infringement in a manner that satisfies 35 U.S.C. §271(b) or (c) are liable,[107] no matter where those acts are performed.

In certain limited situations, persons in the United States are liable for helping persons outside the United States do something that would constitute direct infringement if done in the United States. For example, if someone supplies in or from the United States all or a substantial portion of the components

---

States, its territories, or possessions is not infringement under 35 U.S.C. §271(a). Shockley v. Arcan, Inc., 248 F.3d 1349, 1364, 58 USPQ2d 1692 (Fed. Cir. 2001). *See generally* International Rectifier Corp. v. Samsung Elecs. Co., 361 F.3d 1355, 1360–62, 70 USPQ2d 1124 (Fed. Cir. 2004). Infringement of product claims by an imported product is determined by reference to the form of the product in the United States. Biotec Biologische Naturverpackungen v. Biocorp, Inc., 249 F.3d 1341, 1350–51, 58 USPQ2d 1737 (Fed. Cir. 2001). Whether infringement by offering for sale is within the United States is determined by the location of the contemplated sale. Transocean Offshore Deepwater Drilling, Inc., 617 F.3d, 1309, 96 USPQ2d 1104 (Fed. Cir. 2010).

[105] Biotec Biologische, Naturverpackungen v. Biocorp, Inc., 249 F.3d 1341, 1350–51, 58 USPQ2d 1737 (Fed. Cir. 2001); *Transocean Offshore Deepwater Drilling*, 617 F.3d at 1309, 96 USPQ2d 1104.

[106] 35 U.S.C.A. §272 (2001); *see, e.g.,* National Steel Car, Ltd. v. Canadian Pac. Ry., 357 F.3d 1319, 1325–34, 69 USPQ2d 1641 (Fed. Cir. 2004).

[107] Crystal Semiconductor Corp. v. TriTech Microelectronics Int'l, Inc., 246 F.3d 1336, 1351, 57 USPQ2d 1953 (Fed. Cir. 2001); Lucas Aerospace, Ltd. v. Unison Indus., L.P., 899 F. Supp. 1268, 1286–88 (D. Del. 1995); Nippon Elec. Glass Co. v. Sheldon, 489 F. Supp. 119, 209 USPQ 1023 (S.D.N.Y. 1980).

of a patented invention in a manner to actively induce the combination of the components outside the United States, that person is liable if the combination would constitute infringement if done in the United States.[108] Thus, if a patented invention is the combination of parts A and B, and company X in the United States supplies parts A and B in separate boxes to company Y outside the United States, and instructs company Y how to combine the parts to practice the patented invention, company X is liable for infringement. Similarly, liability for infringement is placed on anyone:

1. supplying in or from the United States any component of a patented invention:
   a. is especially made or especially adapted for use in the patented invention,
   b. that is not a staple article or commodity of commerce suitable for substantial noninfringing use, and
   c. that is not wholly combined;
2. knowing the component is so made or adapted; and
3. intending that the component will be combined outside the United States in a manner that would infringe if done within the United States.[109]

Section 271(f) does not apply to method patents.[110]

---

[108] 35 U.S.C. §271(f)(1). To be supplied from the United States under §271(f), the accused components that are incorporated into infringing devices must have been supplied from the United States. Supplying plans, blueprints or templates for such components does not trigger the statute. Microsoft Corp. v. AT&T Corp., 550 U.S. 437, 457, 82 USPQ2d 1400 (2007) (software copies made outside the United States from a master disk sent from the United States do not infringe under §271(f)); see also Pellegrini v. Analog Devices, Inc., 375 F.3d 1113, 1117–18, 71 USPQ2d 1630 (Fed. Cir.), cert. denied, 543 U.S. 1003 (2004). To be a component of a patented invention under §271(f), the component must be in tangible form if the invention is in tangible form. Microsoft Corp., 550 U.S. at 459–51, 82 USPQ2d 1400 (software in the abstract was not a component of a patented computing device).

[109] 35 U.S.C.A. §271(f)(2) (2001). See generally Rotec Indus. v. Mitsubishi Corp., 215 F.3d 1246, 1257–58, 55 USPQ2d 1001 (Fed. Cir. 2000). Section 271(f)(2) does not require actual combination of the components. Waymark Corp. v. Porta Sys. Corp., 245 F.3d 1364, 1367–68, 58 USPQ2d 1456 (Fed. Cir. 2001).

[110] Cardiac Pacemakers, Inc. v. St. Jude Med., Inc., 576 F.3d 1348, 1364, 91 USPQ2d 1898 (Fed. Cir. 2009), cert. denied, 130 S. Ct. 1088 (2010).

F. During the Term of the Patent

For patent applications filed on or after June 8, 1995, the term of a U.S. patent begins on the date that the patent issues and ends 20 years after the date on which the application that resulted in the patent was filed or, under certain conditions, the date on which an earlier filed application (that is referenced in the later filed application) was filed. Before June 8, 1995, the term of a patent lasted for 17 years from the day the patent was issued.[111] By statute, a patent term can be "adjusted" by the Patent and Trademark Office if the granting of the application was delayed for certain reasons.[112]

In addition, by statute, term extension is available for patents covering certain products that cannot be commercially marketed without the approval of the Food and Drug Administration (e.g., human drugs). Patents for such products may have their term extended to restore the time lost because of the regulatory approval process.[113]

A patent owner may voluntarily shorten the term of a patent by filing a "terminal disclaimer" with the PTO. This is often done to remove an objection that the patent claims are invalid for "double patenting" over a previously granted patent.[114]

---

[111] 35 U.S.C. §154(a)(2). *See generally* Merck & Co. v. Kessler, 80 F.3d 1543, 1547–48, 38 USPQ2d 1347 (Fed. Cir. 1996), *cert. denied*, 519 U.S. 1101 (1997). Regarding whether a patent expires because of a failure to pay maintenance fees, see generally *Ulead Sys. Inc. v. Lex Computer & Mgmt. Corp.*, 351 F.3d 1139, 69 USPQ2d 1097 (Fed. Cir. 2003).

[112] 35 U.S.C. §154(b); Wyeth v. Kappos, 591 F.3d 1364, 93 USPQ2d 1257 (Fed. Cir. 2010).

[113] 35 U.S.C. §§155, 156; *see, e.g.*, PhotoCure ASA v. Kappos, 603 F.3d 1372, 95 USPQ2d 1250 (Fed. Cir. 2010); Ortho-McNeil Pharm., Inc. v. Lupin Pharms., Inc., 603 F.3d 1377, 95 USPQ2d 1246 (Fed. Cir. 2010); Arnold P'ship v. Dudas, 362 F.3d 1338, 1341–42, 70 USPQ2d 1311 (Fed. Cir. 2004) (patent for the combination of active ingredients A and B may be extended if either A or B have not been previously marketed); Pfizer Inc. v. Dr. Reddy's Labs., Ltd., 359 F.3d 1361, 69 USPQ2d 2016 (Fed. Cir. 2004) (extension does not apply to non-pharmaceutical uses of a patented product); Hoechst-Roussel Pharm. Inc. v. Lehman, 109 F.3d 756, 42 USPQ2d 1220 (Fed. Cir. 1997) (no extension for compound that is not actually claimed, even if FDA-approved product would infringe patent); *see also* Merck & Co. v. Kessler, 80 F.3d 1543, 38 USPQ2d 1347 (Fed. Cir. 1996), *cert. denied*, 519 U.S. 1101 (1997) (discussing term extension issues from the transition from a 17-year patent term to a 20-year term in 1995).

[114] 35 U.S.C. §253; *see, e.g.* Boehringer Ingelheim Int'l, GmbH v. Barr Labs., Inc., 592 F.3d 1340, 1346–50, 93 USPQ2d 1417 (Fed. Cir. 2010); Perricone v. Medicis Pharm. Corp., 432 F.3d 1368, 1375, 77 USPQ2d 1321 (Fed. Cir. 2005).

A patent cannot be infringed before it is issued[115] or after its term has expired.[116] Accordingly, making, using, offering for sale, selling, or importing the patented invention before the issue date of the patent or after the exclusionary period ends is not infringement. Similarly, there can be no liability for inducing infringement for acts of inducement that occurred before a patent issues.[117] However, pre-issuance activities may be relevant to show post-issuance infringement.[118]

Expiration of the patent's exclusionary power does not affect a patent owner's right to sue for infringement that occurred during the life of the patent.[119]

II. DEFENSES

A. Claims of Noninfringement

An alleged infringer can introduce evidence to show that the acts complained of do not constitute infringement, including evidence that:

1. the properly interpreted claims do not read on the accused product or process;
2. the alleged infringer is acting within the scope of an actual license;
3. the alleged infringer has an implied license under one of the judicially created doctrines discussed in §I.B of this chapter;

---

[115] See 3 WILLIAM C. ROBINSON, THE LAW OF PATENTS FOR USEFUL INVENTIONS §907 (1890); see, e.g., Johns Hopkins Univ. v. CellPro Inc., 152 F.3d 1342, 1366, 47 USPQ2d 1705 (Fed. Cir. 1998); Hoover Group Inc. v. Custom Metalcraft Inc., 66 F.3d 299, 303–04, 36 USPQ2d 1101 (Fed. Cir. 1995).

[116] Kearns v. Chrysler Corp., 32 F.3d 1541, 1550, 31 USPQ2d 1746 (Fed. Cir. 1994), cert. denied, 514 U.S. 1032 (1995).

[117] Micro Chem. v. Great Plains Chem. Co., 194 F.3d 1250, 1261, 52 USPQ2d 1258 (Fed. Cir. 1999); National Presto Indus. Inc. v. W. Bend Co., 76 F.3d 1185, 1194–96, 37 USPQ2d 1685 (Fed. Cir. 1996).

[118] Chimie v. PPG Indus., Inc., 402 F.3d 1371, 1382, 74 USPQ2d 1321 (Fed. Cir. 2005).

[119] 5 DONALD S. CHISUM, CHISUM ON PATENTS §16.04[4] (2010). Damages cannot be recovered for any infringement that occurred more than six years prior to the filing of the complaint or counterclaim for infringement. 35 U.S.C. §286.

4. the alleged infringer's use is experimental and completely noncommercial;
5. the alleged infringer is acting within the scope of the "safe harbor" of 35 U.S.C. §271(e)(1) because the accused acts are reasonably related to meeting the reporting requirements of the food and drug laws;
6. the alleged infringer is entitled to the "prior inventor" defense for certain method claims under 35 U.S.C. §273;[120]
7. the patent owner is not entitled to apply the doctrine of equivalents because of prosecution history estoppel;
8. the accused product does not infringe under the reverse doctrine of equivalents; or
9. the alleged infringer's use is on a vessel, aircraft, or vehicle of a foreign country that entered the United States temporarily or accidentally (and fulfills the other requirements of 35 U.S.C. §272).

Although, as discussed in §I.C.2 of this chapter, the prior art may limit the applicability of the doctrine of equivalents, it is not a defense to a charge of infringement that the accused infringer is "practicing the prior art."[121]

B. Claims of Invalidity

Only valid patents give the patent owner the right to exclude others from making, using, offering for sale, selling, or

---

[120] Until 2011, the prior inventor defense had previously applied only to patent claims covering "methods of doing or conducting business," 35 U.S.C. §273(a)(3) (2010). For patents that issue after September 16, 2011, the Leahy-Smith America Invents Act, Pub.L. 112-29, H.R. 1249 (2011) expands this defense to cover a prior user of any patented invention where the alleged infringing device or process was in commercial use in the United States more than one year before the effective filing date of the patent (or, if earlier, the date when the invention was first disclosed publicly). The party asserting the defense bears the burden of proof by clear and convincing evidence. The defense requires that the prior use have been in good faith and that the infringing product or method not be "derived from the patentee or persons in privity with the patentee." The defense is not available for inventions owned by an institution of higher learning or a technology transfer organization working with such an institution. *See* Leahy-Smith America Invents Act, Pub.L. 112-29, H.R. 1249 (2011), sec. 5, amending 35 U.S.C. §273.

[121] *In re* Omeprazole Patent Litig., 536 F.3d 1361, 1377, 87 USPQ2d 1865 (Fed. Cir. 2008).

importing the patented invention and the process-patent owner the right to exclude others from importing, using, offering for sale, or selling the products made by the patented process. An invalid patent cannot be infringed.[122] Therefore, an accused infringer who can show that the patent asserted against him or her is invalid cannot be liable for infringement.[123]

There are two ways to establish that a patent is invalid: (1) prove that the patented invention does not meet one or more of the conditions of patentability (discussed in Chapter 4, §I) or (2) prove that the inventor did not satisfy one or more of the requirements of patentability (discussed in Chapter 4, §II). As detailed earlier (see Chapter 3, §IV), a duly issued patent is presumed valid, and one seeking to prove that a patent is invalid must do so by clear and convincing evidence. The first step in analyzing a patent's alleged invalidity is to construe the claims.[124] Generally, each claim at issue must be considered individually.[125]

In addition, at least one nonsubstantive PTO requirement may render a patent for an invention invalid if it is not satisfied: the requirement to obtain a PTO license before filing a foreign patent application regarding the same invention.[126] Also potentially relevant to invalidity, a certificate of correction applied for by the patent owner and issued by the PTO is effective only for causes of action arising after the certificate was issued.[127]

---

[122] See, e.g., Ever-Wear Inc. v. Wieboldt Stores Inc., 427 F.2d 373, 376, 166 USPQ 109 (7th Cir. 1970).

[123] 35 U.S.C. §282. Some accused infringers are precluded from challenging validity. See, e.g., Mentor Graphics Corp. v. Quickturn Design Sys., 150 F.3d 1374, 1377–79, 47 USPQ2d 1683 (Fed. Cir. 1998) (assignor estoppel); Diversey Lever Inc. v. Ecolab Inc., 191 F.3d 1350, 52 USPQ2d 1062 (Fed. Cir. 1999) (consent judgment).

[124] SIBIA Neurosciences v. Cadus Pharm., 225 F.3d 1349, 1355, 55 USPQ2d 1927 (Fed. Cir. 2000); Smiths Indus. Med. Sys. v. Vital Signs, 183 F.3d 1347, 1353, 51 USPQ2d 1415 (Fed. Cir. 1999).

[125] 35 U.S.C. §282; Dayco Prods., Inc. v. Total Containment, Inc., 329 F.3d 1358, 1370–71, 66 USPQ2d 1801 (Fed. Cir. 2003).

[126] 35 U.S.C. §§184–185.

[127] E.I. DuPont de Nemours & Co. v. MacDermid Printing Solutions, 525 F.3d 1353, 1362, 86 USPQ2d 1732 (Fed. Cir. 2008).

EQUITABLE DEFENSES

Patents are enforced, inter alia, through equitable relief, e.g., injunctions issued to enforce the statutory right to prevent future infringement. By statute, injunctive relief in patent cases is available "in accordance with the principles of equity."[1] Judicially created equitable defenses to a charge of infringement include: (1) inequitable conduct before the PTO; (2) patent misuse; (3) laches; and (4) estoppel.[2]

---

[1] 35 U.S.C. §283. 35 U.S.C. §282 identifies unenforceability as a potential defense "in any action involving the validity or infringement of a patent."

[2] The common law shop right, which is based on equitable principles, can also be an infringement defense, McElmurry v. Arkansas Power & Light Co., 995 F.2d 1576, 1580–82, 27 USPQ2d 1129 (Fed. Cir. 1993), as can the doctrine of implied license and its judicially created analog, patent exhaustion. See Chapter 6, §I.A. There are also statutory defenses to a charge of infringement that incorporate equitable principles or that arose from equitable concerns. *See, respectively,* 35 U.S.C. §252 (intervening rights) *and* 35 U.S.C. §273 (earlier inventor defense for method patents under certain circumstances). The earlier inventor defense was created by Congress in 1999. *See generally* 145 CONG. REC. S14696, S14716–17 (Nov. 17, 1999) (section-by-section analysis).

I. Inequitable Conduct Before the PTO

A. The Controlling Authority

In the mid-1940s, the Supreme Court first decided that conduct during the application process may render a subsequently issued patent unenforceable.[3] Such a defense arises when the applicant's actions or omissions constitute "inequitable conduct." The defense originally arose from cases involving "egregious conduct" tantamount to common law fraud, i.e., obtaining a patent through deliberate falsehood.[4] However, as the doctrine developed, courts held that conduct falling short of actual fraud could be sufficiently egregious to warrant the sanction of unenforceability.[5]

A charge of inequitable conduct has always required two elements: (1) a material misstatement or omission during prosecution of the patent at issue or a closely related patent application and (2) that the misstatement or omission was made with intent to deceive the PTO. As discussed in the Federal Circuit's 2011 en banc decision in *Therasense, Inc. v. Becton, Dickinson,* "the standards for intent to deceive and materiality have fluctuated over time."[6]

The inequitable conduct doctrine developed from a desire by the courts to "foster full disclosure to the PTO" during patent prosecution. The Federal Circuit revisited the basic standard in *Therasense* because charges of inequitable conduct had become "a common litigation tactic" and "an absolute plague" on patent litigation.[7]

---

[3] Precision Instrument Mfg. Co. v. Automotive Maint. Mach. Co., 324 U.S. 806 (1945). *See generally* Robert J. Goldman, *Evolution of the Inequitable Conduct Defense in Patent Litigation,* 7 HARV. J.L. & TECH. 37 (1993); Christian Mammen, *Controlling the "Plague": Reforming the Defense of Inequitable Conduct,* 24 BERKELEY TECH. L.J. 1329 (2009).

[4] Therasense, Inc. v. Becton, Dickinson & Co., 649 F.3d 1276, 1285–87, 99 USPQ2d 1065 (Fed. Cir. 2011) (en banc).

[5] Norton v. Curtiss, 433 F.2d 779, 793–94, 167 USPQ 532 (C.C.P.A. 1970); *see also* Robert J. Goldman, Evolution of the Inequitable Conduct Defense in Patent Litigation, 7 HARV. J.L. & TECH. at 52–67 (1993).

[6] *Therasense,* 649 F.3d at 1287–88, 99 USPQ2d 1065; *see* Digital Control, Inc. v. Charles Mach. Works, 437 F.3d. 1309, 1315–16, 77 USPQ2d 1823 (Fed. Cir. 2006) (materiality); Kingsdown Med. Consultants v. Hollister, Inc., 863 F.2d 867, 876, 9 USPQ2d 1384 (Fed. Cir. 1988) (en banc), *cert. denied,* 490 U.S. 1067 (1989) (intent).

[7] *Therasense,* 649 F.3d at 1285–90, 99 USPQ2d 1065.

In *Therasense,* the court adopted a but-for standard for showing materiality:

> This court holds that, as a general matter, the materiality required to establish inequitable conduct is but-for materiality. When an applicant fails to disclose prior art to the PTO, that prior art is but-for material if the PTO would not have allowed a claim had it been aware of the undisclosed prior art. Hence, in assessing the materiality of a withheld reference, the court must determine whether the PTO would have allowed the claim if it had been aware of the undisclosed reference.[8]

The court created an exception to the but-for rule where the patent applicant or others substantively involved in the prosecution of the patent at issue committed "affirmative acts of egregious misconduct":

> Although but-for materiality generally must be proved to satisfy the materiality prong of inequitable conduct, this court recognizes an exception in cases of affirmative egregious misconduct. This exception to the general rule requiring but-for proof incorporates elements of the early unclean hands cases before the Supreme Court, which dealt with "deliberately planned and carefully executed scheme[s]" to defraud the PTO and the courts. When the patentee has engaged in affirmative acts of egregious misconduct, such as the filing of an unmistakably false affidavit, the misconduct is material.[9]

However, the court clearly stated that nondisclosure of prior art alone, whether in an affidavit or not, does not constitute "egregious misconduct":

> Because neither mere nondisclosure of prior art references to the PTO nor failure to mention prior art references in an affidavit constitutes affirmative egregious misconduct, claims of inequitable

---

[8] *Id.* at 1291, 99 USPQ2d 1065.

[9] *Id.* at 1292, 99 USPQ2d 1065 (internal citations omitted). In adopting the but-for materiality standard, the Federal Circuit did not distinguish between an objective standard—what a reasonable examiner would have done—versus a subjective standard—what effect the alleged omission or misrepresentation would have had on the actual examiner of the patent application at issue. However, by phrasing the standard in terms of "the PTO," *Therasense* at least suggests an objective standard, e.g., an examiner following the standards set forth in the PTO's *Manual of Patent Examining Procedure.* By PTO regulation, patent examiners are generally not permitted to testify about prosecution activities. *See* MANUAL OF PATENT EXAMINING PROCEDURE (MPEP) §1701.01; 37 CFR §104, subpart C.

conduct that are based on such omissions require proof of but-for materiality. By creating an exception to punish affirmative egregious acts without penalizing the failure to disclose information that would not have changed the issuance decision, this court strikes a necessary balance between encouraging honesty before the PTO and preventing unfounded accusations of inequitable conduct.[10]

The *Therasense* court reaffirmed its 2008 decision from *Star Scientific Inc. v. R. J. Reynolds Tobacco Co.* that the element of intent means "specific intent to deceive the PTO":

> A finding that the misrepresentation or omission amounts to gross negligence or negligence under a "should have known" standard does not satisfy this intent requirement. "In a case involving nondisclosure of information, clear and convincing evidence must show that the applicant *made a deliberate decision* to withhold a *known* material reference." In other words, the accused infringer must prove by clear and convincing evidence that the applicant knew of the reference, knew that it was material, and made a deliberate decision to withhold it.[11]

Intent and materiality are separate requirements. Although intent may be inferred from circumstantial evidence, a finding of materiality alone will not support an inference of intent to deceive. And, in all events, the finding of intent must be " 'the single most reasonable inference able to be drawn from the evidence.' "[12]

A finding of inequitable conduct renders the entire patent unenforceable, not just the claim for which inequitable conduct was found. A finding of inequitable conduct may be used offensively by the patent challenger in support of counterclaims for unfair competition and, in the case of conduct that amounts to common law fraud, as part of the basis for a claim of antitrust

---

[10] *Id.* at 1292–93, 99 USPQ2d 1065 (internal citations omitted).

[11] *Id.* at 1290, 99 USPQ2d 1065 (internal citations omitted).

[12] *Id.* at 1290, 99 USPQ2d 1065 (quoting *Star Scientific, Inc. v. R. J. Reynolds Tobacco Co.*, 537 F.3d 1357, 1365–71, 88 USPQ2d 1001 (Fed. Cir. 2008) and citing *Larson Mfg. Co. of S.D., Inc. v. Aluminart Prods., Ltd.*, 559 F.3d 1317, 1340, 90 USPQ2d 1257 (Fed. Cir. 2009)).

violation.[13] A finding of inequitable conduct may also support a claim for attorneys' fees under the exceptional case provision of 35 U.S.C. §285.[14]

B. Recurring Substantive and Procedural Issues

Allegations of inequitable conduct must be pled with specificity. The pleading must set forth "the specific who, what, when, where, and how of the material misrepresentation" as well as allegations permitting a reasonable inference that a specific individual (as opposed to a corporation generally) acted with intent to deceive the PTO.[15]

Materiality and intent are factual issues, and must be proved by clear and convincing evidence.[16] However, because the defense is wholly equitable in nature, there is no right to have it tried by a jury. An advisory verdict by a jury as to either element is not binding on the court.[17]

In making a determination of but-for materiality, a court must apply the claim construction rules and burdens of proof used by the PTO during patent prosecution. That is, claims are to be given their broadest reasonable construction and prima facie invalidity can be shown by a preponderance of the evidence.[18]

---

[13] *Therasense*, 649 F.3d 1289, 99 USPQ2d 1065; Dow Chem. Co. v. Exxon Corp., 139 F.3d 1470, 1471, 46 USPQ2d 1120 (Fed. Cir. 1998) (unfair competition); *see* Walker Process Equip. Inc. v. Food Mach. & Chem. Corp., 382 U.S. 172, 178, 147 USPQ 404 (1965); 4 JULIAN O. VON KALINOWSKI ET AL., ANTITRUST LAWS AND TRADE REGULATION §73.03 (2d ed. 2006) (antitrust). Under certain circumstances, inequitable conduct in an earlier application can render unenforceable all claims that issue in a subsequent related application. *See* Nilssen v. Osram Sylvania, Inc., 504 F.3d 1223, 1229–30, 84 USPQ2d 1811 (Fed. Cir. 2007), *cert. denied*, 554 U.S. 903 (2008); Consolidated Aluminum Corp. v. Foseco Int'l Ltd., 910 F.2d 804, 809, 15 USPQ2d 1481 (Fed. Cir. 1990).

[14] Brasseler, U.S.A. I, L.P. v. Stryker Sales Corp., 267 F.3d 1370, 1380, 60 USPQ2d 1482 (Fed. Cir. 2001). With respect to the "exceptional case" standard, see Chapter 8, §V.

[15] Exergen Corp. v. Wal-Mart Stores, Inc., 575 F.3d 1312, 1328–29, 91 USPQ2d 1656 (Fed. Cir. 2009).

[16] Purdue Pharma L.P. v. Boehringer Ingelheim GmbH, 237 F.3d 1359, 1366, 57 USPQ2d 1647 (Fed. Cir. 2001).

[17] American Calcar, Inc. v. American Honda Motor Co., 99 USPQ2d 1137, 1146–47 (Fed. Cir. 2011); Fiskars, Inc. v. Hunt Mfg. Co., 221 F.3d 1318, 1326, 55 USPQ2d 1569 (Fed. Cir. 2000), *cert. denied*, 532 U.S. 972 (2001). See Chapter 9, §III.

[18] *Therasense*, 649 F.3d at 1291–92, 99 USPQ2d 1065.

Although *Therasense* spoke of materiality in terms of disclosing or failing to disclose prior art, the materiality standard also applies to other information relating to the requirements for patentability. Information found to be material has included whether statements in the specification of the patent are true, facts relating to inventorship, and facts that would establish possible bias by those submitting declarations in support of patentability.[19] Misstatements about such information now must be evaluated under the heightened materiality standard.

In adopting a standard of but-for materiality, the Federal Circuit rejected cases in which materiality was measured with reference to the PTO's definition of materiality, set forth in PTO Rule 56, 37 C.F.R. §1.56(b). However, to the extent that Rule 56 will factor into the but-for analysis of materiality—an issue not yet determined by the courts—the rule states that information merely cumulative to what is already before the patent examiner is not material.[20] The Federal Circuit has stated that "[c]lose cases should be resolved by disclosure, not unilaterally by the applicant."[21]

A finding that the pertinent facts were before the PTO precludes a finding of inequitable conduct, whether the facts were disclosed by the applicant or discovered by the PTO during examination of the patent application. However, an applicant may not make a genuine misrepresentation of material fact, and then seek to excuse it as "attorney argument."[22]

---

[19] *See, e.g.*, Hoffmann-La Roche, Inc. v. Promega Corp., 323 F.3d 1354, 1367, 66 USPQ2d 1385 (Fed. Cir. 2003) (statements in the specification); PerSeptive Biosystems, Inc. v. Parmacia Biotech, Inc., 225 F.3d 1315, 1321, 56 USPQ2d 1001 (Fed. Cir. 2000) (inventorship); Ferring B. V. v. Barr Labs., Inc., 437 F.3d 1181, 1200, 78 USPQ2d 1161 (Fed. Cir.), *cert. denied*, 549 U.S. 1015 (2006) (declarant bias). A threshold question is whether a statement alleged to be a material misstatement is, in fact, false or misleading. Scanner Techs. Corp. v. ICOS Vision Sys. Corp. N.V., 528 F.3d 1365 (Fed. Cir. 2008); Young v. Lumenis, Inc., 492 F.3d 1336, 83 USPQ2d 1191 (Fed. Cir. 2007).

[20] *Therasense*, 649 F.3d at 1293–95, 99 USPQ2d 1065; 37 C.F.R. §1.56(b). A misleading affidavit cannot be excused as cumulative because affidavits are inherently material even if cumulative. Refac Int'l, Ltd. v. Lotus Dev. Corp., 81 F.3d 1576, 1583, 38 USPQ2d 1665 (Fed. Cir. 1996).

[21] LaBounty Mfg. v. United States Int'l Trade Comm'n, 958 F.2d 1066, 1076, 22 USPQ2d 1025 (Fed. Cir. 1992).

[22] Innogenetics, N.V. v. Abbott Labs., 512 F.3d 1363, 1378–79, 85 USPQ2d 1641 (Fed. Cir. 2008); *Young v. Lumenis*, 492 F.3d 1336, 1347–49, 83 USPQ2d 1191; Ring Plus, Inc. v. Cingular Wireless Corp., 614 F.3d 1354, 1360–61, 96 USPQ2d 1022 (Fed. Cir. 2010) (affirmative misrepresentations).

Intent may not be inferred from the mere fact that a material misstatement or omission occurred.[23] And *Therasense* emphasized that the burden of proving intent to deceive the PTO is not lessened where the misstatement or omission can be characterized as highly material:

> Intent and materiality are separate requirements. A district court should not use a "sliding scale," where a weak showing of intent may be found sufficient based on a strong showing of materiality, and vice versa. Moreover, a district court may not infer intent solely from materiality. Instead, a court must weigh the evidence of intent to deceive independent of its analysis of materiality. Proving that the applicant knew of a reference, should have known of its materiality, and decided not to submit it to the PTO does not prove specific intent to deceive.[24]

However, in her concurring opinion in *Therasense,* Judge O'Malley agreed with the majority that "intent may not be inferred from materiality alone" but added that evidence of the degree of materiality may be "circumstantial evidence" of intent to deceive:

> While I join this portion of the majority opinion (Part V), I do so with the understanding that the majority does not hold that it is impermissible for a court to consider the level of materiality as circumstantial evidence in its intent analysis. As in all other legal inquiries involving multiple elements, the district court may rely on the same items of evidence in both its materiality and intent inquiries. A district court must, however, reach separate conclusions of intent and materiality and may not base a finding of specific intent to deceive on materiality alone, regardless of the level of materiality.[25]

---

[23] Star Scientific, Inc. v. R. J. Reynolds Tobacco Co., 537 F.3d 1357, 1366–67, 88 USPQ2d 1001 (Fed. Cir. 2008). Even information that may be characterized as misleading does not necessarily imply culpable intent. Alza Corp. v. Mylan Labs., Inc., 391 F.3d 1365, 1372, 73 USPQ2d 1161 (Fed. Cir. 2004); Glaxo, Inc. v. Novopharm, Ltd., 52 F.3d 1043, 1048, 34 USPQ2d 1565 (Fed. Cir.), *cert. denied,* 516 U.S. 988 (1995).

[24] *Therasense,* 649 F.3d at 1290, 99 USPQ2d 1065 (internal citations omitted).

[25] *Id.* at 1297 n.1, 99 USPQ2d 1065 (O'Malley, J., concurring in part and dissenting in part). The views of other members of the Federal Circuit can be seen, e.g., in *Optium Corp. v. Emcore Corp.,* 603 F.3d 1313, 1322, 94 USPQ2d 1925 (Fed. Cir. 2010) (Prost, J., concurring); *Leviton Mfg. v. Universal Sec. Instruments, Inc.,* 606 F.3d 1353, 1368, 95 USPQ2d 1432 (Fed. Cir. 2010) (Prost, J., dissenting); and *Cancer Research Tech. Ltd. v. Barr Labs., Inc.,* 625 F.3d 724, 734–35, 737–38, 96 USPQ2d 1937 (Fed. Cir. 2010) (Prost, J., dissenting).

Where "threshold intent" has been found, courts have inferred intent from the absence of a "credible explanation" for nondisclosure by the patentee.[26] However, *Therasense* instructs that "[t]he absence of a good faith explanation for withholding a material reference does not, by itself, prove intent to deceive."[27] When making a finding regarding intent to deceive the PTO, a court must consider all circumstances, including those indicating good faith.[28]

With respect to subjective evidence of good faith, the Federal Circuit has stated:

> No single factor or combination of factors can be said always to require an inference of intent to mislead; yet a patentee facing a high level of materiality and clear proof that it knew or should have known of that materiality, can expect to find it difficult to establish "subjective good faith" sufficient to prevent the drawing of an inference of intent to mislead. A mere denial of intent to mislead (which would defeat every effort to establish inequitable conduct) will not suffice in such circumstances.[29]

Before *Therasense*, the inequitable conduct analysis required a court to balance the actual degree of materiality and the strength of the evidence of intent to determine whether, as a matter of equity, the patent in suit should be held unenforceable.[30] Although *Therasense* ended the use of the sliding scale to balance materiality and intent, it remains true that the defense

---

[26]Bruno Indep. Living Aids, Inc. v. Acorn Mobility Servs., Ltd., 394 F.3d 1348, 1354, 73 USPQ2d 1593 (Fed. Cir. 2005); *see also* Dayco Prods., Inc. v. Total Containment, Inc., 329 F.3d 1358, 1367, 66 USPQ2d 1801 (Fed. Cir. 2003).

[27]*Therasense*, 649 F.3d at 1291, 99 USPQ2d 1065 (internal citations omitted).

[28]*See, e.g.,* Pfizer, Inc. v. Teva Pharms. USA, Inc., 518 F.3d 1353, 1366–67, 86 USPQ2d 1001 (Fed. Cir. 2008); eSpeed, Inc. v. BrokerTec USA, L.L.C., 480 F.3d 1129, 1137–38, 82 USPQ2d 1183 (Fed. Cir. 2007); Purdue Pharma L.P. v. Endo Pharms., Inc., 438 F.3d 1123, 1134, 77 USPQ2d 1767 (Fed. Cir. 2006). Paragon Podiatry Lab. v. KLM Labs., 984 F.2d 1182, 1190, 25 USPQ2d 1561 (Fed. Cir. 1993); Kingsdown Med. Consultants v. Hollister, Inc., 863 F.2d 867, 876, 9 USPQ2d 1384 (Fed. Cir. 1988), *cert. denied*, 490 U.S. 1067 (1989).

[29]Monsanto Co. v. Bayer Bioscience N.V., 514 F.3d 1229, 85 USPQ2d 1582 (Fed. Cir. 2008); Sanofi-Synthelabo v. Apotex, Inc., 470 F.3d 1368, 81 USPQ2d 1097 (Fed. Cir. 2006); FMC Corp. v. Manitowoc Co., 835 F.2d 1411, 1416, 5 USPQ2d 1112 (Fed. Cir. 1987).

[30]Star Scientific, Inc. v. R. J. Reynolds Tobacco Co., 537 F.3d 1357, 1367, 88 USPQ2d 1001 (Fed. Cir. 2008).

is "an equitable doctrine" and, as such, "hinges on basic fairness."[31] Accordingly, the ultimate determination of whether there was inequitable conduct is committed to the trial court's discretion and, for purposes of appellate review, the court should enter a finding as to the reasons for its conclusion.[32]

II. PATENT MISUSE

A patent is misused when its owner uses it to expand impermissibly the scope of the patent right with anticompetitive effect.[33] Although the patent misuse defense arises from the doctrine of unclean hands, it is not an open-ended defense that arises from any wrongful conduct. Rather, to constitute misuse, the conduct complained of must restrict the use of the patent "in one of the specific ways that have been held to be outside the otherwise broad scope of the patent grant."[34]

A. The Current Scope of the Misuse Defense

The defense of misuse arose from a series of Supreme Court decisions in the first half of the twentieth century that challenged various terms in patent license agreements. For example, the Supreme Court struck down agreements to license patented technology (e.g., a movie projector) only if the licensee agreed to

---

[31] *Therasense*, 649 F.3d at 1292, 99 USPQ2d 1065.

[32] See Bruno Indep. Living Aids, Inc. v. Acorn Mobility Servs., Ltd., 394 F.3d 1348, 1351, 73 USPQ2d 1593 (Fed. Cir. 2005); Purdue Pharma L.P. v. Boehringer Ingelheim GmbH, 237 F.3d 1359, 1366, 57 USPQ2d 1647 (Fed. Cir. 2001). Even where both threshold materiality and threshold intent have been found, a court may still conclude that, taking all circumstances into account, no inequitable conduct occurred. Kemin Foods, L.C. v. Pigmentos Vegetales Del Centro S.A. De C.V., 464 F.3d 1339, 80 USPQ2d 1385 (Fed. Cir. 2006); Kimberly Clark Corp. v. Johnson & Johnson, 745 F.2d 1437, 223 USPQ 603 (Fed. Cir. 1984).

[33] Princo Corp. v. International Trade Comm'n, 616 F.3d 1318, 1326–29, 96 USPQ2d 1233 (Fed. Cir. 2010) (en banc), *cert. denied,* 179 L. Ed. 2d 1209 (2011); Illinois Tool Works, Inc. v. Independent Ink, Inc., 547 U.S. 28, 38, 77 USPQ2d 1801 (2006).

[34] *Princo,* 616 F.3d at 1329, 96 USPQ2d 1233; C. R. Bard, Inc. v. M3 Sys., Inc., 157 F.3d 1340, 1372–73, 48 USPQ2d 1225 (Fed. Cir. 1998), *cert. denied,* 526 U.S. 1130 (1999).

buy unpatented supplies (e.g., the films to be shown on those projectors) from the patent owner.[35] By the early 1970s, the license provisions that were generally recognized as suspect were known informally as the "nine no-nos."[36]

Beginning in the 1980s, the Justice Department, the Federal Trade Commission, and the courts began to move away from rigid per se rules toward an analysis of license terms based on the rule of reason, balancing the potentially procompetitive and anticompetitive effect of the license.[37] The Federal Circuit required that the defense of misuse include proof of anticompetitive effect.[38] And, in 1988, Congress amended the patent statute to expressly declare that certain licensing practices are not misuse.[39]

The Supreme Court has held that certain practices are per se patent misuse, e.g., extending the temporal scope of a patent by requiring a licensee to pay royalties after the patent has expired.[40]

For acts that are neither per se misuse nor statutorily exempted from being misuse, determining if an act constitutes patent misuse involves a two-step inquiry.[41] First, the court must

---

[35] *Princo,* 616 F.3d at 1326, 96 USPQ2d 1233; Motion Picture Patents Co. v. Universal Film Manufacturing Co., 243 U.S. 502, 518 (1917).

[36] *See* FEDERAL TRADE COMMISSION, TO PROMOTE INNOVATION: THE PROPER BALANCE BETWEEN COMPETITION AND PATENT LAW AND POLICY, Chap. 1, at 14–18 (October 2003), available at http://www.ftc.gov/os/2003/10/innovationrpt.pdf. The license terms that potentially gave rise to a misuse defense were: (1) tying the patent license to the purchase of unpatented materials; (2) requiring the licensee to grant back rights under subsequently issued patents; (3) restricting the rights of the licensee to resell patented products; (4) restricting the licensee's commercial activities outside the scope of the patent; (5) an agreement restricting the licensor's right to grant further licenses; (6) mandatory package licenses; (7) royalty provisions not reasonably related to the actual sales by the licensee; (8) restrictions on how the licensee could use a product made by a patented process; and (9) minimum resale price provisions of licensed products. *See* Robert J. Hoerner, *Patent Misuse,* 53 ANTITRUST L.J. 641, 649–54 (1984).

[37] *See id.* at 18–20, 22–23; U.S. DEPARTMENT OF JUSTICE AND FEDERAL TRADE COMMISSION, ANTITRUST GUIDELINES FOR THE LICENSING OF INTELLECTUAL PROPERTY at 16–18 (1995), available at http://www.justice.gov/atr/public/guidelines/0558.htm.

[38] Windsurfing Int'l, Inc. v. AMF, Inc., 782 F.2d 995, 228 USPQ 562 (Fed. Cir.), *cert. denied,* 477 U.S. 905 (1986).

[39] 35 U.S.C. §271(d); *Princo,* 616 F.3d at 1329–31, 96 USPQ2d 1233. The legislative history of the 1988 amendments is discussed in *Princo,* 616 F.3d at 1329–31 and at 1350–51, 96 USPQ2d 1233 (Dyk, J., dissenting).

[40] Brulotte v. Thys Co., 379 U.S. 29, 33, 143 USPQ 264(1964); Virginia Panel Corp. v. MAC Panel Co., 133 F.3d 860, 869, 45 USPQ2d 1225 (Fed. Cir. 1997), *cert. denied* 525 U.S. 815 (1998).

[41] *Id.* at 860, 869, 45 USPQ2d 1225; B. Braun Med., Inc. v. Abbott Labs., 124 F.3d 1419, 1426–27, 43 USPQ2d 1896 (Fed. Cir. 1997); Mallinckrodt, Inc. v. Medipart, Inc., 976 F.2d 700, 708, 24 USPQ2d 1173 (Fed. Cir. 1992).

determine if the act is reasonably within the patent grant.[42] If so, then the act cannot be a misuse because it has not expanded the scope of the patent right.[43] Second, if the act is not reasonably within the patent grant, then the court must determine whether the act has an anticompetitive effect that is not justifiable under the rule of reason.[44]

Regarding the first inquiry, the Federal Circuit stated in its 2010 en banc decision in *Princo Corp. v. International Trade Commission:*

> [C]ourts have noted that the patentee begins with substantial rights under the patent grant—"includ[ing] the right to suppress the invention while continuing to prevent all others from using it, to license others, or to refuse to license, . . . to charge such royalty as the leverage of the patent permits," and to limit the scope of the license to a particular "field of use."[45]

Other acts that have been held to be within the patent right include good faith notification of potential infringement

---

[42] U.S. Philips Corp. v. United States Int'l Trade Comm'n, 424 F.3d 1179, 1197, 76 USPQ2d 1545 (Fed. Cir. 2005), *cert. denied,* 547 U.S. 1207 (2006); *Virginia Panel Corp.,* 133 F.3d at 869, 45 USPQ2d 1225; *B. Braun Med., Inc.,* 124 F.3d at 1426–27, 43 USPQ2d 1896; *Mallinckrodt, Inc.,* 976 F.2d at 708, 24 USPQ2d 1173.

[43] *Princo,* 616 F.3d at 1328, 96 USPQ2d 1233; *U.S. Philips Corp.,* 424 F.3d at 1197, 76 USPQ2d 1545; Monsanto Co. v. McFarling, 363 F.3d 1336, 1341, 70 USPQ2d 1481 (Fed. Cir. 2004), *cert. denied,* 545 U.S. 1139 (2005) ("Monsanto I"); *Virginia Panel Corp.,* 133 F.3d at 869, 45 USPQ2d 1225; *B. Braun Med., Inc.,* 124 F.3d at 1426–27, 43 USPQ2d 1896; *Mallinckrodt, Inc.,* 976 F.2d at 708, 24 USPQ2d 1173.

[44] *Virginia Panel Corp.,* 133 F.3d at 869, 45 USPQ2d 1225; *B. Braun Med., Inc.,* 124 F.3d at 1426–27, 43 USPQ2d 1896; *Mallinckrodt, Inc.,* 976 F.2d at 708, 24 USPQ2d 1173.

[45] *Princo,* 616 F.3d at 1328–29, 96 USPQ2d 1233 (citation omitted). *Princo* addressed allegations of patent misuse arising from joint development and joint package licensing in the electronics standards context. The allegations included improper tying, package licensing, and conspiring to suppress alternative technology. The court concluded that the activities complained of did not constitute patent misuse. Judge Dyk wrote a detailed dissent, which Judge Gajarsa joined. *Id.* at 1341–57, 96 USPQ2d 1233. For other cases relating to alleged misuse arising from not exploiting the patented invention, see Monsanto Co. v. Scruggs, 459 F.3d 1328, 1339, 79 USPQ2d 1813 (Fed. Cir. 2006), *cert. denied,* 127 S. Ct. 2062 (2007) ("Monsanto II"); Cygnus Therapeutics Sys. v. Alza Corp., 92 F.3d 1153, 1160, 39 USPQ2d 1666 (Fed. Cir. 1996); *Monsanto I,* 363 F.3d at 1343, 70 USPQ2d 1481; *In re* Independent Serv. Orgs. Antitrust Litig., 203 F.3d 1322, 1325–28, 53 USPQ2d 1852 (Fed. Cir. 2000), *cert. denied,* 531 U.S. 1143 (2001) (antitrust); Image Tech. Servs., Inc. v. Eastman Kodak Co., 125 F.3d 1195, 1214–20, 44 USPQ2d 1065 (9th Cir. 1997), *cert. denied,* 523 U.S. 1094 (1998) (antitrust).

and threats of suit and injunction,[46] and agreeing to calculate royalties in part on unpatented components of a patented system.[47]

Regarding the second inquiry, determining when an act has an anticompetitive effect not justifiable under the rule of reason is fact intensive, involving consideration of evidence relating to the relevant business; the market power of the patent owner within the relevant market; the condition of the business before and after the anticompetitive act; and the act's history, nature, and effect.[48] For example, when the alleged misuse is a licensing arrangement, the evidence must reveal that the overall effect of the license tends to restrain competition unlawfully in an appropriately defined relevant market.[49]

A misused patent is unenforceable until the improper practice has stopped and the effects of the misuse have dissipated.[50]

B. Standards Setting Organizations

A standards setting organization (SSO) is an organization formed by a group of companies in an industry, who come together to agree on certain technical specifications for the products that they plan to market. For example, an SSO might consist of the makers of personal computers, the makers of video dis-

---

[46] *Virginia Panel Corp.*, 133 F.3d at 869–70, 45 USPQ2d 1225. Threats to void or limit a warranty are not a use of a patent right and thus cannot be patent misuse. *Id.* A patent owner's proposal to act in a manner that would be a misuse is not a misuse when the proposal has been voluntarily and unilaterally revoked before consummation. *Id.* at 871, 45 USPQ2d 1225.

[47] Engel Indus., Inc. v. Lockformer Co., 96 F.3d 1398, 1407–09, 40 USPQ2d 1161 (Fed. Cir. 1996).

[48] *Princo*, 616 F.3d at 1334, 96 USPQ2d 1233; Illinois Tool Works, Inc v. Independent Ink, Inc., 547 U.S. 28, 38, 43, 77 USPQ2d 1801 (2006); *Virginia Panel Corp.*, 133 F.3d at 869, 45 USPQ2d 1225.

[49] Windsurfing Int'l, Inc. v. AMF, Inc., 782 F.2d 995, 1001, 228 USPQ 562 (Fed. Cir.), *cert. denied*, 477 U.S. 905 (1986). *See generally Monsanto II*, 459 F.3d 1328, 1341, 79 USPQ2d 1813; U.S. Philips Corp. v. United States Int'l Trade Comm'n, 424 F.3d 1179, 1198, 76 USPQ2d 1545 (Fed. Cir. 2005), *cert. denied*, 547 U.S. 1207 (2006); USM Corp. v. SPS Techs., Inc., 694 F.2d 505, 512–14, 216 USPQ 959 (7th Cir. 1982), *cert. denied*, 462 U.S. 1107 (1983); *see also* U.S. DEPARTMENT OF JUSTICE AND FEDERAL TRADE COMMISSION, ANTITRUST GUIDELINES FOR THE LICENSING OF INTELLECTUAL PROPERTY at 16–18 (1995), available at http://www.justice.gov/atr/public/guidelines/0558.htm.

[50] *See, e.g., Princo*, 616 F.3d at 1334–39, 96 USPQ2d 1233; *see also* C. R. Bard, Inc. v. M3 Sys., Inc., 157 F.3d 1340, 1372, 48 USPQ2d 1225 (Fed. Cir. 1998), *cert. denied*, 526 U.S. 1130 (1999); United States Gypsum Co. v. National Gypsum Co., 352 U.S. 457, 112 USPQ 340 (1957) Damages may not be recovered solely on the basis of patent misuse. B. Braun Med., Inc. v. Abbott Labs., 124 F.3d 1419, 1427–28, 43 USPQ2d 1896 (Fed. Cir. 1997).

plays and the makers of the controller chips that create the interface between computers and displays. By agreeing on specifications, the participants in an SSO ensure the interoperability of their products.[51]

An SSO is generally governed by an agreement that requires its members to disclose whether they have patents that bear on a standard under consideration and, often, to agree to license such patents on fair, reasonable, and nondiscriminatory terms (FRAND). The purpose of a disclosure and licensing obligations are to prevent a member from obtaining an unfair advantage by inducing the SSO to adopt technology in which that member can later claim exclusive rights. This is sometimes referred to as a patent holdup.[52]

Intentionally failing to meet one's disclosure obligations and then asserting in litigation a patent that should have been disclosed has been found to be patent misuse. In addition to giving rise to potential antitrust liability, the patents at issue have been held unenforceable against products covered by the standard under a variety of legal theories, including waiver, patent misuse, and equitable estoppel.[53]

III. LACHES

The elements underlying the laches defense are: (1) the patent owner unreasonably and inexcusably delayed filing suit for infringement; and (2) the alleged infringer has been materially prejudiced by the delay.[54] Even if the laches elements are proven, the court nevertheless may exercise its discretion to deny the defense after looking at all the relevant

---

[51] See generally U.S. DEPARTMENT OF JUSTICE AND FEDERAL TRADE COMMISSION, ANTITRUST ENFORCEMENT AND INTELLECTUAL PROPERTY RIGHTS: PROMOTING INNOVATION AND COMPETITION at 33–34 (2007), available at http://www.ftc.gov/reports/innovation/P040101PromotingInnovationandCompetitionrpt0704.pdf.

[52] Id. at 34–37.

[53] See, e.g., Qualcomm Inc. v. Broadcom Corp., 548 F.3d 1004, 89 USPQ2d 1321 (Fed. Cir. 2008); see also Joseph Farrell et al., Standard Setting, Patents and Hold-up, 74 ANTITRUST L.J. 603 (2007).

[54] A. C. Aukerman Co. v. R. L. Chaides Constr. Co., 960 F.2d 1020, 1032, 22 USPQ2d 1321 (Fed. Cir. 1992) (en banc).

evidence and weighing the equities.[55] Thus, for example, the patent owner can defeat a laches defense by showing that the alleged infringer acted egregiously.[56] The egregious conduct must be related to the laches facts.

The alleged infringer bears the burden of proving the laches elements by a preponderance of the evidence.[57] However, if the alleged infringer can prove that the delay exceeded six years, the elements of laches are presumed and a burden of going forward with evidence to burst the presumption is imposed on the patent owner, who can meet that burden either by showing that the delay was reasonable or excusable under the circumstances or by showing that the delay did not prejudice the alleged infringer.[58]

The period of delay begins when the patent owner knows or, in the exercise of reasonable diligence, should have known of the alleged infringement.[59] A patent owner should have known of the alleged infringement if it was pervasive, open, and notorious in the patent owner's field of endeavor.[60] For example, sales, publication, marketing, public use, or other conspicuous activity in regard to a product gives rise to an ongoing duty to investigate whether there is infringement, if the product is similar to, or embodies technology similar to, the patented invention.[61] In con-

---

[55] Symantec Corp. v. Computer Assocs. Int'l, Inc., 522 F.3d 1279, 1294, 86 USPQ2d 1449 (Fed. Cir. 2008); State Contracting & Eng'g Corp. v. Condotte Am., Inc., 346 F.3d 1057, 1065, 68 USPQ2d 1481 (Fed. Cir. 2003); see also Eastman Kodak Co. v. Goodyear Tire & Rubber Co., 114 F.3d 1547, 1559, 42 USPQ2d 1737 (Fed. Cir. 1997).

[56] A. C. Aukerman Co., 960 F.2d at 1033, 1038, 22 USPQ2d 1321; Gasser Chair Co. v. Infanti Chair Mfg. Corp., 60 F.3d 770, 775–76, 34 USPQ2d 1822 (Fed. Cir. 1995).

[57] A. C. Aukerman Co., 960 F.2d at 1038–39, 1045, 22 USPQ2d 1321.

[58] A. C. Aukerman Co., 960 F.2d at 1034–39, 22 USPQ2d 1321; Symantec Corp., 522 F.3d 1279, 1294, 86 USPQ2d 1449; Wanlass v. General Elec. Co., 148 F.3d 1334, 1337, 46 USPQ2d 1915 (Fed. Cir. 1998); Hall v. Aqua Queen Mfg. Inc., 93 F.3d 1548, 1556–57, 39 USPQ2d 1925 (Fed. Cir. 1996); Hemstreet v. Computer Entry Sys. Corp., 972 F.2d 1290, 1293, 23 USPQ2d 1860 (Fed. Cir. 1992). Evidence offered to burst the presumption need only be evidence that is sufficient to raise a genuine issue. A. C. Aukerman Co., 960 F.2d at 1038, 22 USPQ2d 1321.

[59] A. C. Aukerman Co., 960 F.2d at 1032, 22 USPQ2d 1321; Ultimax Cement Co, v. CTS Cement Mfg. Corp., 587 F.3d 1339, 1349–50, 92 USPQ2d 1865 (Fed. Cir. 2009); Studiengesellschaft Kohle v. Eastman Kodak Co., 616 F.2d 1315, 206 USPQ 577 (5th Cir.), cert. denied, 449 U.S. 1014 (1980).

[60] Wanlass, 148 F.3d at 1337–39, 46 USPQ2d 1915; Hall, 93 F.3d at 1553, 39 USPQ2d 1925. But see Wanlass v. Fedders Corp., 145 F.3d 1461, 47 USPQ2d 1097 (Fed. Cir. 1998).

[61] Wanlass, 148 F.3d at 1337–39, 46 USPQ2d 1915. But see Fedders Corp., 145 F.3d 1461, 47 USPQ2d 1097. The frequency with which a patent owner should conduct infringement investigations is a function of cost and difficulty. Wanlass, 148 F.3d at 1340, 46 USPQ2d 1915. The duty to investigate may also arise from past dealings between the patent owner and alleged infringers. Id.; Symantec Corp., 522 F.3d at 1294, 86 USPQ2d 1449. Sale of products that give rise to laches must be the same or similar to the products at issue in the suit.

trast, an infringer's policy of secrecy and denial of infringement led a court to find that the infringer failed to prove that the patent owner knew or should have known of the alleged infringement.[62] The patent owner asserting the patent is responsible for the delays of any previous owners of the patent.[63]

The trial court must consider any reasonable excuse offered by the patent owner for delay in commencing suit.[64] Excuses for delay that courts have found reasonable include the following: the patent owner was suing a different party for infringement of the same patent; the patent owner was negotiating a license with the alleged infringer; or a war was going on.[65] The equities may require that the patent owner communicate its reasons for delay to the alleged infringer.[66] Excuses that courts generally have found unreasonable include that the patent owner was too poor, sick, or could not find counsel, and that the alleged infringer was not worth suing because he or she was too poor.[67]

Prejudice to the alleged infringer resulting from the patent owner's delay can be either evidentiary or economic.[68] Examples of evidentiary prejudice may be loss of physical evidence or records, death of a witness, or the unreliability of memories of long past events.[69] Examples of economic prejudice may be damages or loss of investments that would likely have been prevented by earlier suit.[70] Prejudice that arose

---

[62] Eastman Kodak Co. v. Goodyear Tire & Rubber Co., 114 F.3d 1547, 1559, 42 USPQ2d 1737 (Fed. Cir. 1997).

[63] *Id.;* Nordek Corp. v. Garbe Iron Works, Inc., 221 USPQ 587 (N.D. Ill. 1982).

[64] Gasser Chair Co. v. Infanti Chair Mfg. Corp., 60 F.3d 770, 774, 34 USPQ2d 1822 (Fed. Cir. 1995).

[65] *A. C. Aukerman Co.,* 960 F.2d at 1033, 22 USPQ2d 1321; *see* 6 DONALD S. CHISUM, CHISUM ON PATENTS §19.05[2][b] (2010) (collecting cases).

[66] Hall v. Aqua Queen Mfg., Inc., 93 F.3d 1548, 1554, 39 USPQ2d 1925 (Fed. Cir. 1996); Hemstreet v. Computer Entry Sys. Corp., 972 F.2d 1290, 1293, 23 USPQ2d 1860 (Fed. Cir. 1992).

[67] *See* 6 DONALD S. CHISUM, CHISUM ON PATENTS §19.05[2][b] (2010) (collecting cases); as to poverty, *see also Hall,* 93 F.3d at 1554, 39 USPQ2d 1925, and *A. C. Aukerman Co.,* 960 F.2d at 1033, 22 USPQ2d 1321.

[68] *A. C. Aukerman Co.,* 960 F.2d at 1033, 22 USPQ2d 1321; Hearing Components, Inc. v. Shure Inc., 600 F.3d 1357, 1375–76, (Fed. Cir. 2010). The prejudice must be because of and as a result of the patent owner's delay. *Gasser Chair Co.,* 60 F.3d at 774–75, 34 USPQ2d 1822; *see also* Ecolab, Inc. v. Envirochem, Inc., 264 F.3d 1358, 1371–72, 60 USPQ2d 1173 (Fed. Cir. 2001).

[69] Wanlass v. General Elec. Co., 148 F.3d 1334, 1337, 46 USPQ2d 1915 (Fed. Cir. 1998); *A. C. Aukerman Co.,* 960 F.2d at 1033, 22 USPQ2d 1321.

[70] State Contracting & Eng'g Corp. v. Condotte Am., Inc., 346 F.3d 1057, 1066, 68 USPQ2d 1481 (Fed. Cir. 2003); *Wanlass,* 148 F.3d at 1337, 46 USPQ2d 1915; *A. C. Aukerman Co.,* 960 F.2d at 1033, 22 USPQ2d 1321.

because of actions before the beginning of the delay period are irrelevant.[71]

If laches is established, the patent owner is precluded from recovering for all infringement by the infringer that occurred before the complaint was filed and from obtaining an injunction regarding products sold before the complaint was filed.[72] The patent owner is not, however, estopped from obtaining an injunction for products sold after the complaint was filed or from recovering postfiling damages.[73]

In addition to the conventional defense of laches, "prosecution laches" may bar enforcement of patent claims that issued after an unreasonable and unexplained delay in prosecution of the patents in suit.[74]

IV. ESTOPPEL

If established, the defense of equitable estoppel precludes the patent owner from recovering from the alleged infringer for all past and prospective infringement, and from obtaining an injunction against the alleged infringer.[75]

---

[71] *State Contracting & Eng'g Corp.*, 346 F.3d at 1066, 68 USPQ2d 1481; *Hall*, 93 F.3d at 1556–57, 39 USPQ2d 1925.

[72] Odetics Inc. v. Storage Tech. Corp., 185 F.3d 1259, 1272–74, 51 USPQ2d 1225 (Fed. Cir. 1999); Leinoff v. Louis Milona & Sons, 726 F.2d 734, 741, 220 USPQ 845 (Fed. Cir. 1984).

[73] *Id.*

[74] Symbol Techs., Inc. v. Lemelson Med., Educ. & Research Found., L.P., 422 F.3d 1378, 1386, 76 USPQ2d 1354 (Fed. Cir.), *amended on reh'g in part by* 429 F.3d 1051, 1052 (Fed. Cir. 2005) (extending laches holding of unenforceability to all claims of the asserted patents); *see also* Symbol Techs., Inc. v. Lemelson Med. Educ. & Research Found., L.P., 277 F.3d 1361, 1363–68, 61 USPQ2d 1515 (Fed. Cir.), *cert. denied,* 537 U.S. 825 (2002); *In re* Bogese, 303 F.3d 1362, 1367, 64 USPQ2d 1448 (Fed. Cir. 2002).

[75] *See generally* A. C. Aukerman Co. v. R. L. Chaides Constr. Co., 960 F.2d 1020, 1041, 22 USPQ2d 1321 (Fed. Cir. 1992) (en banc). Equitable estoppel is an absolute bar to an infringement claim. Scholle Corp. v. Blackhawk Molding Co., 133 F.3d 1469, 1471, 45 USPQ2d 1468 (Fed. Cir. 1998). Equitable estoppel should not be confused with legal estoppel. For the distinction, see Wang Labs., Inc. v. Mitsubishi Elecs. of Am., 103 F.3d 1571, 1581–82, 41 USPQ2d 1263 (Fed. Cir.), *cert. denied,* 522 U.S. 818 (1997) (an equitable estoppel-style implied license). An implied license, as discussed in Chapter 6, §I.A., usually is in the nature of a legal estoppel. *Id.* For the elements of equitable estoppel-style implied license, see Winbond Elec. Corp. v. United States Int'l Trade Comm'n, 262 F.3d 1363, 1374, 60 USPQ2d 1029, *corrected,* 275 F.3d 1344 (Fed. Cir. 2001).

Equitable estoppel focuses on what the alleged infringer was led reasonably to believe by the patent owner's conduct.[76] Three elements underlie the usual defense of equitable estoppel:

1. through misleading conduct, the patent owner leads the alleged infringer reasonably to infer that the patent owner does not intend to enforce its patent against the alleged infringer;
2. the alleged infringer relies on the patent owner's misleading conduct; and
3. because of its reliance, the alleged infringer will be materially prejudiced if the patent owner is allowed to proceed with its claim.[77]

Misleading conduct includes specific statements, action, inaction, or silence where there was an obligation to speak.[78] Reliance requires that the alleged infringer had a relationship or communication with the patent owner that lulls the alleged infringer into a sense of security in taking some action.[79] Material prejudice can be either evidentiary or economic.[80]

Unlike the defense of laches, a six-year delay in bringing suit does not give rise to any presumption under an equitable estoppel defense,[81] although it may be relevant to assessing

---

[76] A. C. Aukerman Co., 960 F.2d at 1034, 22 USPQ2d 1321.

[77] Id. at 1028, 22 USPQ2d 1321; see id. at 1042 n.17, 22 USPQ2d 1321, for another type of equitable estoppel defense.

[78] Aspex Eyewear Inc. v. Clariti Eyewear, Inc., 605 F.3d 1305, 1310–12, 94 USPQ2d 1856 (Fed. Cir. 2010); Scholle Corp., 133 F.3d at 1473, 45 USPQ2d 1468; A. C. Aukerman Co., 960 F.2d at 1028, 1042, 22 USPQ2d 1321. No general obligation exists to answer an infringer's questions regarding possible infringement, but such a duty could arise under certain circumstances. Scholle Corp., 133 F.3d at 1472, 45 USPQ2d 1468.

[79] A. C. Aukerman Co. 960 F.2d at 1042–43, 22 USPQ2d 1321; see, e.g., B. Braun Med., Inc. v. Abbott Labs., 124 F.3d 1419, 1425, 43 USPQ2d 1896 (Fed. Cir. 1997); (relationship regarding a noninfringing product was not sufficient); Hall v. Aqua Queen Mfg., Inc., 93 F.3d 1548, 1558, 39 USPQ2d 1925 (Fed. Cir. 1996) (alleged infringer may have acted with belief patent was invalid and not in reliance on patent owner's conduct).

[80] A. C. Aukerman Co., 960 F.2d at 1043, 22 USPQ2d 1321; see, e.g., ABB Robotics, Inc. v. GMFanuc Robotics Corp., 52 F.3d 1062, 1065, 34 USPQ2d 1597 (Fed. Cir.), cert. denied, 516 U.S. 917 (1995).

[81] A. C. Aukerman Co., 960 F.2d at 1043, 22 USPQ2d 1321; see also Scholle Corp. v. Blackhawk Molding Co., 133 F.3d 1469, 1473, 45 USPQ2d 1468 (Fed. Cir. 1998); ABB Robotics, Inc., 52 F.3d at 1063, 34 USPQ2d 1597.

whether the patent owner's conduct is misleading.[82] The alleged infringer must prove the equitable estoppel elements (absent allegations of fraud or intentional misconduct) by a preponderance of the evidence.[83]

Even if all three elements are established, the court must consider any other evidence respecting the equities of the parties when deciding whether to exercise its discretion to bar the suit because of equitable estoppel.[84]

---

[82] A. C. Aukerman Co., 960 F.2d at 1042, 22 USPQ2d 1321.

[83] Vanderlande Indus. Nederland BV v. United States Int'l Trade Comm'n, 366 F.3d 1311, 1324, 70 USPQ2d 1696 (Fed. Cir. 2004); A. C. Aukerman Co., 960 F.2d at 1045–46, 22 USPQ2d 1321.

[84] A. C. Aukerman Co., 960 F.2d at 1043, 22 USPQ2d 1321; Aspex Eyewear Inc. v. Clariti Eyewear, Inc., 605 F.3d 1305 1313–14, 94 USPQ2d 1856 (Fed. Cir. 2010).

REMEDIES

Remedies in actions for patent infringement are (1) injunctive relief against ongoing or future infringement; (2) monetary damages for past infringement, together with prejudgment interest; (3) increased damages for willful infringement; and (4) attorney fees.[1]

---

[1]The general rule is remedies for infringement are only available after the patent issues. *See, e.g.,* Johns Hopkins Univ. v. CellPro Inc., 152 F.3d 1342, 1366, 47 USPQ2d 1705 (Fed. Cir.

Section 283 of Title 35 permits courts to "grant injunctions in accordance with the principles of equity to prevent the violation of any right secured by patent, on such terms as the court deems reasonable." Before the Supreme Court's 2006 decision in *eBay Inc. v. MercExchange, LLC*,[2] injunctive relief generally consisted of an order barring further infringement of the patent at issue. Since *eBay*, equitable relief may also include mandatory royalties in lieu of such an order.[3]

Section 284 of Title 35 mandates that the patent owner be awarded "damages adequate to compensate for the infringement, but in no event less than a reasonable royalty . . . together with interest and costs." Compensatory damages are awarded to restore a patent owner to the position he or she would have occupied if no infringement had occurred.[4] Compensatory awards generally are a combination of the patent owner's lost profits or, in the alternative, a "reasonable royalty". Damages may be increased "up to three times the amount found or assessed" at the discretion of the district court.[5]

Attorney's fees may be awarded to the "prevailing party," either the patent owner or the accused infringer, in "exceptional cases."[6]

1998). However, 35 U.S.C. §154(d) grants patent owners provisional rights, i.e., the right to collect a reasonable royalty for activities beginning when a patent application that subsequently issues has been published by the PTO, if the accused infringer had actual notice of the published application and if the asserted claims of the issued patent are "substantially identical" to the claims that were published. *See* Stephens v. Tech Int'l, Inc., 393 F.3d 1269, 1275–76, 73 USPQ2d 1369 (Fed. Cir. 2004).

[2] 547 U.S. 388, 78 USPQ2d 1577 (2006).

[3] MercExchange, LLC v. eBay Inc., 500 F. Supp. 2d 556, 585, 83 USPQ2d 1688 (E.D. Va. 2007); Paice LLC v. Toyota Motor Corp., 504 F.3d 1293, 1313–14, 85 USPQ2d 1001 (Fed. Cir. 2007), *cert. denied*, 553 U.S. 1032 (2008); Amado v. Microsoft Corp., 517 F.3d 1353, 1361–62, 86 USPQ2d 1090 (Fed. Cir. 2008); *compare* Innogenetics, N.V. v. Abbott Labs., 512 F.3d 1363, 1380–81, 85 USPQ2d 1641 (Fed. Cir. 2008) (not an abuse of discretion to deny injunction where damages sought included royalty for future infringement).

[4] Aro Mfg. Co. v. Convertible Top Replacement Co., 377 U.S. 476, 512, 141 USPQ 681 (1964) (hereafter "Aro II"); Rite-Hite Corp. v. Kelley Co., 56 F.3d 1538, 1544–45, 35 USPQ2d 1065 (Fed. Cir.), *cert. denied*, 516 U.S. 867 (1995) (en banc). *See generally* Roger D. Blair & Thomas F. Cotter, *An Economic Analysis of Damages Rules in Intellectual Property Law*, 39 Wm. & Mary L. Rev. 1585 (1998).

[5] 35 U.S.C. §284.

[6] *Id.* §285.

I. INJUNCTIONS

The remedy of an injunction against further infringement for the life of the patent has been available to courts pursuant to statute since 1819.[7] From the early days of the patent system into the nineteenth and early twentieth centuries, injunctive relief was generally granted as a matter of course. Injunctive relief is consistent with principles of equity and the notion that infringement may cause irreparable injury to the patent owner's statutory right to exclude others from practicing the patented invention.[8]

Injunctive relief barring further infringement remains the norm, but is no longer granted as a matter of course. In *eBay*,[9] the Supreme Court held that courts may not automatically grant injunctive relief absent a determination that the facts of the case satisfy the traditional four-part test applied generally in civil litigation.

A. Permanent Injunctions

In patent cases before *eBay,* the general rule had been that an injunction barring further infringement would issue in favor of a patent owner whose patent had been found infringed, valid, and enforceable. The rationale for this rule was that (1) the patent statute grants the patent owner the "right to exclude" others from practicing the patented invention without permission in the United States during the term of the patent;[10] and (2) courts had long rejected the concept of compulsory licensing of patent rights.[11] These two principles created a presumption

---

[7] The Patent Act of 1819 granted the federal courts "[u]pon any bill in equity [the] . . . authority to grant injunctions, according to the course and principles of courts of equity . . . on such terms and conditions as the said courts may deem fit and reasonable." Act of Feb. 15, 1819, ch. 19, 3 Stat. 481, 481–82 (1819) (codified at 35 U.S.C. §283).

[8] *See* Note, *Injunctive Relief in Patent Infringement Suits,* 112 U. Pa. L. Rev. 1025, 1041–43 (1964); Smith Int'l Inc. v. Hughes Tool Co., 718 F.2d 1573, 1577–78, 1580–81, 219 USPQ 686 (Fed. Cir.), *cert. denied,* 464 U.S. 996, 220 USPQ 385 (1983).

[9] 547 U.S. 388, 394, 78 USPQ2d 1577 (2006).

[10] 35 U.S.C. §154.

[11] Continental Paper Bag Co. v. Eastern Paper Bag Co., 210 U.S. 405, 423 (1908).

that a permanent injunction should issue absent extraordinary circumstances.[12] By contrast, compulsory licensing in various forms has long been a feature of the copyright statute.[13]

In *eBay,* the Supreme Court repudiated the general rule. Instead, courts must determine whether the patent owner has demonstrated that:

1. it will suffer irreparable injury if the infringer is not enjoined;
2. remedies available at law, such as monetary damages, are inadequate to compensate for that injury;
3. considering the balance of hardships between the patent owner and the adjudicated infringer, a remedy in equity is warranted; and,
4. the public interest would not be disserved by a permanent injunction.[14]

The various concurring opinions in *eBay* disagreed about the extent to which its decision would depart from the general rule of ordering injunctions in most patent cases. Chief Justice Roberts, writing for himself and Justices Scalia and Ginsburg, suggested in one concurring opinion that the departure should be minimal, given the difficulty of protecting the right to exclude with monetary remedies.[15] These justices suggested deference to the historical practice of granting injunctions in the vast majority of patent cases.[16]

However, in a separate concurrence, Justice Kennedy, writing for himself and Justices Stevens, Souter, and Breyer, suggested a more substantial departure.[17] While historically injunctions may have been appropriate in most cases, today's cases present different considerations.[18] An injunction may not be appropriate

---

[12]Tate Access Floors v. Maxcess Techs., 222 F.3d 958, 971–72, 55 USPQ2d 1513 (Fed. Cir. 2000); Richardson v. Suzuki Motor Co., 868 F.2d 1226, 1247, 9 USPQ2d 1913 (Fed. Cir. 1989), *cert. denied,* 493 U.S. 853 (1989); W. L. Gore & Assocs. Inc. v. Garlock, Inc., 842 F.2d 1275, 1281, 6 USPQ2d 1277 (Fed. Cir. 1988).

[13]17 U.S.C. §115.

[14]eBay Inc. v. MercExchange, LLC, 547 U.S. 388, 391, 78 USPQ2d 1577 (2006).

[15]*Id.* at 395, 78 USPQ2d 1577.

[16]*Id.; see also* Robert Bosch LLC v. Pylon Mfg. Corp., ____ F.3d ____, 2011 WL 4834266 (Fed. Cir. (Del.) Oct. 13, 2011), *5–6.

[17]*Id.* at 395–97, 78 USPQ2d 1577.

[18]*Id.* at 396, 78 USPQ2d 1577.

where, for example, the patent owner is using the patent not as a basis for producing and selling goods, but rather to generate license fees, or where the patented invention is "but a small component" of the product that would be subject to injunction.[19] In the former case, an injunction could be used as a bargaining tool to charge exorbitant license fees, and in the latter, legal damages may be sufficient to compensate for infringement and an injunction may not serve the public interest.[20]

Since *eBay*, a majority of courts have continued to grant a permanent injunction as part of a final judgment for the patent owner.[21] While most courts have continued to grant an injunction in cases where the patent owner and the infringer are competitors,[22] some courts have denied injunctions in such cases.[23] In cases where the patent owner and infringer are not competitors, courts have both granted[24] and denied injunctions.[25]

Courts have found that the patent owner and infringer are competitors in situations where the patent owner does not sell a product covered by the patent in suit, but sells a product that

---

[19] *eBay Inc.*, 547 U.S. at 396, 78 USPQ2d 1577.

[20] *Id.* at 396–97, 78 USPQ2d 1577.

[21] In 2011, the Federal Trade Commission published a report that included extensive analysis of remedies in patent infringement cases. FEDERAL TRADE COMMISSION, THE EVOLVING IP MARKETPLACE: ALIGNING PATENT NOTICE AND REMEDIES WITH COMPETITION (2011), available at http://www.ftc.gov/os/2011/03/110307patentreport.pdf. Appendix B to the report is a study of district court permanent injunction decisions through 2010. *Id.* at 253–79. The cases tabulated in that report show that between the 2006 decision in *eBay* and March 2010, 55 reported decisions granted permanent injunctions after trial, while 21 decisions denied such relief. *Id.* at 272–78.

[22] *See, e.g.*, Robert Bosch LLC, 2011 WL 4834266, at *7–8; Broadcom Corp. v. Qualcomm Inc., 543 F.3d 683, 701–04, 88 USPQ2d 1641 (Fed. Cir. 2008) (affirming grant of an injunction against an indirect competitor); TiVo, Inc. v. Echostar Commc'ns Corp., 446 F. Supp. 2d 664 (E.D. Tex. 2006), *aff'd in part, rev'd in part, and remanded*, 516 F.3d 1290, 85 USPQ2d 1801 (Fed. Cir.), *cert. denied*, 555 U.S. 888 (2008).

[23] *See, e.g.*, Innogenetics, N.V. v. Abbott Labs., 512 F.3d 1363, 1380–81, 85 USPQ2d 1641 (Fed. Cir. 2008); ResQNet.com, Inc. v. Lansa, Inc., 533 F. Supp. 2d 397, 420–21 (S.D.N.Y. 2008).

[24] *See, e.g.*, Commonwealth Scientific & Indus. Research Org. v. Buffalo Tech. Inc., 492 F. Supp. 2d 600, 606–07 (E.D. Tex. 2007); Monsanto Co. v. Parr, 545 F. Supp. 2d 836 (N.D. Ind. 2008).

[25] *See, e.g.*, Paice LLC v. Toyota Motor Corp., 504 F.3d 1293, 85 USPQ2d 1001 (Fed. Cir. 2007), *cert. denied*, 553 U.S. 1032 (2008); Amado v. Microsoft Corp., 517 F.3d 1353, 1361, 86 USPQ2d 1090 (Fed. Cir. 2008); z4 Techs., Inc. v. Microsoft Corp., 434 F. Supp. 2d 437, 81 USPQ2d 1737 (E.D. Tex. 2006); MercExchange, LLC v. eBay, Inc., 500 F. Supp. 2d 556, 83 USPQ2d 1688 (E.D. Va. 2007); Finisar Corp. v. DirecTV Group, Inc., 523 F.3d 1323, 86 USPQ2d 1609 (Fed. Cir. 2008).

competes with the infringing product.[26] Although the prospect of lost sales by the patentee or its licensees alone is generally not sufficient, a factor found to be persuasive is likely loss of market share, particularly where the purchase of the infringing product locks in potential customers to the infringing supplier for the future.[27] The likelihood of price erosion is evidence of irreparable harm, as is damage to goodwill and reputation.[28] In a situation where the patent owner was a government-funded technology licensing organization, a court also found persuasive the argument that the patent owner could not fairly enforce its licensing program in the absence of an injunction.[29]

Circumstances that do not amount to sound reasons for denying a permanent injunction include that the patent owner has been willing to license the patent in suit to others, that the infringer's sales are small in comparison with the patent owner's sales, that the infringer would be put out of business, or that the infringer has stopped infringing.[30] A patent owner's failure to move for a preliminary injunction does not weigh against the owner's right to a permanent injunction after trial.

Circumstances that may lead to the denial of an injunction include finding that the patent owner and infringer are not competitors;[31] determining that a mandatory payment by the infringer to the patent owner or a prospective royalty is more equitable;[32] finding that the damages awarded included com-

---

[26] *See, e.g., Broadcom Corp.* 543 F.3d at 703, 88 USPQ2d 1641; *TiVo Inc.*, 446 F. Supp. 2d at 667.
[27] *Id.*

[28] Sanofi-Synthelabo v. Apotex, Inc., 470 F.3d 1368, 1382–83, 81 USPQ2d 1097 (Fed. Cir. 2006) (price erosion); i4i Ltd. P'ship v. Microsoft Corp., 598 F.3d 831, 93 USPQ2d 1943 861–62 (Fed. Cir. 2009) (loss of market share, change of business strategy), *aff'd*, 131 S. Ct. 2238, 98 USPQ2d 1857 (2011); Emory Univ. v. Nova Biogenetics, Inc., No. 1:06-CV-1041, 2008 WL 2945476, at *4 (N.D. Ga. July 25, 2008) (damage to goodwill and reputation).

[29] Commonwealth Scientific & Indus. Research Org. v. Buffalo Tech. Inc., 492 F. Supp. 2d 600, 606–07 (E.D. Tex. 2007).

[30] Robert Bosch LLC, 2011 WL 4834266, at 7–8. Acumed LLC v. Stryker Corp., 551 F.3d 1323, 1327–29, 89 USPQ2d 1612 (Fed. Cir. 2008) (licensing); Windsurfing Int'l Inc. v. AMF Inc., 782 F.2d 995, 1003 n.2, 228 USPQ 562 (Fed. Cir.), *cert. denied*, 477 U.S. 905 (1986).

[31] *See* MercExchange, LLC v. eBay Inc., 500 F. Supp. 2d 556, 572, 83 USPQ2d 1688 (E.D. Va. 2007); z4 Techs., Inc. v. Microsoft Corp., 434 F. Supp. 2d 437, 440, 81 USPQ2d 1737 (E.D. Tex. 2006.

[32] Paice LLC v. Toyota Motor Corp., 504 F.3d 1293, 1313–14, 85 USPQ2d 1001 (Fed. Cir. 2007), *cert. denied*, 553 U.S. 1032 (2008); *Innogenetics, N.V.*, 512 F.3d at 1380–81, 85 USPQ2d 1641; Foster v. American Mach. & Foundry Co., 492 F.2d 1317, 1324, 182 USPQ 1 (2d Cir.), *cert. denied*, 419 U.S. 833, 183 USPQ 321 (1974).

pensation for future infringement, e.g., for infringement causing lost follow-on sales in the future;[33] finding that infringing products were sold during a laches period;[34] finding that the patented invention is a small component of the product incorporating the invention;[35] and substantial injury to the public interest.[36] Courts may not grant injunctions merely to punish infringers or to compensate for litigation costs.[37]

With respect to the public interest and threatened harm to third parties, the court may delay the effective date of the injunction to lessen the inconvenience caused by the entry of an injunction.[38]

B. Preliminary Injunctions

In the mid-twentieth century, preliminary injunctions in patent infringement cases to bar infringement during the pendency of the action were very difficult to obtain. A patent owner had to demonstrate that there was no reasonable doubt that the patent was both valid and infringed,[39] and that he or she would suffer irreparable harm. The most acceptable way to satisfy the validity test was for the patent owner to show that the patent previously had been adjudicated valid. To show irreparable harm, the patent owner was required to establish that the defendant was either insolvent or about to become insolvent, or that the patent owner would suffer some drastic business reversal during the course of litigation.[40] For the purpose of a preliminary

---

[33] Innogenetics, N.V. v. Abbott Labs., 512 F.3d 1363, 1380–81, 85 USPQ2d 1641 (Fed. Cir. 2008); Trans-World Mfg. Corp. v. Al Nyman & Sons Inc., 750 F.2d 1552, 1565, 224 USPQ 259 (Fed. Cir. 1984); *see, e.g.,* Odetics Inc. v. Storage Tech. Corp., 14 F. Supp. 2d 785, 47 USPQ2d 1573 (E.D. Va. 1998), *aff'd in part, rev'd in part,* 185 F.3d 1259, 51 USPQ2d 1225 (Fed. Cir. 1999).

[34] *Odetics, Inc.,* 185 F.3d at 1272–74, 51 USPQ2d 1225.

[35] *Paice LLC,* 504 F.3d at 1303, 85 USPQ2d 1001; *z4 Techs., Inc.,* 434 F. Supp. 2d at 440, 81 USPQ2d 1737).

[36] *See* MercExchange, LLC v. eBay Inc., 401 F.3d 1323, 1338–39, 74 USPQ2d 1225 (Fed. Cir. 2005), *vacated and remanded,* 547 U.S. 388, 78 USPQ2d 1577 (2006); *z4 Tech., Inc.,* 434 F. Supp. 2d at 444.

[37] *Innogenetics, N.V.,* 512 F.3d at 1380–81 n.8, 85 USPQ2d 1641

[38] i4i Ltd. P'ship v. Microsoft Corp., 598 F.3d 831, 863–64, 93 USPQ2d 1943 (Fed. Cir. 2009).

[39] *See* Note, *Injunctive Relief in Patent Infringement Suits,* 112 U. PA. L. REV. 1025, 1030 (1964).

[40] *Id.* at 1032–35.

injunction, it was not presumed that the patent owner would be harmed irreparably by ongoing infringement. Consequently, the test for obtaining a preliminary injunction in patent infringement cases was very difficult. By contrast, in the trademark area, if a trademark owner made a reasonable showing that the trademark was valid and infringed, it was presumed that the injury to the trademark right would be irreparable.[41] The same was true for copyrights.[42]

Against this background, the Federal Circuit, in its 1983 decision in *Smith International Inc. v. Hughes Tool Co.*, ruled that "[w]here validity and continuing infringement have been clearly established . . . immediate irreparable harm is presumed."[43] The court adopted for the patent area the same rule of irreparable harm that was already the law with respect to copyright matters.[44]

In its October 2011 decision in *Robert Bosch LLC v. Pylon Mfg. Corp.*, the Federal Circuit confirmed that the Supreme Court's decision in *eBay* has eliminated the presumption of irreparable harm.[45] However, the Federal Circuit was equally clear that *eBay* "does not swing the pendulum in the opposite direction. . . . [I]t does not follow that courts should entirely ignore the fundamental nature of patents as property rights granting the owner the right to exclude. . . . While the patentee's right to exclude cannot justify an injunction, it should not be ignored either."[46] The court reaffirmed the continued applicability of its pre-*eBay* case law on the analysis of whether injunctive relief should be granted.[47]

---

[41] *E.g.,* Frisch's Rest. Inc. v. Elby's Big Boy, 670 F.2d 642, 649–50, 214 USPQ 15 (6th Cir.), *cert. denied,* 459 U.S. 916 (1982); Johnson & Johnson v. Carter-Wallace Inc., 631 F.2d 186, 189–92, 208 USPQ 169 (2d Cir. 1980).

[42] *E.g.,* Roper Corp. v. Litton Sys. Inc., 757 F.2d 1266, 1271, 225 USPQ 345 (Fed. Cir. 1985); Apple Computer Inc. v. Formula Int'l Inc., 725 F.2d 521, 525, 221 USPQ 762 (9th Cir. 1984); Apple Computer Inc. v. Franklin Computer Corp., 714 F.2d 1240, 1254, 219 USPQ 113 (3d Cir. 1983), *cert. dismissed,* 464 U.S. 1033 (1984).

[43] Smith Int'l Inc. v. Hughes Tool Co., 718 F.2d 1573, 1581, 219 USPQ 686 (Fed. Cir.), *cert. denied,* 464 U.S. 996, 220 USPQ 385 (1983).

[44] *Smith Int'l Inc.,* 718 F.2d at 1581 n.7, 219 USPQ 686.

[45] *Robert Bosch LLC,* 2011 WL 4834266 at *4.

[46] *Id.* at *5.

[47] *Id.* at *6.

A preliminary injunction is a drastic and extraordinary remedy that is not to be routinely granted.[48] This does not mean that a preliminary injunction must be rare or practically unattainable,[49] but, rather, that preliminary injunctions are not granted as a matter of right and must be thoroughly justified.[50] The decision to grant or deny a preliminary injunction is committed to the discretion of the trial court, and is reviewed for abuse of discretion.[51]

The purpose of a preliminary injunction is to preserve the status quo until a trial on the merits can be held.[52] The courts apply a four-factor test:

1. whether the movant has sufficiently established a reasonable likelihood of success on the merits;
2. whether the movant would suffer irreparable harm if the injunction were not granted;
3. whether the balance of hardships tips in the movant's favor; and
4. what impact, if any, the injunction would have on the public interest.[53]

Each factor must be weighed and assessed against the other factors and circumstances and against the form and magnitude of the relief sought.[54] No factor or circumstance can be ignored

---

[48] Intel Corp. v. ULSI Sys. Tech. Inc., 995 F.2d 1566, 1568, 27 USPQ2d 1136 (Fed. Cir. 1993), cert. denied, 510 U.S. 1092 (1994).

[49] Polymer Techs. Inc. v. Bridwell, 103 F.3d 970, 977, 41 USPQ2d 1185 (Fed. Cir. 1996).

[50] Id.

[51] Abbott Labs. v. Sandoz, Inc., 544 F.3d 1341, 1344–45, 89 USPQ2d 1161 (Fed. Cir. 2008); Amazon.com, Inc. v. Barnesandnoble.com, Inc., 239 F.3d 1343, 1350, 57 USPQ2d 1747 (Fed. Cir. 2001). An abuse of discretion may be found when the decision is based on an error of law, a clearly erroneous finding of fact, or a clear error of judgment in weighing the factors. Abbott Labs, 544 F.3d at 1345, 89 USPQ2d 1161.

[52] Abbott Labs., 544 F.3d at 1344–45, 89 USPQ2d 1161.

[53] Id.; Amazon.com, Inc., 239 F.3d at 1350, 57 USPQ2d 1747; Purdue Pharma L.P. v. Boehringer Ingelheim GmbH, 237 F.3d 1359, 1363, 57 USPQ2d 1647 (Fed. Cir. 2001).

[54] Intel Corp. v. ULSI Sys. Tech. Inc., 995 F.2d 1566, 1568, 27 USPQ2d 1136 (Fed. Cir. 1993), cert. denied, 510 U.S. 1092 (1994); Amazon.com, Inc., 239 F.3d at 1350, 57 USPQ2d 1747; Hybritech Inc. v. Abbott Labs., 849 F.2d 1446, 1451, 7 USPQ2d 1191 (Fed. Cir. 1988). Regarding procedural matters relating to injunctions, the Federal Circuit generally will apply the law of the regional circuit in which the district court sits. Digital Equip. Corp. v. Emulex Corp., 805 F.2d 380, 382–83 n.3, 231 USPQ 779 (Fed. Cir. 1986). But see Texas Instruments v. Tessera Inc., 231 F.3d 1325, 1328, 56 USPQ2d 1674 (Fed. Cir. 2000) (Federal Circuit law applied regarding request to enjoin continued participation in an ITC proceeding.).

when determining whether the requested preliminary injunction should issue.[55] Although it is preferable that all factors be considered when determining a denial of the requested preliminary injunction, the district court may deny the request based on the movant's failure to establish either of the first two factors.[56]

Regarding likelihood of success on the merits, a patent owner will show a reasonable likelihood of success on the merits if, in light of the presumptions and burdens that apply during trial, the patent owner clearly shows that (a) it will likely prove infringement, and (b) its claim will likely withstand a challenge to the validity and enforceability of the patent.[57] The court's finding regarding the likelihood of success factor may be based on a tentative claim construction.[58] A defendant can avoid a showing of a likelihood of success by demonstrating a substantial question of invalidity.[59] A showing of a substantial question of invalidity can be made on a lesser showing than the clear and convincing standard required to prove invalidity at trial.[60]

Regarding irreparable harm, the court may rely on the same types of injury that will support the entry of a permanent injunction, including loss of market share during the pendency of the litigation, price erosion, loss of goodwill, and other market oppor-

---

[55] Illinois Tool Works Inc. v. Grip-Pak, Inc., 906 F.2d 679, 681, 15 USPQ2d 1307 (Fed. Cir. 1990).

[56] National Steel Car, Ltd. v. Canadian Pac. Ry., 357 F.3d 1319, 1325, 69 USPQ2d 1641 (Fed. Cir. 2004); Jeneric/Pentron Inc. v. Dillon Co., 205 F.3d 1377, 1380, 54 USPQ2d 1086 (Fed. Cir. 2000); Eli Lilly & Co. v. American Cyanamid Co., 82 F.3d 1568, 1571, 38 USPQ2d 1705 (Fed. Cir. 1996); *Texas Instruments*, 231 F.3d at 1329, 56 USPQ2d 1674.

[57] Anton/Bauer Inc. v. PAG. Ltd., 329 F.3d 1343, 1348, 66 USPQ2d 1675 (Fed. Cir. 2003); *Amazon.com, Inc.* 239 F.3d at 1358–59, 57 USPQ2d 1747; Nutrition 21 v. United States, 930 F.2d 867, 869–70, 18 USPQ2d 1347 (Fed. Cir. 1991). If the alleged infringer challenges validity, the patent owner must show that the defense lacks substantial merit. Oakley, Inc. v. Sunglass Hut Int'l, 316 F.3d 1331, 1340, 65 USPQ2d 1321 (Fed. Cir. 2003); Tate Access Floors v. Interface Architectural Res., 279 F.3d 1357, 1365, 61 USPQ2d 1647 (Fed. Cir. 2002); *Purdue Pharma L.P.*, 237 F.3d at 1363, 57 USPQ2d 1647.

[58] International Commc'n Materials v. Ricoh Co., 108 F.3d 316, 41 USPQ2d 1957 (Fed. Cir. 1997). The court is not obligated to construe claims conclusively and finally during a preliminary injunction proceeding. Sofamor Danek Group v. DePuyMotech, 74 F.3d 1216, 1221, 37 USPQ2d 1529 (Fed. Cir. 1996). The court may exercise its discretion and conclusively construe the claims at a later stage. *Id.; see also Oakley, Inc.*, 316 F.3d at 1347–48, 65 USPQ2d 1321 (Dyk, J., concurring).

[59] *Amazon.com, Inc.*, 239 F.3d at 1350, 57 USPQ2d 1747. *But see Abbott Labs.*, 544 F.3d at 1363–71, 89 USPQ2d 1161.

[60] Erico Int'l Corp. v. Vutec Corp., 516 F.3d 1350, 1356, 86 USPQ2d 1030 (Fed. Cir. 2008); *Amazon.com, Inc.*, 239 F.3d at 1358, 57 USPQ2d 1747.

tunities.[61] "[T]he fact that a patentee has licensed others under its patents does not mean that unlicensed infringement must also be permitted while the patents are litigated."[62]

To the extent that a rebuttable presumption of harm remains after *eBay*, only a clear showing of validity and infringement raises that presumption.[63] Circumstances that have been considered in rebutting the presumption include that the alleged infringer has or will soon stop the accused infringing acts; the patent owner's delay in bringing suit; the patent owner's licensing of the patent in suit; the patent owner's practice of the patent; the patent owner's large market share in comparison with that of the alleged infringer; and the alleged infringer's inability to pay money damages.[64] Circumstances that do not rebut the presumption include the fact that other infringers may be in the market; that the patent owner is inexperienced in business; or that the market for goods covered by the patent is small.[65]

Regarding the balance of hardships, the court must balance the harm to the patent owner from the denial of the preliminary

---

[61] *Abbott Labs.*, 544 F.3d at 1361–62, 89 USPQ2d 1161. *Compare* Sanofi-Synthelabo v. Apotex, Inc., 470 F.3d 1368, 1382–83, 81 USPQ2d 1097 (Fed. Cir. 2006) (finding irreparable harm based on price erosion and loss of goodwill) *with* Eli Lilly & Co. v. American Cyanamid Co., 82 F.3d 1568, 1578–79, 38 USPQ2d 1705 (Fed. Cir. 1996) (finding no irreparable harm based on lost research opportunities).

[62] *Abbott Labs.*, 544 F.3d at 1361–62, 89 USPQ2d 1161.

[63] Anton/Bauer Inc. v. PAG Ltd., 329 F.3d 1343, 1353, 66 USPQ2d 1675 (Fed. Cir. 2003); Purdue Pharma L.P. v. Boehringer Ingelheim GmbH, 237 F.3d 1359, 1363, 57 USPQ2d 1647 (Fed. Cir. 2001); Hybritech Inc. v. Abbott Labs., 849 F.2d 1446, 1456, 7 USPQ2d 1191 (Fed. Cir. 1988); H. H. Robertson Co. v. United Steel Deck Inc., 820 F.2d 384, 390, 2 USPQ2d 1926 (Fed. Cir. 1987); Nutrition 21 v. United States, 930 F.2d 867, 871, 18 USPQ2d 1347 (Fed. Cir. 1991).

[64] Polymer Techs., Inc. v. Bridwell, 103 F.3d 970, 974–75, 41 USPQ2d 1185 (Fed. Cir. 1996); High Tech Med. Instrumentation v. New Image Indus., 49 F.3d 1551, 1556–57, 33 USPQ2d 2005 (Fed. Cir. 1995); Rosemount Inc. v. United States Int'l Trade Comm'n, 910 F.2d 819, 821, 15 USPQ2d 1569 (Fed. Cir. 1990); *Hybritech Inc.*, 849 F.2d at 1456–57, 7 USPQ2d 1191; T. J. Smith & Nephew Ltd. v. Consol. Med. Equip., 821 F.2d 646, 648, 3 USPQ2d 1316 (Fed. Cir. 1987); Roper Corp. v. Litton Sys., 757 F.2d 1266, 1273, 225 USPQ 345 (Fed. Cir. 1985); B.F. Goodrich Flight Sys. v. Insight Instruments, 22 USPQ2d 1832, 1844 (S.D. Ohio 1992), *aff'd without op.*, 991 F.2d 810 (Fed. Cir. 1993). The alleged infringer's ability to pay money damages does not preclude the grant of a preliminary injunction. *Polymer Techs. Inc.*, 103 F.3d at 975, 41 USPQ2d 1185; *Roper Corp.*, 757 F.2d at 1269 n.2, 225 USPQ 345. Irreparable harm is particularly likely when the market for the patented product is in decline. Bell & Howell Document Mgmt. Prods. v. Altek Sys., 132 F.3d 701, 708, 45 USPQ2d 1033 (Fed. Cir. 1997).

[65] *Polymer Techs. Inc.*, 103 F.3d at 974–76, 41 USPQ2d 1185. Suing one infringer at a time is not inconsistent with being irreparably harmed. *Id.* at 975, 41 USPQ2d 1185. Failure to bring suit against other alleged infringers is relevant only when it indicates unreasonable delay, willingness to accept money damages, or indifference to enforcing the patent. *Id.* at 976, 41 USPQ2d 1185.

injunction against the harm to the alleged infringer if the injunction is entered.[66] Threatened harm to the accused infringer that was preventable and arose from a calculated decision to sell an infringing product may be discounted.[67] Circumstances that are considered include the effect on the patent owner's market share and business reputation and goodwill, and the effect on the alleged infringer's overall sales and its employees.[68] That the patent will expire soon is not relevant.[69]

Regarding the public interest, courts typically focus on whether there exists some critical public interest that would be harmed by the grant of an injunction.[70]

C. Stays of Injunctions Pending Appeal

Until the early 1980s, after a trial on the merits resulted in a decision for the patent owner, it was common for an infringer to obtain a stay of an injunction pending appeal to a higher tribunal by posting an adequate bond. It was not uncommon for the appellate process, including the denial of a writ of certiorari, to take one or two years from the date of entry of the judgment enjoining further infringement. Hence, because of the length of time required to prosecute a patent case from trial through appeals, and the inhospitableness to patents in many of the regional circuits, a typical perception in the business community was that enough time, money, and effort could, as a practical matter, successfully forestall injunctive relief.[71]

---

[66] *Bell & Howell Document Mgmt. Prods.*, 132 F.3d at 707–08, 45 USPQ2d 1033; PPG Indus. Inc. v. Guardian Indus. Corp, 75 F.3d 1558, 1567, 37 USPQ2d 1618 (Fed. Cir. 1996); *Hybritech Inc.*, 849 F.2d at 1457, 7 USPQ2d 1191; *see, e.g.,* Oakley, Inc. v. Sunglass Hut Int'l, 316 F.3d 1331, 1345–46, 65 USPQ2d 1321 (Fed. Cir. 2003).

[67] *Abbott Labs.*, 544 F.3d at 1362, 89 USPQ2d 1161; Sanofi-Synthelabo v. Apotex, Inc., 470 F.3d 1368,1383, 81 USPQ2d 1097 (Fed. Cir. 2006).

[68] *See, e.g.,* Illinois Tool Works Inc. v. Grip-Pak Inc., 906 F.2d 679, 683–84, 15 USPQ2d 1307 (Fed. Cir. 1990); Atlas Powder Co. v. Ireco Chems., 773 F.2d 1230, 1234, 227 USPQ 289 (Fed. Cir. 1985); Critikon Inc. v. Becton Dickinson Vascular Access Inc., 28 USPQ2d 1362, 1371 (D. Del. 1993); Tensar Corp. v. Tenax Corp., 24 USPQ2d 1605, 1614 (D. Md. 1992).

[69] *Atlas Powder Co.*, 773 F.2d at 1234, 227 USPQ 289 ("Patent rights do not peter out as the end of the patent term . . . is approached").

[70] *Hybritech Inc.*, 849 F.2d at 1458, 7 USPQ2d 1191; *see also PPG Indus. Inc.*, 75 F.3d at 1567, 37 USPQ2d 1618; *Critikon Inc.*, 28 USPQ2d at 1370–71.

[71] Herbert F. Schwartz, *Injunctive Relief in Patent Cases*, 50 ALB. L. REV. 565, 566–67 (1986).

This trend reversed early in 1985. In *Shiley Inc. v. Bentley Laboratories*,[72] *S. C. Johnson Inc. v. Carter-Wallace Inc.*,[73] and *Crucible Inc. v. Stora Kopparbergs Bergslags, A.B.*,[74] the respective district courts declined to stay injunctions during the appeals. However, the district courts in *Shiley*[75] and *S. C. Johnson*[76] did allow each defendant a transition period during which the defendant could seek a stay in the court of appeals or comply with the injunction. In both of these cases, the defendants made motions in the Federal Circuit seeking a stay of the injunction, and in both, without rendering a written decision, the court declined to grant a stay.[77]

The best-known case in which the Federal Circuit declined a stay of injunction probably is *Polaroid Corp. v. Eastman Kodak Co.*[78] The district court held seven Polaroid patents valid and infringed by Kodak's instant cameras and film.[79] Of those seven patents, five had not expired as of the date of the court's decision.[80] Despite Kodak's showing that a permanent injunction would inconvenience millions of camera owners who would no longer be able to obtain film, and might lead to the closing of Kodak's instant photography factories, the district court declined to stay the injunction but set the effective date of its order 90 days later, giving Kodak time to appeal or to stop infringing those five Polaroid patents.[81] Kodak moved in the Federal Circuit to stay

---

[72] 601 F. Supp. 964, 225 USPQ 1013 (C.D. Cal. 1985), *stay pending appeal denied*, 782 F.2d 992, 228 USPQ 543 (Fed. Cir.), *aff'd on the merits*, 794 F.2d 1561, 230 USPQ 112 (Fed. Cir. 1986), *cert. denied*, 479 U.S. 1087 (1987).

[73] 225 USPQ 968 (S.D.N.Y. 1985) (order denying motion for stay pending appeal), *stay pending appeal denied*, No. 85-2191 (Fed. Cir. July 9, 1985). The injunction against which the infringer sought a stay was granted in a decision on the merits. S. C. Johnson Inc. v. Carter-Wallace Inc., 225 USPQ 1022 (S.D.N.Y. 1985), *aff'd in part and vacated and remanded in part*, 781 F.2d 198, 228 USPQ 367 (Fed. Cir. 1986).

[74] 226 USPQ 842 (W.D. Pa. 1985), *aff'd in part and remanded in part sub nom.* Kloster Speedsteel, A.B. v. Crucible Inc., 793 F.2d 1565, 230 USPQ 81 (Fed. Cir. 1986), *cert. denied*, 479 U.S. 1034 (1987).

[75] 601 F. Supp. at 971, 225 USPQ 1013.

[76] 225 USPQ at 973.

[77] *Shiley Inc.*, 782 F.2d 992, 228 USPQ 543; *S. C. Johnson*, No. 85-2191 (Fed. Cir. July 9, 1985) (order denying motion for stay pending appeal).

[78] 641 F. Supp. 828, 228 USPQ 305 (D. Mass. 1985), *aff'd*, 789 F.2d 1556, 229 USPQ 561 (Fed. Cir.), *cert. denied*, 479 U.S. 850 (1986).

[79] *Id.* at 877–78, 228 USPQ 305.

[80] *Id.*

[81] *See id.* at 878, 228 USPQ at 342 (memorandum of decision and order).

the injunction pending an appeal on the merits. At the request of the court, the case was fully briefed on an accelerated schedule and argued on the merits two days before the injunction was to take effect. One day after the hearing and final submission to the court on the merits, Kodak's motion to stay the injunction was denied.[82] On the following day, Kodak unsuccessfully sought relief from the U.S. Supreme Court.[83]

However, in 2006, after the Supreme Court's decision in *eBay,* the Federal Circuit granted a stay of injunction in another high profile case that implicated millions of consumers. In *TiVo Inc. v. EchoStar Communications Corp.,*[84] the patents in suit related to digital video recording (DVR) features of satellite TV services. TiVo prevailed at trial on patents relating to both the hardware and software aspects of the DVR. The district court entered a permanent injunction.[85] EchoStar moved to stay the injunction pending appeal. In addition to its arguments on the merits of its anticipated appeal, EchoStar emphasized not only that the balance of harms favors a stay, but also that the public interest favors a stay because the injunction would have resulted in more than three million U.S. households losing their ability to use the digital video recording features of their satellite TV services.[86] The Federal Circuit granted the stay, finding that "EchoStar has met its burden of showing that there is a substantial case on the merits and that the harm factors militate in its favor."[87] TiVo, however, prevailed on appeal.[88]

---

[82] Polaroid Corp. v. Eastman Kodak Co., No. 86-604 (Fed. Cir. Jan. 7, 1986) (order denying motion to stay injunction pending appeal).

[83] Eastman Kodak Co. v. Polaroid Corp., No. A-530 (U.S. Jan. 8, 1986) (Powell, J.) (denying application to stay injunction). The Federal Circuit ultimately affirmed the district court's decision on the merits. *Polaroid Corp.,* 789 F.2d 1556, 229 USPQ 561. The Supreme Court denied certiorari on October 6, 1986. Eastman Kodak Co. v. Polaroid Corp., 479 U.S. 850 (1986).

[84] 446 F. Supp. 2d 664 (E.D. Tex. 2006), *aff'd in part, rev'd in part and remanded,* 516 F.3d 1290, 85 USPQ2d 1801 (Fed. Cir. 2008).

[85] *Id.* at 671.

[86] Emergency motion to stay the district court's injunction at 20, brief of defendants-appellants, *TiVo Inc. v. EchoStar Commc'ns Corp.,* No. 2006-1574 (Fed. Cir. Aug. 18, 2006).

[87] *TiVo Inc. v. EchoStar Commc'ns Corp.,* No. 2006-1574 (Fed. Cir. Oct. 3, 2006) (order granting emergency motion to stay injunction pending appeal).

[88] *TiVo Inc. v. EchoStar Commc'ns Corp.,* 516 F.3d 1290, 1312, 85 USPQ2d 1801 (Fed. Cir. 2008).

When deciding whether to grant a stay of an injunction pending an appeal,[89] a court considers four factors:

1. whether the stay applicant has made a strong showing that the applicant is likely to succeed in the appeal;
2. whether the stay applicant will be irreparably injured if the stay is not granted;
3. whether issuing a stay will substantially injure the other parties interested in the appeal; and
4. the public interest.[90]

The four factors need not be given equal weight.[91]

Regarding the first factor, something less than a strong showing will suffice if the harm to the stay applicant is great enough.[92] Circumstances that have been found relevant under the second factor include that the applicant would have to lay off employees, become insolvent, or suffer corporate death.[93] Circumstances that have not been found relevant include that the applicant would lose market share and suffer damage to its reputation.[94] Regarding the third factor, circumstances that have been considered relevant include the effect of a stay on the patent owner's ability to execute on its judgment[95] and the fact that the patent owner has

---

[89] The Federal Circuit applies the same factors regardless of whether it is deciding to stay a preliminary or a permanent injunction pending appeal. *See, e.g.,* Critikon v. Becton Dickinson Vascular Access, nonprecedential order of Aug. 26, 1993 (Fed. Cir.).

[90] Standard Havens Prods. v. Gencor Indus., 897 F.2d 511, 512, 13 USPQ2d 2029 (Fed. Cir. 1990), *cert. denied,* 506 U.S. 817 (1992); *see, e.g.,* Purdue Pharma L.P. v. Endo Pharms. Inc., 71 USPQ2d 1539, 1540–41 (S.D.N.Y. 2004); Odetics Inc. v. Storage Tech. Corp., 14 F. Supp. 2d 785, 797–800, 47 USPQ2d 1573 (E.D. Va. 1998), *aff'd in part, rev'd in part,* 185 F.3d 1259, 51 USPQ2d 1225 (Fed. Cir. 1999).

[91] *Standard Havens Prods.,* 897 F.2d at 512, 13 USPQ2d 2029.

[92] *Id.* at 512–13, 13 USPQ2d 2029; *see, e.g.,* E.I. DuPont Nemours & Co. v. Phillips Petroleum, 835 F.2d 277, 278–79, 5 USPQ2d 1109 (Fed. Cir. 1987). For an example of the result when a court concludes that there is almost no chance the applicant will succeed on appeal, see *Polaroid Corp. v. Eastman Kodak Co.,* 228 USPQ 305, 343 (D. Mass. 1985).

[93] *Standard Havens Prods.,* 897 F.2d at 515–16, 13 USPQ2d 2029; Pall Corp. v. Micron Separations Inc., 792 F. Supp. 1298, 1328 (D. Mass. 1992), *aff'd in part, rev'd in part, modified in part, remanded, stay vacated,* 66 F.3d 1211, 36 USPQ2d 1225 (Fed. Cir. 1995), *cert. denied,* 520 U.S. 1115 (1997); *In re* Hayes Microcomputer Prods. Patent Litig., 766 F. Supp. 818, 822–23, 20 USPQ2d 1836 (N.D. Cal. 1991), *aff'd,* 982 F.2d 1527, 25 USPQ2d 1241 (Fed. Cir. 1992).

[94] *See generally* Laitram Corp. v. Rexnord Inc., 15 USPQ2d 1161, 1175 (E.D. Wis. 1990), *rev'd on other grounds,* 939 F.2d 1533, 19 USPQ2d 1367 (Fed. Cir. 1991).

[95] *Standard Havens Prods.,* 897 F.2d at 515, 13 USPQ2d 2029.

licensed others.[96] Under the fourth factor, public access to the infringing products is considered.[97]

A stay of injunction pending appeal may mandate the payment into escrow of a royalty for infringement that takes place during the stay, should the underlying judgment be affirmed. Such a royalty is not necessarily limited by the reasonable royalty standard for prejudgment infringement.[98]

If an injunction is not stayed pending appeal, the patent owner must post a bond in an amount sufficient to compensate the infringer, should the infringer's appeal be successful.[99]

D. Scope of Injunction and Contempt

An injunction must be specific regarding the enjoined conduct. A typical form of injunction bars further infringement by the products or processes actually litigated or colorable imitations of those products or processes.[100] An injunction may not enjoin acts that are not infringing or are not likely to be infringing.[101] An

---

[96] *E.I. DuPont de Nemours & Co.*, 835 F.2d at 278, 5 USPQ2d 1109; *Hayes Microcomputer Prods. Patent Litig.*, 766 F. Supp. at 823, 20 USPQ2d 1836.

[97] *Compare Pall Corp.*, 792 F. Supp. at 1328 ("various important scientific and medical applications") *with Laitram Corp.*, 15 USPQ2d at 1175–76 ("Public policy favors the innovator, not the copier").

[98] Amado v. Microsoft Corp., 517 F.3d 1353, 1361–62, 86 USPQ2d 1090 (Fed. Cir. 2008); *see, e.g.,* Creative Internet Advertising Corp. v. Yahoo, Inc., No. 6:07 civ. 354-JDL (E.D. Tex December 9, 2009).

[99] Cargill, Inc. v. Sears Petroleum & Transp. Corp., No. 5:03 CV 0530 (DEP), 2004 WL 3507329, at *11 n.9 (N.D.N.Y. Aug. 27, 2004) (citing Fed. R. Civ. P. 62(c)); *see* Endress + Hauser, Inc. v. Hawk Measurement Sys. Pty. Ltd., 932 F. Supp. 1147, 1148–50 (S.D. Ind. 1996).

[100] Fed. R. Civ. P. 65(d); International Rectifier Corp. v. IXYS Corp., 383 F.3d 1312, 1315–18, 72 USPQ2d 1571 (Fed. Cir. 2004); Oakley, Inc. v. Sunglass Hut Int'l, 316 F.3d 1331, 1346–47, 65 USPQ2d 1321 (Fed. Cir. 2003). An injunction can be denied if specific language cannot be drafted. *See generally* Fuji Photo Film Co. v. Jazz Photo Corp., 394 F.3d 1368, 1380, 73 USPQ2d 1678 (Fed. Cir. 2005).

[101] Johns Hopkins Univ. v. CellPro Inc., 152 F.3d 1342, 1365–66, 47 USPQ2d 1705 (Fed. Cir. 1998). Regarding contempt proceedings, see *Tegal Corp. v. Tokyo Electron Co.*, 248 F.3d 1376, 58 USPQ2d 1791 (Fed. Cir. 2001) and *Additive Controls & Measurement Sys. v. Flowdata*, 154 F.3d 1345, 47 USPQ2d 1906 (Fed. Cir. 1998). A concern that an enjoined infringer would attempt to design around a permanent injunction, which would result in numerous contempt hearings, is not a reason for denying a permanent injunction. MercExchange, LLC v. eBay Inc., 401 F.3d 1323, 1339, 74 USPQ2d 1225 (Fed. Cir. 2005), *vacated and remanded,* 547 U.S. 388, 78 USPQ2d 1577 (2006).

injunction can reach extraterritorial acts if the injunction prevents infringement.[102]

The remedy for violation of an injunction is a motion for contempt. A party facing such a motion may not defend on the grounds of having made a good faith attempt to comply with the injunction, although such good faith may factor into the consideration of penalties, if any, for violation of the injunction.[103] Although the alleged vagueness of the terms of the injunction may provide a defense to a charge of contempt, the issue of vagueness should first be raised on appeal from the entry of the injunction or on motion to clarify the injunction brought before the court that issued it. Similarly, the issue of alleged overbreadth of the injunction should not be raised for the first time on motion for contempt.[104]

In its 2011 en banc decision in *TiVo Inc. v. Echostar Corp.*, the Federal Circuit set forth the requirements for a contempt proceeding against a product that purports to be a "design-around" of a product already enjoined:

> The primary question on contempt should be whether the newly accused product is so different from the product previously found to infringe that it raises "a fair ground of doubt as to the wrongfulness of the defendant's conduct." The analysis must focus not on differences between randomly chosen features of the product found to infringe in the earlier infringement trial and the newly accused product, but on those aspects of the accused product that were previously alleged to be, and were a basis for, the prior finding of infringement, and the modified features of the newly accused product. Specifically, one should focus on those elements of the adjudged infringing products that the patentee previously contended, and proved, satisfy specific limitations of the asserted claims. Where one or more of those elements previously found to infringe has been modified, or removed, the court must make an inquiry into whether that modification is significant.[105]

---

[102] *Johns Hopkins Univ.*, 152 F.3d at 1366–67, 47 USPQ2d 1705. Upon a finding of patent infringement, the U.S. International Trade Commission can prohibit infringing products from entering the United States. 19 U.S.C. §1337(d).

[103] TiVo Inc. v. Echostar Corp., 98 USPQ2d 1413,1420–21 (Fed. Cir. 2011) (en banc).

[104] *Id.* at 1424–25, 1427–28.

[105] *Id.* at 1422 (internal citations omitted).

If the modification was, in fact, significant, then contempt is inappropriate and the issue of infringement of the modified device or process should be litigated in a new, separate trial.[106] The analysis for the significance of the differences, if any, is as follows:

> The significance of the differences between the two products is much dependent on the nature of the products at issue. The court must also look to the relevant prior art, if any is available, to determine if the modification merely employs or combines elements already known in the prior art in a manner that would have been obvious to a person of ordinary skill in the art at the time the modification was made. A nonobvious modification may well result in a finding of more than a colorable difference. Where useful, a district court may seek expert testimony in making the determination. The analysis may also take account of the policy that legitimate design-around efforts should always be encouraged as a path to spur further innovation. But an assertion that one has permissibly designed around a patent should not be used to mask continued infringement. Determining the requisite level of difference is a question of fact.[107]

The patent owner bears the burden of proving violation of the injunction and that the purported design around meets every element of the claimed invention. The burden of proof as to both is clear and convincing evidence.[108]

II. MONETARY DAMAGES

The purpose of a damages award is to put the patent owner in the economic position it would have been in the absence of infringement. As stated by the Supreme Court:

> [The patent owner's damages] have been defined by this Court as "compensation for the pecuniary loss he [the patentee] has suf-

---

[106] *Id.*

[107] *Id.* (internal citations omitted).

[108] *Id.* at 1422–23.

fered from the infringement, without regard to the question whether the defendant has gained or lost by his unlawful acts." They have been said to constitute "the difference between his pecuniary condition after the infringement, and what his condition would have been if the infringement had not occurred." The question to be asked in determining damages is "how much had the Patent Holder and Licensee suffered by the infringement. And that question [is] primarily: had the Infringer not infringed, what would Patent Holder-Licensee have made?"[109]

Accordingly, the issue in determining damages is not what the infringer made, but what the patent owner lost.[110] As with all tort damages, the patent owner's right to recover is limited by rules of proximate causation and objectively reasonable foreseeability.[111] The patent owner has the burden of proving damages by a preponderance of the evidence.[112] Although the patent owner need not prove the amount of damages to a certainty, damages awards must be predicated on sound economic proofs.[113]

The two traditional measures of monetary damages awarded under 35 U.S.C. §284 are lost profits and royalties, either established or hypothetical.[114]

When the patent owner is attempting to exploit its patent commercially, the general rule is that damages are to be measured by lost profits, provided they can be fairly estimated.[115] Lost profits are the appropriate measure where the patent owner

---

[109] Aro Mfg. Co. v. Convertible Top Replacement Co. 377 U.S. 476, 507, 141 USPQ 681 (1964) (*Aro II*).

[110] Rite-Hite Corp. v. Kelley Co., 56 F.3d 1538, 1545–46, 35 USPQ2d 1065 (Fed. Cir.), *cert. denied*, 516 U.S. 867 (1995) (en banc); *see Aro II*, 377 U.S. at 507–08, 141 USPQ 681.

[111] *Rite-Hite Corp.*, 56 F.3d at 1544–47, 35 USPQ2d 1065. Examples of consequences that are too remote to be compensable are an inventor's heart attack and a patent-owning corporation's loss of value in its common stock. *Id.; see also* Micro Chem., Inc. v. Lextron, Inc., 318 F.3d 1119, 1125–26, 65 USPQ2d 1695 (Fed. Cir. 2003); Minco Inc. v. Combustion Eng'g, Inc., 95 F.3d 1109, 1118, 40 USPQ2d 1001 (Fed. Cir. 1996).

[112] Lucent Techs., Inc. v. Gateway, Inc., 580 F.3d 1301, 1324, 92 USPQ2d 1555 (Fed. Cir. 2009), *cert. denied sub nom.* Microsoft Corp. v. Lucent Techs., Inc., 130 S. Ct. 3324 (2010); Vulcan Eng'g Co. v. FATA Aluminum, Inc., 278 F.3d 1366, 1376, 61 USPQ2d 1545 (Fed. Cir.), *cert. denied*, 537 U.S. 814 (2002).

[113] Riles v. Shell Exploration & Prod. Co., 298 F.3d 1302, 1311, 63 USPQ2d 1819 (Fed. Cir. 2002); *Minco Inc.*, 95 F.3d at 1118, 40 USPQ2d 1001.

[114] King Instruments Corp. v. Perego, 65 F.3d 941, 947–52, 36 USPQ2d 1129 (Fed. Cir. 1995), *cert. denied*, 517 U.S. 1188 (1996); *Rite-Hite Corp.*, 56 F.3d at 1544–45, 1554, 35 USPQ2d 1065.

[115] Del Mar Avionics Inc. v. Quinton Instrument Co., 836 F.2d 1320, 1326–27, 5 USPQ2d 1255 (Fed. Cir. 1987); Polaroid Corp. v. Eastman Kodak Co., 16 USPQ2d 1481, 1484 (D. Mass. 1990).

and infringer compete in the same market. When the patent owner sells a product that is not covered by the patent, lost profits may also be recovered if the infringing product caused the patent owner to lose sales of the nonpatented product.[116] A patent owner who does not sell a product may nonetheless be entitled to lost profits only if the patent owner can meet the commensurately heavy burden of proving that it would have sold a product but for the infringement.[117]

Either the patent owner or an exclusive licensee may be awarded damages. A patent owner cannot recover profits lost by its nonexclusive licensee.[118]

A reasonable royalty is appropriate where there is an established royalty for the patented invention or where lost profits cannot be sufficiently proved or are otherwise inappropriate as the measure of damages.[119] Subject to the rules of proximate cause and reasonable foreseeability, the Federal Circuit has approved other measures of damages, at least in dicta.[120] In no event may damages be "less than a reasonable royalty."[121]

Each joint tortfeasor is liable for the full amount of general damages, up to a full single recovery.[122] Neither lost profits nor

---

[116] Siemens Med. Solutions USA, Inc. v. Saint-Gobain Ceramics & Plastics, Inc., 637 F.3d 1269, 1288, 97 USPQ2d 1897 (Fed. Cir. 2011). With respect to nonpatented products, see Micro Chem., Inc., 318 F.3d at 1125–26, 65 USPQ2d 1695; Rite-Hite Corp., 56 F.3d at 1544–49, 35 USPQ2d 1065.

[117] Hebert v. Lisle Corp., 99 F.3d 1109, 1119–20, 40 USPQ2d 1611 (Fed. Cir. 1996).

[118] Weinar v. Rollform Inc., 744 F.2d 797, 223 USPQ 369 (Fed. Cir. 1984), cert. denied, 470 U.S. 1084 (1985) (exclusive licensee); cf. Rite-Hite Corp., 56 F.3d at 1551–54, 35 USPQ2d 1065. Poly-America, L.P. v. GSE Lining Tech., Inc., 383 F.3d 1303, 1310–12, 72 USPQ2d 1685 (Fed. Cir. 2004) (nonexclusive licensee).

[119] Del Mar Avionics Inc., 836 F.2d at 1328, 5 USPQ2d 1255.

[120] For an example of an alternative theory of compensation, see Mars, Inc. v. Coin Acceptors, Inc., 527 F.3d 1359, 1365, 87 USPQ2d 1076 (Fed. Cir. 2008) (failure to claim profits lost by wholly owned subsidiary precludes recovery of such profits); Minco Inc. v. Combustion Eng'g Inc., 95 F.3d 1109, 1120–21, 40 USPQ2d 1001 (Fed. Cir. 1996) (patent owner did not carry its burden of proving that the infringing product was an important factor in the sale of the infringer's business); compare with Rodime PLC v. Seagate Tech. Inc., 174 F.3d 1294, 1307–08, 50 USPQ2d 1429 (Fed. Cir. 1999) (patent owner's damages limited by the traditional theory of compensation it presented), cert. denied, 528 U.S. 1115 (2000). See generally Transclean Corp. v. Bridgewood Servs., Inc., 290 F.3d 1364, 1375–77, 62 USPQ2d 1865 (Fed. Cir. 2002).

[121] 35 U.S.C. §284; Crystal Semiconductor Corp. v. TriTech Microelectronics Int'l, 246 F.3d 1336, 57 USPQ2d 1953 (Fed. Cir. 2001); see also Dow Chem. Co. v. Mee Indus., Inc., 341 F.3d 1370, 1381, 68 USPQ2d 1176 (Fed. Cir. 2003) ("The statute is unequivocal that the district court must award damages in an amount no less than a reasonable royalty").

[122] Shockley v. Arcan, Inc., 248 F.3d 1349, 1364, 58 USPQ2d 1692 (Fed. Cir. 2001). A party jointly liable for general damages who was not found to have willfully infringed is not jointly liable for willfulness damages. Crystal Semiconductor, 246 F.3d at 1361, 57 USPQ2d 1953.

a reasonable royalty may be used to compensate the patent holder for litigation costs or fees.[123]

The trial court's choice of methodology for calculating damages is reviewed for abuse of discretion. The determination of the amount of damages is an issue of fact, reviewed under the clearly erroneous standard if found by the court and under the substantial evidence standard if found by a jury. "A jury's decision with respect to an award of damages must be upheld unless the amount is grossly excessive or monstrous, clearly not supported by the evidence, or based only on speculation or guesswork."[124]

A. Lost Profits

The prevailing party in a successful suit for patent infringement is entitled to an award of profits lost because of diverted sales, price erosion, and increased costs, where provable.[125] Such an award is usually composed of profits lost by the patent owner rather than profits made by the infringer.[126]

To recover lost profits damages, a patent owner must show a reasonable probability that, but for the infringement, the patent owner would have made some or all of the infringer's sales.[127] It is unnecessary for the patent owner to rule out the possibility that purchasers might have bought another product.[128] A patent

---

[123] Mahurkar v. C. R. Bard, Inc., 79 F.3d 1572, 1580–81, 38 USPQ2d 1288 (Fed. Cir. 1996). Attorneys' fees may be awarded for noncompensatory purposes in exceptional cases. 35 U.S.C. §285, as discussed in Chapter 8, §§IV and V.

[124] Lucent Techs., Inc. v. Gateway, Inc., 580 F.3d 1301, 1310, 92 USPQ2d 1555 (Fed. Cir. 2009), *cert. denied sub nom.* Microsoft Corp. v. Lucent Techs., Inc., 130 S. Ct. 3324 (2010) (internal quotations and citations omitted). With respect to findings by a court, see Fed. R. Civ. P. 52(a)(6).

[125] Minco Inc. v. Combustion Eng'g Inc., 95 F.3d 1109, 1118, 40 USPQ2d 1001 (Fed. Cir. 1996); Central Soya Co. v. George A. Hormel & Co., 723 F.2d 1573, 1579, 220 USPQ 490 (Fed. Cir. 1983); Lam Inc. v. Johns-Manville Corp., 718 F.2d 1056, 1065, 219 USPQ 670 (Fed. Cir. 1983).

[126] Aro Mfg. Co. v. Convertible Top Replacement Co., 377 U.S. 476, 502–07, 141 USPQ 681 (1964) (Aro II). *But see* Kori Corp. v. Wilco Marsh Buggies & Draglines, 761 F.2d 649, 653–55, 225 USPQ 985 (Fed. Cir.), *cert. denied*, 474 U.S. 902 (1985) (damages award approximated lost profits by comparing the patent owner's claimed damages with the infringer's historical profits).

[127] Siemens Med. Solutions USA, Inc. v. Saint-Gobain Ceramics & Plastics, Inc., 637 F.3d 1269, 1287, 97 USPQ2d 1897 (Fed. Cir. 2011); *Crystal Semiconductor Corp.* 246 F.3d at 1353, 57 USPQ2d 1953.

[128] Rite-Hite Corp. v. Kelley Co., 56 F.3d. 1538, 1545, 35 USPQ2d 1065 (Fed. Cir.), *cert. denied*, 516 U.S. 867 (1995) (en banc); Kaufman Co. v. Lantech Inc., 926 F.2d 1136, 17 USPQ2d 1828, 1831 (Fed. Cir. 1991).

owner ordinarily cannot recover lost profits when the patent owner merely licenses the patents to a related entity that makes or sells the patented product.[129]

A widely used test for a patent owner to prove entitlement to lost profits damages was articulated by former Chief Judge Markey, then of the Court of Customs and Patent Appeals, sitting by designation in the Sixth Circuit in *Panduit Corp. v. Stahlin Bros. Fibre Works:*[130]

> To obtain as damages the profits on sales he would have made absent the infringement, i.e., the sales made by the infringer, a patent owner must prove: (1) demand for the patented product, (2) the absence of acceptable noninfringing substitutes, (3) his manufacturing and marketing capability to exploit the demand, and (4) the amount of the profit he would have made.

Although the Federal Circuit has said that the *Panduit* analysis is not necessarily the only way to prove lost profits,[131] the *Panduit* factors generally remain the starting point for such a claim.[132]

If the patent owner and a single infringer are the only parties supplying products to the relevant market, then the first two *Panduit* factors are satisfied. If the patent owner can also show the third and fourth *Panduit* elements, then but-for causation is presumed. The infringer may rebut the presumption by showing that the patent owner reasonably would not have made some or all of the infringer's sales.[133]

Demand for the patented product. Assuming that the patent owner and the infringer sell substantially the same product at substantially the same prices, proof of a significant number of sales by the patent owner or the infringer is deemed

---

[129]Mars, Inc. v. Coin Acceptors, Inc., 527 F.3d 1359, 1365, 87 USPQ2d 1076 (Fed. Cir. 2008); Poly-America L.P. v. GSE Lining Tech., Inc., 383 F.3d 1303, 1311, 72 USPQ2d 1685 (Fed. Cir. 2004).

[130]575 F.2d 1152, 1156, 197 USPQ 726 (6th Cir. 1978).

[131] *Rite-Hite Corp.* 56 F.3d at 1545, 35 USPQ2d 1065; State Indus. Inc. v. Mor-Flo Indus. Inc., 883 F.2d 1573, 1577–80, 12 USPQ2d 1026 (Fed. Cir. 1989), *cert. denied,* 493 U.S. 1022 (1990).

[132] *Siemens Med. Solutions USA, Inc.,* 637 F.3d at 1287, 97 USPQ2d 1897. *State Indus. Inc.,* 883 F.2d at 1577,12 USPQ2d 1026.

[133]Micro Chem., Inc. v. Lextroon, Inc., 318 F.3d 1119, 1124–25, 65 USPQ2d 1695 (Fed. Cir. 2003).

compelling evidence of demand.[134] However, a substantial difference in price between the infringing and patented product may indicate that the market for the good at issue is segmented, and properly may lead to a finding that there was not demand for the patented goods at the infringer's historical selling price.[135]

Absence of acceptable noninfringing substitutes. The second *Panduit* factor has evolved into a requirement that the patent owner show "either that (1) the purchasers in the marketplace generally were willing to buy the patented product because of the advantages provided by the patented features, or (2) the specific purchasers of the infringing product purchased on that basis."[136] Available noninfringing substitutes of significantly higher cost are not considered acceptable substitutes for the purpose of calculating damages.[137]

Proof of a long-felt need for the patented invention in the liability trial may be extrapolated into proof of lack of acceptable substitutes.[138] Market surveys showing that large numbers of the infringer's purchasers would have purchased the patent owner's device may be considered.[139] Testimony by third parties that they would have bought from the patent holder absent the infringement[140] or that purchasers considered other features of the infringer's product more important than the patented invention[141] may also be probative.

---

[134] Gyromat Corp. v. Champion Spark Plug Co., 735 F.2d 549, 552, 222 USPQ 4 (Fed. Cir. 1984).

[135] BIC Leisure Prods. v. Windsurfing Int'l, Inc., 1 F.3d 1214, 1218–19, 27 USPQ2d 1671 (Fed. Cir. 1993); Crystal Semiconductor Corp. v. TriTech Microelectronics Int'l, 246 F.3d 1336, 1357, 57 USPQ2d 1953 (Fed. Cir. 2001).

[136] Standard Havens Prods. v. Gencor Indus., 953 F.2d 1360, 1373, 21 USPQ2d 1321 (Fed. Cir. 1991), *cert. denied,* 506 U.S. 817 (1992).

[137] *Gyromat Corp.,* 735 F.2d at 553–54, 222 USPQ 4; *Crystal Semiconductor Corp.* 246 F.3d at 1356, 57 USPQ2d 1953. Third party infringing substitutes can become acceptable noninfringing substitutes when the patent owner settles with the third party, but the transformation is not retroactive. Pall Corp. v. Micron Separations Inc., 66 F.3d 1211, 1222–23, 36 USPQ2d 1225 (Fed. Cir. 1995), *cert. denied,* 520 U.S. 1115 (1997).

[138] Micro Motion Inc. v. Exac Corp., 761 F. Supp. 1420, 1424, 19 USPQ2d 1001 (N.D. Cal. 1991); Panduit Corp. v. Stahlin Bros. Fibre Works, 575 F.2d 1152, 1162, 197 USPQ 726 (6th Cir. 1978).

[139] Bio-Rad Labs. v. Nicolet Instrument Corp., 739 F.2d 604, 616, 222 USPQ 654 (Fed. Cir.), *cert. denied,* 469 U.S. 1038 (1984).

[140] Livesay Window Co. v. Livesay Indus., 251 F.2d 469, 473, 116 USPQ 167 (5th Cir. 1958).

[141] TP Orthodontics Inc. v. Professional Positioners Inc., 20 USPQ2d 1017, 1023 (E.D. Wis. 1991).

A patent owner may address the second *Panduit* factor using a market share approach, in which the infringing sales are divided according to sales that would have been made by the patent owner and sales that would have gone to those who sold noninfringing alternatives.[142] In appropriate cases, the sales for which lost profits are not awarded according to market share may be subject to a reasonable royalty.[143]

For a product to be an acceptable noninfringing alternative, it must have been available during the time for which damages are sought. A product may be available even if it has not been sold in the marketplace. If the product has not been on the market, however, the trier of fact may reasonably infer that it was not available. An infringer may overcome this inference with proof of availability. For example, lost profits have been precluded by proof that, had it not infringed, the infringer forseeably would have used a noninfringing process, which it had the ability and incentive to use during the time for which damages were sought:

> [A] fair and accurate reconstruction of the "but for" market also must take into account, where relevant, alternative actions the infringer forseeably would have undertaken had he not infringed. Without the infringing product, a rational would-be infringer is likely to offer an acceptable noninfringing alternative, if available, to compete with the patent owner rather than leave the market altogether. The competitor in the "but for" marketplace is hardly likely to surrender its complete market share when faced with a patent, if it can compete in some other lawful manner. Moreover, only by comparing the patented invention to its next-best available alternative(s)— regardless of whether the alternative(s) were actually produced and sold during the infringement—can the court discern the market value of the patent owner's exclusive right.[144]

In contrast, an infringer's design-around product that took many months to design, test, and implement has been held to

---

[142] *Crystal Semiconductor Corp.*, 246 F.3d at 1360–61, 57 USPQ2d 1953; BIC Leisure Prods. v. Windsurfing Int'l, Inc., 1 F.3d 1214, 1218–19, 27 USPQ2d 1671 (Fed. Cir. 1993).

[143] State Indus. Inc. v. Mor-Flo Indus., Inc., 883 F.2d 1573, 1577–78, 12 USPQ2d 1026 (Fed. Cir. 1998); *Crystal Semiconductor*, 246 F.3d at 1353, 57 USPQ2d 1953.

[144] Grain Processing Corp. v. American Maize-Prods., 185 F.3d 1341, 1350–53, 51 USPQ2d 1556 (Fed. Cir. 1999).

have been not available.[145] The relevant market for acceptable alternatives includes the patented invention and excludes alternatives with significantly different characteristics or disparately different prices.[146]

Manufacturing and marketing capability to meet the incremental demand. The third *Panduit* factor can be met by proving that the patent owner possessed adequate manufacturing and marketing capability to meet the additional demand.[147] Even if adequate manufacturing capacity did not exist during the period of infringement, proof of an ability to expand to meet the additional demand is sufficient.[148]

The amount of profits lost. The final element of proof called for in *Panduit* is the quantum of profit the patent owner would have made.[149] Where diversion of sales is proven, lost profits from those sales are measured by multiplying the marginal profit lost on the diverted sales by the sales total that the patent owner would have garnered.[150]

Marginal profit lost is determined by three factors: (1) the number of sales that would have been made by the patent owner but for infringement; (2) the price at which the patent owner

---

[145] Micro Chem., Inc. v. Lextron, Inc., 318 F.3d 1119, 1122–23, 65 USPQ2d 1695 (Fed. Cir. 2003). An infringer who chooses to wait until after trial to disclose and market its noninfringing alternative product can be denied relief under Fed. R. Civ. P. 60(b)(6) from an adverse damages judgment. Fiskars, Inc. v. Hunt Mfg. Co., 279 F.3d 1378, 1382–83, 61 USPQ2d 1851 (Fed. Cir. 2002).

[146] Siemens Med. Solutions USA, Inc. v. Saint-Gobain Ceramics & Plastics, Inc., 637 F.3d 1269, 1288–89, 97 USPQ2d 1897 (Fed. Cir. 2011); *see also* DePuy Spine, Inc. v. Medtronic SofamorDanek, Inc., 567 F.3d 1314, 1330–32, 90 USPQ2d 1865 (Fed. Cir. 2009).

[147] Fonar Corp. v. General Elec. Co., 107 F.3d 1543, 1553, 41 USPQ2d 1801 (Fed. Cir.), *cert. denied, motion granted,* 522 U.S. 908 (1997); Kearns v. Chrysler Corp., 32 F.3d 1541, 1551–52, 31 USPQ2d 1746 (Fed. Cir. 1994), *cert. denied,* 514 U.S. 1032 (1995); Bio-Rad Labs. v. Nicolet Instrument Corp., 739 F.2d 604, 616, 222 USPQ 654 (Fed. Cir.), *cert. denied,* 469 U.S. 1038 (1984); Yarway Corp. v. Eur-Control USA Inc., 775 F.2d 268, 276–77, 227 USPQ 352 (Fed. Cir. 1985).

[148] *Bio-Rad Labs.,* 739 F.2d at 616, 222 USPQ 654; Livesay Window Co. v. Livesay Indus., 251 F.2d 469, 473, 116 USPQ 167 (5th Cir. 1958); Polaroid Corp. v. Eastman Kodak Co., 16 USPQ2d 1481, 1510–25 (D. Mass. 1990), *correction for clerical errors,* 17 USPQ2D 1711 (D. Mass. 1991).

[149] Panduit Corp. v. Stahlin Bros. Fibre Works, 575 F.2d 1152, 1156–57, 197 USPQ 726 (6th Cir. 1978). In *Panduit,* the Court of Appeals affirmed the denial of lost profits because the patent owner was unable to prove the amount of its profit, in particular because it was unable to prove the cost of manufacturing and selling the additional volume in the but-for world. *Id.*

[150] King Instruments Corp. v. Otari Corp., 767 F.2d 853, 864, 226 USPQ 402 (Fed. Cir. 1985), *cert. denied,* 475 U.S. 1016 (1986); Paper Converting Mach. Co. v. Magna-Graphics, 745 F.2d 11, 22, 223 USPQ 591 (Fed. Cir. 1984); Gyromat Corp. v. Champion Spark Plug Co., 735 F.2d 549, 554–55, 222 USPQ 4 (Fed. Cir. 1984); Lam Inc. v. Johns-Manville Corp., 718 F.2d 1056, 1065, 219 USPQ 670 (Fed. Cir. 1983).

would have made those sales; and (3) the marginal cost to the patent owner of those sales.[151]

Gross sales of the infringer may be proven from the infringer's business records, public records, figures accumulated by trade associations, or other reliable sources. While uncertainties that arise from the infringer's failure to keep comprehensive or accurate records are resolved in favor of the patentee,[152] the patent owner cannot meet its burden of proof with guesswork and speculation.[153]

When the patented feature makes up only a portion of the product, there may be a question as to whether the patentee should be awarded the entire profit on the product or only a proportionate share of that profit. Under the entire market value rule, the entire marginal profit for the product is used to compute damages if the patent-related feature is the basis for customer demand. The entire market value rule encompasses physically separate unpatented components that are sold together with the patented component if the unpatented components function together with the patented component to produce a desired end product or result (convoyed sales).[154] The entire market value rule does not encompass separate unpatented components that are sold together with the patented component only as a matter of convenience or business advantage.[155]

---

[151] Minnesota Mining & Mfg. Co. v. Johnson & Johnson Orthopaedics, Inc., 976 F.2d 1559, 1579, 24 USPQ2d 1321 (Fed. Cir. 1992).

[152] Beatrice Foods v. New England Printing & Lithographing Co., 899 F.2d 1171, 1175–76, 14 USPQ2d 1020 (Fed. Cir. 1990); Lam Inc. v. Johns-Manville Corp., 718 F.2d 1056, 1065, 219 USPQ 670 (Fed. Cir. 1983).

[153] Oiness v. Walgreen Co., 88 F.3d 1025, 1029–31, 39 USPQ2d 1304 (Fed. Cir. 1996), *cert. denied*, 519 U.S. 1112 (1997); *see also* Riles v. Shell Exploration & Prod. Co., 298 F.3d 1302, 1311, 63 USPQ2d 1819 (Fed. Cir. 2002).

[154] Rite-Hite Corp. v. Kelley Co., 56 F.3d. 1538, 1549–51, 35 USPQ2d 1065 (Fed. Cir.), *cert. denied*, 516 U.S. 867 (1995) (en banc); *see also* Juicy Whip, Inc. v. Orange Bang, Inc., 382 F.3d 1367, 1371–73, 72 USPQ2d 1385 (Fed. Cir. 2004) ("[A] functional relationship between a patented device and an unpatented material used with it is not precluded by the fact that the device can be used with other materials or that the unpatented material can be used with other devices").

[155] *Rite-Hite Corp.*, 56 F.3d at 1550–51, 35 USPQ2d 1065. Lost profits may be recovered, however, for past and future lost sales of repair parts, which the Federal Circuit refers to as derivative sales. *See, e.g.,* Carborundum v. Molten Metal Equip. Innovations, 72 F.3d 872, 881–82, 37 USPQ2d 1169 (Fed. Cir. 1995); *see also* King Instruments Corp. v. Otari Corp., 767 F.2d 853, 865, 226 USPQ 402 (Fed. Cir. 1985), *cert. denied*, 475 U.S. 1016 (1986).

In calculating marginal profit, only a reasonable approximation must be proven, and any uncertainty regarding the amount is resolved against the infringer.[156] The margin of profit is determined by subtracting from expected revenue the incremental or marginal costs, not full absorption costs, that the patent holder would have incurred as a result of the increased sales. Expected revenue is the expected price multiplied by expected sales.[157]

Preinfringement prices are generally used in calculating lost revenue so that the patent owner is not penalized because of price erosion caused by illegal competition.[158] Price erosion may be taken into account where prices would have increased in the absence of infringement.[159] To prove price erosion, or to justify the use of preinfringement prices in a market where prices declined during the period of the infringement, the patentee must show that higher prices would not have substantially reduced demand in the but-for world.[160]

Incremental costs are those costs that would have increased with a rise in sales volume. Normally, only variable costs, such as direct labor and materials, are taken into account. Not included are fixed costs, such as insurance; property taxes; and administrative, management, and noncommission sales expenses.[161] Courts have approved various methods for calculating incremental

---

[156] Minco, Inc. v. Combustion Eng'g Inc., 95 F.3d 1109, 1118, 40 USPQ2d 1001 (Fed. Cir. 1996); Del Mar Avionics, Inc. v. Quinton Instrument Co., 836 F.2d 1320, 1326, 5 USPQ2d 1255 (Fed. Cir. 1987); *King Instruments Corp.,* 767 F.2d at 864, 226 USPQ 402; Paper Converting Mach. Co. v. Magna-Graphics, 745 F.2d 11, 22, 223 USPQ 591 (Fed. Cir. 1984); Gyromat Corp. v. Champion Spark Plug Co., 735 F.2d 549, 554–55, 222 USPQ 4 (Fed. Cir. 1984).

[157] *Paper Converting Mach. Co.,* 745 F.2d at 22, 223 USPQ 591; *Lam Inc.,* 718 F.2d at 1059, 219 USPQ 670.

[158] Yale Lock Co. v. Sargent, 117 U.S. 536, 552–53 (1886); Crystal Semiconductor Corp. v. TriTech Microelectronics Int'l, 246 F.3d 1336, 1357–61, 57 USPQ2d 1953 (Fed. Cir. 2001); TWM Mfg. Co. v. Dura Corp., 789 F.2d 895, 898, 229 USPQ 525 (Fed. Cir.), *cert. denied,* 479 U.S. 852 (1986); *Lam Inc.,* 718 F.2d at 1065, 219 USPQ 670. If the patent owner reduced its price to meet the infringer's competition, it is not necessary to show that the patent owner knew the competition was infringing. Vulcan Eng'g Co. v. FATA Aluminum, 278 F.3d 1366, 1377, 61 USPQ2D 1545 (Fed. Cir.), *cert. denied,* 537 U.S. 814 (2002).

[159] Ericsson, Inc. v. Harris Corp., 352 F.3d 1369, 1378–79, 69 USPQ2d 1109 (Fed. Cir. 2003); Fiskars, Inc. v. Hunt Mfg. Co., 221 F.3d 1318, 1325, 55 USPQ2d 1569 (Fed. Cir. 2000), *cert. denied,* 532 U.S. 972 (2001); *Minco Inc.,* 95 F.3d at 1120, 40 USPQ2d 1001; Kalman v. Berlyn Corp., 914 F.2d 1473, 1485, 16 USPQ2d 1093 (Fed. Cir. 1990); *Lam Inc.,* 718 F.2d at 1065, 219 USPQ 670.

[160] *Crystal Semiconductor,* 246 F.3d at 1357, 57 USPQ2d 1953. The degree to which demand varies with price is elasticity of demand. Polaroid Corp v. Eastman Kodak Co., 16 USPQ2d 1481, 1505–06 (D. Mass. 1990), *corrected for clerical errors,* 17 USPQ2D 1711 (D. Mass. 1991).

[161] Panduit Corp. v. Stahlin Bros. Fibre Works, 575 F.2d 1152, 1156–57, 197 USPQ 726 (6th Cir. 1978); *see, e.g., Polaroid Corp.,* 16 USPQ2d at 1526.

costs of making the additional sales in the but-for world, including linear regression[162] and an account analysis of the accounting records of the patentee to determine which costs would be fixed and which costs would be variable as volume increased.[163] The patentee's costs may be proven by his or her historical financial records if they are sufficiently detailed; otherwise, they may be reconstructed by expert testimony.[164] Where proving the patentee's costs is not possible, profits of the infringer or normal industry profit margins may be examined as evidence of the patentee's lost profits.[165] Once the patent owner has established his or her profit margin, it is up to the infringer to prove that the patent owner's proofs are unreasonable.[166]

The patent owner may also recover lost profits from lost sales including price erosion and damages for the patentee's actual sales during the period of the infringement, to the extent that such price erosion was caused by competition from the infringing product.[167] Where appropriate, the patent owner may also recover lost profits for sales of nonpatented products (convoyed sales) that would have been made but for the infringement.[168]

Reduced sales growth can also be considered in calculating the quantity of lost sales.[169] Other methods of projecting lost revenues, such as analyzing the pricing and sales policies that

---

[162] Minnesota Mining & Mfg. Co. v. Johnson & Johnson Orthopaedics, 976 F.2d 1559, 1579–80, 24 USPQ2d 1321 (Fed. Cir. 1992).

[163] Paper Converting Mach. Co. v. Magna-Graphics Corp., 745 F.2d 11, 22, 223 USPQ 591 (Fed. Cir. 1984); King Instruments Corp. v. Otari Corp., 767 F.2d 853, 864, 226 USPQ 402 (Fed. Cir. 1985), cert. denied, 475 U.S. 1016 (1986); Ryco, Inc. v. Ag Bag Corp., 857 F.2d 1418, 1428, 8 USPQ2d 1323 (Fed. Cir. 1988).

[164] W. L. Gore & Assocs. Inc. v. Carlisle Corp., 198 USPQ 353, 359 (D. Del. 1978).

[165] Kori Corp. v. Wilco Marsh Buggies & Draglines, 761 F.2d 649, 655, 225 USPQ 985 (Fed. Cir.), cert. denied, 474 U.S. 902 (1985).

[166] Paper Converting Mach. Co., 745 F.2d 11, 21, 223 USPQ 591; Lam Inc. v. Johns-Manville Corp., 718 F.2d 1056, 1065, 219 USPQ 670 (Fed. Cir. 1983); John O. Butler Co. v. Block Drug Co., 620 F. Supp. 771, 778–79, 226 USPQ 855 (N.D. Ill. 1985). But see Pall Corp. v. Micron Separations, Inc., 66 F.3d 1211, 1223, 36 USPQ2d 1225 (Fed. Cir. 1995), cert. denied, 520 U.S. 1115 (1997) (court chose a lower margin than asserted by the patent owner).

[167] Crystal Semiconductor v. TriTech Microelectronics Int'l, 246 F.3d 1336, 1357–61, 57 USPQ2d 1953 (Fed. Cir. 2001); Lam Inc. 718 F.2d at 1064–65, 219 USPQ 670; Polaroid Corp. v. Eastman Kodak Co., 16 USPQ2d 1481, 1504–09 (D. Mass. 1990), correction for clerical errors, 17 USPQ2D 1711 (D. Mass. 1991).

[168] Rite-Hite Corp. v. Kelley Co., 56 F.3d 1538, 1548–49, 35 USPQ2d 1065 (Fed. Cir.), cert. denied, 516 U.S. 867 (1995); Central Soya Co. v. George A. Hormel & Co., 723 F.2d 1573, 1579, 220 USPQ 490 (Fed. Cir. 1983); Paper Converting Mach. Co., 745 F.2d at 23, 223 USPQ 591; Kori Corp., 761 F.2d at 656, 225 USPQ 985.

[169] Lam Inc., 718 F.2d at 1068, 219 USPQ 670. Regarding future lost profits, see generally Shockley v. Arcan, Inc., 248 F.3d 1349, 1362–64, 58 USPQ2d 1692 (Fed. Cir. 2001).

the patentee would practice as a rational patent-based mono-polist, are acceptable.[170] Damage to the market due to sales of inferior infringing products also has been considered.[171]

B. Reasonable Royalty

If lost profits are not claimed or proved, damages are measured by a royalty, either an established royalty if one exists or by a reasonable royalty[172]

If an established royalty exists for the patented invention, that rate is usually the best measure of damages.[173]

35 U.S.C. §284 provides that damages shall be "no less than a reasonable royalty for the use made of the invention by the infringer." Thus, reasonable royalty is "a floor beneath which the courts are not authorized to go."[174] For example, a reasonable royalty may be higher than an established royalty if the patent owner can prove that widespread infringement made the established royalty artificially low.[175]

---

[170]Yale Lock Co. v. Sargent, 117 U.S. 536, 552–53 (1886); *see* TWM Mfg. Co. v. Dura Corp., 789 F.2d 895, 902, 229 USPQ 525 (Fed. Cir.), *cert. denied*, 479 U.S. 852 (1986); *Lam Inc.*, 718 F.2d at 1065, 219 USPQ 670.

[171] *Lam Inc.*, 718 F.2d at 1068, 219 USPQ 670.

[172]Wordtech Sys., Inc. v. Integrated Networks Solutions, Inc., 609 F.3d 1308, 1319, 95 USPQ2d 1619 (Fed. Cir. 2010); Dowagiac Mfg. Co. v. Minn. Moline Plow Co., 235 U.S. 641, 648 (1915); *Rite-Hite Corp.*, 56 F.3d at 1554, 35 USPQ2d 1065; Hanson v. Alpine Valley Ski Area Inc., 718 F.2d 1075, 1078, 219 USPQ 679 (Fed. Cir. 1983) (citing Panduit Corp. v. Stahlin Bros. Fibre Works, 575 F.2d 1152, 1157, 197 USPQ 726 (6th Cir. 1978).

[173]Nickson Indus., Inc. v. Rol Mfg. Co., 847 F.2d 795, 798, 6 USPQ2d 1878 (Fed. Cir. 1988). A single licensing agreement is not sufficient proof of an established royalty. Trell v. Marlee Elecs. Corp., 912 F.2d 1443, 1446, 16 USPQ2d 1059 (Fed. Cir. 1990); *Hanson*, 718 F.2d at 1078, 219 USPQ 679. A royalty established for a limited license is not an established royalty for an unlimited license. Monsanto Co. v. Ralph, 382 F.3d 1374, 1383–84, 72 USPQ2d 1515 (Fed. Cir. 2004) (infringing use broader than use authorized by established limited licenses). Offers to license at a given rate, particularly offers made after infringement began and litigation was threatened or probable, do not demonstrate an established rate. *Hanson*, 718 F.2d at 1078, 219 USPQ 679; Deere & Co. v. International Harvester, 710 F.2d 1551, 1557, 218 USPQ 481 (Fed. Cir. 1983).

[174]Del Mar Avionics Inc. v. Quinton Instruments Co., 836 F.2d 1320, 1326, 5 USPQ2d 1255 (Fed. Cir. 1987); *see e.g., Polaroid Corp. v. Eastman Kodak Co.*, 16 USPQ2d 1481, 1532–33, (D. Mass. 1990), *correction for clerical errors*, 17 USPQ2D 1711 (D. Mass. 1991), in which the court awarded a reasonable royalty for the periods in which lost profits would have been lower than the royalty determined by the court.

[175] *Nickson Indus., Inc.* 847 F.2d at 798, 6 USPQ2d 1878 (citing Trio Process Corp. v. L. Goldstein's Sons, Inc., 533 F.2d 126, 129–30, 189 USPQ 561 (3d Cir.1976)); Bio-Rad Labs., Inc. v. Nicolet Instrument Corp., 739 F.2d 604, 617, 222 USPQ 654 (Fed. Cir.), *cert. denied*, 469 U.S. 1038 (1984).

The 1970 district court decision in *Georgia-Pacific Corp. v. United States Plywood Corp.* set forth a "list of evidentiary facts relevant, in general, to the determination of the amount of a reasonable royalty for a patent license":

1. The royalties received by the patentee for the licensing of the patent in suit, proving or tending to prove an established royalty.
2. The rates paid by the licensee for the use of other patents comparable to the patent in suit.
3. The nature and scope of the license, as exclusive or non-exclusive; or as restricted or non-restricted in terms of territory or with respect to whom the manufactured product may be sold.
4. The licensor's established policy and marketing program to maintain his patent monopoly by not licensing others to use the invention or by granting licenses under special conditions designed to preserve that monopoly.
5. The commercial relationship between the licensor and licensee, such as, whether they are competitors in the same territory in the same line of business; or whether they are inventor and promoter.
6. The effect of selling the patented specialty in promoting sales of other products of the licensee; the existing value of the invention to the licensor as a generator of sales of his non-patented items; and the extent of such derivative or convoyed sales.
7. The duration of the patent and the term of the license.
8. The established profitability of the product made under the patent; its commercial success; and its current popularity.
9. The utility and advantages of the patent property over the old modes or devices, if any, that had been used for working out similar results.
10. The nature of the patented invention; the character of the commercial embodiment of it as owned and produced by the licensor; and the benefits to those who have used the invention.

11. The extent to which the infringer has made use of the invention; and any evidence probative of the value of that use.

12. The portion of the profit or of the selling price that may be customary in the particular business or in comparable businesses to allow for the use of the invention or analogous inventions.

13. The portion of the realizable profit that should be credited to the invention as distinguished from non-patented elements, the manufacturing process, business risks, or significant features or improvements added by the infringer.

14. The opinion testimony of qualified experts.

15. The amount that a licensor (such as the patentee) and a licensee (such as the infringer) would have agreed upon (at the time the infringement began) if both had been reasonably and voluntarily trying to reach an agreement; that is, the amount which a prudent licensee— who desired, as a business proposition, to obtain a license to manufacture and sell a particular article embodying the patented invention—would have been willing to pay as a royalty and yet be able to make a reasonable profit and which amount would have been acceptable by a prudent patentee who was willing to grant a license.[176]

The Federal Circuit has characterized the *Georgia-Pacific* factors as a "comprehensive (but unprioritized and often overlapping) list of relevant factors" and has noted that the hypothetical negotiation approach to estimating a reasonable royalty is more common than other methods.[177] The court has also stated that "the flexible analysis of all applicable *Georgia-Pacific*

---

[176] Georgia-Pacific Corp. v. United States Plywood Corp., 318 F. Supp. 1116, 1120, 166 USPQ 235 (S.D.N.Y. 1970), *modified and aff'd sub nom.* Georgia-Pacific Corp. v. United States Plywood-Champion Papers, Inc., 446 F.2d 295, 170 USPQ 369 (2d Cir.), *cert. denied*, 404 U.S. 870, 171 USPQ 322 (1971).

[177] ResQNet.com, Inc. v. Lansa, Inc., 594 F.3d 860, 868–69, 93 USPQ2d 1553 (Fed. Cir. 2010); Lucent Techs., Inc. v. Microsoft Corp., 580 F.3d 1304, 1324–25, 92 USPQ2d 1555 (Fed. Cir. 2009); Rite-Hite Corp. v. Kelley Co., 56 F.3d 1538, 1554–55, 35 USPQ2d 1065 (Fed. Cir.), *cert. denied*, 516 U.S. 867 (1995). In *Lucent*, the court also discussed an analytical method which estimates a royalty based on the infringer's projected profits when the infringement began. *Id.*

factors provides a useful and legally required framework for assessing the damages award" in appropriate cases.[178]

Before 2000, decisions of the Federal Circuit expressed concern that the hypothetical negotiation construct would result in damages too low to adequately compensate the patent owner.[179] In *Stickle v. Heublein Inc.* (1983), the court stated:

> As a final matter we would add that the trial court may award an amount of damages greater than a reasonable royalty so that the award is "adequate to compensate for the infringement." As stated in *Panduit Corp. v. Stahlin Bros. Fibre Works, supra,* 575 F.2d at 1158, 197 USPQ at 731:
>
> [T]he infringer would have nothing to lose, and everything to gain if he could count on paying only the normal, routine royalty non-infringers might have paid. As said by this court in another context, the infringer would be in a "heads-I-win, tails-you-lose" position.
>
> Such an increase, which may be stated by the trial court either as a reasonable royalty *for an infringer* (as in *Panduit*) or as an increase in the reasonable royalty determined by the court, is left to its sound discretion.[180]

Accordingly, the Federal Circuit cautioned courts to be mindful of the facts that might make the hypothetical negotiation different from an actual license negotiation.[181] In particular, the hypothetical negotiation analysis "permits and often requires a court to look to events and facts that occurred after and that could not have been known to or predicted by the hypothesized negotiators."[182]

Beginning in the 2000s, however, the decisions of the Federal Circuit placed increased emphasis on the economic sound-

---

[178] *Id.,* 580 F.3d at 1335, 92 USPQ2d 1555.

[179] Fromson v. Western Litho Plate & Supply Co., 853 F.2d 1568, 1576, 7 USPQ2d 1606 (Fed. Cir. 1988); *see also Rite-Hite Corp.,* 56 F.3d at 1554 n.6, 35 USPQ2d 1065.

[180] Stickle v. Heublein Inc., 716 F.2d 1550, 1563, 219 USPQ 377 (Fed. Cir. 1983); *accord* Maxwell v. J. Baker Inc., 86 F.3d 1098, 1110, 39 USPQ2d 1001 (Fed. Cir. 1996), *cert. denied,* 520 U.S. 1115 (1997).

[181] For example, the court stated that "emphasis on an individual inventor's lack of money or manufacturing capacity" when hypothetically negotiating against a large corporation "should be rejected as the disservice it is to the public interest in technological advancement." *Fromson,* 853 F.2d at 1575, 7 USPQ2d 1606.

[182] *Lucent Techs., Inc.,* 580 F.3d at 1333–34, 92 USPQ2d 1555 (internal quotes omitted).

ness upon which a finding of a reasonable royalty was based. For example, in *Riles v. Shell Exploration & Production Co.*, the court stated:

> A "reasonable royalty" contemplates a hypothetical negotiation between the patentee and the infringer at a time before the infringement began. Again, this analysis necessarily involves some approximation of the market as it would have hypothetically developed absent infringement. This analysis, in turn, requires sound economic and factual predicates.[183]

The Federal Circuit's more recent decisions have emphasized the need to determine with as much precision as possible the economic footprint of the claimed invention in the marketplace.[184]

The Federal Circuit has not affirmatively stated how this is to be done.[185] However, the court has reversed damages awards where:

(1) arguments about a reasonable royalty were based on license agreements that were not strictly comparable to the alleged hypothetical royalty. In this regard, the court has distinguished the economic considerations that lead to a license agreement based on a lump sum payment as opposed to a running royalty, as well as distinguishing actual licenses that were directed to patents other than the patents in suit and products other than those substantially similar to the products accused of infringement;[186]

---

[183] 298 F.3d 1302, 1311, 1313, 63 USPQ2d 1819 (Fed. Cir. 2002).

[184] ResQNet.com, Inc. v. Lansa, Inc., 594 F.3d 860, 869, 93 USPQ2d 1553 (Fed. Cir. 2010); Uniloc USA, Inc. v. Microsoft Corp., 632 F.3d 1292, 1317, 98 USPQ2d 1203 (Fed. Cir. 2011); *see also Lucent Techs., Inc.*, 580 F.3d at 1335–36, 92 USPQ2d 1555.

[185] The Federal Trade Commission's 2011 report on patent damages contains an extensive discussion of the law of reasonable royalty as it now exists and how the law might better reflect economic principles. *See* FEDERAL TRADE COMMISSION, THE EVOLVING IP MARKETPLACE: ALIGNING PATENT NOTICE AND REMEDIES WITH COMPETITION 137–212 (2011), available at http://www.ftc. gov/os/2011/03/110307patentreport.pdf.

[186] *See Lucent Techs., Inc.*, 580 F.3d at 1324–32, 92 USPQ2d 1555 (comparable licenses); *ResQNet.com, Inc.*, 594 F.3d at 869, 93 USPQ2d 1553 (comparable licenses); Wordtech Sys., Inc. v. Integrated Network Solutions, 609 F.3d 1308, 1318–22 (Fed. Cir. 2010) (comparable licenses).

(2) the alleged royalty was based on the entire market value of the accused device while the patent in suit covered only limited features of that device;[187]

(3) in a case where the entire market value rule did not apply, the patent owner argued that the royalty sought at trial was reasonable by comparing it to the amount of the accused infringer's total sales;[188] and

(4) the alleged royalty was based on the arbitrary "25 percent rule of thumb," under which the patent owner is awarded 25 percent of the infringer's projected profits at the time of the hypothetical negotiation.[189]

Further, the court has strongly encouraged trial courts to perform a gatekeeping function by ruling inadmissible before trial damages claims based on fundamentally flawed arguments.[190]

The hypothetical licensing negotiation takes place at the time infringement began.[191] The royalty award can take the form of a hypothetically negotiated lump sum based on expected future sales.[192] Some courts have said that a reasonable royalty

---

[187] *Uniloc USA, Inc.*, 632 F.3d at 1318–21, 98 USPQ2d 1203.

[188] *Id.* at 1320–21, 98 USPQ2d 1203.

[189] *Id.* at 1312–18, 98 USPQ2d 1203 (25% rule of thumb).

[190] *Id.* at 1315–18, 98 USPQ2d 1203 (ruling that 25% rule of thumb is an inadmissible methodology and suggesting in dicta that absent "a basis in fact to associate the royalty rates used in prior licenses to the particular hypothetical negotiation at issue in the case," such licenses should be excluded as well. *See also* two cases in which Chief Judge Rader, sitting as a trial judge by designation, has granted motions in limine with respect to damages: *Cornell Univ. v. Hewlett-Packard Co.*, 609 F. Supp. 2d 279 (N.D.N.Y. 2009); and *IP Innovation L.L.C. v. Red Hat, Inc.*, 705 F. Supp. 2d 687 (E.D. Tex. 2010). *But see* Microsoft Corp. v. i4i Ltd. P'ship, 598 F. 3d 831, 852–56, 93 USPQ2d 1943 (Fed. Cir. 2010) (affirming denial of *Daubert* motion to exclude expert testimony where methodology was sound).

[191] Wang Labs. Inc. v. Toshiba Corp., 993 F.2d 858, 869–70, 26 USPQ2d 1767 (Fed. Cir. 1993); *see also* Riles v. Shell Exploration & Prod. Co., 298 F.3d 1302, 1311, 1313, 63 USPQ2d 1819 (Fed. Cir. 2002); Panduit Corp. v. Stahlin Bros. Fibre Works, 575 F.2d 1152, 1158, 197 USPQ 726 (6th Cir. 1978). The Federal Trade Commission's 2011 report contains an extensive discussion of the theory of damages and suggests that, as a matter of economics, the proper timeframe for the hypothetical negotiation is at a time *before* the actual infringement began, when the accused infringer had to choose between developing its product with the feature later accused of infringement, using an available alternative, or forgoing use of the infringing functionality altogether. *See* FEDERAL TRADE COMMISSION, THE EVOLVING IP MARKETPLACE: ALIGNING PATENT NOTICE AND REMEDIES WITH COMPETITION 189–91 (2011), available at .http://www.ftc.gov/os/2011/03/110307patentreport.pdf

[192] Lucent Techs., Inc. v. Microsoft Corp., 580 F.3d 1304, 1325–32, 92 USPQ2d 1555 (Fed. Cir. 2009).

should leave an infringer with a reasonable profit,[193] but the law does not require that an infringer be permitted to make a profit.[194] Further, a hypothetical profit must be determined as of the time of the hypothetical negotiations. It is irrelevant that, taking into consideration subsequent events, the infringer actually made little or no profit or that the reasonable royalty yields a damage award larger than an infringer's actual profits.[195]

A court may properly rely on internal memoranda projecting anticipated profits before infringement began.[196] A court also may rely on proof of an infringer's actual profits as probative of anticipated profits.[197] Increased profitability and estimated cost savings from use of the patented invention also may be considered.[198] The impact on the respective bargaining positions of the willing licensee and willing licensor of anticipated collateral sales of a noninfringing product line, the desire to maintain market position, and the desire to enter a new market should also be taken into account.[199]

---

[193] Hanson v. Alpine Valley Ski Area, Inc., 718 F.2d 1075, 1081, 219 USPQ 679 (Fed. Cir. 1983); Georgia-Pacific Corp. v. United States Plywood Corp., 318 F. Supp. 1116, 1120, 166 USPQ 235 (S.D.N.Y. 1970), *modified and aff'd sub nom.*, Georgia-Pacific Corp. v. United States Plywood-Champion Papers, Inc., 446 F.2d 295, 170 USPQ 369 (2d Cir.), *cert. denied*, 404 U.S. 870, 171 USPQ 322 (1971).

[194] Monsanto Co. v. Ralph, 382 F.3d 1374, 1384, 72 USPQ2d 1515 (Fed. Cir. 2004).

[195] Rite-Hite Corp v. Kelley Co., 56 F.3d 1538, 1555, 35 USPQ2d 1065 (Fed. Cir.), *cert. denied*, 516 U.S. 867 (1995); State Indus., Inc. v. Mor-Flo Indus., Inc., 883 F.2d 1573, 1580, 12 USPQ2d 1026 (Fed. Cir. 1989), *cert. denied*, 493 U.S. 1022 (1990) ("There is no rule that a royalty be no higher than the infringer's net profit margin"); Golight, Inc. v. Wal-Mart Stores, Inc., 355 F.3d 1327, 1338, 69 USPQ2d 1481 (Fed. Cir. 2004).

[196] TWM Mfg. Co. v. Dura Corp., 789 F.2d 895, 900, 229 USPQ 525 (Fed. Cir.), *cert. denied*, 479 U.S. 852 (1986). Similarly, internal memoranda projecting future sales before infringement began may be relied on. Interactive Pictures v. Infinite Pictures, 274 F.3d 1371, 1384–85, 61 USPQ2d 1152 (Fed. Cir. 2001).

[197] Trans-World Mfg. Corp. v. Al Nyman & Sons, 750 F.2d 1552, 1568, 224 USPQ 259 (Fed. Cir. 1984); *see also* State Contracting & Eng'g Corp. v. Condotte Am., 346 F.3d 1057, 1072, 68 USPQ2d 1481 (Fed. Cir. 2003); *TWM Mfg. Co.*, 789 F.2d at 899, 229 USPQ 525.

[198] Deere & Co. v. International Harvester Co., 710 F.2d 1551, 1558, 218 USPQ 481 (Fed. Cir. 1983).

[199] Micro Chem., Inc. v. Lextron, Inc., 317 F.3d 1387, 1393, 65 USPQ2d 1532 (Fed. Cir. 2003); Interactive Pictures v. Infinite Pictures, 274 F.3d 1371,1385–86, 61 USPQ2d 1152 (Fed. Cir. 2001), *cert. denied*, 537 U.S. 825 (2002); *State Indus. Inc.*, 883 F.2d at 1580; *Deere & Co.*, 710 F.2d at 1559, 218 USPQ 481; Radio Steel & Mfg. Co. v. MTD Prods., 788 F.2d 1554, 1557, 229 USPQ 431 (Fed. Cir. 1986); *Trans-World Mfg. Corp.*, 750 F.2d at 1568, 224 USPQ 259; Arriflex Corp. v. Aaton Cameras, Inc., 225 USPQ 487, 489 (S.D.N.Y. 1984); Mosinee Paper Corp. v. James River Corp. of Va., 22 USPQ2d 1657, 1661–62 (E.D. Wis. 1992); Micro Motion Inc. v. Exac Corp., 761 F. Supp. 1420, 1435, 19 USPQ2d 1001 (N.D. Cal. 1991). The condition of the patent owner's business also may be relevant to the hypothetical negotiations. Rodime PLC v. Seagate Tech. Inc., 174 F.3d 1294, 1308, 50 USPQ2d 1429 (Fed. Cir. 1999), *cert. denied*, 528 U.S. 1115 (2000).

Courts have divided about the extent to which a royalty paid to settle an infringement claim may be used as evidence of a reasonable royalty.[200] That the patentee might have accepted less than a reasonable royalty rate or that the infringer would not have accepted a license at that rate is of little relevance.[201]

Availability to the infringer of acceptable alternatives to the patented device may decrease the royalty rate.[202] The infringer's election to infringe and its withdrawal from the business after enforcement of an injunction are evidence of the absence of noninfringing alternatives.[203]

The royalty base may include damages for bundled or convoyed sales where appropriate.[204]

A jury may choose a royalty rate between the rates proffered by the parties.[205]

When assessing a reasonable royalty after trial for the purpose of a compulsory or going-forward license in lieu of an

---

[200] *Compare* ResQNet.com, Inc. v. Lansa, Inc., 594 F.3d 860, 872, 93 USPQ2d 1553 (Fed. Cir. 2010) ("the most reliable license in this record arose out of litigation") *with* Hanson v. Alpine Valley Ski Area, Inc., 718 F.2d 1075, 1078, 219 USPQ 679 (Fed. Cir. 1983). As to whether such licenses are inadmissible under Fed. R. Evid. 408 if one party objects, so to their use at trial, see Alpex Computer Corp. v. Nintendo Co., 770 F. Supp. 161, 163–67, 20 USPQ2d 1782 (S.D.N.Y. 1991), *reaffirmed on reconsideration*, No. 86 Civ. 1749 (KMW), 1994 U.S. Dist. LEXIS 3343 (S.D.N.Y. Mar. 16, 1994), *vacated in part*, No. 86 Civ. 1749 (KMW), 1994 U.S. Dist. LEXIS 9963 (S.D.N.Y. July 19, 1994); *see also* Alpex Computer Corp. v. Nintendo Co., 34 USPQ2d 1167, 1201–03 (S.D.N.Y. 1994), *aff'd in part, rev'd in part*, 102 F.3d 1214, 40 USPQ2d 1667 (Fed. Cir. 1996), *cert. denied*, 521 U.S. 1104 (1997). *But see* Studiengesellschaft Kohle v. Dart Indus., 862 F.2d 1564, 1570–73, 9 USPQ2d 1273 (Fed. Cir. 1988); Century Wrecker Corp. v. E. R. Buske Mfg. Co., 898 F. Supp. 1334, 1338–42 (N.D. Iowa 1995).

[201] *TWM Mfg. Co.*, 789 F.2d at 899, 229 USPQ 525; *Hanson*, 718 F.2d at 1081, 219 USPQ 679; Panduit Corp. v. Stahlin Bros. Fibre Works, 575 F.2d 1152, 1158–59, 197 USPQ 726 (6th Cir. 1978).

[202] Riles v. Shell Exploration & Prod. Co., 298 F.3d 1302, 1312, 63 USPQ2d 1819 (Fed. Cir. 2002); Minco Inc. v. Combustion Eng'g, Inc., 95 F.3d 1109, 1119, 40 USPQ2d 1001 (Fed. Cir. 1996). Regarding an alternative that was not available at the time of the hypothetical negotiation, see *Micro Chem., Inc.*, 317 F.3d at 1393–94, 65 USPQ2d 1532.

[203] *TWM Mfg. Co.*, 789 F.2d at 900, 229 USPQ 525.

[204] Fujifilm Corp. v. Benun, 605 F.3d 1366, 1373, 95 USPQ2d 1985 (Fed. Cir.), *cert. denied*, 131 S. Ct. 829 (2010); *Interactive Pictures*, 274 F.3d at 1385, 61 USPQ2d 1152; *see also* Rite-Hite Corp. v. Kelley Co., 56 F.3d 1538, 1549–51, 35 USPQ2d 1065 (Fed. Cir.), *cert. denied*, 516 U.S. 867 (1995) (standard for awarding damages for convoyed sales in the lost profits context).

[205] Spectralytics, Inc. v. Cordis Corp., 99 USPQ2d 1012, 1020 (Fed. Cir. 2011); Fuji Photo Film Co. v. Jazz Photo Corp., 394 F.3d 1368, 1378, 73 USPQ2d 1678 (Fed. Cir. 2005).

injunction, courts may assess a royalty or determine a royalty rate different from that used to calculate damages.[206]

C. Mixed Awards

The Federal Circuit has approved mixed awards, which use lost profits as the measure of damages on the part of the infringing sales that the patent owner proved it could have made and a reasonable royalty as the damages measure on the remainder.[207] The practice of mixing awards is derived from the equitable notion that because each act of infringement is separately compensable, losses incurred by infringers on some infringing sales should not be used to diminish awards based on other profitable sales in computing lost profits.[208] Damages awards have been split between lost profits and reasonable royalties where the patent owner would have chosen to or been able to sell to some but not all of the infringer's customers,[209] where the patent owner would have chosen to penetrate some but not all of the infringer's geographic sales areas,[210] and where a reasonable royalty would have exceeded lost profits in some but not all of the years of infringement.[211] It is an abuse of discretion for a court not to consider royalty damages for infringing sales for which lost profits are unavailable.[212]

---

[206]Amado v. Microsoft Corp., 517 F.3d 1353, 1361–62, 86 USPQ2d 1090 (Fed. Cir. 2008); Paice LLC v. Toyota Motor Corp., 504 F.3d 1293, 1317, 85 USPQ2d 1001 (Fed. Cir. 2007), *cert. denied,* 128 S. Ct. 2430 (2008).

[207]Crystal Semiconductor Corp. v. TriTech Microelectronics Int'l, 246 F.3d 1336, 1354, 57 USPQ2d 1953 (Fed. Cir. 2001); State Indus., Inc. v. Mor-Flo Indus., Inc., 883 F.2d 1573, 1577 12 USPQ2d 1026 (Fed. Cir. 1989), *cert. denied,* 493 U.S. 1022 (1990); Siemens Med. Solutions USA, Inc. v. Saint-Gobain Ceramics and Plastics, Inc., 637 F.3d 1269, 1288–89, 97 USPQ2d 1897 (Fed. Cir. 2011).

[208] *See* Crosby Steam Gage & Valve Co. v. Consolidated Safety Valve Co., 141 U.S. 441, 457 (1891).

[209] *See, e.g.,* Radio Steel & Mfg. Co. v. MTD Prods., 788 F.2d 1554, 1555–57, 229 USPQ 431 (Fed. Cir. 1986); Micro Motion Inc. v. Exac Corp., 761 F. Supp. 1420, 1426–27, 19 USPQ2d 1001 (N.D. Cal. 1991); Polaroid Corp. v. Eastman Kodak Co., 16 USPQ2d 1481, 1532–33 (D. Mass. 1990), *correction for clerical errors,* 17 USPQ2d 1711 (D. Mass. 1991).

[210]Broadview Chem. Corp. v. Loctite Corp., 311 F. Supp. 447, 164 USPQ 419 (D. Conn. 1970).

[211]H. K. Porter Co. v. Goodyear Tire & Rubber Co., 536 F.2d 1115, 191 USPQ 486 (6th Cir. 1976); *Polaroid Corp.,* 16 USPQ2d at 1490.

[212] *Siemens Med. Solutions USA, Inc.,* 637 F.3d at 1290, 97 USPQ2d 1897.

III. MARKING OR ACTUAL NOTICE—
A PREREQUISITE TO RECOVERING DAMAGES

A patent owner that directly or indirectly sells patented articles and that seeks to recover damages for any infringement that occurred prior to the filing of the lawsuit for infringement must plead and prove compliance with the marking or actual notice requirements of 35 U.S.C. §287(a).[213] Damages may be recovered from the time when marking in compliance with Section 287(a) began or from the time actual notice was given, whichever came first.[214]

Before September 2011, marking in compliance with Section 287(a) required the patent owner (or one making or selling any patented article for or under the patent owner)[215] to fix on the patented article the word "patent" (or the abbreviation "pat.") together with the patent's number or, when that cannot be done,[216] to fix to the patented article or to the package that contains the patented article a label containing a like notice.[217] The purpose behind the marking requirement is to give patent

---

[213] *See generally* Dunlap v. Schofield, 152 U.S. 244, 247–48 (1894); Maxwell v. J. Baker Inc., 86 F.3d 1098, 1111 (Fed. Cir. 1996); American Med. Sys. v. Medical Eng'g Corp., 6 F.3d 1523, 1537, 28 USPQ2d 1321 (Fed. Cir. 1993), *cert. denied*, 511 U.S. 1070 (1994); Calmar Inc. v. Emson Research Inc., 850 F. Supp. 861, 867 (C.D. Cal. 1994). If there are no products for the patent owner to mark, then recovery is not limited by Section 287(a). Texas Digital Sys., Inc. v. Telegenix, Inc., 308 F.3d 1193, 1219–20, 64 USPQ2d 1812 (Fed. Cir. 2002) (patent owner did not make or sell the patented product), *cert. denied*, 538 U.S. 1058 (2003). The notice provisions of Section 287(a) do not apply to patents that only claim processes or methods. Crystal Semiconductor Corp. v. TriTech Microelectronics Int'l, 246 F.3d 1336, 1353, 57 USPQ2d 1953 (Fed. Cir. 2001); *see, e.g.*, State Contracting & Eng'g Corp. v. Condotte Am., 346 F.3d 1057, 1073–74, 68 USPQ2d 1481 (Fed. Cir. 2003).

[214] *American Med. Sys.*, 6 F.3d at 1536–37, 28 USPQ2d 1321. There is no liability for post-notice repair of products that were sold prior to notice. Fonar Corp. v. Gen. Elec. Co., 107 F.3d 1543, 1554–55 (Fed. Cir. 1997).

[215] *See, e.g.*, Amsted Indus. Inc. v. Buckeye Steel Castings Co., 24 F.3d 178, 184–85, 30 USPQ2d 1462 (Fed. Cir. 1994). When there is a failure to mark by one other than the patent owner, a rule of reason approach is used and substantial compliance may satisfy Section 287(a). *Maxwell*, 86 F.3d at 1111–12. In such situations, the trier of fact may consider whether the patent owner made reasonable efforts to ensure compliance with the statute. *Id.*

[216] *Compare* Rutherford v. Trim-Tex Inc., 803 F. Supp. 158, 25 USPQ2d 1866 (N.D. Ill. 1992), *with* John L. Rie Inc. v. Shelly Bros. Inc., 366 F. Supp. 84, 181 USPQ 157 (E.D. Pa. 1973).

[217] 35 U.S.C. §287(a) (2001). A manifestly obvious typographical error in the patent number has been held not to be a failure to comply with §287(a) when interested members of the public are not prevented from discerning the number. Allen Eng'g Corp. v. Bartell Indus., 299 F.3d 1336, 1355–56, 63 USPQ2d 1769 (Fed. Cir. 2002).

owners incentive to mark their products and thereby place the world on notice of the existence of the patent.[218] Marking must be substantially consistent and continuous, but there is no time by when it must begin.[219] There is no duty to mark for patents that include only method claims.[220] Compliance with Section 287(a) is a question of fact.[221]

In September 2011, the America Inventions Act amended 35 U.S.C. § 287(a) to allow the patent owner another way to provide constructive notice: by adding to the word "patent" on a product or its packaging "an address of a posting on the Internet, accessible to the public without charge for accessing the address, that associates the patented article with the number of the patent."[222] Actual notice sufficient to satisfy Section 287(a) "requires the affirmative communication of a specific charge of infringement by a specific accused product or device."[223] The patent owner need not make an unqualified charge of infringement.[224] Section 287(a)'s requirement is met by a communication that is sufficiently specific regarding the patent owner's belief that there may be infringement.[225] Whether actual notice was given is determined by focusing on the actions of the patent owner, not by focusing on the knowledge of the infringer.[226]

---

[218] *Amsted Indus. Inc.,* 24 F.3d at 185, 30 USPQ2d 1462; *American Med. Sys.,* 6 F.3d at 1538, 28 USPQ2d 1321. The marking statute also aids the public in identifying what articles are patented, which helps avoid innocent infringement. Nike Inc. v. Wal-Mart Stores, 138 F.3d 1437, 1443, 46 USPQ2d 1001 (Fed. Cir. 1998), *cert. denied and motion granted,* 528 U.S. 946, 120 S. Ct. 363 (1999).

[219] *American Med. Sys.,* 6 F.3d at 1537, 28 USPQ2d 1321; *see also Maxwell,* 86 F.3d at 1111. Regarding a possible de minimis exception, see *Hazeltine Corp. v. Radio Corp. of Am.,* 20 F. Supp. 668, 671–72 (S.D.N.Y. 1937).

[220] Crystal Semiconductor Corp. v. TriTech Microelectronics Int'l, 246 F.3d 1336, 1353, 57 USPQ2d 1953 (Fed. Cir. 2001).

[221] *Maxwell,* 86 F.3d at 1111. *See, e.g.,* ADC Telecomms. Inc. v. Siecor Corp., 954 F. Supp. 820, 832–33 (D. Del. 1997) (denying summary judgment); Clancy Sys. Int'l v. Symbol Techs., 953 F. Supp. 1170, 42 USPQ2d 1290 (D. Colo. 1997) (granting summary judgment); Loral Fairchild Corp. v. Victor Co. of Japan, Ltd., 906 F. Supp. 813 (E.D.N.Y. 1995) (same).

[222] *See* Leahy-Smith America Invents Act, Pub. L. 112-29, H.R. 1249 (2011), sec. 16 ("virtual marking") and sec. 16(4) for the effective date of the amendment.

[223] *Amsted Indus. Inc.,* 24 F.3d at 187, 30 USPQ2d 1462. *See, e.g.,* M-S Cash Drawer Corp. v. Block & Co., 26 USPQ2d 1472 (C.D. Cal. 1992). Actual notice under §287(a) is not coextensive with the requirements for creating an actual controversy under the Declaratory Judgment Act. SRI Int'l v. Advanced Tech. Labs., 127 F.3d 1462, 1470, 44 USPQ2d 1422 (Fed. Cir. 1997). *See generally* Gart v. Logitech, Inc., 254 F.3d 1334, 1345–46, 59 USPQ2d 1290 (Fed. Cir. 2001), *cert. denied,* 534 U.S. 1114 (2002). Regarding the requirements for creating an actual controversy, see Chapter 3, §I.B.

[224] *Gart,* 254 F.3d at 1346, 59 USPQ2d 1290.

[225] *Id.*

[226] *Amsted Indus. Inc.,* 24 F.3d at 187, 30 USPQ2d 1462.

Thus, it is irrelevant that the infringer knew of the patent or knew that he or she was infringing.[227] Notice must come from the patent owner, not somebody closely associated with the patent owner.[228]

False marking. Before September 2011, 35 U.S.C §292 provided:

> Whoever marks upon, or affixes to, or uses in advertising in connection with any unpatented article, the word "patent" or any work or number importing that the same is patented, for the purpose of deceiving the public . . . [s]hall be fined not more than $500 for every such offense.

"The two elements of a §292 false marking claim were (1) marking an unpatented article and (2) intent to deceive the public."[229]

The statute applied to products that are marked with the numbers of patents that had subsequently expired or patents that do not cover the product on which they are marked.[230] " 'When the statute refers to an "unpatented article" the statute means that the article in question is not covered by at least one claim of each patent with which the article is marked.' "[231]

Section 292 thus established a *qui tam* action, in which a private plaintiff could sue on behalf of the government as well as himself.[232]

The enactment of the Leahy-Smith America Invents Act in September 2011 should substantially curtail actions for false marking. Now, only the United States may bring an action seeking to assess a civil fine. A private plaintiff seeking to bring suit must prove that it has suffered "competitive injury" as a result of the false marking, and can recover only "damages adequate to compensate" for that injury. The listing of expired patents

---

[227] *Id.; see also Gart*, 254 F.3d at 1346, 59 USPQ2d 1290.

[228] Lans v. Digital Equip. Corp., 252 F.3d 1320, 1326–28, 59 USPQ2d 1057 (Fed. Cir. 2001).

[229] Forest Grp., Inc. v. Bon Tool Co., 590 F.3d 1295, 1300, 93 USPQ2d 1097 (Fed. Cir. 2009).

[230] Pequignot v. Solo Cup Co., 608 F.3d 1356, 1361–62, 95 USPQ2d 1501 (Fed. Cir. 2010).

[231] Juniper Networks, Inc. v. Shipley, 643 F.3d 1346, 1350, 98 USPQ2d 1491 (Fed. Cir. 2011) (citation omitted). Although a website can be an unpatented article, the statute does not apply to a website that falsely describes what a patent covers, unless the alleged unpatented invention is used to operate the website itself. *Id.*

[232] Stauffer v. Brooks Brothers, Inc., 619 F.3d 1321, 1324–28, 96 USPQ2d 1304 (Fed. Cir. 2010).

that once covered the product is no longer a violation of the statute.[233]

Allegations of false marking are subject to the heightened pleading requirements of Rule 9(b) of the Federal Rules of Civil Procedure.[234] Evidence that a manufacturer has taken reasonable steps to change its packaging after the expiration of a patent may demonstrate a lack of intent to deceive.[235]

IV. INCREASED DAMAGES

Damages may be increased up to three times at the discretion of the district court under 35 U.S.C. §284. Provisions allowing treble damages have been in force since enactment of the Patent Act of 1793.[236] Trebling was mandatory before the enactment of the 1836 act.[237]

Increased damages, which are punitive rather than compensatory,[238] serve as a deterrent to the tort of infringement.[239] Accordingly, increased damages awards are based on the culpable nature of conduct that forms the basis of the award.[240]

---

[233] Leahy-Smith America Invents Act, Pub. L. 112-29, H.R. 1249 (2011), sec. 16, amending 35 U.S.C. §292, effective as to all actions pending on the date of enactment or brought thereafter.

[234] In re BP Lubricants USA, 637 F.3d 1307, 1309, 97 USPQ2d 2025 (Fed. Cir. 2011).

[235] See, e.g., Laughlin Prods., Inc. v. ETS, Inc., 257 F. Supp. 2d 863, 871 (N.D. Tex. 2002), aff'd, 68 F. App'x 976 (Fed. Cir. 2003); Promote Innovation LLC v. Ortho-McNeill Pharm., LLC, No. 11 Civ. 607, 2011 WL 2837421, at *2 (D.N.J. July 14, 2011); Public Patent Found., Inc. v. GlaxoSmithKline Consumer Healthcare, L.P., No 09 Civ. 5881 (RMB), slip op. at 25 (S.D.N.Y. August 10, 2011).

[236] Act of July 4, 1936, ch. 357, §14, 5 Stat. 117 (1936) ("it shall be in the power of the court to render judgment for any amount above . . . the actual damages . . . not exceeding three times the amount thereof"); Act of July 8, 1870, ch. 230, §55, 16 Stat. 201 (1870).

[237] Act of Feb. 21, 1793, ch. 11, §5, 1 Stat. 318 (1793); Act of Apr. 17, 1800, ch. 25, §3, 2 Stat. 37, 38 (1800); Act of July 4, 1836, ch. 357, §14, 5 Stat. 117 (1836).

[238] Jurgens v. CBK, Ltd., 80 F.3d 1566, 1569–71, 38 USPQ2d 1397 (Fed. Cir. 1996); Crystal Semiconductor Corp. v. TriTech Microelectronics Int'l, 246 F.3d 1336, 1361, 57 USPQ2d 1953 (Fed. Cir. 2001). This can be contrasted with the award of increased damages in trademark actions, which may not be punitive and must be based on showing actual harm. 15 U.S.C. §1117 (damages, including increased damages, "shall constitute compensation and not a penalty"); Electronics. Corp. of Am. v. Honeywell, Inc., 358 F. Supp. 1230, 1233, 179 USPQ 73 (D. Mass), aff'd, 487 F.2d 513, 180 USPQ 97 (1st Cir. 1973), cert. denied, 415 U.S. 960 (1974).

[239] Rite-Hite Corp. v. Kelley Co., 819 F.2d 1120, 1125–26, 2 USPQ2d 1915 (Fed. Cir. 1987).

[240] Id. The patent owner must present evidence of culpable behavior. Norian Corp. v. Stryker Corp., 363 F.3d 1321, 1332, 70 USPQ2d 1508 (Fed. Cir. 2004); In re Seagate Tech., LLC, 497 F.3d 1360, 1371, 83 USPQ2d 1865 (Fed. Cir. 2007), cert. denied, 552 U.S. 1230 (2008).

A district court's decision to increase damages requires two steps: (1) finding clear and convincing evidence that the infringement was willful (or that other circumstances justify an enhanced award), and (2) determining from the totality of the circumstances that damages should be increased.[241] The district court should explain the basis for increasing damages, or for not increasing damages when there has been a finding of willful infringement.[242]

A. Willful Infringement

Patent infringement itself is a strict liability tort.[243] However, the infringer's intent and reasonable beliefs are the primary focus of a willful infringement inquiry. Willfulness includes reckless behavior.[244] Until 2007, a potential infringer having actual notice[245] of a patent had an affirmative duty of due care to avoid

---

[241] i4i Ltd. P'ship v. Microsoft Corp., 598 F.3d 831, 858–59, 93 USPQ2d 1943 (Fed. Cir. 2010), aff'd on other grounds, 131 S. Ct. 2238, 98 USPQ2d 1857 (2011) ("Although a finding of willfulness is a prerequisite for enhancing damages under §284, the standard for deciding whether—and by how much—to enhance damages is set forth in Read [Corp. v. Portec, Inc., 970 F.2d 816, 828, 23 USPQ2d 1426 (Fed. Cir. 1992)], not Seagate"); see also Spectralytics, Inc. v. Cordis Corp., 99 USPQ2d 1012, 1021–22 (Fed. Cir. 2011); Jurgens, 80 F.3d at 1570, 38 USPQ2d 1397; State Indus. Inc. v. Mor-Flo Indus. Inc., 948 F.2d 1573, 1576, 20 USPQ2d 1738 (Fed. Cir. 1991) (two–step process).

[242] Read Corp. v. Portec Inc., 970 F.2d 816, 828, 23 USPQ2d 1426 (Fed. Cir. 1992). Failure to explain the basis for an award of increased damages can be harmless error where the appellate court can discern reasons for the award from the record. Metabolite Labs., Inc. v. Laboratory Corp. of Am. Holdings, 370 F.3d 1354, 1370–71, 71 USPQ2d 1081 (Fed. Cir. 2004), cert. dismissed, 548 U.S. 124, 79 USPQ2d 1065 (2006).

[243] In re Seagate Tech., LLC, 497 F.3d at 1369, 83 USPQ2d 1865.

[244] Knorr-Bremse Systeme Fuer Nutzfahrzeuge GmbH v. Dana Corp., 383 F.3d 1337, 1342–43, 72 USPQ2d 1560 (Fed. Cir. 2004) (en banc); In re Seagate Tech., 497 F.3d at 1371.

[245] An infringer cannot willfully infringe a patent of which it is unaware. Gustafson Inc. v. Intersystems Indus. Prods., 897 F.2d 508, 511, 13 USPQ2d 1972 (Fed. Cir. 1990). Actual notice has been deemed to have occurred where the patentee offered the infringer a license, where verbal notice of infringement was accompanied by presentation of a copy of the patent, and where there was notification by a third party even if that party opined that the patent was invalid. See, e.g., Great N. Corp. v. Davis Core & Pad Co., 782 F.2d 159, 167, 228 USPQ 356 (Fed. Cir. 1986); American Original Corp. v. Jenkins Food Corp., 774 F.2d 459, 465, 227 USPQ 299 (Fed. Cir. 1985); Ralston Purina Co. v. Far-Mar-Co., 772 F.2d 1570, 1577, 227 USPQ 177 (Fed. Cir. 1985); see also Imonex Servs., Inc. v. W. H. Munzprufer Dietmar Trenner GmbH, 408 F.3d 1374, 1377–78, 74 USPQ2d 1936 (Fed. Cir. 2005) (actual notice of patents to defendants was found by plaintiff's displaying products marked with patent number at trade shows attended by defendants' employees, widespread distribution of advertising literature that stated the products were patented, and correspondence with defendants' employees about defendants' use of patented products). Awareness that a patent is pending is insufficient to support a finding of willfulness. Conopco Inc. v. May Dep't Stores Co., 46 F.3d 1556, 1562, 32 USPQ2d 1225 (Fed. Cir. 1994), cert. denied, 514 U.S. 1078 (1995).

infringement of that patent.[246] Failure to perform the duty could have subjected the infringer to a finding of willfulness.[247]

In *In re Seagate*,[248] the Federal Circuit abolished the affirmative duty of due care, creating a two-part test for assessing willfulness. To establish willful infringement, the patent owner must show by clear and convincing evidence that:

1. the infringer acted despite an objectively high likelihood that its action constituted infringement of a valid patent; and,
2. the objectively defined risk was either known or so obvious that it should have been known.[249]

The state of mind of the accused infringer is not relevant to the first threshold inquiry. The objectively defined risk of the second inquiry is determined by the record developed in the infringement proceeding.[250] A willfulness claim ordinarily is restricted to the infringer's prelitigation conduct.[251] Whether a willfulness claim based solely on conduct occurring solely after litigation began is sustainable depends on the facts of each case.[252]

Seeking and obtaining competent legal advice before initiating possibly infringing activity may be an important factor in determining willful infringement. Before September 2011, there was no rule, however, that an opinion letter from counsel precluded a finding of willful infringement, or that lack of an opinion letter mandated a finding of willfulness.[253] Effective

---

[246] *Knorr-Bremse Systeme* 383 F.3d at 1345, 72 USPQ2d 1560.

[247] *In re Seagate Tech.*, 497 F.3d at 1368–69, 83 USPQ2d 1865.

[248] *Id.*, 497 F.3d at 1370–72, 83 USPQ2d 1865.

[249] *Id.* at 1371, 83 USPQ2d 1865.

[250] *Id.*

[251] *Id.* at 1374, 83 USPQ2d 1865.

[252] *Id.*

[253] Knorr-Bremse Systeme Fuer Nutzfahrzeuge GmbH, 383 F.3d 1337, 1346–47, 72 USPQ2d 1560 (Fed. Cir. 2004); Rolls-Royce Ltd. v. GTE Valeron Corp., 800 F.2d 1101, 1109–10, 231 USPQ 185 (Fed. Cir. 1986); *see, e.g.,* Vulcan Eng'g Co. v. FATA Aluminum, Inc., 278 F.3d 1366, 1379, 61 USPQ2d 1545 (Fed. Cir.) (infringer, who had initiated infringing activity, sought legal advice promptly after receiving notice of infringement), *cert. denied,* 537 U.S. 814 (2002); LNP Eng'g Plastics v. Miller Waste Mills, 275 F.3d 1347, 1357, 61 USPQ2d 1193 (Fed. Cir. 2001); Kori Corp. v. Wilco Marsh Buggies & Draglines, 761 F.2d 649, 656, 225 USPQ 985 (Fed. Cir.), *cert. denied,* 474 U.S. 902 (1985); Central Soya Co. v. George A. Hormel & Co., 723 F.2d 1573, 1577, 220 USPQ 490 (Fed. Cir. 1983); Underwater Devices Inc. v. Morrison-Knudsen Co., 717 F.2d 1380, 1389–90, 219 USPQ 569 (Fed. Cir. 1983).

September 2011, the Leahy-Smith America Invents Act adds a section to the patent statute stating that the failure to obtain an opinion of counsel or the failure to introduce such an opinion "may not be used to prove that the accused infringer willfully infringed the patent or that the infringer intended to induce infringement of the patent."[254]

Defenses prepared for trial are not equivalent to competent legal opinions that qualify as an exercise of a potential infringer's duty of due care to avoid infringement.[255]

If a party accused of infringement elects to waive the attorney-client privilege and rely on the advice of counsel as a defense to willfulness, the focus is not on the legal correctness of the opinion, but rather on whether the opinion was sufficient to demonstrate that the objectively defined risk of infringement was either known or that it should have been known.[256] Thus, relevant facts include:

1. when the infringer sought the advice;
2. what the infringer knew about counsel's independence, skill, and competence to provide the opinion;
3. what the infringer knew about the nature and extent of the analysis performed by counsel; and
4. what the infringer knew and had concluded about the credibility, value, and reasonableness of the opinion.[257]

The Federal Circuit delineated objective evidence of an adequate opinion from counsel in *Underwater Devices Inc. v. Morrison-Knudsen Co.*[258] In that case, the infringer had obtained an opinion that failed to rise to the level of competent legal advice:

---

[254] Leahy-Smith America Invents Act, Pub. L. 112-29, H.R. 1249 (2011), sec. 17, adding 35 U.S.C. §298.

[255] Crystal Semiconductor Corp. v. TriTech Microelectronics Int'l, 246 F.3d 1336, 1351–52, 57 USPQ2d 1953 (Fed. Cir. 2001).

[256] *In re* Seagate Tech., LLC, 497 F.3d 1360, 1371, 83 USPQ2d 1865 (Fed. Cir. 2007). Before *Seagate,* opinions were used to determine whether an infringer believed that a court might reasonably hold the patent invalid, not infringed, or unenforceable. Johns Hopkins Univ. v. Cell-Pro Inc., 152 F.3d 1342, 1364, 47 USPQ2d 1705 (Fed. Cir. 1998).

[257] *Johns Hopkins Univ.,* 152 F.3d at 1364, 47 USPQ2d 1705; SRI Int'l v. Advanced Tech. Labs, 127 F.3d 1462, 1464–68, 44 USPQ2d 1422 (Fed. Cir. 1997); Thorn EMI N. Am. Inc. v. Micron Tech. Inc., 837 F. Supp. 616, 620, 29 USPQ2d 1872 (D. Del. 1993).

[258] 717 F.2d 1380, 1390, 219 USPQ 569 (Fed. Cir. 1983).

Had [the opinion] contained within its four corners a patent validity analysis, properly and explicitly predicated on a review of the file
histories of the patents at issue, and an infringement analysis that,
inter alia, compared and contrasted the potentially infringing
method or apparatus with the patented inventions, the opinion
may have contained sufficient internal indicia of credibility to
remove any doubt that M-K in fact received a competent opinion.[259]

Factors bearing on the competency of an opinion letter
include whether counsel examined the file history of the patent,
whether the opinion was oral or written, whether the opinion
came from in-house or outside counsel, whether the opinion
came from a patent attorney, whether the opinion was detailed
or merely conclusory, and whether material information was
withheld from the attorney.[260] A competent opinion may not be
probative on the issue of willfulness if the infringer subsequently
made significant design changes[261] or did not rely on counsel's
advice.[262]

When an accused infringer relies on the advice of counsel
as a defense to a charge of willful infringement, the infringer
waives attorney-client privilege and work product immunity.[263]
The waiver applies to privileged communications with opinion
counsel, not trial counsel. Absent exceptional circumstances,
trial counsel's work product is not subject to the waiver.[264]

In addition to an opinion of counsel, other factors that have
been considered when determining the issue of willful infringement include evidence of outrageous conduct in response to

---

[259] *Id.* at 1390, 219 USPQ 569. Another opinion in that case was held inadequate because it
contained "only bald, conclusory and unsupported remarks regarding validity and infringement." *Id.* at 1385, 219 USPQ 569.

[260] *See, e.g., SRI Int'l,* 127 F.3d at 1465–67, 44 USPQ2d 1422; Read Corp. v. Portec Inc., 970
F.2d 816, 828–29, 23 USPQ2d 1426 (Fed. Cir. 1992); Ortho Pharm. Corp. v. Smith, 959 F.2d
936, 944–45, 22 USPQ2d 1119 (Fed. Cir. 1992); Minnesota Mining & Mfg. Co. v. Johnson &
Johnson Orthopaedics, 976 F.2d 1559, 1580–81, 24 USPQ2d 1321 (Fed. Cir. 1992).

[261] Critikon Inc. v. Becton Dickinson Vascular Access Inc., 120 F.3d 1253, 1259, 43 USPQ2d
1666 (Fed. Cir. 1997), *cert. denied,* 523 U.S. 1071 (1998).

[262] *See, e.g., In re* Hayes Microcomputer Prods. Patent Litig., 982 F.2d 1527, 1543–44, 25
USPQ2d 1241 (Fed. Cir. 1992); Radio Steel & Mfg. Co. v. MTD Prods., 788 F.2d 1554, 1559, 229
USPQ 431 (Fed. Cir. 1986); Central Soya Co. v. George A. Hormel & Co., 723 F.2d 1573, 1577,
220 USPQ 490 (Fed. Cir. 1983).

[263] *In re* Seagate Tech., LLC, 497 F.3d 1360, 1372–75, 83 USPQ2d 1865 (Fed. Cir. 2007).

[264] *Id.* at 1374–75, 83 USPQ2d 1865.

the patent owner's charges of infringement, evidence of copying versus attempts to design around the patent, and evidence of frivolous litigation defenses versus substantial challenges to the patent.[265]

An infringer's bad faith that is unrelated to the duty to avoid infringing another's patent rights is not relevant to determining if willful infringement has occurred. Thus, for example, misconduct during litigation is not relevant to determining whether the infringement was willful. Such misconduct, however, may be a factor in deciding how much to increase damages if willful infringement is found, and may be the basis for other awards such as attorney fees.[266]

B. Increasing Damages

A finding of willful infringement does not mandate increasing damages. The paramount factor in granting increased damages and the amount of the increase is the egregiousness of the infringer's conduct based on all the facts and circumstances.[267] Factors that have been considered include: whether the infringer deliberately copied; whether the infringer with knowledge of the patent formed a good faith belief that the patent was invalid, not infringed, or unenforceable; the infringer's behavior as a party to the litigation; the infringer's size and financial condition; the closeness of the case; the duration of the infringer's misconduct; whether the infringer took any remedial action; the infringer's motivation for harm; and whether the infringer attempted to conceal its misconduct. These are sometimes referred to as the *Read* factors.[268]

The decision whether to enhance damages is based on the totality of the circumstances.[269] When making the discretionary decisions whether to increase damages and by how much, within

---

[265] *See, e.g., SRI Int'l*, 127 F.3d at 1468, 44 USPQ2d 1422 ("delays, silences, misinformation, non-responses, and various other means of 'putting SRI off as long as possible' ").

[266] Jurgens v. CBK, Ltd., 80 F.3d 1566, 1570–71, 38 USPQ2d 1397 (Fed. Cir. 1996); i4i Ltd. P'ship v. Microsoft Corp., 598 F.3d 831, 859, 93 USPQ2d 1943 (Fed. Cir. 2010).

[267] Read Corp. v. Portec Inc., 970 F.2d 816, 826, 23 USPQ2d 1426 (Fed. Cir. 1992).

[268] *See, e.g.,* Spectralytics, Inc. v. Cordis Corp., 99 USPQ2d 1021, 1022 (Fed. Cir. 2011).

[269] *Read Corp.,* 970 F.2d at 826, 23 USPQ2d 1426.

the normal constraints of a jury trial, a judge may consider evidence that was not available to the jury.[270]

V. ATTORNEY FEES

The traditional American rule requires that each party to a lawsuit bear its own litigation expenses, including attorney fees.[271] In 1946, the patent statute was amended to provide one of the statutory exceptions to this general rule. This amendment was designed to "discourage infringement of a patent by anyone thinking that all he would be required to pay if he loses the suit would be a royalty."[272] However, the Senate Committee on Patents said that "[i]t is not contemplated that the recovery of attorney's fees will become an ordinary thing in the patent suits."[273] The statutory provision for attorney fees was revised in 1952 by adding the words "in exceptional cases." Codified at Section 285, this amendment was seen "as expressing the intention of the present statute as shown by its legislative history and as interpreted by the courts."[274] Attorney fees are compensatory, not punitive.[275] When an action has both patent and nonpatent claims, fees can only be awarded under Section 285 for litigating the patent claims.[276] Expert witness fees cannot be awarded under Section 285.[277]

---

[270]Advanced Cardiovascular Sys. v. Medtronic, Inc., 265 F.3d 1294, 1310, 60 USPQ2d 1161 (Fed. Cir. 2001).

[271]Alyeska Pipeline Co. v. Wilderness Soc'y, 421 U.S. 240, 247 (1975).

[272]35 U.S.C.A. §70 (1946); S. Rep. No. 1503, 79th Cong., 2d Sess. 1, 2, *reprinted in* 1946 U.S.C.C.A.N. 1386, 1387.

[273]*Id.* 35 U.S.C.A. §70 (1946)

[274]S. Rep. No. 1979, 82d Cong., 2d Sess., *reprinted in* 1952 U.S.C.C.A.N. 2394, 2423.

[275]Knorr-Bremse Systeme Fuer Nutzfahrzeuge GmbH, 383 F.3d 1337, 1347, 72 USPQ2d 1560 (Fed. Cir. 2004). Attorney fees can be awarded even if there were no actual damages. *Id.*

[276]Gjerlov v. Schuyler Labs. Inc., 131 F.3d 1016, 1025, 44 USPQ2d 1881 (Fed. Cir. 1997). Breach of a patent license agreement might, or might not, be so intertwined with patent infringement issues that Section 285 would apply. *Id. But see* Interspiro USA Inc. v. Figgie Int'l Inc., 18 F.3d 927, 933, 30 USPQ2d 1070 (Fed. Cir. 1994).

[277]Amsted Indus. v. Buckeye Steel Castings, 23 F.3d 374, 30 USPQ2d 1470 (Fed. Cir. 1994). *See generally* Daniel W. McDonald & Matthew A. Doscotch, *Why Aren't Expert Fees Recoverable in Exceptional Patent Cases?* 84 J. PAT. & TRADEMARK OFF. SOC'Y 255 (2002). A party may waive the right to object to an award of expert witness fees by failing to raise the objection. *See, e.g.,* Evident Corp. v. Church & Dwight Co., Inc., 399 F.3d 1310, 1315 n.2, 73 USPQ2d 1910 (Fed. Cir. 2005).

There are three requirements for an award of fees under Section 285: (1) the case must be exceptional, (2) the fees must be reasonable, and (3) the fees may be awarded only to the prevailing party.[278] The issue is committed to the discretion of the trial court.[279]

Exceptional case. The standard for finding a case "exceptional" is set forth in *Brooks Furniture Manufacturing, Inc. v. Dutailier International, Inc.*:

> A case may be deemed exceptional when there has been some material inappropriate conduct related to the matter in litigation, such as willful infringement, fraud or inequitable conduct in procuring the patent, misconduct during litigation, vexatious or unjustified litigation, conduct that violates Fed. R. Civ. P. 11, or like infractions. Absent misconduct in conduct of the litigation or in securing the patent, sanctions may be imposed against the patentee only if both (1) the litigation is brought in subjective bad faith, and (2) the litigation is objectively baseless.[280]

The prevailing party must establish the exceptional nature of the case by clear and convincing evidence. Whether a case is exceptional is a question of fact, reviewable for clear error.[281]

The standard for a finding that litigation was objectively baseless is the same standard required for a finding of willfulness under *Seagate*:

> [P]roof of willful infringement permitting enhanced damages requires at least a showing of *objective recklessness*. . . . Accordingly,

---

[278] Machinery Corp. of Am. v. Gullfiber AB, 774 F.2d 467, 470–72, 227 USPQ 368 (Fed. Cir. 1985). Regarding the relationship between awarding increased damages and awarding attorney fees, see *Jurgens v. CBK, Ltd.*, 80 F.3d 1566, 1573 n.4, 38 USPQ2d 1397 (Fed. Cir. 1996). Attorney fees also can be awarded pursuant to an agreement of the parties. *See, e.g.*, Embrex v. Serv. Eng'g Corp., 216 F.3d 1343, 1351, 55 USPQ2d 1161 (Fed. Cir. 2000).

[279] *Machinery Corp. of Am.*, 774 F.2d at 470–72, 227 USPQ 368 (which list discretion as one of four requirements); iLOR, LLC v. Google, Inc., 631 F.3d 1372, 1376, 97 USPQ2d 1597 (Fed. Cir. 2011); *see also* Medtronic Navigation, Inc. v. BrainLAB Medizinsiche Computersysteme GmbH, 603 F.3d 943, 953, 95 USPQ2d 1065 (Fed. Cir. 2010) (on appeal, Federal Circuit will examine record with care because of the impact of sanctions on the parties and their counsel).

[280] 393 F.3d 1378, 1381, 73 USPQ2d 1457 (Fed. Cir. 2005) (internal citations omitted); *iLOR, LLC*, 631 F.3d at 1376–77, 97 USPQ2d 1597.

[281] *Machinery Corp. of Am.*, 774 F.2d at 470–72, 227 USPQ 368; Superior Fireplace Co. v. Majestic Prods. Co., 270 F.3d 1358, 1376, 60 USPQ2d 1668 (Fed. Cir. 2001); *iLOR, LLC*, 631 F.3d at 1376, 97 USPQ2d 1597.

to establish willful infringement, a patentee must show by clear and convincing evidence that the infringer acted despite an *objectively high likelihood that its actions constituted infringement of a valid patent.* . . . . *The state of mind of the accused infringer is not relevant to this objective inquiry.* If this *threshold* objective standard is satisfied, the patentee *must also* demonstrate that this objectively defined risk (determined by the record developed in the infringement proceeding) was either known or so obvious that it should have been known to the accused infringer.[282]

With respect to a claim for attorney fees by an accused infringer from an unsuccessful patent owner, "[t]o be objectively baseless, the infringement allegations must be such that 'no reasonable litigant could reasonably expect success on the merits.' "[283]

Litigation misconduct may make a case exceptional, whether or not the underlying suit was objectively baseless. Merely failing to prevail in the litigation, or taking positions that were ultimately not adopted by the court or jury, does not constitute litigation misconduct. Rather a finding of litigation misconduct requires "unethical or unprofessional conduct by a party or his attorneys during the course of adjudicative proceedings"[284]

Under the Leahy-Smith America Invents Act of 2011, if an infringer asserts the defense of prior commercial use and "subsequently fails to establish a reasonable basis for asserting the defense," the trial court "shall find the case exceptional for the purpose of awarding attorney fees" under Section 285.[285]

---

[282] *iLOR, LLC*, 631 F.3d at 1377, 97 USPQ2d 1597 (quoting *In re* Seagate Tech., LLC, 497 F.3d 1360 (Fed. Cir. 2007)) (emphasis in original).

[283] Dominant Semiconductors Sdn. Bhd. v. OSRAM GmbH, 524 F.3d 1254, 1260, 86 USPQ2d 1480 (Fed. Cir. 2008) (citation omitted); *iLOR, LLC*, 631 F.3d at 1376, 97 USPQ2d 1597.

[284] Old Reliable Wholesale, Inc. v. Cornell Corp., 635 F.3d 539, 549–50, 97 USPQ2d 1993 (Fed. Cir. 2011); McNeil-PPC, Inc. v. L. Perrigo Co., 337 F.3d 1362, 1371–73, 67 USPQ2d 1649 (Fed. Cir. 2003), *cert. denied*, 540 U.S. 1107 (2004) (not litigation misconduct to assert patent later found invalid). Examples of conduct found to constitute litigation misconduct include making " 'multiple, repeated misrepresentations . . . to the Court,' " ICU Med., Inc. v. Alaris Med. Sys., Inc., 558 F.3d 1368, 1380, 90 USPQ2d 1072 (Fed. Cir. 2009); *see also* Mathis v. Spears, 857 F.2d 749, 8 USPQ2d 1029 (Fed. Cir. 1988) (vexatious litigation tactics combined with the assertion of a patent obtained by "blatantly misleading" the PTO); Rambus Inc. v. Infineon Techs. AG, 318 F.3d 1081, 1106, 65 USPQ2d 1705 (Fed. Cir.), *cert. denied*, 540 U.S. 874 (2003); Brasseler U.S.A. I, L.P. v. Stryker Sales Corp., 267 F.3d 1370, 1380, 60 USPQ2d 1482 (Fed. Cir. 2001).

[285] Leahy-Smith America Invents Act, Pub. L. 112-29, H.R. 1249 (2011), sec. 5, amending 35 U.S.C. §273 by the addition of a new subsection (f). This amendment applies only to patents issued after the enactment of the statute, i.e., after September 16, 2011.

Determination of a reasonable fee. Calculation of the amount of a reasonable fee starts with "the number of hours reasonably expended on the litigation multiplied by a reasonable hourly rate."[286] Generally, a reasonable rate corresponds to the prevailing rates in the relevant community. If the prevailing party had a good reason for using nonlocal counsel, however, then the comparison may be to prevailing rates in the attorney's business location.[287] To assess the number of hours reasonably expended, courts look to the number of attorneys involved and their cumulative hours.[288]

Once this lodestar amount is determined, the courts consider other factors that may adjust the fee upward or downward, including the results obtained; the attorney's normal billing rate; difficulty and novelty of the case; time and labor involved; loss of other business; fees customarily charged for similar services; whether it is a fixed or contingent fee; reputation, experience, and ability of counsel; fees paid to opposing counsel; and expenses and advancements.[289] In appropriate cases, the award may include attorney fees incurred by a nonparty that assisted in the case and assumed some of the legal expenses.[290]

When appropriate, there can be joint and several liability for the fees.[291]

Prevailing party. A patent owner who recovers damages or obtains an injunction has prevailed.[292] An alleged infringer

---

[286]Hensley v. Eckerhart, 461 U.S. 424, 433 (1983). When plaintiff's lawsuit was frivolous, the award to defendant may include attorney fees incurred in preparing defenses that the court never needed to resolve. *Brasseler U.S.A. I, L.P.*, 267 F.3d at 1386, 60 USPQ2d 1482.

[287]Howes v. Medical Components Inc., 761 F. Supp. 1193, 1195–97, 17 USPQ2d 1591 (E.D. Pa. 1990) (attorneys fees for a lawsuit in Philadelphia were awarded based on reasonable rates in New York City, where the prevailing party's trial counsel practiced).

[288] *See, e.g., id.* at 1197–99, 17 USPQ2d 1591; Stryker Corp. v. Intermedics Orthopedics Inc., 898 F. Supp. 116 (E.D.N.Y. 1995).

[289] *Hensley,* 461 U.S. at 434. Northcross v. Board of Educ. of Memphis City Sch., 611 F.2d 624, 642 (6th Cir. 1979), *cert. denied,* 447 U.S. 911 (1980); Swann v. Charlotte-Mecklenburg Bd. of Educ., 66 F.R.D. 483 (W.D.N.Y. 1975). *See generally* Junker v. Eddings, 396 F.3d 1359, 1365–66, 73 USPQ2d 1850 (Fed. Cir.), *cert. denied,* 545 U.S. 1128 (2005).

[290]Automated Bus. Cos. v. NEC Am., 202 F.3d 1353, 1355–56, 53 USPQ2d 1601 (Fed. Cir. 2000).

[291]Evident Corp. v. Church & Dwight Co., 399 F.3d 1310, 1315–17, 73 USPQ2d 1910 (Fed. Cir. 2005).

[292]Gentry Gallery Inc. v. Berkline Corp., 134 F.3d 1473, 1480, 45 USPQ2d 1498 (Fed. Cir. 1998).

has prevailed if the patent in suit is adjudged invalid or not infringed.[293] When neither party clearly has prevailed, district courts have discretion to allow in part or to deny attorney fees.[294]

VI. PREJUDGMENT AND POST-JUDGMENT INTEREST

In *General Motors Corp. v. Devex Corp.*, the Supreme Court held prejudgment interest ordinarily should be awarded where necessary to afford a patentee full compensation for infringement, "absent some justification for withholding such an award."[295] The Court suggested that it might be appropriate to limit prejudgment interest when the patent owner had been responsible for undue delay in prosecuting the lawsuit.[296] Nonetheless, the Court upheld the district court's ruling that a patentee had not caused undue delay even though the case had been litigated for over 25 years.

Since *General Motors,* only one decision denying prejudgment interest based on undue delay has been upheld by the Federal Circuit, in *Crystal Semiconductor Corp. v. TriTech Microelectronics Int'l.* To support the denial of prejudgment interest, the undue delay must prejudice the alleged infringer.[297] Although *General Motors* leaves open the possibility that other circumstances may allow prejudgment interest to be denied, the Federal Circuit has

---

[293] Manildra Milling Corp. v. Ogilvie Mills Inc., 76 F.3d 1178, 1182–83, 37 USPQ2d 1707 (Fed. Cir. 1996); *see also* Inland Steel Co. v. LTV Steel Co., 364 F.3d 1318, 70 USPQ2d 1472 (Fed. Cir. 2004) (defendant prevailed when stayed case was dismissed after patent determined invalid in a PTO reexamination).

[294] *See, e.g.,* Slimfold Mfg. Co. Inc. v. Kinkead Indus. Inc., 932 F.2d 1453, 1459, 18 USPQ2d 1842 (Fed. Cir. 1991); Beckman Instruments Inc. v. LKB Produkter AB, 892 F.2d 1547, 1553–54, 13 USPQ2d 1301 (Fed. Cir. 1989).

[295] 461 U.S. 648, 656–67, 217 USPQ 1185 (1983); Sensonics Inc. v. Aerosonic Corp., 81 F.3d 1566, 1574, 38 USPQ2d 1551 (Fed. Cir. 1996) ("[P]rejudgment interest is the rule, not the exception").

[296] *General Motors Corp.,* 461 U.S. at 656–57, 217 USPQ 1185.

[297] Crystal Semiconductor Corp. v. TriTech Microelectronics Int'l, 246 F.3d 1336, 1361–62, 57 USPQ2d 1953 (Fed. Cir. 2001); *see also* Lummus Indus. Inc. v. D.M. & E. Corp., 862 F.2d 267, 275, 8 USPQ2d 1983 (Fed. Cir. 1988) (requirement of prejudicial delay).

approved of only one such circumstance.[298] Denying prejudgment interest because of calculation difficulties is error.[299]

Calculating prejudgment interest involves three elements: (1) the principal amount for which interest is awarded, (2) the interest rate, and (3) the method used to accrue interest (i.e., compound or simple interest).[300]

The principal amount must consist only of compensatory damages (i.e., damages based on lost profits or reasonable royalty) and not enhanced damages.[301] Further, prejudgment interest may be awarded only for damages already suffered.[302] The district court has the power to award prejudgment interest on attorney fees, if awarded.[303]

District courts have broad discretion in deciding what interest rate to apply.[304] The rate may be higher than the generally established commercial rates (e.g., T-bill or prime)[305] if

---

[298] The Federal Circuit held that it was not error to deny prejudgment interest during a four-year stay that the patent owner had sought. Uniroyal Inc. v. Rudkin-Wiley Corp., 939 F.2d 1540, 1546, 19 USPQ2d 1432 (Fed. Cir. 1991). *But compare* Allen Archery, Inc. v. Browning Mfg. Co., 898 F.2d 787, 791–92, 14 USPQ2d 1156 (Fed. Cir. 1990) (abuse of discretion to deny prejudgment interest during a stay that the patent owner initially opposed). As to other circumstances proposed by infringers, see *Radio Steel & Mfg. Co.* v. *MTD Prods.*, 788 F.2d 1554, 1557, 229 USPQ 431 (Fed. Cir. 1986); *T. D. Williamson Inc. v. Laymon*, 723 F. Supp. 587, 611, 13 USPQ2d 1417 (N.D. Okla. 1989), *aff'd without op.*, 923 F.2d 871, 18 USPQ2d 1575 (Fed. Cir. 1990), *cert. dismissed*, 500 U.S. 901 (1991).

[299] *Sensonics Inc.*, 81 F.3d at 1574, 38 USPQ2d 1551.

[300] *See generally* Michael S. Knoll, *A Primer on Prejudgment Interest*, 75 TEX. L. REV. 293 (1996).

[301] Gyromat Corp. v. Champion Spark Plug Co., 735 F.2d 549, 554–55, 222 USPQ 4 (Fed. Cir. 1984); Lam Inc. v. Johns-Manville Corp., 718 F.2d 1056, 1066, 219 USPQ 670 (Fed. Cir. 1983).

[302] Oiness v. Walgreen Co., 88 F.3d 1025, 1033, 39 USPQ2d 1304 (Fed. Cir. 1996), *cert. denied*, 519 U.S. 1112 (1997).

[303] Mathis v. Spears, 857 F.2d 749, 760–61, 8 USPQ2d 1029 (Fed. Cir. 1988). *See, e.g.*, Water Techs. Corp. v. Calco, Ltd., 714 F. Supp. 899, 909, 11 USPQ2d 1410 (N.D. Ill. 1989); Gardiner v. Gendel, 727 F. Supp. 799, 806, 14 USPQ2d 2043 (E.D.N.Y. 1989), *aff'd without op.*, 976 F.2d 746 (Fed. Cir. 1992).

[304] Laitram Corp. v. NEC Corp., 115 F.3d 947, 955, 42 USPQ2d 1897 (Fed. Cir. 1997); *Lam Inc.*, 718 F.2d at 1066, 219 USPQ 670.

[305] Decisions applying the T-bill rate include *Laitram Corp.*, 115 F.3d at 955, 42 USPQ2d 1897; *Fonar Corp. v. General Elec. Co.*, 902 F. Supp. 330, 354, 41 USPQ2d 1088 (E.D.N.Y. 1995), *aff'd in part and rev'd in part*, 107 F.3d 1543, 41 USPQ2d 1801 (Fed. Cir.), *cert. denied, motion granted*, 522 U.S. 908 (1997); *Polaroid Corp. v. Eastman Kodak Co.*, 16 USPQ2d 1481, 1540–41 (D. Mass. 1990); and *W. L. Gore & Assocs. v. Garlock Inc.*, 10 USPQ2d 1628, 1631 n.10 (N.D. Ohio 1989). Decisions applying the prime rate include *Maxwell v. J. Baker Inc.*, 879 F. Supp. 1007, 1009 (D. Minn. 1995); *Lemelson v. General Mills*, 968 F.2d 1202, 1206, 23 USPQ2d 1284 (Fed. Cir. 1992), *cert. denied*, 506 U.S. 1053 (1993); and *ALM Surgical Equip. Inc. v. Kirschner Med. Corp.*, 15 USPQ2d 1241, 1257 (D.S.C. 1990).

the patent owner affirmatively demonstrates that a higher rate should apply.[306] State statutory rates also have been applied.[307]

Courts have broad discretion in deciding whether to award simple or compound interest.[308] Courts also have discretion to compound interest on a pre- or post-tax basis.[309]

Post-judgment interest is governed by statute. The Federal Circuit defers to the regional circuits for interpretation of the post-judgment interest statute.[310]

---

[306] *Lam Inc.*, 718 F.2d at 1066, 219 USPQ 670. This demonstration often involves proving the rate that the patent owner received on contemporaneous investments. *See, e.g.,* Micro Motion Inc. v. Exac Corp., 761 F. Supp. 1420, 1436, 19 USPQ2d 1001 (N.D. Cal. 1991); Beckman Instruments Inc. v. LKB Produkter AB, 703 F. Supp. 408, 410, 8 USPQ2d 1605 (D. Md. 1988), *aff'd in part, vacated in part, and remanded,* 892 F.2d 1547, 13 USPQ2d 1301 (Fed. Cir. 1989). This demonstration also may involve proving the rate that the patent owner paid to borrow money during the infringing period. *See, e.g.,* Mobil Oil Corp. v. Amoco Chems. Corp., 915 F. Supp. 1333, 1371–72 (D. Del. 1994); Smith Corona Corp. v. Pelikan Inc., 784 F. Supp. 452, 484–85 (M.D. Tenn. 1992), *aff'd without op.,* 1 F.3d 1252 (Fed. Cir. 1993). The rate the infringer paid to borrow money during the period of infringement also may be relevant. *See generally In re* Mahurkar Double Lumen Hemodialysis Patent Litig., 831 F. Supp. 1354, 1394–95 (N.D. Ill. 1993), *aff'd,* 71 F.3d 1573, 37 USPQ2d 1138 (Fed. Cir. 1995).

[307] *See, e.g.,* Brooktree Corp. v. Advanced Micro Devices Inc., 757 F. Supp. 1101, 1102, 18 USPQ2d 1703 (S.D. Cal. 1990); Ortloff Corp. v. Gulsby Eng'g Inc., 706 F. Supp. 1295, 1309, 8 USPQ2d 1873 (S.D. Tex. 1988), *aff'd without op.,* 884 F.2d 1399, 13 USPQ2d 1335 (Fed. Cir. 1989). For examples of other rates applied, see 7 DONALD S. CHISUM, CHISUM ON PATENTS §20.03[4] [a] [v] (2011).

[308] Rite-Hite Corp. v. Kelley Co., 56 F.3d 1538, 1555, 35 USPQ2d 1065 (Fed. Cir. 1987), *cert. denied,* 516 U.S. 867 (1995). Gyromat Corp. v. Champion Spark Plug Co., 735 F.2d 549, 557, 222 USPQ 4 (Fed. Cir. 1984). Decisions awarding compound interest include *Polaroid Corp v. Eastman Kodak Co.,* 16 USPQ2d 1481, 1540–41 (D. Mass 1985), *correction for clerical errors,* 17 USPQ2d 1711 (D. Mass. 1990) and *Johns-Manville Corp. v. Guardian Indus. Corp.,* 718 F. Supp. 1310, 1317, 13 USPQ2d 1684 (E.D. Mich. 1989), *aff'd without op.,* 925 F.2d 1480 (Fed. Cir. 1991). Decisions awarding simple interest include *In re Hayes Microcomputer Prods. Patent Litig.,* 766 F. Supp. 818, 824, 20 USPQ2d 1836 (N.D. Cal. 1991), *aff'd,* 982 F.2d 1527, 25 USPQ2d 1241 (Fed. Cir. 1992) and *Bandag Inc. v. Al Bolser Tire Stores Inc.,* 228 USPQ 211, 212 (W.D. Wash. 1985), *aff'd without op.,* 809 F.2d 788 (Fed. Cir. 1986).

[309] *See. e.g.,* Electro Scientific Indus., Inc. v. Gen. Scanning Inc., 247 F.3d 1341, 1354, 58 USPQ2d 1498 (Fed. Cir. 2001) (post-tax); *Polaroid Corp.,* 16 USPQ2d at 1540–41 (pre-tax). For an economist's explanation of the difference between the two methods, *see* Franklin M. Fisher & R. Craig Romaine, *Janis Joplin's Yearbook and the Theory of Damages,* 5 J. ACCT., AUDITING & FIN. 145 (1990).

[310] 28 U.S.C. §1961(a); Taltech Ltd. v. Esquel Enters. Ltd., 604 F.3d 1324, 1634–35, 95 USPQ2d 1257 (Fed. Cir. 2010).

Chapter 9

CASE MANAGEMENT AND JURY TRIALS

I. CASE MANAGEMENT

Although the Federal Circuit was charged with bringing uniformity to substantive patent law, the court has deferred to the law of the regional circuits with respect to issues of procedure, "so long as they do not: (1) pertain to patent law; (2) bear an essential relationship to matters committed to our exclusive control by statute; or (3) clearly implicate the jurisprudential responsibilities of this court in a field within its exclusive jurisdiction."[1]

The best example of a procedural matter that pertains to patent law is the construction of patent claims, discussed in Chapter 5. As a result of the Federal Circuit and Supreme Court decisions in *Markman,* district courts are now required to consider how and when they will address the issue of claim construction before an action is submitted to the jury.[2] Generally, however, within the framework provided by the patent statute, the statutes governing judicial procedure, the Federal Rules of Civil Procedure and Federal Rules of Evidence, and local court rules, district courts have substantial latitude in case management of patent infringement actions.

Much has been written on the subject, with substantial input from the bench, the bar, and academics. For example, publications of the Federal Judicial Center, the publicly funded research arm of the federal judiciary, include a chapter on intellectual property litigation in the *Manual for Complex Litigation (Fourth)* and a 2011 pocket guide for federal judges on compensatory damages in patent infringement cases. In 2009, the Center published a 650-page judicial guide to patent case management.[3] Helpful volumes are also available from commercial publishers.[4]

---

[1]Bose Corp. v. JBL, Inc., 274 F.3d 1354, 1360, 61 USPQ2d 1216 (Fed. Cir. 2001), *cert. denied,* 537 U.S. 880 (2002) (citations omitted); *see also* Midwest Indus., Inc. v. Karavan Trailers, Inc., 175 F.3d 1356, 1359–61, 50 USPQ2d 1672 (Fed. Cir. 1999); Panduit Corp. v. All States Plastic Mfg. Co., 744 F.2d 1564, 1572–76, 223 USPQ 465, 471 (Fed. Cir. 1984).

[2]See Chapter 5, §III.

[3]The Federal Judicial Center publications are available for free download from www.fjc.gov, as well as for purchase in hard copy. *See* FEDERAL JUDICIAL CENTER, MANUAL FOR COMPLEX LITIGATION 4TH (2004); WILLIAM S. ROOKLEDGE ET AL., COMPENSATORY DAMAGES ISSUES IN PATENT INFRINGEMENT CASES: A POCKET GUIDE FOR FEDERAL DISTRICT COURT JUDGES (2011); PETER S. MENELL ET AL., PATENT CASE MANAGEMENT JUDICIAL GUIDE (2009).

[4] *See, e.g.,* COMPLEX LITIGATION COMMITTEE OF THE AMERICAN COLLEGE OF TRIAL LAWYERS, ANATOMY OF A PATENT CASE (BNA 2009).

Nevertheless, at the end of the day, case management remains largely an art, not a science. For example, patent infringement actions are tried in the Northern District of California, where, by local rule, contentions discovery and claim construction occur early in the action.[5] Such actions are also tried in the Southern District of New York, where, by local rule, contentions discovery does not happen until the end of fact discovery and, in the absence of a local rule, the timing of claim construction is left to the discretion of individual judges.[6] The recommendations of commentators and the case management preferences of other courts may be instructive or helpful, but they are not dispositive.

To add briefly to this discussion, in the authors' experience, the following procedural issues recur in most patent infringement actions: (1) education of the court about the technology underlying the patents in suit; (2) identification of contentions to determine and possibly narrow what is truly in dispute; (3) determination of whether all issues should be tried together or whether bifurcation, separate trials, or other procedures are desirable; and (4) pretrial motions to limit issues and evidence at trial.

A. Judicial Education About the Underlying Technology

The challenge of coming to grips with the technology underlying the patents in suit is not new. A generation ago, Simon H. Rifkind, a retired district court judge in private practice, wrote that "patent litigation has a poor reputation. . . . [M]any judges, and most lawyers, harbor the belief that patent litigation demands of the participants a very wide acquaintance with esoteric bodies of special knowledge and scientific training." And, although Judge Rifkind ultimately disagreed with that belief, he conceded that "some effort is frequently necessary to acquire the rudiments of the vocabulary used in a particular science."[7]

As the patent law has developed, the challenge of learning about the technology at issue is compounded by legal standards that require the court and jury to reason with the technological

---

[5] N.D. Cal. Patent Local Rules 3 and 4 (2010).
[6] S.D. N.Y. Local Civil Rule 33.3(c).
[7] Simon H. Rifkind, *The Romance Discoverable in Patent Cases,* 16 F.R.D. 253, 253–54 (1954).

facts of the case from the standpoint of a person having ordinary skill in the art to which the patent pertains.[8]

The procedural tools available to educate the court are discussed in Chapter 5, §III.A, in connection with claim construction, because that is where the issue often arises for the first time. However, courts have included separate provisions for an in-court technology tutorial as part of a standard case management order. Other courts have asked the parties to prepare a joint video submission that the court can refer to in chambers.[9] There is also literature directed to helping courts understand technical evidence.[10]

With respect to case management in anticipation of trial, the parties generally introduce evidence to educate the jury about the underlying science as part of their cases in chief, e.g., through the testimony of the inventor of the patent in suit or the testimony of a technical expert. Where pretrial proceedings raise significant concerns about juror comprehension, the Federal Rules include the options of having the action tried in the first instance by a special master, or the appointment of a court-appointed technical expert.[11]

B. Contentions Discovery

Among judicial districts that have adopted uniform local rules for patent cases, the trend is to require the parties to

---

[8] *See, e.g.,* KSR Int'l Co. v. Teleflex Inc., 550 U.S. 398, 406, 417–418, 82 USPQ2d 1385 (2007) (nonobviousness under 35 U.S.C. §103); Sanofi-Synthelabo v. Apotex, Inc., 550 F.3d 1075, 1082, 89 USPQ2d 1370 (Fed. Cir. 2008), *cert. denied,* 130 S. Ct. 493 (2009) (anticipation under 35 U.S.C. §102); Pandrol USA, LP v. Airboss Ry. Prods., 424 F.3d 1161, 1165, 76 USPQ2d 1524 (Fed. Cir. 2005) (written description under 35 U.S.C. §112); Transocean Offshore Deepwater Drilling, Inc. v. Maersk Contractors USA, Inc., 617 F.3d 1296, 1305–07, 96 USPQ2d 1104 (Fed. Cir. 2010) (enablement under 35 U.S.C. §112); Green Edge Enters., LLC v. Rubber Mulch etc., LLC, 620 F.3d 1287, 1296–97, 96 USPQ2d 1425 (Fed. Cir. 2010) (best mode under 35 U.S.C. §112); Enzo Biochem, Inc. v. Applera Corp., 599 F.3d 1325, 1332–33, 94 USPQ2d 1321 (Fed. Cir. 2010), *cert. denied,* 180 L. Ed. 2d 844 (2011) (indefiniteness under 35 U.S.C. §112).

[9] For an example of such an order from the District of Delaware, see http://www.ded. uscourts.gov/LPSmain.htm > "Forms" > "Form Scheduling Order—Patent," ¶9.

[10] *See, e.g.,* FEDERAL JUDICIAL CENTER, REFERENCE MANUAL ON SCIENTIFIC EVIDENCE, THIRD EDITION (2011), available on www.fjc.gov.

[11] *See, e.g.,* Festo Corp. v. Shoketsu Kinzoku Kogyo Kabushiki Co., 72 F.3d 857, 864–66, 37 USPQ2d 1161 (Fed. Cir. 1995) (special master); Monolithic Power Sys., Inc. v. O2 Micro Int'l Ltd., 558 F.3d 1341, 1348, 90 USPQ2d 1001 (Fed. Cir. 2009) (court-appointed expert).

serve at least preliminary contentions concerning the bases for the plaintiff's allegations of infringement and the defendant's allegations of invalidity at the beginning of the action.[12]

In response to the Federal Circuit's expressed interest in having district courts diligently exercise a gatekeeping function with respect to patent damages claims, at least one court has required the parties to provide damages discovery and an expert report "earlier than normal," to allow the court to consider the legal sufficiency of the parties' contentions.[13]

C. Bifurcation, Separate Trials, and Related Procedures

Commentators, including experienced trial judges, have considered bifurcation an option where the complexity of the issues warrants the procedure.[14] There are many published decisions dealing with bifurcating patent jury trials, including decisions that consider whether to separate damages issues from liability issues,[15] and how to handle the issues of willfulness.[16]

---

[12] As of July 2011, local patent rules have been adopted in the following judicial districts: N.D. Cal., S.D. Cal., N.D. Ga., D. Idaho, N.D. Ill., S.D. Ind., D. Mass., D. Minn., E.D. Mo., E.D.N.C., W.D.N.C., D.N.J., N.D. Ohio., S.D. Ohio, W.D. Pa., E.D. Tex., N.D. Tex. (Dallas Div.), S.D. Tex, E.D. Wash., and W.D. Wash. For a survey of the similarities and differences among these local rules, see Grace Pak, *Balkanization of the Local Patent Rules and a Proposal to Balance Uniformity and Local Experimentation*, 2 AM. UNIV. INTELL. PROP. BRIEF 44 (Spring 2011), http://www.ipbrief.net/volume2/issue3/IPB_Pak.pdf.

[13] Oracle Am., Inc. v. Google, Inc., No. 3:10-cv-03561-WHA, 2011 WL 2976449 at *10, (N.D. Cal. July 22, 2011) (order granting in part motion to strike damage report).

[14] *See, e.g.*, William W. Schwarzer, *Reforming Jury Trials*, 132 F.R.D. 575, 594–95 (1991); Avern Cohn, *Thoughts on Jury Trial in a Patent Case*, 6 PROCEEDINGS OF THE INTELLECTUAL PROPERTY LAW SECTION OF THE STATE BAR OF MICHIGAN 4 (1994).

[15] Examples of decisions granting a motion to bifurcate include Dutch Branck of Streamserve Dev., AB v. Exstream Software, LLC, No. Civ. 08-343-SLR, 2009 WL 2705932 (D. Del. Aug. 26, 2009); Cherdak v. Stride Rite Corp., 396 F. Supp. 2d 602 (D. Md. 2005); Princeton Biochemicals Inc. v. Beckman Instruments Inc., 180 F.R.D. 254, 256–60, 45 USPQ2d 1757 (D.N.J. 1997). Examples of decisions denying a motion to bifurcate include Computer Assocs. Int'l Inc. v. Simple.com Inc., 247 F.R.D. 63, 67 (E.D.N.Y. 2007); Crown Packaging Tech., Inc. v. Rexam Beverage Can Co., 498 F. Supp. 2d 734, 737–38 (D. Del. 2007); Classen Immunotherapies, Inc. v. King Pharms., Inc., 403 F. Supp. 2d 451 (D. Md. 2005); THK Am. Inc. v. NSK Co., 151 F.R.D. 625, 29 USPQ2d 2020 (N.D. Ill. 1993); Output Tech. Corp. v. Dataproducts Corp., 22 USPQ2d 1072, 1073 (W.D. Wash. 1991).

[16] *See, e.g.*, Neorx Corp. v. Immunomedics Inc., 28 USPQ2d 1395, 1396 (D.N.J. 1993) (citing Quantum Corp. v. Tandon Corp., 940 F.2d 642, 643 (Fed. Cir. 1991)); *see also, e.g.*, F&G Scrolling Mouse, L.L.C. v. IBM Corp., 190 F.R.D. 385, 391–92 (M.D.N.C. 1985); Novopharm Ltd. v. Torpharm Inc., 181 F.R.D. 308, 311–12 (E.D.N.C. 1998); *Princeton Biochemicals Inc.*, 180 F.R.D. 254, 45 USPQ2d 1757, 1762–63; Laitram Corp. v. Hewlett-Packard Co., 791 F. Supp. 113, 116–18, 22 USPQ2d 1597 (E.D. La. 1992).

Another option for a court is to allow discovery to proceed on all issues, but then to bifurcate. In cases with multiple parties, it may be appropriate to try common issues—e.g., validity of the patent in suit—with all parties, while bifurcating issues of damages or infringement for subsequent and separate hearing.[17] A court may address concerns about overlapping evidence by conducting a multiple-phase trial with the same jury.[18]

In addition, for cases with issues that are tried only to the court, such as the defense of inequitable conduct, those issues are often the subject of a separate hearing, before, during or after the trial.

Bifurcation of claims in a patent infringement action is not barred by the Seventh Amendment. However, where an equitable claim shares common issues of fact with claims that are properly triable to a jury, such as claims based on state law for fraud and unjust enrichment, a bench trial of the equitable claim first is barred by the Seventh Amendment.[19] Antitrust counterclaims in patent infringement actions are often based on the contention that the patent owner has asserted in litigation a patent obtained by deliberate fraud on the United States Patent and Trademark Office (PTO) as part of an attempt to monopolize, or has asserted in litigation a patent known to be invalid or unenforceable, again as part of an attempt to monopolize.[20] In such cases, there may be an overlap between the facts relating to the antitrust claim, for which there is a right to a jury trial, and facts relating to the equi-

---

[17] Intel Corp. v. Commonwealth Scientific & Indus. Research Org., No. Civ. 6:06-cv-324, 2008 WL 5378037 (E.D. Tex. Dec. 23, 2008).

[18] See, e.g., Haney v. Timesavers Inc., 26 USPQ2d 1159, 1160 (D. Or. 1992) (one-week hiatus between phases); Armstrong Mfg. Co. v. Wright Mach. Tool Co. Inc., 22 USPQ2d 1960 (D. Or. 1992) (two-week hiatus between phases); Laitram Corp., 791 F. Supp. at 118, 22 USPQ2d 1597 (no hiatus).

[19] Shum v. Intel Corp., 499 F.3d 1272, 1279, 83 USPQ2d 1933 (Fed. Cir. 2007).

[20] See, e.g., In re Innotron Diagnostics, 800 F.2d 1077, 1084–86, 231 USPQ 178 (Fed. Cir. 1986) ("The district court noted cases reflecting the now standard practice of separating for trial patent issues and those raised in an antitrust counterclaim"); Walker Process Equip., Inc. v. Food Mach. & Chem. Corp., 382 U.S. 172 (1965) (fraud); Handgards, Inc. v. Ethicon, Inc., 601 F.2d 986 (9th Cir. 1979) (knowing assertion of an invalid patent); Beacon Theatres, Inc. v. Westover, 359 U.S. 500 (1959); Paragon Podiatry Lab. v. KLM Labs., 984 F.2d 1182, 25 USPQ 2d 1561 (Fed. Cir. 1993); Gardco Mfg. Inc. v. Herst Lighting Co., 820 F.2d 1209, 2 USPQ 2d 2015 (Fed. Cir. 1987).

table defense of patent unenforceability, for which there is no right to a jury trial.[21] District courts have divided on whether, in such cases, it better serves interests of efficiency and fairness to try the patent issues first, particularly where the plaintiff's claim is for equitable relief only, or to try all issues in a single trial.[22]

Although courts have substantial discretion with respect to the sequence of trial of separate issues, trying infringement first and then trying validity only if there is a finding of infringement, a proposal from the late 1980s,[23] appears untenable as a matter of law in light of the Supreme Court's 1993 ruling in *Cardinal Chemical Co. v. Morton International Inc.* Both issues must be dealt with because of the public interest in disposing of invalid patents.[24]

D. Pretrial Motions to Limit Issues or to Exclude Expert Testimony

Subject to the provisions of Rule 56 of the Federal Rules of Civil Procedure, and the controlling authorities interpreting that rule,[25] the substantive issues of patent validity, infringement,

---

[21] Beacon Theatres, Inc. v. Westover, 359 U.S. 500 (1959) (antitrust claim); American Calcar, Inc. v. American Honda Motor Co., 651 F.3d 1318, 1332–36 99 USPQ2d 1137 (Fed. Cir. 2011) (inequitable conduct claim); *see, e.g.,* Purdue Pharma L.P v. Endo Pharms., Inc., 00 Civ. 8029 (SHS) (S.D.N.Y. Dec. 10, 2002) (granting bifurcation); Celgene Corp. v. Barr Labs., Inc., No. 07-286(SDW), 2008 WL 2447354, at *2–3 (D.N.J. June 13, 2008) (denying bifurcation); and Climax Molybdenum Co. v. Molychem, LLC, 414 F. Supp. 2d 1007, 1014 (D. Colo. 2005) (denying bifurcation).

[22] *See, e.g.,* Purdue Pharma L.P v. Endo Pharms., Inc., 00 Civ. 8029 (SHS) (S.D.N.Y. Dec. 10, 2002) (granting bifurcation); Celgene Corp. v. Barr Labs., Inc., No. 07-286(SDW), 2008 WL 2447354, at *2–*3 (D.N.J. June 13, 2008) (denying bifurcation); and Climax Molybdenum Co. v. Molychem, LLC, 414 F. Supp. 2d 1007, 1014 (D. Colo. 2005) (denying bifurcation).

[23] Howard T. Markey, *On Simplifying Patent Trials,* 116 F.R.D. 369 (1987).

[24] 508 U.S. 83, 26 USPQ2d 1721 (1993). Although the better practice is for the district court to decide all litigated issues, if a patent is held not infringed and invalidity has been raised only as an affirmative defense, the district court has the discretion not to decide the invalidity issue. Hill-Rom Co. v. Kinetic Concepts Inc., 209 F.3d 1337, 1343–44, 54 USPQ2d 1437 (Fed. Cir. 2000); Multiform Desiccants Inc. v. Medzam, Ltd., 133 F.3d 1473, 1481, 45 USPQ2d 1429 (Fed. Cir. 1998).

[25] Anderson v. Liberty Lobby, Inc., 477 U.S. 242 (1986); Celotex Corp. v. Catrett, 477 U.S. 317 (1986).

and enforceability are all subject to disposition before trial on motion for full or partial summary judgment.[26]

With respect to motions in limine to exclude expert testimony, the admissibility of such testimony is governed by Federal Rules of Evidence, Rule 702, and the Supreme Court's *"Daubert* trilogy" of cases interpreting that rule. The Federal Circuit has stated:

> Under *Daubert v. Merrell Dow Pharmaceuticals, Inc.,* 509 U.S. 579, 597, 113 S. Ct. 2786, 125 L. Ed. 2d 469 (1993), and Rule 702, courts are charged with a "gatekeeping role," the objective of which is to ensure that expert testimony admitted into evidence is both reliable and relevant. *See also Kumho Tire Co. v. Carmichael,* 526 U.S. 137, 149, 119 S. Ct. 1167, 143 L. Ed. 2d 238 (1999) (holding that Rule 702 applies not only to "scientific" testimony, but to all expert testimony). Patent cases, like all other cases, are governed by Rule 702. There is, of course, no basis for carving out a special rule as to experts in patent cases.

The decision to admit expert testimony is committed to the discretion of the district court and is reviewed for abuse of discretion.[27]

The Federal Circuit has, however, addressed two issues that may be unique to patent cases. The first is the patent law expert. The second issue relates to expert methodology in calculating patent damages.

---

[26]Examples of decisions granting and denying such motions include KSR Int'l Co. v. Teleflex Inc., 550 U.S. 398, 82 USPQ2d 1385 (2007) (summary judgment of obviousness); Transocean Offshore Deepwater Drilling Inc. v. Maersk Contractors USA Inc., 617 F.3d 1296, 96 USPQ2d 1104 (Fed. Cir. 2010) (reversing summary judgment of obviousness); Billups-Rothenberg Inc. v. Associated Reg'l & Univ. Pathologists Inc., 642 F.3d 1301, 98 USPQ2d 1578 (Fed. Cir. 2011) (affirming summary judgment of anticipation); Crown Packaging Tech. Inc. v. Ball Metal Beverage Container Corp., 635 F.3d 1373, 98 USPQ2d 1244 (Fed. Cir. 2011) (reversing summary judgment of anticipation); Creative Compounds LLC v. Starmark Labs., 651 F.3d 1303, 99 USPQ2d 1168 (Fed. Cir. 2011) (affirming summary judgment of infringement); Warner-Lambert Co. v. Teva Pharms. USA Inc., 418 F.3d 1326, 75 USPQ2d 1865 (Fed. Cir. 2005) (reversing summary judgment of infringement); Paragon Podiatry Lab. v. KLM Labs., 984 F.2d 1182, 25 USPQ2d 1561 (Fed. Cir. 1993) (affirming summary judgment of inequitable conduct); Leviton Mfg. Co. v. Universal Sec. Instruments Inc., 606 F.3d 1353, 95 USPQ2d 1432 (Fed. Cir. 2010) (reversing summary judgment of inequitable conduct).

[27]Sundance, Inc. v. DeMonte Fabricating, Ltd., 550 F.3d 1356, 1360, 89 USPQ2d 1535 (Fed. Cir. 2008). In addition to the *Daubert* and *Kumho* decisions, the third case in the trilogy is General Elec. Co. v. Joiner, 522 U.S. 136 (1997). *See generally* Margaret A. Berger, *The Supreme Court's Trilogy on the Admissibility of Expert Testimony, in* FEDERAL JUDICIAL CENTER, REFERENCE MANUAL ON SCIENTIFIC EVIDENCE 9 (2d ed. 2000).

A party may wish to use a patent law expert to educate the jury, as a factual matter, about practices and procedures in the PTO. A defense of patent invalidity is often structured for trial as a question of whether the PTO's decision to issue the patent in suit was correct or incorrect. But the PTO generally does not permit patent examiners to testify about patent prosecution matters.[28] Thus, there is no live witness from the PTO to explain how the application for the patent in suit was examined. The next best alternative is expert testimony about how patent applications are examined in general.

The potential problem with even factual testimony by a patent law expert for either party is that the expert may be understood as expressing an opinion on the substantive issue of patent validity. This would, of course, invade the province of the court and the jury, couching legal argument as expert opinion.[29]

Some courts will permit such testimony, carefully circumscribing the permissible scope of examination.[30] An alternative is to provide a neutral source of information to the jury about patent examination procedure. One possibility is to include this in pretrial instructions to the jury. Other courts, by agreement of the parties, will use a teaching aid such as the Federal Judicial Center's 2002 video *An Introduction To The Patent System*.[31]

Another possible role for a patent law expert is to testify with respect to the issues of validity or infringement of the patent in suit. Such testimony is inadmissible unless the expert qualifies as a person of ordinary skill in the pertinent technical art, without regard to the expert's legal training and work as a patent attorney.[32]

In the area of patent damages, a *Daubert* challenge is appropriate to test whether the expert is qualified and whether the

---

[28] *See* 37 C.F.R pt. 104, subpart C; MANUAL OF PATENT EXAMINING PROCEDURE (MPEP) §1701.01 (8th ed. 2001, rev. July 2010).

[29] *Sundance, Inc.*, 550 F.3d. at 1365 n.8, 89 USPQ2d 1535.

[30] *Id.* at 1364 n.7, 89 USPQ2d 1535.

[31] The Federal Judicial Center video may be downloaded from http://www.fjc.gov/public/home.nsf/pages/557. For an example of a district court order limiting the testimony of patent law experts to exceptional circumstances in view of the court's intention to show the video, see Judge Robinson's "Additional Civil Trial Guidelines for Patent Cases" (2010), available at http://www.ded.uscourts.gov/SLRmain.htm.

[32] *Sundance, Inc.*, 550 F.3d. at 1360–65, 89 USPQ2d 1535. *See generally* Laurence H. Pretty, *The Current Role for the Patent Expert and Its Boundaries*, 89 J. PAT. & TRADEMARK OFF. SOC'Y 886 (2007).

expert's proposed methodology of calculating damages is sound.[33] A mere disagreement among the parties as to the soundness of the expert's conclusions goes to the weight to be accorded the opinion, not to its admissibility.[34] However, the Federal Circuit has ruled that certain damages methodologies are inadmissible as a matter of law, e.g., the use of a 25 percent rule of thumb to estimate a baseline royalty. An expert opinion relying on an impermissible methodology may be excluded on a motion in limine or a motion to strike the expert's proffered opinion.[35]

II. JURY TRIALS

The first jury was empaneled in a United States patent case in 1804, during the presidency of Thomas Jefferson.[36] The history of involvement by average Americans in the resolution of patent disputes is substantial. Their role also is controversial and viewed with ambivalence within the community of attorneys. Although the Constitution entitles litigants in most patent cases to jury trials,[37] the complexity of patent cases can undermine the jurors' ability to understand the issues and decide them fairly.

---

[33] Micro Chem., Inc. v. Lextron, Inc., 317 F.3d 1387, 1391–94, 65 USPQ2d 1532 (Fed. Cir. 2003).

[34] i4i Ltd. P'ship v. Microsoft Corp, 598 F.3d 831, 852–54, 93 USPQ2d 1943 (Fed. Cir. 2010), aff'd, 131 S. Ct. 2238 (2011).

[35] Uniloc USA, Inc. v. Microsoft, Corp., 632 F.3d 1292, 1315, 98 USPQ2d 1203 (Fed. Cir. 2011); see also Oracle Am., Inc. v. Google, Inc., No. 3:10-cv-03561-WHA, 2011 WL 2976449 (N.D. Cal. July 22, 2011) (order granting in part motion to strike damages report). See generally, FEDERAL TRADE COMMISSION, THE EVOLVING IP MARKETPLACE: ALIGNING PATENT NOTICE AND REMEDIES WITH COMPETITION (2011), pp. 194–204, available at http://www.ftc.gov/os/2011/03/110307patentreport.pdf.

[36] Reutgen v. Kanowrs, Fed. Cas. 11,710 (C.C.D. Pa. 1804). Although earlier cases may exist (see this chapter, §I), this is the earliest reported case of which the authors are aware. There are earlier reported, non-U.S. patent jury cases. See, e.g., The King v. Arkwright, Webster's Patent Cases, p. 64 (1785).

[37] There is no right to a jury trial when the plaintiff patent owner seeks only an injunction, regardless of whether the defendant makes any counterclaim or asserts any affirmative defense. In re Technology Licensing Corp., 423 F.3d 1286, 1290–91, 76 USPQ2d 1450 (Fed. Cir. 2005). Although there is no Federal Circuit precedent on this issue, some district courts have held that there is no right to a jury trial in an action brought under 35 U.S.C. §271(e)(2) involving only possible future infringement and where the plaintiff seeks only an injunction. See, e.g., Sanofi-Synthelabo v. Apotex Inc., 64 USPQ2d 1684 (S.D.N.Y. 2002). See generally Brian D. Coggio & Timothy E. DeMasi, The Right to a Jury Trial Under the Waxman-Hatch Act—The Question Revisited and Resolved, 57 FOOD & DRUG L.J. 155 (2002).

Legal scholars have often focused on the jurors' ability to comprehend the evidence and the instructions. Even in fairly simple patent cases, the nature of patent law requires the jurors to answer very complex intellectual questions, and to do so from the standpoint of a person of ordinary skill in a technical art.[38]

A. Reliance on Juries

From 1790 to 1793, the first patent act required juries to assess damages in patent cases.[39] In 1793, the second patent act changed the way patent damages were assessed.[40] Under this act, patent actions, which were actions at law, could use juries as fact-finding bodies. Thus the parties to a patent action had the right to a jury trial unless it was waived.[41]

During the 1800s, the use of juries in patent trials declined dramatically. This decline likely began in 1819, when federal courts were given the equitable power to grant injunctions in patent cases.[42] Although there were many ways for a court sitting in equity to involve a jury in the process,[43] there was no right to a jury trial in equity.

Actions in equity, although beneficial, did not immediately replace actions at law because there was a significant disadvantage for a patent owner who brought an action in equity. Specifically, a court sitting in equity could not compensate the patent owner for damages sustained by the patent owner because of the infringement.[44] This disadvantage was removed in 1870,

---

[38] *See* note 8, supra, and notes 50 and 52, infra.

[39] Act of April 10, 1790.

[40] Act of February 21, 1793.

[41] *See generally* Gary M. Ropski, *Constitutional and Procedural Aspects of the Use of Juries in Patent Litigation* (pts. 1–2), 58 J. PAT. OFF. SOC'Y 609, 673 (1976); 7 DONALD S. CHISUM, CHISUM ON PATENTS §20.02[1] (2011).

[42] Act of February 15, 1819. Before this act, a patent owner could obtain equitable relief in state court or in federal court only when there was diversity of citizenship. 7 DONALD S. CHISUM, CHISUM ON PATENTS §20.02[1] [c] (2011).

[43] 7 DONALD S. CHISUM, CHISUM ON PATENTS §20.02[1] [c] (2011).

[44] The court could order an accounting to divest the infringer of all the profits it made by virtue of the infringement, but there might not be any profits. *See generally* Birdsall v. Coolidge, 93 U.S. 64, 68–69 (1876).

when federal courts were given the power to award damages in patent actions in equity.[45] Not surprisingly, by 1890, almost all patent actions were brought in equity,[46] where there was no right to a jury.

The merger of law and equity in 1937 did not return juries to a prominent role in patent trials. When a patent owner sought equitable relief, courts often first tried the equitable claim (which generally included the same factual issues as the legal claim), resulting in patent owners being collaterally estopped from having the facts underlying their legal claims tried by a jury.[47] Thus, it is not very surprising that in 1940 (the first year such statistics were gathered), only 2.5 percent of all patent cases that were tried were tried to a jury.[48]

In 1959, the Supreme Court held that the right to trial by jury must be recognized for issues historically tried by juries.[49] No longer was the patent owner who sought equitable relief effectively barred from obtaining a jury trial.[50] Although the parties in a patent suit had a right to a jury trial on certain issues after 1959, the use of juries in patent trials increased slowly. From 1960 through 1970, more than 95 percent of patent trials were to the bench.[51] This apparent reluctance to embrace jury trials was probably due, at least in part, to a "fear of the unknown."[52] By the 1970s, however, scholarly and practical inter-

---

[45] Act of July 8, 1870.

[46] 3 WILLIAM C. ROBINSON, THE LAW OF PATENTS FOR USEFUL INVENTIONS §932 n.5 (1890).

[47] See generally Ralph W. Launius, Some Aspects of the Right to Trial by Jury in Patent Cases, 49 J. PAT. & TRADEMARK OFF. SOC'Y 112 (1967); Kennedy v. Lakso Co., 414 F.2d 1249, 1251–52, 163 USPQ 136 (3d Cir. 1969); Thermo-Stitch Inc. v. Chemi-Cord Processing Corp., 294 F.2d 486, 488–90, 131 USPQ 1 (5th Cir. 1961).

[48] Gary M. Ropski, Constitutional and Procedural Aspects of the Use of Juries in Patent Litigation (pts. 1–2), 58 J. PAT. & TRADEMARK OFF. SOC'Y 609, 610 (1976). Similarly, only 3.4% of the patent cases that were tried from 1940–59 were tried to a jury. Id.

[49] See Kennedy, 414 F.2d at 1252, 163 USPQ 136 (citing Beacon Theatres Inc. v. Westover, 359 U.S. 500 (1959)).

[50] B. R. Pravel, Jury Trials in Patent Cases, PATENT LAW ANNUAL 23 (Southwestern Legal Found. 1970).

[51] Ropski, 58 J. PAT. & TRADEMARK OFF. SOC'Y at 611 (1976)

[52] Pravel, PATENT LAW ANNUAL 23, 33; remarks of Don W. Martens at the 10th Annual Judicial Conference of the United States Court of Appeals for the Federal Circuit, 146 F.R.D. 205, 375 (1993) ("[Patent lawyers] used to always have a fear of juries").

est in patent jury trials was growing.[53] From 1975 through 2009, the last year for which statistics are currently available, the percentages of patent cases that were tried to a jury increased from 11.9 percent to 69.3 percent.[54]

As these statistics reflect, it is now common to have a jury involved in a patent trial.[55] Trying a patent case to a jury, though, can present special problems, including: (1) the jurors' ability to comprehend the evidence; (2) the jurors' role, if any, in deciding legal issues; (3) the court's choice of form of verdict; and (4) the adequacy of the instruction to the jurors on the law they are to apply.

B. Juror Comprehension

While patent law itself always calls for sophisticated reasoning, the concern with juror comprehension is reduced in cases that involve simple technology. In patent cases involving complex technology, however, jurors may be confronted with remarkably complex evidence concerning inventions produced

---

[53] *See, e.g.,* George B. Newitt & Jon O. Nelson, *The Patent Lawyer and Trial by Jury,* 1 J. MARSHALL J. PRAC. & PROCEDURE 59 (1967); *Launius,* 49 J. PAT. & TRADEMARK OFF. SOC'Y; *Pravel,* PATENT LAW ANNUAL 23; Donald Zarley, *Jury Trials in Patent Litigation,* 20 DRAKE L. REV. 242 (1971); Ernest E. Figari, *Jury Trials in a Patent Context,* PATENT LAW ANNUAL 189 (Southwestern Legal Found. 1974); *Ropski,* 58 J. PAT. & TRADEMARK OFF. SOC'Y 609 (1976); James M. Wetzel, *A Survey of Patent Jury Litigation for the Last Fifteen Years,* 10 INTELL. PROP. L. REV. 378 (1978); V. Bryan Medlock, Jr., *The Patent Jury Trial, in* PATENT & TRADEMARK LITIGATION INSTITUTE at M-1 (American Patent Law Ass'n. 1978). It probably is not merely coincidental that the interest in jury trials arose after the 1960s. During that decade, fewer than one out of four patents that were tried to the bench were found valid and, of the ones found valid, the odds were three to one that the appellate court would reverse the district court. *Wetzel,* 10 INTELL. PROP. L. REV. 378; *see also* Duane Burton, *Patent Jury Charge, in* CONTINUING LEGAL EDUCATION INSTITUTE ON PATENT JURY LITIGATION at J-1, J-26 (American Patent Law Ass'n. 1981) (between 1953 and 1972, the patent owner prevailed at trial only 27% of the time).

[54] Statistics compiled from Director of Administration, Office of U.S. Courts, Table C-4, Annual Report. The 2000 and 2007–2009 statistics are based on a September-ending number, which was the only one available, unlike the rest of these statistics, which are based on a December-ending number.

[55] For some empirical research regarding differences between judge and jury resolution of patent cases, see Kimberly A. Moore, *Judges, Juries, and Patent Cases—An Empirical Peek Inside the Black Box,* 11 FED. CIR. B.J. 209 (2001). Regarding who asks for a jury, see Kimberly A. Moore, *Jury Demands: Who's Asking?* 17 BERKELEY TECH. L.J. 847 (2002).

by the best minds in biogenetics, physics, computer technology, and the like.[56]

Whether a complexity exception to the Seventh Amendment would allow the court to keep complex technical issues from the jury is an unresolved question in patent law that raises strong responses.[57] Complexity, at times, calls for unusual creativity, and in this area of the law one right answer sometimes might not exist. The attorneys' and the court's insight and acumen, therefore, can make a real and right difference. Until a complexity exception is recognized, jurors will be called upon to resolve complex technical disputes.

The attorneys and the court have a duty to conduct the trial in a way that educates the jurors and gives them com-

---

[56] As one Federal Circuit Judge said in an interview:

In a simple patent case, if the claims are sufficiently straightforward and the case is sufficiently non-technical and you want to give it to the jury, I can't get too excited about it. But if you've got some of these terribly complex technologies and you take that to a lay jury, I just don't know whether that's sensible.

An Interview with Federal Circuit Judge S. Jay Plager, 5 J. PROPRIETARY RIGHTS 2, 10 (1993). *See also* the remarks of District Judge T. S. Ellis III:

In my experience, juries in [the Eastern District of Virginia] appear to have no difficulty comprehending the technology involved in product and method patents involving mechanical devices. Jury comprehension is also not a problem, in my experience, in patent cases involving business methods, computer applications, design patents and some manufacturing methods or processes. At the same time, however, there is clearly a jury comprehension problem in patent cases involving such highly complex matters as transistor circuitry, microchip fabrication, and chemical compounds and formulae.

T. S. Ellis III, *Judicial Management of Patent Litigation in the United States: Expedited Procedures and Their Effects,* 9 FED. CIR. B.J. 541, 547 n.15 (2000). District Judge Claudia Wilken, deciding to use a court-appointed expert in the trial of a case involving a complex electronics patent, stated:

While a court-appointed expert would not be appropriate in every case, having presided over a trial with the same technology at issue, the Court found the technology particularly complex and difficult to understand.

Monolithic Power Sys., Inc., v. O2 Micro Int'l Ltd., 2007 WL 3231709, at * 7 (N.D. Cal. Oct. 30, 2007).

[57] *See, e.g.,* SRI Int'l v. Matsushita Elec. Corp. of Am., 775 F.2d 1107, 1126–32, 227 USPQ 577 (Fed. Cir. 1985) (comments of Federal Circuit Judges Howard T. Markey and Pauline Newman); *In re* Japanese Elec. Prods. Antitrust Litig., 631 F.2d 1069, 1079 (3d Cir. 1980); *In re* U.S. Fin. Sec. Litig., 609 F.2d 411, 432 (9th Cir. 1979).

prehensible evidence.[58] The bar offers many continuing legal education programs and practical journal articles aimed at enhancing the litigator's ability to try a patent case to a jury.[59] As discussed in this chapter in §I.A, the Federal Rules of Civil Procedure and the Federal Rules of Evidence also provide for the appointment of special masters and independent experts to assist the jury where appropriate. As with case management, there is a substantial body of literature about trial management, most of which considers how to enhance the ability of the jury to understand and decide the issues for which the jury is responsible at trial.[60]

C. The Jurors' Role

While some commentators believe that the job of the trial court is to ensure that a jury does no more than decide disputed factual questions,[61] the reality is that trial courts often allow a patent jury to resolve legal questions on the way to its verdict. If the trial court wants or is willing to restrict the jury's

---

[58] See Ninth Circuit Jury Trial Improvement Committee, Second Report: Recommendations and Suggested Best Practices (2006); see also remarks of Federal Circuit Judge Haldane Robert Mayer at the 11th Annual Judicial Conference of the United States Court of Appeals for the Federal Circuit, 153 F.R.D. 177, 252 (1994).

[59] See, e.g., AMERICAN BAR ASSOCIATION, PRINCIPLES FOR JURIES AND JURY TRIALS (2005); Susan J. Macpherson and Elissa Krauss, Tools to Keep Jurors Engaged, 44 TRIAL 32 (2008).

[60] See FEDERAL JUDICIAL CENTER, MANUAL FOR COMPLEX LITIGATION (FOURTH) (2004); WILLIAM S. ROOKLEDGE ET AL., COMPENSATORY DAMAGES ISSUES IN PATENT INFRINGEMENT CASES: A POCKET GUIDE FOR FEDERAL DISTRICT COURT JUDGES (2011); PETER S. MENELL ET AL., PATENT CASE MANAGEMENT JUDICIAL GUIDE (2009); see also William W Schwarzer, Reforming Jury Trials, 132 F.R.D. 575, 577–78 (1991); Avern Cohn, Thoughts on Jury Trial in a Patent Case, 6 PROCEEDINGS OF THE INTELLECTUAL PROPERTY LAW SECTION OF THE STATE BAR OF MICHIGAN 4 (1994); Paul R. Michel & Michelle Rhyu, Improving Patent Jury Trials, 6 FED. CIR. B.J. 89, 104 (1996); COMPLEX LITIGATION COMMITTEE OF THE AMERICAN COLLEGE OF TRIAL LAWYERS, ANATOMY OF A PATENT CASE (BNA 2009).

[61] See, e.g., remarks of Professor Rochelle Dreyfuss at the 11th Annual Judicial Conference of the United States Court of Appeals for the Federal Circuit, To What Extent Must Juries Be Used in Patent Cases? 153 F.R.D. 177, 245 (1994).

decision-making role to resolving disputed factual issues relating to a legal claim, then the court may, inter alia:

1. order a separate and prior[62] nonjury trial of the inequitable conduct defense;[63]
2. order a concurrent trial of the inequitable conduct defense (i.e., nonjury inequitable conduct defense in the morning; other issues to jury in the afternoon);[64]
3. order a separate and prior nonjury trial of the equitable defenses of laches and equitable estoppel;[65] and
4. order a separate and prior nonjury trial of the equitable defense of patent misuse.[66]

In addition to withholding the equitable defenses from the jury, the court may want, or be willing, to keep the purely legal

---

[62] Ordering a separate nonjury trial subsequent to a jury trial also is possible. *See, e.g.,* LNP Eng'g Plastics v. Miller Waste Mills, 275 F.3d 1347, 1350, 61 USPQ2d 1193 (Fed. Cir. 2001). Such a procedure might be useful if the court found a factual issue in dispute relating to a legal claim to be intertwined with the equitable defense. *See generally* Mag Instrument Inc. v. J. Baxter Brinkmann Int'l Corp., 123 F.R.D. 543, 546–47, 10 USPQ2d 1387 (N.D. Tex. 1988).

[63] *See, e.g.,* Agfa Corp. v. Creo Prods., Inc., 451 F.3d 1366, 1372–73, 79 USPQ2d 1385 (Fed. Cir. 2006); Gardco Mfg. Inc. v. Herst Lighting Co., 820 F.2d 1209, 1211–13, 2 USPQ2d 2015 (Fed. Cir. 1987). The court may also use the jury in an advisory capacity. *See, e.g.,* American Calcar, Inc. v. American Honda Motor Co., 651 F.3d 1318, 1332–36, 99 USPQ2d 1137, 1146-47 (Fed. Cir. 2011); Duro-Last, Inc. v. Custom Seal, Inc., 321 F.3d 1098, 1110, 66 USPQ2d 1025 (Fed. Cir. 2003). If a jury determines factual questions that are common to both legal and equitable claims, however, the court is bound by those determinations when deciding the equitable claim. Cabinet Vision v. Cabnetware, 129 F.3d 595, 44 USPQ2d 1683 (Fed. Cir. 1997) (court could not treat as advisory a jury's factual finding regarding fraud-based antitrust counterclaim when deciding the inequitable conduct defense); Therma-Tru Corp. v. Peachtree Doors Inc., 44 F.3d 988, 994–95, 33 USPQ2d 1274 (Fed. Cir. 1995). With the agreement of the parties, the inequitable conduct defense can be completely or partially submitted to the jury for verdict. *See generally* Hupp v. Siroflex of Am. Inc., 122 F.3d 1456, 1465, 43 USPQ2d 1887 (Fed. Cir. 1997). *See, e.g.,* Hebert v. Lisle Corp., 99 F.3d 1109, 1114–17, 40 USPQ2d 1611 (Fed. Cir. 1996); *see also* Juicy Whip, Inc. v. Orange Bang, Inc., 292 F.3d 728, 735–36, 746 n.3, 63 USPQ2d 1251 (Fed. Cir.), *cert. denied,* 537 U.S. 1019 (2002).

[64] Avco Corp. v. PPG Indus., Nos. 90-10316-y and 90-10688-y (D. Mass. 1990).

[65] A. C. Aukerman Co. v. R. L. Chaides Constr. Co., 960 F.2d 1020, 1028, 22 USPQ2d 1321 (Fed. Cir. 1992) ("As equitable defenses, laches and equitable estoppel are matters committed to the sound discretion of the trial judge"). *See generally* Dewey Elecs. Corp. v. Montage Inc., 117 F.R.D. 73, 3 USPQ2d 1229 (M.D. Pa. 1987).

[66] *In re* Yarn Processing Patent Validity Litig., 472 F. Supp. 170, 205 USPQ 758 (S.D. Fla. 1979).

issues from jurors. The Federal Circuit has characterized many of the issues that routinely arise in patent cases as follows:

Questions of Law

1. statutory subject matter;[67]
2. indefinite claiming;[68]
3. prosecution history estoppel, and, if estoppel is found, the degree to which estoppel will limit use of the doctrine of equivalents to prove infringement;[69]
4. implied license;[70] and
5. repair or reconstruction.[71]

Questions of Fact

1. utility;[72]
2. novelty (anticipation);[73]
3. derivation (not an original inventor);[74]
4. abandonment;[75]

---

[67] Prometheus Labs., Inc. v. Mayo Collaborative Servs., 628 F.3d 1347, 1353, 97 USPQ2d 1097 (Fed. Cir. 2010), *cert. granted*, 180 L. Ed. 2d 844 (2011); *In re* Ferguson, 558 F.3d 1359, 90 USPQ2d 1035 (Fed. Cir. 2009), *cert. denied*, 130 S. Ct. 3541 (2010).

[68] Young v. Lumenis, Inc., 492 F.3d 1336, 1345, 83 USPQ2d 1191 (Fed. Cir. 2007); Halliburton Energy Servs. Inc., v. M-I LLC, 514 F.3d 1244, 1249, 85 USPQ2d 1654 (Fed. Cir. 2008).

[69] Cybor Corp. v. FAS Techs. Inc., 138 F.3d 1448, 1460, 46 USPQ2d 1169 (Fed. Cir. 1998) (en banc); Spine Solutions, Inc. v. Medtronic Sofamor Danek USA, 620 F.3d 1305, 1317, 96 USPQ2d 1640 (Fed. Cir. 2010); Festo Corp. v. Shoketsu Kinzoku Kogyo Kabushiki Co., 344 F.3d 1359, 1367, 68 USPQ2d 1321 (Fed. Cir. 2003), *cert. denied*, 541 U.S. 988 (2004).

[70] Monsanto Co. v. Scruggs, 459 F.3d 1328, 1336, 79 USPQ2d 1813 (Fed. Cir. 2006); Zenith Elecs. Corp. v. PDI Commc'n Sys., 522 F.3d 1348, 1360, 86 USPQ2d 1513 (Fed. Cir. 2008).

[71] Fuji Photo Film Co. v. International Trade Comm'n, 474 F.3d 1281, 1289, 82 USPQ2d 1495 (Fed. Cir. 2007).

[72] Juicy Whip, Inc. v. Orange Bang, Inc., 185 F.3d 1364, 1365, 51 USPQ2d 1700 (Fed. Cir. 1999); *In re* '318 Patent Infringement Litig., 583 F.3d 1317, 1323, 92 USPQ2d 1385 (Fed. Cir. 2009).

[73] Orion IP, LLC v. Hyundai Motor Am., 605 F.3d 967, 974, 95 USPQ2d 1297 (Fed. Cir. 2010); Z4 Techs., Inc. v. Microsoft Corp., 507 F.3d 1340, 1347, 85 USPQ2d 1340 (Fed. Cir. 2007), *cert. dismissed*, 553 U.S. 1028 (2008).

[74] International Rectifier Corp. v. IXYS Corp., 361 F.3d 1363, 1376, 70 USPQ2d 1209 (Fed. Cir. 2004); Brand v. Miller, 487 F.3d 862, 869, 82 USPQ2d 1705 (Fed. Cir. 2007).

[75] Aristocrat Techs. Austl. Pty. Ltd. v. International Game Techs., 543 F.3d 657, 661, 88 USPQ2d 1458 (Fed. Cir. 2008), *cert. denied*, 129 S. Ct. 2791 (2009); Encyclopaedia Britannica, Inc. v. Alpine Elecs. of Am., Inc., 609 F.3d 1345, 1349, 95 USPQ2d 1660 (Fed. Cir. 2010).

5. inadequate written description;[76]
6. best mode;[77]
7. infringement (both literal and under the doctrine of equivalents);[78]
8. reverse doctrine of equivalents;[79]
9. amount of lost profits;[80]
10. reasonable royalty;[81]
11. willful infringement;[82] and
12. marking.[83]

Questions of Law That Are Based on Underlying Questions of Fact

1. enablement;[84]
2. nonobviousness;[85]

---

[76] Spine Solutions, Inc. v. Medtronic Sofamor Danek USA, Inc., 620 F.3d 1305, 1312, 96 USPQ2d 1640 (Fed. Cir. 2010); Ariad Pharms., Inc. v. Eli Lilly & Co., 598 F.3d 1336, 1343, 94 USPQ2d 1161 (Fed. Cir. 2010) (en banc).

[77] Green Edge Enters., LLC v. Rubber Mulch etc., LLC, 620 F.3d 1287, 1296, 96 USPQ2d 1425 (Fed. Cir. 2010); Ajinomoto Co. v. Int'l Trade Comm'n, 597 F.3d 1267, 1272, 94 USPQ2d 1055 (Fed. Cir. 2010).

[78] Lazare Kaplan Int'l, Inc. v. Photoscribe Techs., Inc., 628 F.3d 1359, 97 USPQ2d 1437 (Fed. Cir. 2010); Becton, Dickinson & Co. v. Tyco Healthcare Group, 616 F.3d 1249, 1253, 95 USPQ2d 1752 (Fed. Cir. 2010); Adams Respiratory Therapeutics, Inc. v. Perrigo Co., 616 F.3d 1283, 1291, 96 USPQ2d 1041 (Fed. Cir. 2010); Festo Corp. v. Shoketsu Kinzoku Kogyo Kabushiki Co., 493 F.3d 1368, 1377, 83 USPQ2d 1385 (Fed. Cir. 2007), cert. denied, 553 U.S. 1093 (2008).

[79] SRI Int'l v. Matsushita Elec. Corp. of Am., 775 F.2d 1107, 1125, 227 USPQ 577 (Fed. Cir. 1985) (en banc). But see Amgen Inc. v. Hoechst Marion Roussel, Inc., 314 F.3d 1313, 1351, 65 USPQ2d 1385 (Fed. Cir. 2003), which states that the reverse doctrine of equivalents is equitable in nature.

[80] Rite-Hite Corp. v. Kelley Co., 56 F.3d 1538, 1544, 35 USPQ2d 1065 (Fed. Cir. 1995) (en banc), cert. denied, 516 U.S. 867 (1995).

[81] Fujifilm Corp. v. Benun, 605 F.3d 1366, 1372, 95 USPQ2d 1985 (Fed. Cir. 2010); Wordtech Sys., Inc. v. Integrated Networks Solutions, Inc., 609 F.3d 1308, 1318, 95 USPQ2d 1619 (Fed. Cir. 2010).

[82] i4i Ltd. P'ship v. Microsoft Corp., 598 F.3d 831, 859, 93 USPQ2d 1943 (Fed. Cir. 2010), aff'd, 131 S. Ct. 2238 (2011); SEB S.A. v. Montgomery Ward & Co., 594 F.3d 1360, 1380, 93 USPQ2d 1617 (Fed. Cir. 2010), aff'd, 131 S. Ct. 2060 (2011).

[83] Funai Elec. Co. v. Daewoo Elecs. Corp., 616 F.3d 1357, 1373, 96 USPQ2d 1329 (Fed. Cir. 2010); Minks v. Polaris Indus., Inc. 546 F.3d 1364, 1375, 89 USPQ2d 1102 (Fed. Cir. 2008).

[84] Ortho-McNeil Pharm., Inc. v. Mylan Labs., Inc., 520 F.3d 1358, 1365, 86 USPQ2d 1196 (Fed. Cir. 2008); Alza Corp. v. Andrx Pharms., LLC, 603 F.3d 935, 939, 94 USPQ2d 1823 (Fed. Cir. 2010).

[85] Rolls-Royce, PLC v. United Techs. Corp., 603 F.3d 1325, 1338, 95 USPQ2d 1097 (Fed. Cir. 2010); Western Union Co. v. Moneygram Payment Sys., Inc., 626 F.3d 1361, 97 USPQ2d 1263 (Fed. Cir. 2010).

   3. 102(b) public-use bar;[86]
   4. 102(b) on-sale bar;[87]
   5. 102(b) printed publication bar;[88] and
   6. prior inventor.[89]

D. Form of Verdict

The choice of the form of verdict is left to the trial court's sound discretion.[90] If the court chooses to illuminate the jury's decision making, then the court will employ a special verdict[91] or a general verdict accompanied by interrogatories.[92] A simple general verdict, while acceptable,[93] is rare in intellectual property cases.

If a general verdict is used, however, it should be in multiple parts to lead the jury through the principal issues in the

---

[86] Motionless Keyboard Co. v. Microsoft Corp., 486 F.3d 1376, 1383, 82 USPQ2d 1801 (Fed. Cir. 2007), cert. denied, 552 U.S. 1131 (2008); Clock Spring, L.P. v. Wrapmaster, Inc., 560 F.3d 1317, 1324, 90 USPQ2d 1212 (Fed. Cir. 2009).

[87] Gemmy Indus. Corp. v. Chrisha Creations Ltd., 452 F.3d 1353, 1358, 79 USPQ2d 1172 (Fed. Cir. 2006); Delaware Valley Floral Group, Inc. v. Shaw Rose Nets, LLC, 597 F.3d 1374, 1379, 94 USPQ2d 1064 (Fed. Cir. 2010).

[88] ResQNet.com, Inc. v. Lansa, Inc., 594 F.3d 860, 865, 93 USPQ2d 1553 (Fed. Cir. 2010); Orion IP, LLC v. Hyundai Motor Am., 605 F.3d 967, 974, 95 USPQ2d 1297 (Fed. Cir. 2010).

[89] Monsanto Co. v. Mycogen Plant Sci., Inc., 261 F.3d 1356, 1362, 59 USPQ2d 1930 (Fed. Cir. 2001); Solvay S.A. v. Honeywell Int'l, Inc., 622 F.3d 1367, 1375, 96 USPQ2d 1870 (Fed. Cir. 2010).

[90] Weinar v. Rollform Inc., 744 F.2d 797, 809, 223 USPQ 369 (Fed. Cir. 1984), cert. denied, 470 U.S. 1084 (1985). See generally Kimberly A. Moore, Juries, Patent Cases, and a Lack of Transparency, 39 Hous. L. Rev. 779 (2002) (arguing that the Federal Circuit should mandate the use of meaningful special verdict forms).

[91] Fed. R. Civ. P. 49(a); see also Warner-Jenkinson Co. v. Hilton Davis Chem. Co., 520 U.S. 17, 39 n.8 (1997) (noting that "in cases that reach the jury, a special verdict and/or interrogatories on each claim element could be very useful in facilitating review, uniformity, and possibly postverdict judgments as a matter of law"); see, e.g., Tronzo v. Biomet, Inc., 318 F.3d 1378, 1379, 65 USPQ2d 1861 (Fed. Cir. 2003); Minnesota Mining & Mfg. Co. v. Chemque, Inc., 303 F.3d 1294, 1299, 64 USPQ2d 1270 (Fed. Cir. 2002), cert. dismissed, 538 U.S. 972 (2003).

[92] Fed. R. Civ. P. 49(b).

[93] Structural Rubber Prods. Co. v. Park Rubber Co., 749 F.2d 707, 720, 223 USPQ 1264 (Fed. Cir. 1984); see, e.g., Deks v. Atlas Bolt & Screw Co., 14 USPQ2d 1077 (Fed. Cir. 1989) (unpublished). See generally Paul R. Michel & Michelle Rhyu, Improving Patent Jury Trials, 6 FED. CIR. B.J. 89, 95 (1996) (Judge Michel noted that the "[u]se of special verdicts and interrogatories that direct juries to sequentially address the specific issues presented could greatly enhance the rationality, reliability, and predictability of jury verdicts").

case.[94] Even though the Federal Rules of Civil Procedure do not provide for such a procedure, the Federal Circuit has approved its use in patent cases.[95]

Another form of verdict that has been used in patent cases consists of instructive interrogatories.[96] This form of verdict was used in *Railroad Dynamics, Inc. v. A. Stucki Co.*[97] In general, such a form of verdict consists of questions that are composed of, or accompanied by, instructions as to which party has what burden of proof and other relevant information. The form should conform to the proofs and arguments presented at trial.[98]

Good verdict forms should take the jurors logically through the case. Plaintiffs usually want very general forms, whereas defendants usually want very detailed forms. Because of the tension between these two positions, it is difficult to recommend good verdict forms. Certainly, minimum requirements include careful attention to the use of clear language, the avoidance of leading questions, and the use of unbiased language. Sample jury verdict forms are appended to several of the model jury instructions discussed in the following section, e.g., those prepared by the National Jury Instruction Project and the Northern District of California.

---

[94] Avern Cohn, *Thoughts on Jury Trial in a Patent Case,* 6 PROCEEDINGS OF THE INTELLECTUAL PROPERTY LAW SECTION OF THE STATE BAR OF MICHIGAN 4 (1994). Judge Cohn believes that a set of special questions keyed to the differences between the parties usually will make a general verdict unnecessary. *Id.* When a party argues multiple theories, it may be useful to use a form of verdict that distinguishes between the theories. *See generally* Mitsubishi Elec. Corp. v. Ampex Corp., 190 F.3d 1300, 1303–04, 51 USPQ2d 1910 (Fed. Cir. 1999), *cert. denied,* 529 U.S. 1054 (2000). Regardless of its decision on validity, the jury should decide infringement issues that are tried. Hebert v. Lisle Corp., 99 F.3d 1109, 1114, 40 USPQ2d 1611 (Fed. Cir. 1996).

[95] *Structural Rubber Prods. Co.,* 749 F.2d at 720, 223 USPQ 1264. *See generally* McGinley v. Franklin Sports, Inc., 262 F.3d 1339, 1358–59, 60 USPQ2d 1001 (Fed. Cir. 2001) (Michel, J., dissenting).

[96] Robert I. Berdon, *Instructive Interrogatories: Helping the Civil Jury to Understand,* 55 CONN. BAR J. 179 (1981).

[97] 727 F.2d 1506, 220 USPQ 929 (Fed. Cir.), *cert. denied,* 469 U.S. 871 (1984). The instructive interrogatories used in that case can be found at 727 F.2d at 1521–22. The Federal Circuit's discussion of these interrogatories can be found at 727 F.2d at 1515–17.

[98] *See, e.g.,* Motorola Inc. v. Interdigital Tech. Corp., 121 F.3d 1461, 1467, 43 USPQ2d 1481 (Fed. Cir. 1997).

E. Adequately Instructing the Jurors on the Law They Are to Apply

It is essential that the jury be adequately instructed on the law it is asked to apply.[99] The Federal Circuit reviews the adequacy of the jury instructions for prejudicial legal error.[100]

The jury instructions, when read as a whole, must be both legally correct and sufficiently comprehensive to address the factual issues in dispute.[101] No instruction should be given regarding a proposition of law about which no competent evidence was introduced.[102] It is the trial court's duty to give meaningful instructions that can be understood and given effect once the jury resolves the disputed factual issues.[103]

Model jury instructions serve as a useful starting point for drafting instructions for a specific case.[104] Although the Federal Circuit has not developed them,[105] model jury instructions that exist for patent cases have been suggested by:

1. the Federal Circuit Bar Association;[106]
2. the Patent Litigation Committee of the American Intellectual Property Law Association;[107]

---

[99] *See generally Railroad Dynamics Inc.,* 727 F.2d at 1515, 220 USPQ 929.

[100] *See, e.g.,* Lisle Corp. v. A.J. Mfg. Co., 398 F.3d 1306, 1316, 73 USPQ2d 1891 (Fed. Cir. 2005); Texas Digital Sys., Inc. v. Telegenix, Inc., 308 F.3d 1193, 1201, 64 USPQ2d 1812 (Fed. Cir. 2002), *cert. denied,* 538 U.S. 1058 (2003). Prejudicial error is error that appears to the court to be inconsistent with substantial justice. Environ Prods. v. Furon Co., 215 F.3d 1261, 1265, 55 USPQ2d 1038 (Fed. Cir. 2000).

[101] Biodex Corp. v. Loredan Biomedical Inc., 946 F.2d 850, 853–54, 20 USPQ2d 1252 (Fed. Cir. 1991), *cert. denied,* 504 U.S. 980 (1992). On appellate review, attention is given to the instruction's "clarity, objectivity, and adequacy, taken as a whole." United States Surgical Corp. v. Ethicon Inc., 103 F.3d 1554, 1564, 41 USPQ2d 1225 (Fed. Cir.), *cert. denied,* 522 U.S. 950 (1997).

[102] DMI Inc. v. Deere & Co., 802 F.2d 421, 429, 231 USPQ 276 (Fed. Cir. 1986).

[103] Sulzer Textil A.G. v. Picanol N.V., 358 F.3d 1356, 1365, 69 USPQ2d 1961 (Fed. Cir. 2004); Structural Rubber Prods. Co. v. Park Rubber Co., 749 F.2d 707, 723, 223 USPQ 1264 (Fed. Cir. 1984).

[104] Edward J. Devitt, *Ten Practical Suggestions About Federal Jury Instructions,* 38 F.R.D. 75, 77 (1966).

[105] *See generally* Gerald J. Mossinghoff & Donald R. Dunner, *Increasing Certainty in Patent Litigation: The Need for Federal Circuit Approved Pattern Jury Instructions,* 83 J. PAT. OFF. & TRADEMARK SOC'Y 431 (2001).

[106] FEDERAL CIRCUIT BAR ASSOCIATION MODEL PATENT JURY INSTRUCTIONS (2010).

[107] AMERICAN INTELLECTUAL PROPERTY LAW ASSOCIATION'S MODEL PATENT JURY INSTRUCTIONS (2008).

3. the Intellectual Property Litigation Committee of the Section of Litigation of the American Bar Association;[108]
4. the Fifth Circuit;[109]
5. the Eleventh Circuit;[110]
6. the United States District Court for the District of Delaware;[111]
7. the United States District Court for the Northern District of California;[112]
8. the Minnesota Intellectual Property Law Association;[113]
9. the National Jury Instruction Project;[114]
10. Burton;[115]
11. Horwitz;[116]
12. Sand;[117] and
13. O'Malley.[118]

---

[108] MODEL JURY INSTRUCTIONS: PATENT LITIGATION (2005).

[109] FIFTH CIRCUIT PATTERN JURY INSTRUCTIONS (CIVIL CASES) (2006). The Ninth Circuit withdrew its model patent jury instructions in 1997. MANUAL OF MODEL CIVIL JURY INSTRUCTIONS FOR THE DISTRICT COURTS OF THE NINTH CIRCUIT, p. 301 (2001).

[110] ELEVENTH CIRCUIT PATTERN JURY INSTRUCTIONS (CIVIL CASES) (2005).

[111] UNIFORM JURY INSTRUCTIONS FOR PATENT CASES IN THE UNITED STATES DISTRICT COURT FOR THE DISTRICT OF DELAWARE (1993). These instructions have not been adopted by the court as standard instructions.

[112] MODEL PATENT JURY INSTRUCTIONS FOR THE NORTHERN DISTRICT OF CALIFORNIA (2007). These instructions have been adopted by the court as model instructions.

[113] INTELLECTUAL PROPERTY JURY INSTRUCTIONS (1998). This is a collection of instructions actually used by the Minnesota District Court and some uniform instructions from the District of Delaware.

[114] MODEL PATENT JURY INSTRUCTIONS (2009).

[115] 1 DUANE BURTON, JURY INSTRUCTIONS IN INTELLECTUAL PROPERTY CASES ch. 20 (1999 & Supp. 2007). This is a collection of instructions that were given in a number of cases.

[116] 3 ETHAN HORWITZ & LESTER HORWITZ, PATENT LITIGATION: PROCEDURES & TACTICS ch. 11 (2003).

[117] 4 LEONARD B. SAND ET AL., MODERN FEDERAL JURY INSTRUCTIONS ch. 86 (2003).

[118] 3A KEVIN F. O'MALLEY ET AL., FEDERAL JURY PRACTICE AND INSTRUCTIONS 158 (5th ed. 2001 & Supp. 2007).

ANNOTATED BIBLIOGRAPHY

Specialized Reporters & Newsletters

The Bureau of National Affairs publishes The United States Patents Quarterly (USPQ), which dates back to 1929. USPQ and USPQ2d report cases and decisions relating to patent, trademark, and copyright law. Many, but not all, of these cases are also reported in the more familiar reporters published by West Publishing Company. Because some patent cases and decisions are published only in USPQ, it is not uncommon for the parties involved in patent litigation to cite or refer to this reporter system.

In addition, the Bureau of National Affairs publishes BNA's Patent, Trademark & Copyright Journal (PTCJ). PTCJ, published weekly in both paper and electronic formats, contains synopses of recent cases, intellectual property legislation, and various association activities.

Government Works

CODE OF FEDERAL REGULATIONS. Chapter 1 of Title 37 contains the PTO's regulations.

MANUAL OF PATENT EXAMINING PROCEDURE (8th ed. 2001, rev. July 2010) (MPEP). This work, intended as a handbook for patent examiners, is a comprehensive, frequently revised, and annotated treatment of patent examining procedures and, in Chapter 2100, the PTO's summary of the law governing patentability. The MPEP is available online at http://www.uspto.gov/web/offices/pac/mpep/index.htm.

THE FEDERAL JUDICIAL CENTER is the research and education agency for the Federal Courts. The Center publishes a number of titles relevant to patents and patent litigation, some of which are available for free download. Search "patents" at http://www.fjc.gov/library/fjc_catalog.nsf

The Leahy-Smith America Invents Act

The full text of the bill, Pub.L. 112-29, H.R. 1249 (2011), is available from the Government Printing Office at http://www. gpo.gov/fdsys/pkg/BILLS-112hr1249enr/pdf/BILLS-112 hr1249enr.pdf. The House Report accompanying the bill, House Rept. No. 112-98 (112th Cong., 1st Sess.) (2011) can be found at http://www.gpo.gov/fdsys/pkg/CRPT-112hrpt98/ pdf/CRPT-112hrpt98-pt1.pdf.

Patent Databases

LEXIS (www.lexis.com) has the following database files that are particularly useful for the patent lawyer:

> PATENTS, which contains the full text of U.S. patents issued since 1975; and IPOMNI, which contains, among other things, patent, trademark, and copyright cases decided by the Supreme Court (since 1850), regional circuit courts of appeals (since 1938), district courts (since 1948), Court of Customs and Patent Appeals (1952–1982), Court of Claims (1960–1982), Claims Court (1982–1992), U.S. Court of Federal Claims (since 1992), and Federal Circuit (since 1982).

> TOTAL PATENT – Full text and bibliographic/abstract authorities for issued patents.

DIALOG (www.dialog.com) contains over eighteen databases of U.S. and foreign patents in bibliographic and/or full-text formats, issued over various time periods:

CLAIMS/U.S. Patents provides access to U.S. pregrant applications and patents issued by the PTO since 1950.

DERWENT World Patents Index and World Patents First View provide patent information from 40+ countries, most since 1963.

INPADOC/Family and Legal Status contains patent family and legal status information on patents in 66 countries.

WESTLAW (www.westlaw.com) contains patent databases under its Practice-Area Materials: Intellectual Property heading, including CLAIMS, Derwent World Patent Index, and INPADOC. Additionally, any decision reported in West's familiar reporter systems is retrievable.

GOOGLE PATENTS (www.google.com/patents) provides access to issued U.S. patents

MICROPATENT (www.micropatent.com) provides access to U.S. patent file histories and copies of patents and published patent applications.

Internet Websites

www.cafc.uscourts.gov—U.S. Court of Appeals for the Federal Circuit—recent precedential and non-precedential decisions and orders, court rules, court calendars and dispositions, and notices

www.delphion.com—patent offices worldwide

www.uspto.gov—U.S. Patent & Trademark Office

www.epo.org—European Patent Office

www. jpo.go.jp—Japanese Patent Office

www.wipo.int—World Intellectual Property Organization

www.patentlogistics.com/FetchPatent.php—U.S.Patent Fetcher

www.patentlogistics.com/FetchApp.php—U.S.Patent Application Fetcher

Patents and Patent Law Blogs

http://ip-updates.blogspot.com/—IP Updates blog of IP news and information

http://patentlaw.typepad.com/patent/—Patently-O: Patent law blog of patent decisions, news, and information

patentdocs.typepad.com/patent_docs – Biotechnology and pharmaceutical patent news

Journals

Although scholarly articles relating to patent law frequently appear in general, school-affiliated law reviews, patent law and patent practice articles are more commonly found in specialized journals. Many of these journals are now available online from LexisNexis or from the online subscription service HeinOnLine (http://home.heinonline.org/content/list-of-libraries/). Some of these titles are:

JOURNAL OF THE PATENT AND TRADEMARK OFFICE SOCIETY, first published in 1918 (under the name JOURNAL OF THE PATENT OFFICE SOCIETY).

The AMERICAN INTELLECTUAL PROPERTY LAW ASSOCIATION QUARTERLY JOURNAL, first published in 1973.

IDEA, first published in 1957 (under the name THE PATENT, TRADEMARK, AND COPYRIGHT JOURNAL OF RESEARCH AND EDUCATION). INTELLECTUAL PROPERTY & TECHNOLOGY LAW JOURNAL, first published in 1988 (under the name THE JOURNAL OF PROPRIETARY RIGHTS).

BERKELEY TECHNOLOGICAL LAW JOURNAL, first published in 1986 (under the name HIGH TECHNOLOGY LAW JOURNAL) by Boalt Hall School of Law, University of California.

HARVARD JOURNAL OF LAW & TECHNOLOGY, first published in 1988.

FEDERAL CIRCUIT BAR JOURNAL, first published in 1991.

Books and Treatises

MARTIN J. ADELMAN, PATENT LAW PERSPECTIVES (originally published 1970, updated regularly). This nine-volume, loose-leaf treatise is a thoughtful collection of patent cases and editorial commentary regarding the decisions. Online version available from LexisNexis.

AMERICAN BAR ASSOCIATION, 200 YEARS OF ENGLISH & AMERICAN PATENT, TRADEMARK & COPYRIGHT LAW (1977).

WILLIAM R. BALLARD, THERE IS NO MYSTERY ABOUT PATENTS (1946).

GREGORY J. BATTERSBY & CHARLES W. GRIMES, LICENSING ROYALTY RATES (2011)

J. W. BAXTER & JOHN P. SINNOTT, WORLD PATENT LAW AND PRACTICE (originally published 1968, updated regularly).

DONALD S. CHISUM, CHISUM ON PATENTS (originally published 1978, updated regularly). This eleven-volume, loose-leaf treatise is a good resource for patent law. It contains a comprehensive treatment of the case law and has a bibliography that exceeds 50 pages and an additional eight-volume guide to the Federal Circuit's patent-related decisions. Online version available from LexisNexis.

BARRY L. GROSSMAN & GARY M. HOFFMAN (EDS.), PATENT LITIGATION STRATEGIES HANDBOOK (3d ed 2010 & Supps.).

ETHAN HORWITZ & LESTER HORWITZ, PATENT LITIGATION: PROCEDURES & TACTICS (originally published1971, updated regularly). This three-volume loose-leaf work is designed primarily as a practical guide for patent litigators. Online version available from LexisNexis.

LESTER HORWITZ & ETHAN HORWITZ (EDS.), INTELLECTUAL PROPERTY COUNSELING AND LITIGATION (originally published 1988, updated regularly). This seven-volume, loose-leaf treatise includes several chapters on patent law written by leading practitioners. Online version available from LexisNexis

IRVING KAYTON (ED.), PATENT PRACTICE (8th ed. 2004). This six-volume, loose-leaf treatise, which is updated regularly, is an excellent introduction to patent practice, that is, practice before the Patent and Trademark Office.

JOHN S. KENYON ET AL., PATENT DAMAGES LAW AND PRACTICE (2011, updated regularly).

JOHN GLADSTONE MILLS III ET AL., PATENT LAW FUNDAMENTALS (2d ed. 1986, updated regularly). This five-volume, loose-leaf treatise is a good treatment of patent law. (Formerly authored by Peter D. Rosenberg.) Online version available from Westlaw.

R. CARL MOY, MOY'S WALKER ON PATENTS (4th ed. 2003, updated regularly). (Formerly published as Lipscomb's Walker on Patents.)

WILLIAM C. ROBINSON, THE LAW OF PATENTS FOR USEFUL INVENTIONS (1890). This three-volume treatise contains the best theoretical treatment of patent law. It is a good starting place for serious historical research.

JEROME ROSENSTOCK, PATENT INTERFERENCE PRACTICE HANDBOOK (2011, updated regularly).

JEROME ROSENSTOCK, THE LAW OF CHEMICAL AND PHARMACEUTICAL INVENTION: PATENT AND NONPATENT PROTECTION (3d ed. 2011, updated regularly).

JOHN W. SCHLICHER, PATENT LAW: LEGAL AND ECONOMIC PRINCIPLES (2d ed. 2011, updated regularly).

Among the many works on drafting patent claims or prosecuting patent applications are the following:

IRAH H. DONNER, PATENT PROSECUTION: LAW, PRACTICE, AND PROCEDURE (7th ed. 2011, updated regularly). (Formerly published as PATENT PROSECUTION: PRACTICE AND PROCEDURE BEFORE THE U.S. PATENT OFFICE.)

ROBERT C. FABER, LANDIS ON MECHANICS OF PATENT CLAIM DRAFTING (6th ed. 2011, updated regularly).

JEFFREY G. SHELDON, HOW TO WRITE A PATENT APPLICATION (2d ed. 2011).

TABLE OF CASES

*References are to chapter and note numbers (e.g., **4**: 47 refers to note 47 in Chapter 4). Alphabetization is letter-by-letter (e.g., "Goldenberg" precedes "Golden Blount").*

INDEX

*References are to chapter and section numbers (e.g., **6:** I.C.2, I.E refers to sections I.C.2 and I.E of Chapter 6). Alphabetization is word-by-word (e.g., "Ex parte" precedes "Examination").*

P

ABOUT THE AUTHORS

Herbert F. Schwartz has specialized in intellectual property litigation since 1964, and has represented clients in trial and appellate courts throughout the United States in all areas of intellectual property law. Mr. Schwartz is of counsel to and a retired partner of the law firm of Ropes & Gray LLP, and former member and Managing Partner, of the intellectual property law firm of Fish & Neave LLP, which merged into Ropes & Gray LLP in 2005. Mr. Schwartz received a B.S. in Electrical Engineering from the Massachusetts Institute of Technology in 1957, and an M.A. in Applied Economics from the University of Pennsylvania, and LL.B. from the University of Pennsylvania Law School in 1964, where he was an editor of the Law Review and a member of the Order of the Coif.

Mr. Schwartz is an Adjunct Professor of Law at the University of Pennsylvania Law School and New York University Law School, and has taught courses on patent, trademark, trade secret, and unfair competition law since 1981. He is co-author, with Judge Pauline Newman, F. Scott Kieff, and Henry E. Smith of the casebook, *Principles of Patent Law.*

Mr. Schwartz also is a fellow of the American College of Trial Lawyers, a fellow of the American Bar Foundation, and a member of the American Law Institute. He was named as one of the *Lawdragon 500 Leading Lawyers in America* (2005); *Litigator of the Year* (*Managing Intellectual Property,* 1999) and identified as one of the *100 Most Influential Lawyers in America* (*The National Law Journal,* 1997 and 2000). He has been listed in The Best Lawyers in America since it was first published and in Euromoney's *Guide to the World's Leading Patent Law Experts* and *Guide to the World's Leading Trademark Law Practitioners.* He has acted as a Special Master in federal court patent litigation, testified several times before Congress at its invitation on issues

357

relating to patent law reform, and has served on the Advisory Board for BNA's *Patent, Trademark & Copyright Journal.*

Robert J. Goldman received his B.S. in Engineering and his law degree from Columbia University, both in 1977 in a joint degree program. He joined Fish & Neave in 1977, and remained at that firm until its merger with Ropes & Gray LLP in 2005. He is a member of the New York and California bars, and currently is resident in Ropes & Gray's Silicon Valley office.

Mr. Goldman has specialized in intellectual property trials and appeals for his entire career, representing clients in patent, trademark, copyright, and trade secret cases. He represented Polaroid Corporation in its landmark patent infringement action against Eastman Kodak Company relating to instant photography. That action resulted in a permanent injunction against Kodak's infringement and the largest litigated patent damages award to that time, $873 million.

Mr. Goldman has also tried cases relating to pharmaceuticals, medical devices, computer systems, information technologies, and integrated circuits. He is listed in *The Best Lawyers in America* and in *Chambers* (USA and Global) for IP litigation.

Mr. Goldman regularly writes and speaks on intellectual property issues. He has been an Associate Adjunct Professor of Law at Fordham University in New York, teaching Patent Law, and has taught Patent Law and Patent Litigation as a Lecturer in Law at Stanford University. He also teaches trial practice for the National Institute of Trial Advocacy (NITA)

Intellectual Property Titles from BNA Books

Biotechnology and the Federal Circuit
by Kenneth J. Burchfiel

*Computer and Intellectual Property
Crime: Federal and State Law*
by A. Hugh Scott

Constructing and Deconstructing Patents
by Irah H. Donner

Copyright Law Deskbook
by Robert W. Clarida

Drafting Patent License Agreements
by Brian G. Brunsvold,
Dennis P. O'Reilley,
and D. Brian Kacedon

*Drafing Patents for Litigation
and Licensing*
by Bradley C. Wright, Editor-in-Chief

*Electronic and Software Patents:
Law and Practice*
Steven W. Lundberg, Stephen C.
Durant,
and Ann M. McCrackin
Editors-in-Chief

*Harmon on Patents:
Black-Letter Law and Commentary*
by Robert L. Harmon

Intellectual Property Law in Cyberspace
by G. Peter Albert, Jr. and AIPLA

*Intellectual Property, Software, and
Information Licensing: Law and Practice*
by Xuan-Thao N. Nguyen,
Robert W. Gomulkiewicz,
and Danielle Conway-Jones

*Intellectual Property Taxation:
Transaction and Litigation Issues*
by Jeffrey A. Maine
and Xuan-Thao N. Nguyen

Intellectual Property Technology Transfer
Aline C. Flower
Editor-in-Chief

*International Patent Litigation:
A Country-by-Country Analysis*
Edited by Michael N. Meller,
William O. Hennessey

*McCarthy's Desk Encyclopedia of
Intellectual Property*
by J. Thomas McCarthy,
Roger E. Schechter,
and David J. Franklyn

Patents and the Federal Circuit
by Robert L. Harmon,
Cynthia A. Homon,
and Charles M. McMahon

Patent Law and Practice
by Herbert F. Schwartz
and Robert J. Goldman

Patent Infringement Remedies
by Lawrence M. Sung

Patent Litigation Strategies Handbook
Barry L. Grossman and
Gary M. Hoffman,
Editors-in-Chief

*Patent Prosecution: Law, Practice,
and Procedure*
by Irah H. Donner

Patent, Trademark, and Copyright Laws
Edited by Jeffrey M. Samuels

*Patent, Trademark, and
Copyright Regulations*
Edited by James D. Crowne

Pharmaceutical Patent Law
by John R. Thomas

*Products Comparison Manual for
Trademark Users*
by Francis M. Pinckney
and David R. Higgins

*Trademark Dilution: Federal, State,
and International Law*
by David S. Welkowitz

Trademark Infringement Remedies
Brian E. Banner, Editor-in-Chief

Trademark Litigation Practice
by David S. Fleming
and John T. Gabrielides

For details on these and other related titles, please visit the BNA Books Web site at *bna.com/bnabooks.com* or call 1-800-960-1220 to request a catalog. All books are available on a 30-day free examination period.